PENGUIN BOOKS

NEW DEALS

Robert B. Reich teaches business, law, and political economy at the John F. Kennedy School of Government at Harvard University. He is the author of the best-selling *The Next American Frontier*. John D. Donahue is an economics consultant as well as a doctoral fellow at Harvard's Center for Business and Government.

NEW DEALS

The Chrysler Revival and the American System

ROBERT B. REICH

JOHN D. DONAHUE

PENGUIN BOOKS

PENGUIN BOOKS
Viking Penguin Inc., 40 West 23rd Street,
New York, New York 10010, U.S.A.
Penguin Books Ltd, Harmondsworth,
Middlesex, England
Penguin Books Australia Ltd, Ringwood,
Victoria, Australia
Penguin Books Canada Limited, 2801 John Street,
Markham, Ontario, Canada L3R 1B4
Penguin Books (N.Z.) Ltd, 182–190 Wairau Road,
Auckland 10, New Zealand

First published in the United States of America by
Times Books, a division of Random House, Inc. 1985
Published in Penguin Books 1986
Reprinted by arrangement with Times Books,
a division of Random House Inc.

LIBRARY OF CONGRESS CATALOGING IN PUBLICATION DATA
Reich, Robert B.
New deals.
Bibliography: p.
Includes index.
1. Chrysler Corporation—Finance. 2. Loans—United
States—Government guaranty. 3. Automobile industry
and trade—Government policy—United States.
4. Industry and state—United States. I. Donahue,
John D. II. Title.
[HD9710.U54C475   1986]   338.7′6292′0973   86-9344
ISBN 0 14 00.8983 7 (pbk.)

Printed in the United States of America by
R. R. Donnelley & Sons Company, Harrisonburg, Virginia
Set in Times Roman

For our parents

CONTENTS

NEW
DEALS

When thy wares went forth out of the seas, thou filledst many people; thou didst enrich the kings of the earth with the multitude of thy riches and of thy merchandise.

In the time when thou shalt be broken by the seas in the depths of the waters thy merchandise and all thy company in the midst of thee shall fall.

All the inhabitants of the isles shall be astonished at thee, and their kings shall be sore afraid, they shall be troubled in their countenance.

The merchants among the people shall hiss at thee; thou shalt be a terror, and never shalt be any more.

—**Ezekiel 27:33–36**

My problems are the problems of the country.

—**Lee Iacocca** to the Senate
Banking Committee, September 1979

INTRODUCTION

1.

I n the midst of the industrial troubles that poisoned Jimmy Carter's reelection bid and plagued the early Reagan years, the federal government saved a car company. Chrysler was front-page news. Citizens sensed from the start that for good or for ill, something significant was happening to the American system. Indeed, the Chrysler rescue was the most visible economic initiative of the one-term Democratic interregnum in what would be twenty years of Republican rule. Public help continued, albeit by altered means, well into the 1980's.

The basic facts are clear enough: The Chrysler Corporation, the fourteenth-biggest industrial firm in America, was hurtling toward bankruptcy in 1979. The stricken automaker came to Washington for help and persuaded the government to guarantee its loans. Chrysler bled cash all through 1980 and 1981, but the fresh money let it continue a retooling campaign. In 1982, a year of dismal car sales, Chrysler broke even. In 1983 it made record profits and paid back the guaranteed loans. By 1984 it was thriving: It had sold more than 2 million vehicles, earned a stunning $2.4 billion, and restored thousands of workers to the payroll. Innovative products and sophisticated production processes were reclaiming for Chrysler its tarnished reputation for superior design.

But beneath the basic story lies a profusion of richly revealing detail; beyond it extend fundamental issues of principle and precedent. The Chrysler bailout marked a turning point in American capitalism. Never before had the government so clearly and explicitly offered so much help to a single troubled firm. The decision to intervene was controversial. It still is. The rescue demonstrably kept Chrysler going—without draining the Treasury—but many Americans remain unsure of what to make of it. What lessons can be distilled from this exceptional enterprise? What guidance does it offer for the future? And what does it suggest about how the American system of finance, labor, and government responds when major corporations and their networks of dependents are imperiled by economic change?

Politics is a filter for our collective history. Politics transforms experience into metaphor. The Chrysler bailout has attained a symbolic status in American politics, but it remains a curiously mercurial symbol. A loathsome instance of government meddling with the free market; an inspiring model of cooperation among business, labor, and government; an overblown but routine specimen of the nation's incoherent industrial development policy—these judgments and more have been extracted from the same set of facts. The rescue is displayed as a symbol of America's failed past, its vibrant future, and its muddled present.

In part this tangle of interpretations reflects the human tendency to let opinions govern observation instead of the other way around. The Chrysler episode is rich enough to offer evidence, if harvested selectively, to support almost any conclusion that ideology dictates. But more important, the very novelty and complexity of the rescue, and the limited attention some of its defining details have so far received, confound consensus.

The debate over the Chrysler bailout will no doubt endure. What we think we have learned from the experience will go on shaping our ideas about how best to deal with economic stress. The model will be pressed urgently into service with the next major downturn in the business cycle. But without a better understanding of what happened and why, the lessons will still slip by us, and the political debate will remain myopic.

What happened? What are we to make of it?

2.

This book has three related goals. First, and most simply, it assembles a record. It fills in the outlines of an episode that is often oversimplified; it describes precedents and the context that shaped the rescue. In the process it punctures some myths and presents a number of surprises.

For instance: Chrysler was no exemplar of excellent management through much of the postwar era, yet the firm's decline and renewal were not a simple matter of switching from bad management to good. The cash crisis that precipitated Chrysler's plea for public help had a great deal to do with its exceptional vulnerability, as the smallest of the "Big Three" carmakers, to the turbulence of the late 1970's. Corporate folklore misses much of the story. Chrysler's chairman, Lee Iacocca—while an executive of uncommon talent—was no single-handed savior, nor has he ever cast himself as such. Indeed, the key products and strategies that powered Chrysler's recovery were inherited from John Riccardo, Iacocca's predecessor. The charismatic chairman provided superb leadership and a flair for marketing that honed the strategy and galvanized the organization, but attributing it all to Iacocca trivializes the firm's renaissance.

Another: The rescue began as an unexceptional bid for a low-profile tax subsidy—the sort of solicitation that American companies routinely make of government. The government's insistence *this* time on an aboveboard program of loan guarantees—not the provision of public aid—was the crucial departure from the norm.

Another: The aid to Chrysler was accompanied by meticulous oversight. Chrysler gave the government veto power over most management decisions. Had company executives later balked at the terms of the deal, the government was empowered to take control of Chrysler's board of directors and force management changes. Yet for all this, the collaboration between Chrysler managers and public officials remained civil, often even cordial.

Another: During the time it was subsidized and supervised by the government, Chrysler shrank dramatically. Public officials are widely thought to be unable to impose or condone economic hardship; here they did so unflinchingly. They endorsed, even insisted on austerity. The bulk of the money to fund the turnaround came not from the government-backed loans but from internal cutbacks. And the biggest cost savings came from simply jettisoning pieces of the company.

Another: Trade protection and tax subsidies arranged by the Reagan administration funneled much more money to Chrysler (at a much higher public cost) than did the loan guarantee program. The free-market enthusiasts extended the limited Chrysler rescue into a less visible but vastly more expensive bailout for the entire automobile industry.

What follows here offers the reader an extensive account of the events. We first summarize the Chrysler story from the company's beginning in the 1920's to the troubles of the late 1970's. It is here that the seeds of Chrysler's downfall are to be found, in the accretion of claims and commitments the firm took on and in the shocks that made those burdens unsustainable. We trace the genesis of Chrysler's bid for public assistance and the precise nature of the government's response. Congress balked at letting a bankruptcy court settle Chrysler's fate, but it was equally reluctant to endorse a simple bailout. What emerged was a hybrid between bankruptcy and bailout. We explore, in some detail, what happened once the Loan Guarantee Act was passed—the choreography of a new set of deals among Chrysler's constituents. We appraise the roles played in Chrysler's struggle to survive by managers, workers, lenders, dealers, and suppliers; by elected and appointed public officials and the civil service bureaucrats who carried out the government's program; and by the teams of lawyers and investment bankers who shaped the action. Finally, we recount the company's return to profitability and the awkward politics of recovery. This record should equip the reader to make informed judgments about the Chrysler case itself.

The record is also valuable for the insights it offers beyond the immediate Chrysler episode. The second and more fundamental goal of this book is to reveal—using the Chrysler story as a vehicle—some of the key processes and institutions that undergird our complex mixed economy in the last decades of the twentieth century and how this intricate organizational skein is changing in response to new pressures.

Chrysler stirred things up. The trauma of the firm's near collapse and the Herculean effort required to rescue it compelled groups to cooperate in unaccustomed ways. Private managers, hired consultants, and federal bureaucrats together drafted and refined Chrysler's operating plans. The secretary of the treasury bargained with labor leaders and briefed rank-and-file delegates. A senior unionist joined the firm's board of directors. Senators and Cabinet officials negotiated with small-town bankers. These odd juxtapositions uncover the institutional workings of our economy. By disrupting the often opaque processes of business and government as usual, the rescue did much to reveal the pattern of economic organization we have chosen and to suggest how it is evolving. One can stress too much the singularity of the rescue. In many ways it was no sharp break with the past; rather, it was a dramatic culmination of trends that had been long under way in the relationships among American business, labor, finance, and government.

Institutional borders, for example, have become strikingly porous. No clean lines mark where the public sector ends and the private begins, where banking and finance become management, where management becomes politics, where politics takes shape from citizens' fears and hopes. The central organizations in our society are also less rigidly hierarchical than many assume. "Business," "labor," "finance," and "government" are commonly cast as monolithic blocs of authority and interests, with decisions taken at the top of each hierarchy defining the course of the economy. Some commentators call for more collaboration among these blocs; others worry that interlocking elites already conspire against the rest of us. But the picture that emerges is far messier and more interesting. While Chrysler's Lee Iacocca, the Auto Workers' Douglas Fraser, and Treasury Secretary G. William Miller all figured prominently in the drama, many of the central actors were deep inside the bureaucracies of business, labor, and government. They could be found on congressional staffs, in local unions, in the bowels of the Treasury. Through their control over pivotal details and day-to-day decisions, these lower-level officials steered the action and shaped the outcome. They bargained, analyzed, cooperated and stonewalled, jockeyed for influence, and formed alliances that frequently had very little to do with their formal roles. The rescue—indeed, the broader evolution of America's political economy—can perhaps be best understood as a series of improvisations on the part of individuals endowed more with tenacity and nitty-gritty information than with formal authority.

These organizational entrepreneurs operate, however, within dense matrices of codes and precedents. The Chrysler rescue illustrates how, for example, the seniority system defines workers' claims on their jobs and limits what kinds of deals labor leaders can consider. It shows how our decentralized financial system—combined with the bankruptcy laws—grants small lenders substantial power over larger lenders when a borrower gets in trouble. It shows how banks in other nations can strongly affect decisions concerning whether and how troubled firms in the United States will survive. It illuminates the pervasive influence of the Federal Reserve System. In short, it shows how these organizational *patterns*—rather than grand pronouncements of high corporate and public officials—govern our institutions' response to economic stress.

The Chrysler episode also illustrates the quiet economic potence of legal structures. Laws define the market. The accretion of laws, each with its own rationale and history, forms a framework for commercial dealings. Bankruptcy law obviously drove the process for Chrysler. But strategies were also rooted in tax codes, securities laws, antitrust decisions, and trade rules. These laws shape the arena within which ailing firms and industries struggle for survival. Without a basic appreciation of these legal structures the American system remains mysterious.

Finally, the story displays the convergent evolution of two once-distinct responses to economic failure: bankruptcy and bailout. Bankruptcy codes have been broadened and extended to bias the process in favor of keeping troubled firms in business, often by compelling a wide circle of constituents to share the cost of recovery. At the same time, unconditional public rescues for failing firms have given way in recent years to more sophisticated interventions that hinge on sacrifice from creditors, employees, and other constituents. Bankruptcy and bailout, at least for large firms, are coming to look much the same.

The third goal of this book—a good deal more ambitious than the other two—is to fuel a broader debate on how we as a nation should deal with the challenge of economic change. This is by no means a new debate. We explore here the history of bankruptcy and bailout in the United States and abroad and the issues surrounding the application, extension, or suspension of the codes governing commercial failure. The debate has gained spirit as the United States has come to share more intimately the growing pains of the international economy. The world market is increasingly integrated. This integration offers rich benefits but exposes the once-sheltered American economy to external pressures. Oil shocks, import surges, swings in currency values, international debt crises, and other external factors can impose on Americans an imperative to change. How we deal with these pressures in the years to come will put our principles and institutions to the test.

The notion that the public should step in to save a stumbling corporate giant is anathema to many people on both the right and the left of the political spectrum. (The Chrysler rescue was opposed by an odd alliance encompassing the conservative National Taxpayers Union and Ralph Nader's Congress Watch.) To the right, it represents an unwarranted intrusion into the workings of the free market; to the left, a noxious instance of private managers foisting onto the public the consequences of incompetence. These positions have little to do with the mundane evidence, and political purists know where they stand on the matter—precisely where they stood on the day in 1979 when the Chrysler rescue was proposed.

Yet for many Americans closer to the center of the ideological spectrum, the issue is less easily put to rest. Most agree that as a general matter the government should not subsidize failing firms. But the specifics give them pause. What about a major employer, in a basic industry, whose problems can plausibly be attributed to government regulations, external shocks, and appalling bad luck? What of the networks of innocent suppliers, dealers, and creditors? What if the costs to the public of accommodating the company's failure—unemployment compensation, pension guarantees, welfare expenditures, lost tax revenues—would add up to substantially more than the public cost of the rescue? What if the company's constituents all agree to share the cost of turning it around?

Chrysler's renaissance has quieted the critics and surprised the skeptics. Americans respect what works. But the pendulum of public opinion may well swing too far. An unexamined success is a perilous precedent. We risk applying phantom lessons to the next round of new deals wrought in the next economic crisis. The Chrysler episode offers evidence—illustrative, if not conclusive—on how we can step in to help preserve failing enterprises. Perhaps more valuably, it sharpens the debate on whether, and when, we should want to.

I

THE FALL

1.

Hindsight can tempt us to oversimple accounts of what happened and why. The knots of cause and consequence concerning Chrysler's rise and decline—like the real story of any human organization—are forbiddingly tangled and invite resort to a tractable fable: Bad management and bad luck brought Chrysler down; public cash and new leadership restored it. This is probably as close to true as any short sentence can be. But to understand Chrysler's troubles of the late 1970's and to appreciate the stakes in the public debate over the bailout, it is worth examining briefly what kind of organization Chrysler was and how it got that way.

The firm's origins and the tone of its first several decades were in large measure the products of the energy and vision of its founder, Walter P. Chrysler. His autobiography, *Life of an American Workman*, begins: "Being a machinist, I have always wanted to know how things work. . . . All my training, instincts, and aptitudes have combined to make me want to penetrate the workings of any machines I see."[1] The first half of the book is partly about Indian scares in Ellis, Kansas, partly about relatives and friends at work and in the town band, but mostly about machines—making them, using them, and fixing them. It reveals a man typical of the pioneers of the auto industry: a passionate tinkerer, bluntly ambitious, literal-minded, superbly competent, and confident to the point of cockiness. "There is in manufacturing a creative joy that only poets are supposed to know," he wrote. "Some day I'd like to show a poet how it feels to design and build a railroad locomotive."[2] (This was about as close as Walter Chrysler ever came to philosophical rumination, except perhaps his comment, concerning the "noble instrument" he played for years, that "you could play a solo on the tuba, but you were likely to be the only one who cared for it."[3])

At the age of eighteen Chrysler signed on as a machine shop apprentice with the Union Pacific Railroad. Four years later he was a journeyman mechanic; after another six years he turned in his union card when he became foreman in a shop of ninety mechanics. He was thirty-three years old, and chief engineer of the Chicago Great Western Railroad, when an encounter in Chicago changed his life. This American workman met a new machine: an ivory and red four-door 1908 Locomobile with built-in oil lamps. The price: $5,000, or about eight times his savings. But, he wrote, "I never stopped to ask myself if I should, if I could afford to go in hock to buy that car. All I asked myself was: Where could I raise the money? . . . I was a machinist and these self-propelled vehicles were by all odds the most astonishing machines that had ever been offered to men."*[4]

Soon after buying his first car, Walter Chrysler quit the railroad and joined a manufacturing firm, the American Locomotive Company. He rose within two years to the position of works manager and the lofty annual salary of $12,000. One of the directors of American Locomotive was also an officer of the General Motors Corporation. In 1911 he arranged for Chrysler to be offered the job of works manager for the Buick division. Although it meant swallowing a 50 percent pay cut, Chrysler took the job and moved to Michigan. On arriving at Buick, Chrysler was exhilarated by the potential of the young industry he was joining, a rich ferment of grand plans, vaunting egos, and round after round of astonishing technological leaps. But he was distressed by the waste, inefficiency, and sloppy management he found at the plant. Three years later, though, "the Buick factory had become something to make any man who worked there proud," and Walter Chrysler was commanding a salary of $25,000. William Durant, the founder of GM,

---

*Van Vechten, Chrysler's banker friend who reluctantly financed his purchase of the Locomobile, later headed a consortium of bankers that hired Chrysler for $1 million a year to turn around the Willys-Overland Company.

asked Walter Chrysler to sign on as head of the Buick division in 1916.[5] General Motors, Buick, and Walter Chrysler all prospered for several years, but Chrysler gradually became concerned at the pace and, to his mind, incoherence of GM's growth. By 1919 Chrysler had developed an amicable but unshakable disagreement with Billy Durant's strategy and was convinced that GM was "expanding too fast by far . . . buying things and budgeting this and budgeting that until it seemed, to me, we might come to a dismal ending."[6] He resigned, sold his GM stock, and—a wealthy man at forty-five—went into early retirement.

But in less than a year he resolved to return to work. (He claimed his emergence from retirement was based in part on his wife's irritation at having him sitting around the house all day, smoking cigars with his friends.)[7] He quickly found a way to make himself useful: "John N. Willys was in trouble in 1920; his Willys-Overland Company was in terrible shape. That year the company was making cars that not many people seemed to want. . . . The company was headed for the rocks. Bankers wanted back the money they had loaned the company."[8] Willys-Overland "had saddled itself with an airplane plant, with a harvester company, and with other subsidiaries, almost none of which were doing it any good. . . . The company had to make better automobiles if it was to survive."[9] A syndicate of bankers hired Chrysler to take control of Willys-Overland for a salary of $1 million. He later wrote: "All that was bad in the Willys-Overland Corporation was due, really, to lack of competition, to the wartime boom and its easy money. Prosperity had made some of its officials too tolerant of things that, in any better-managed corporation, would have been regarded as shocking."[10] Willys had vastly overordered on plant, equipment, and parts. Chrysler's first priority was to cut those commitments back to manageable levels. He "travelled everywhere that parts were made, talked over long-distance telephone wires until my voice became hoarse; argued; cajoled; and in a few months I had cut the company's debt by millions."[11]

In the course of developing a new car for Willys, Chrysler met Fred Zeder, Owen Skelton, and Carl Breer, three young engineers whom he came to consider "parts of a single, extraordinary engineering intelligence." He hired them and set them to work on a special project: developing an entirely new automobile. John Willys apparently shared neither Chrysler's strategy nor his enthusiasm for the team of Zeder, Skelton, and Breer; Chrysler said Willys "sometimes seemed to feel that the company's problems could be met by a couple of new gadgets and a coat of paint." Disputes over the role and design of the new car lasted well into the drafting of preliminary blueprints, and eventually Chrysler "determined that somewhere, somehow, I was going to make a kind of automobile that—I was beginning to feel pretty strongly—was unlikely to be made in the Willys plants."[12] Chrysler arranged for Zeder, Skelton, and Breer to abandon their half-finished blueprints, set up the trio as a separate engineering firm, and ensconced them in an old building in Newark, New Jersey, to work unimpeded on Walter Chrysler's grand project.

At about this time some of the bankers who had solicited Chrysler's assistance on Willys-Overland asked him to take control of another failing firm, the Maxwell Motor Company. The situation was in many respects similar to that of Willys: The war and the boom that followed it had tempted Maxwell into an unsound expansion program. In this case Chrysler was persuaded to scale down his customary seven-figure salary to a modest $100,000 and to accept as a substitute a large package of stock options. In 1922 he signed on as chairman of the Maxwell reorganization and management committee.[13] He immediately persuaded the bankers to extend new loans to Maxwell and to forgive much of the old debt in exchange for stock and stock options. He raised more funds by hurriedly redesigning Maxwell's line of cars and slashing the price. Maxwell was put through a friendly reorganization, and by late spring of 1922 it was owned by the reorganization committee headed by Walter P. Chrysler.

While workdays were devoted to rescuing Maxwell, Chrysler continued to spend weekends in the Newark shop with Zeder, Skelton, and Breer. The prototype car was ready for road testing. "Under an old car's shabby hood we had hidden the unsuspected power of our new high-compression engine. Zeder and his boys had outdone themselves. You could tell that any time a traffic cop's uplifted palm stopped you in a group of cars. It was the most fun if this shabby old testing car was halted between a couple of big ones, with snooty chauffeurs at their wheels. At the whistle's sound we would be past the cop and on our way, while behind us, openmouthed, our chance rivals would just be getting ready to go into second gear."[14] Chrysler persuaded the board of the reorganized Maxwell Motor Company to build a car around Zeder's high-compression engine—presumably no difficult sales job for the chairman and major stockholder. The car was to be called the Chrysler.

The new machine was to be unveiled at the 1924 New York Automobile Show. But a few weeks before the event officials announced that only cars already on the market could be shown. Maxwell was not yet fully tooled up to make the Chrysler—indeed, the firm was counting on favorable publicity from the show to pry loose from its bankers a much needed new loan to finish setting up the production lines—so Walter Chrysler arranged to rent the entire lobby of the Commodore Hotel, traditional host to auto industry insiders, and set up a display of Chrysler prototypes. Maxwell's new car stole the show; $5 million in financing was quickly arranged, and the Chrysler Six went into full-scale production. Before the year was out, it was outselling the line of cars still bearing the Maxwell name. Thirty-two thousand Chrysler cars were sold the first year at a profit of more than $4 million. In 1925 the name of the Maxwell Motor Company was changed to the Chrysler Corporation.[15]

The next year there were four Chrysler models: the 50, the 60, the 70, and the Imperial 80. The numbers signified, with a measure of swagger for 1926, the speed each model could reach on a good stretch of road. (The Ford Model T, which set the standards of the time, could manage thirty-five miles per hour.) Ford shut down for nine months of retrenchment in 1926 to replace the Model T with the Model A, which Henry Ford hoped would quash General Motors' challenge to his company's dominance. The dearth of Fords invited Chrysler to fill the breach. In 1927 the Chrysler Corporation sold 192,000 cars and was ranked fifth in the industry.

By then Walter Chrysler had "done plenty of figuring, and knew that to exercise our full manufacturing power and talents we would have to acquire plants that would cost, if we had to build them, about $75,000,000. Where and how were we going to round up that kind of money? Every time we gave the matter thought, we found our heads full of visions of the splendid plants of the Dodge Brothers."[16] Dodge was then owned by Dillon, Read & Company, a New York banking firm that had bought it from the Dodge brothers' widows. The company that made the "Dependable Dodge" retained the reputation for reliability and superb engineering that it had earned under John and Horace Dodge.

Following some months of corporate courtship and a final five-day bargaining marathon at the Ritz, Chrysler bought Dodge for $170 million, most of it in Chrysler stock. It was the biggest acquisition ever at the time, and it increased Chrysler's size fivefold in one day. The day the deal was closed, July 31, 1928, canvas banners proclaiming "Chrysler Corporation, Dodge Division" were slung across the Dodge plants in Detroit and its suburbs, including the main attraction, the vast Dodge Main assembly plant in Hamtramck just north of the city.[17]

Once the Dodge deal had been made, however, Chrysler and K. T. Keller—who succeeded him as president and later as chairman—"with many disastrous cases of industrial over-expansion in mind, made a kind of pact never to tolerate expansion of the Chrysler Corporation more than ten per cent in any year."[18] In particular, Chrysler chose to forgo the extensive vertical integration—producing instead of buying the materials and components that went into its cars—that Ford and, especially, GM were pursuing. Walter Chrysler opted for "shallow" integration and continued to buy a large fraction of his parts from independent suppliers. This meant more of the money buyers paid for a Chrysler car was passed on to other firms than was the case at Ford and GM. But it also left Chrysler freer to change models and designs since it had no vast network of parts plants to keep in business once they had tooled up to make a part. This turned out to be a marked advantage in the era of rapid technical advance in the auto industry.[19]

In 1929 the company sold 450,543 cars.[20] It weathered the Depression better than most businesses, surviving through three years of salary cuts and retrenchment to set a new sales record in 1933.[21] Walter Chrysler was unbending in his fixation on the future of his company. "No matter how gloomy the outlook," he wrote, "I never cut one single penny from the budget of our research department. . . . The reason for that is something any modern industrialist knows and understands. Its research work is what will be keeping any soundly managed industry alive and healthy five and ten years in the future."[22] The company was profitable in 1934 and 1935, and in 1937, the last year of Walter Chrysler's chairmanship, it paid off the last of the bonds it had issued to buy Dodge. The Chrysler Corporation was free of any debt, any mortgage, even any preferred stock standing between its assets and its shareholders.

Walter Chrysler died in 1940, leaving a legacy of aggressive innovation and engineering excellence.

2.

During World War II the Chrysler Corporation, along with the rest of Detroit, converted wholesale to war production. The assembly lines that had made Chryslers, Plymouths, and Dodges now churned out defense hardware, including 100 miles of submarine nets and 3 billion rounds of small-arms ammunition. But Chrysler was best known for B-29 bomber engines (it made 18,000), Bofors antiaircraft guns (60,000), and, most significant for the firm's future, medium and heavy tanks (25,000).[23] The company won an outstanding reputation for reliability and prompt delivery during the war, and its tank operation was awarded a special Army-Navy award for excellence.[24]

But it did notably less well in adapting to peacetime production. Chrysler was slow in readying new models to meet the postwar boom and ran at only three-fourths capacity during the first half of 1948. *Fortune* magazine questioned whether Chairman K. T. Keller and his team of vice-presidents "lack some of that competitive fire and restless ambition that drove the company, under Walter Chrysler, to constant experimentation and innovation."[25] Chrysler captured 22 percent of the American car market in 1951 but then entered a long downward trend that would take it below 10 percent in 1962. In 1953 it yielded second place in market share to Ford, a position it has never regained.

One factor behind Chrysler's lackluster performance in the postwar era, paradoxically, was its tradition of outstanding engineering. The auto industry was maturing. By the late 1940's most of the fundamental innovations had been made, and competition no longer centered on contests between engineering shops. In the postwar United States cars were less machines for getting from here to there than the American dream rendered in metal, glass, and rubber. The auto industry had become a marketer's game. But Chrysler was slow catching on.

Other auto companies introduced sleeker low-slung cars in 1949; Chrysler's offering was an inch and a half higher than prewar models. President Keller disdained what he saw as the passing fad for novel styling and defended the unfashionably high-roofed Chrysler with the observation that "there are many parts of the country containing millions of people where both the men and ladies are in the habit of getting behind the wheel, or on the back seat, wearing hats." He was more concise on another occasion: "Chrysler builds cars to sit in, not to piss over."[26] The company defied the reign of styling at its peril; Chrysler's market stagnated. At the same time its customer base shifted to a "downscale" clientele of somewhat older, more conservative, and less affluent buyers who valued the dependability of solid design and could live without the glitter.

Many firms founder when the entrepreneurs who launched them give way to the next generation of managers. The entrepreneurs, driven by daring and highly individual vision, bucked the system and created something new. But they are typically unsuited by temperament to sustain an established system; if they do not die off, they are often forced out. The new managers are system builders. They substitute method for vision, organization for daring.

The man who would first face the task of adapting Chrysler to the modern car market was L. L. "Tex" Colbert, a lawyer hired by Walter Chrysler in 1929 and subjected to an extended practical education in the making of motorcars. The firm's two previous chiefs had thought of the auto business in terms of steel and grease and rubber and glass; Colbert was the first of what would be a long line of helmsmen oriented principally to law and finance. During World War II Colbert headed the Dodge airplane plant, and he was named head of the Dodge division at the war's end. He became president of Chrysler in 1950, but it was not until 1956, when Keller resigned from the chairmanship, that Colbert had a free hand at the head office. One of his first moves in his campaign to pull Chrysler into the modern world was the eminently modern expedient of hiring some consultants. Early in Colbert's presidency McKinsey & Company, the management consulting firm, submitted a voluminous report with three main recommendations: Develop international operations, centralize management, and keep the engineering department in its place.[27] Chrysler was quickly launched on an expansion campaign, at first mostly domestic. Colbert built three new assembly plants, new transmission and stamping facilities, and a new proving ground, spending $936 million on facilities between 1953 and 1958. This kind of expansion couldn't be financed out of retained earnings, and in 1954 Chrysler entered a $250 million, ten-year loan agreement with the Prudential Insurance Company.[28]

Colbert sought to banish Chrysler's boring image. If its heritage of exceptional design suffered as a result, such was the price of success in the modern auto industry. The 1955 line came out in 173 different color combinations, including two-tone and three-tone versions. The 1956 line featured optional built-in record players. Finally, the 1957 Chryslers—the models that introduced fins to family cars—were long, low, stylish, and of manifestly indifferent design and manufacture. But they sold. Chrysler posted record sales and near-record earnings in 1957.

But it was not long before Chrysler stumbled seriously for the first time. The recession of 1958 hit it hard. The management reforms Colbert had planned were unevenly realized, and Chrysler's organization kept fixed costs high and margins low. Its predominantly blue-collar customers, moreover, were the first to drop out of the car market when times turned bad. Chrysler sold only 704,000 cars in 1958—a drop of just about half from the year before—and lost $34 million for the year. Sales rose somewhat in 1959, but Chrysler's recovery was feeble compared to the market as a whole; the company again lost money. Its market share fell for the second year in a row, to 11.3 percent. (Six years earlier it had been 20 percent.)[29] Colbert's days as Chrysler's steersman were numbered.

William C. Newburg, Colbert's successor, served as president for only nine weeks before questionable business links with suppliers forced him from office in 1960. The company continued to founder. In 1961, after several executives at other auto firms had declined Chrysler's offers, board member George Love persuaded his fellows to assign to the presidency a forty-two-year-old administrative vice-president named Lynn Townsend. (Love agreed to adopt an active chairmanship to shepherd the young Townsend through his early years in charge.) The new president had joined Chrysler only in 1957, after spending ten years as the Chrysler auditor for the accounting firm of Touche Ross.

3.

Lynn Townsend was articulate, open, and—as his discreet but, for Detroit, daring sideburns advertised—moderately flamboyant. He was also an exceptionally acute financial analyst. An accountant by training, Townsend displayed a strategic sense and a preoccupation with marketing that distinguished him from his predecessors. Chrysler's problems were plain enough: high costs, an eroding market share, and consequently precarious finances. He quickly set about tightening operations: consolidating the Chrysler and Plymouth divisions, closing redundant plants and cutting white-collar jobs by a quarter, and buying a new IBM computer to replace 700 clerks.[30] The first line of cars to come under his influence —and that of the stylist Elwood Engel, whom Townsend had lured away from Ford—were the 1963 models. They were widely judged to be more skillfully designed, better built, and more aggressively sold than any recent Chrysler offerings. Townsend also instituted a five-year, 50,000-mile warranty—which Ford and GM considered reckless but nonetheless copied—and the "pentastar" symbol for Chrysler, put on display throughout the nation in a rush program of dealer "signage."[31] Chrysler seemed at last to be embracing the new era in automaking with style and flair.

Consolidation soon gave way to expansion. The 1960's were a time of exuberant growth. American companies spawned divisions, launched international operations, developed new products. Their managers cherished the conviction that the U.S. economy would continue to grow indefinitely (with the government's discrete "fine tuning" of taxes, the budget, and the money supply), consumers would continue their uninhibited spending, and the future belonged to the biggest and the boldest. Early in 1963 Townsend announced that Chrysler would begin a ten-year expansion plan with a $700 million budget. A year later the timetable was to shrink to four years and the budget was to swell to $1 billion. By late 1965 the budget was $1.7 billion—a sixfold rise from the annual spending rate originally planned.[32] A new vice-president was hired and charged with revitalizing Chrysler's neglected and enfeebled dealer network. Major new factories went up in the mid-1960's: a car assembly plant in Belvidere, Illinois; a truck plant outside St. Louis; a huge stamping plant in Sterling, Michigan; foundries in Detroit and Kokomo, Indiana. A new subsidiary, the Chrysler Credit Corporation (later the Chrysler Financial Corporation), was founded in 1964 to provide a reliable source of credit to Chrysler dealers and customers. Chrysler's capital spending in 1964 equaled Ford's and was 51 percent as great as GM's. In 1965 a sale of new common stock—the first since 1928—netted $262 million to help finance Chrysler's growth.[33]

Chrysler expanded into other products. An auto-leasing subsidiary was launched in 1962. Chrysler Realty was set up in 1967 to manage and market land for Chrysler dealerships; it soon developed into a diversified real estate enterprise that owned luxury housing, shopping centers, student dormitories, and a large stake in the Big Sky resort center in Montana. Chrysler Defense settled down to churning out M-60 battle tanks for the Army. Chrysler Chemical added new plants and products, and Chrysler Marine, long a major manufacturer of high-quality inboard engines, began making outboards and pleasure boats; soon Chrysler Marine dealerships were selling boats and motors directly to the public. A wholly owned subsidiary, Airtemp, grew precipitously as demand for the air conditioners it turned out skyrocketed in the prosperous sixties.[34] Chrysler early on had a hand in America's space program. In 1952 it lent twenty engineers to the government to work with Wernher von Braun. Chrysler built the rockets that Alan Shepard and Virgil Grissom rode on the first suborbital flights in the Mercury program. Under Townsend, the company set up a separate space division and became prime contractor for the Saturn booster rocket.[35] "Townsend was probably the most creative and energetic leadership Chrysler ever had, Iacocca included," a veteran of nearly thirty years with Chrysler recalled. "When he started out, he had a company flat on its tail, with just about every problem it was possible for a car company to have: falling market share, quality problems, fading image, all of it. So Townsend did two things: He got the quality up and instituted the best, gutsiest warranty the industry had ever seen. We had good cars, they sold, and the company made a lot of money. Townsend also thought that if he was going to serve the shareholders right, he had to turn Chrysler into a multinational company. You have to remember this was in the days when everyone in American business knew perfectly well that you either went multinational or you withered away."[36]

What distinguished Townsend and his presidency most sharply from the old Chrysler Corporation was this relentless drive to become an international company. While still an assistant vice-president, Townsend had led a company task force to appraise the options for expanding overseas. Once installed in the president's office, he set himself to seizing opportunities abroad. He established Chrysler International in Geneva, essentially a coordinating center for foreign ventures. In 1963 he increased Chrysler's holdings in Simca—France's second-biggest carmaker—from 25 percent to 64 percent. Two years later Chrysler acquired a large stake in the British auto firm controlled by Lord Rootes. Rootes claimed nearly 10 percent of the British market; it eventually became known as Chrysler U.K. when Townsend upped his stake into a controlling position. Around the same time Chrysler bought into the Spanish truckmaker Barreiros S.A. and built or bought operations in Peru, Brazil, Colombia, Venezuela, and Argentina. In 1961 about 4 percent of Chrysler's vehicles were made outside North America; in 1967 about 24 percent were.[37] By the end of the decade Chrysler had plants in eighteen countries.[38]

Chrysler's North American auto operations at first improved markedly under Townsend. After a triumphant 1965 he was named chief executive officer (CEO); he became chairman of the board the next year. Most observers credited the firm's renewed fortunes in part to exceptionally good design on the compact Plymouth Valiant and Dodge Dart. (This line, built around the celebrated straight-six engine, would be one of Detroit's most enduring successes of the postwar era.) But at least as important was a new attention to marketing. Solid products and aggressive salesmanship raised Chrysler's market share gratifyingly from its 1962 low.* It reached 16 percent in 1968, inspiring *The New York Times* to an uncharacteristic burst of enthusiasm: "If the Chrysler Corporation's silver cloud has a murky lining, it is a hard one to detect. Almost every move made by Lynn Townsend and his management since 1961 seems to have been the correct one."[40] In a feature on Chrysler's "Comeback by the Numbers," *Fortune* magazine hailed the chairman's knack for monitoring and guiding the company through its

---

*The new stress on marketing was not an unalloyed success, however. One campaign took the theme "The Dodge Rebellion" and featured cowgirls cavorting in white Stetsons. *Fortune* magazine commented that by tradition, "owners of Dodge cars are about as far from rebellious as it is possible to be, and the unfortunate Dodge Rebellion campaign left them confused about their car's image and resentful of Chrysler's threat to their own image."[39]

accounts. "The numbers live for Lynn Townsend," the magazine proclaimed, charting Chrysler's impressive metamorphosis from a stodgy purveyor of "practical" transportation to a full-line car company with modern designs and a refurbished image.[41]

Profits on sales were still thin at Chrysler in 1968, compared to Ford and GM. But this was in part because the number three company was spending heavily to build up capacity. Townsend's goal was to stay "facilitized" to accommodate the upper ranges of Chrysler's computer projections of the auto market. Expansion was planned or under way at Highland Park, Kokomo, and Trenton, Michigan, and a new 200,000-car capacity assembly plant was scheduled to be built in New Stanton, Pennsylvania. On paper Chrysler seemed robust. Between 1961 and 1968 its assets had nearly tripled (see Appendix A, Figure 1A). Shareholders' equity had climbed from $700 million to $1.8 billion, and Chrysler's debt burden, as a percentage of equity, had fallen from 35 percent to less than 20 percent.[42] Board member George Love—Townsend's first advocate on the board and predecessor as chairman—said of Townsend, "He is the right fellow because he is figure-minded. It used to be possible to control the company through personal contact. But when a company gets this big you no longer know all the people. You can't see that so-and-so is loafing, so you need a man for whom figures live. You control the company by a knowledge of figures. Townsend can spot trouble through the figures."[43]

Yet there were hidden perils in managing by the numbers. One was the tendency for production targets, rather than for car buyers, to dictate how many Dodges, Chryslers, and Plymouths were produced. Townsend the accountant remained more closely attuned to the judgment of financial analysts than previous chairmen, less willing to depart from the rather short-term definitions of corporate success invoked by Wall Street. At that time analysts valued a car company primarily by its daily shipments, quarterly dividends, and annual market share. Certainly neither Townsend nor anyone else at Chrysler ever set a policy of neglecting longer-term factors for the sake of boosting short-term financial results. But under Townsend the priority became shipping volume, and in tough times that priority tended to overwhelm all others. When sales slipped, Chrysler suffered out-of-control inventories.

When dealer orders fell short of the shipping targets, plant managers would meet targets by building cars anyway and shunting them to what was termed the "sales bank." This was a euphemism for "inventory." Holding some unsold cars in corporate hands was in principle a reasonable way to buffer random variations in sales in order to keep production running smoothly. But as Chrysler's head office continued to push higher production targets, the sales bank offered a repository for cars built without dealer orders. The link between manufacturing and marketing became attenuated, and discipline within the firm began to erode. If the auto market was soft, or if a particular model was selling sluggishly, the sales bank spared managers the sense of urgency they might have felt had a weak market meant idle factories. Instead, rented fields and parking lots around Detroit began filling up with Chrysler cars and trucks.

The sales bank system eventually wounded Chrysler in several ways. Most obviously, the company had already paid to make the stockpiled cars but collected nothing on them while they sat in storage. Hundreds of millions of dollars in idle assets were tied up in the sales bank. Second, the bulging inventory allowed quantity to swamp quality at the plants, particularly during the end-of-the-quarter drive to meet shipping targets. Robert Anderson recalled his days as head of manufacturing under Townsend: "We'd sit in Hamtramck making phone calls to all our plants and field offices across the country and when we'd find someplace to ship a car we'd ship it to get it off the line. These cars weren't bought on the last day of the quarter; they were just shipped." Dan Popa, at one time the head controller at the Hamtramck plant, said, "We shipped cars at the end of a quarter we never should have. In the last hour of overtime work on an end-of-quarter shift, we'd ship out hundreds of dogs."[44]

Third, the sales bank put enormous stress on Chrysler's dealers and sales staff. Robert McCurry, former vice-president for U.S. automotive sales, said that the system "was opposed by the great majority of the sales staff, but by the late 1970's it became an accepted way of doing business even though we didn't like it. It had to be very expensive, and the pressures put on dealers to accept cars for which they had no orders made it difficult to build a good relationship with the dealer body."[45] "They would build cars with no buyer," one Chrysler dealer recalled, "and then they'd call all their district representatives together and lock each one in a hotel room with a telephone and tell him to call his dealers. All day. We're only talking about twelve, sixteen dealers per road man. The pressure was pretty heavy: 'You're my only customer. What's going to happen if you don't take the cars? The company will go out of business; I'll lose my job; you'll lose your dealership.' They'd call several times a day, using all the angles and arguments. They'd wear the dealers down."[46] Fourth, and most subtly, the sales bank undermined morale. One former Chrysler executive put it succinctly: It "makes it hard to control quality when guys in the plant see you parking cars out in the mud."[47]

4.

By 1970 the American automobile industry, like the national economy, was showing signs of strain. Inflation was inching upward, as was unemployment. The muscle cars of the 1960's had become a vanishing species as insurance rates climbed. Imports were increasing; by 1970 more than 400,000 Volkswagen Beetles were being sold in the United States, and an obscure Japanese automaker named Toyota was beginning to make inroads.

There was another trend in the making, even more ominous, although few recognized it at the time. A revolutionary government had nationalized Libya's oilfields in 1968. Two years later Libya became the first third world government to force a Western oil company to accept a price increase; a barrel of Libyan crude went from $2.23 to $2.53. It was also in 1970 that the United States' domestic production of oil peaked. The days of easy oil were over. Although prices did not suddenly rise, the Nixon administration—anticipating price increases—abandoned restrictions on imported oil. These quotas, in force for eleven years, had limited oil imports to about 18 percent of total use. Within two years after they had been lifted, the United States was importing 30 percent of the oil it consumed.

These larger trends would soon converge to subject the American car industry to a decade of unprecedented peril. Uncertainty and sharp changes are anathema to automakers, by the nature of the manufacturing process. Companies must plan their production far in advance. As they develop new product lines, they spend heavily for tooling and plants. They depend absolutely on the eventual appearance, two to five years down the road, of demand for cars of the same type and size as the projections that guided the investment plans. Contracts with suppliers and unionized employees are founded on expectations of future markets. When the costs of investment and revenues from sales fail to coincide neatly, automakers must rely on debt—long-term notes and bonds sold to investors, short-term commercial paper held mostly by institutions like pension funds and insurance companies, and direct loans from banks—to even out cash flows. The need to service debt narrows the margin for error. Balancing all these commitments is inherently a delicate proposition. Upheaval in the economy renders it much more risky. And in the 1970's it was *most* hazardous for Chrysler, the smallest full-line carmaker, as it tried to play in the same competitive arena as Ford and General Motors.

The gradual shift toward small cars that marked the early 1970's would seem to favor Chrysler, which had the first domestic compact and the largest proportion of small-car sales. (This compact was the Dodge Dart/Plymouth Valiant, which was still a very big machine by European standards.) But in absolute numbers Chrysler had too few small cars and too many big cars for sale. And, as one Chrysler director glumly summarized the matter, "the big 1969 cars were turkeys."[48] Because profits on compacts and intermediates were much smaller than on full-size cars, moreover, Chrysler watched its earnings plummet 70 percent between 1968 and 1969 (see Figure 1, below). In the last quarter of 1969 Chrysler posted a $4 million loss, the first since 1961; the last quarter a year earlier had seen $122 million in earnings. For the whole year Chrysler paid out thirteen cents a share more to its stockholders as dividends than it earned; this amounted to slow liquidation. It could not continue.

Townsend laid off 12,000 of the 140,000 U.S. employees. (The dismissed workers included hundreds of trainees enrolled in a joint business-government training program promoted by the National Association of Businessmen. Townsend, whose outside volunteer

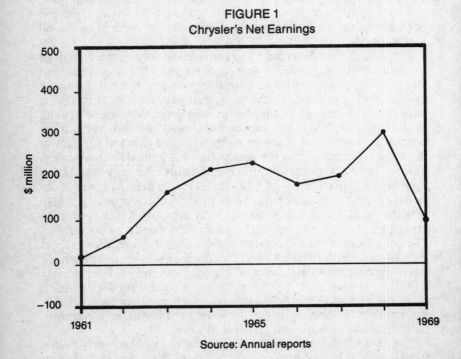

FIGURE 1
Chrysler's Net Earnings

Source: Annual reports

interests were claiming a growing portion of his time, had recently been appointed head of this alliance.) The dividend was cut by 70 percent. Chrysler's renegade computer system, which had made a bad situation worse by fouling up scheduling and shipping orders, was overhauled. The 1970 model big cars were restyled, and two of Chrysler's ten assembly plants were readied to switch to small cars in case the compact fad continued.[49]

Hard on the heels of Chrysler's particular troubles came a general slump. The economy softened, and overall car sales in the first months of 1970 dropped 13 percent from 1969, undercutting Townsend's recovery campaign. Chrysler cut prices and sold aggressively, maintaining its market share at the expense of profits. Townsend's expansion program, however, had little slack. There was no more modest plan to fall back on. When profits could no longer feed the investment flow, Chrysler had to suspend work on the expansion at Kokomo Transmission and the construction of the New Stanton assembly plant.[50] Then, to keep from cutting deeper into the expansion budget, Chrysler had to take on $200 million in long-term debt in early 1970.

Early in 1970 Virgil Boyd was removed from the presidency and installed in the new, substantially ceremonial position of vice-chairman. Boyd's replacement as president was John J. Riccardo, an accountant who had previously been Chrysler's third-ranking officer, head of the North American automotive division. Riccardo was intense, occasionally abrasive, intelligent, and driven. He had been with Chrysler for ten years. Previously he, just like Townsend, had been the chief Chrysler auditor with Touche Ross; in fact, the two men had worked together on accounting projects. At the end of the first quarter of 1970 Chrysler was operating at 68 percent of capacity. It had laid off 6 percent of its white-collar workers and 9 percent of its blue-collar workers. The stock price was down by half from its 1968 peak. But Riccardo was sanguine. Speaking to the shareholders for the first time at the 1970 annual meeting, he said, "I have never felt more confident about the long-range future of our company. . . . We have every reason to expect that the 1970's will be as remarkable for our industry as the 1960's have been."[51] (He would turn out to be right.)

Riccardo quickly set out to reverse Chrysler's setback. He cut budgets, personnel, and dividends. He earned the nickname the Flamethrower in the process, but he reduced Chrysler's costs by $150 million.[52] Townsend's program of diversification and domestic and foreign expansion had drained Chrysler's cash reserves and pumped up the debt load. By 1970 the number three auto company was carrying $790 million in long-term debt—more than General Motors. Chrysler had little choice but to go easy on investment for a while. Between 1970 and 1972 it invested in new plant and equipment at somewhat less than half the rate it had averaged in the late sixties. This meant shelving plans for a domestic subcompact and postponing planned investments in automation to match Ford and GM. Instead of building its own line of cheap little cars to compete against the ubiquitous Volkswagen Beetles, Chrysler bought them from abroad, put Dodge and Plymouth labels on them, and resold them. Along with captive imports from its European subsidiaries, Chrysler began marketing the Colt, made by Mitsubishi, the Japanese car company in which Chrysler had recently bought a 15 percent stake.

The first phase of the turnaround plan was discouraging. The country slid into a recession that would prove severe by the standards of the 1960's. Real gross national product declined in 1970 for the first time since 1958. Chrysler had counted on its foreign branches to augment U.S. earnings. But its subsidiaries in Brazil, Britain, and Spain were losing money, and sales were slumping in France. Imported cars seized a preposterous 14.7 percent of the American market in 1970, embarrassingly close to Chrysler's 15.1 percent share. One Chrysler official, skeptical of the turnaround plan's prospects, told *The Wall Street Journal,* "This isn't 1961 all over again. The things that were easy to fix have been fixed."[53]

In June 1970 the Penn Central Railroad went bankrupt, defaulting on $82 million in commercial paper—unsecured corporate IOUs— and throwing the paper market into a panic. Brokers and analysts pored over portfolios, looking nervously for other companies with shaky earnings that were heavily dependent on selling commercial paper. Chrysler qualified, and there was a run on the short-term debt of Chrysler's financial subsidiary. Chrysler Financial borrowed from the money markets and extended credit to dealers and buyers; if its cash dried up, so would the parent company's sales. Townsend joined John McGillicuddy—the chairman of Manufacturers Hanover, Chrysler's lead bank, which organized its loans—for a cross-country campaign to restore confidence in the firm's essential soundness. Chrysler's bankers finally agreed to make available $275 million in new lines of credit for Chrysler Financial, a backup that readmitted the finance company to the commercial paper market. Chrysler Financial further boosted its cash position by selling $170 million in "receivables."[54] (Consumer loans backed by so sturdy a claim as a first lien on an automobile are often considered marketable financial assets and can be sold to investors in order to raise immediate cash.)* With the finance company's crisis finally subdued, it could resume underwriting car sales and lubricating Chrysler's cash flow.

In 1970 a second development rattled the auto industry, inflicting the worst shocks on the smallest of the Big Three: A new set of federal regulations was issued. The public had come to assume that America's carmakers had essentially solved the problems of mass production and now could be called on to pay for their sins. Ralph Nader had launched his damning appraisal of American cars' safety records five years earlier. Nader's indictment, and the scandal-sparking clumsiness of the industry's response, had dimmed Detroit's image and inspired the first automobile regulations. The National Traffic and Motor Vehicle Safety Act of 1966 had authorized the secretary of transportation to set and enforce minimum auto safety standards. (In practice, the head of the National Highway and Traffic Safety Administration was to implement the legislation.) By 1970 regulations issued under the act covered car components from hood latches to hubcaps.[56] Then the Clean Air Act amendments of 1970 encoded Americans' resurgent concern for environmental integrity and replaced the earlier auto emissions policy—which mostly involved exhortation to build cleaner cars—with strict standards and timetables for compliance. By the 1975 model year, mile-for-mile emissions of hydrocarbons, carbon monoxide, and nitrogen oxides would have to fall drastically from uncontrolled levels. Congress intended to spur the development of pollution-reducing technology by confronting the auto companies with tough new regulations.

The auto industry, especially Chrysler, protested vigorously that the new safety and emissions standards were unneeded, or impossible to meet, or unduly rigid in substance or timing. Chrysler filed suit in 1972 against a rule requiring all cars sold after 1975 to be equipped with air bags to protect passengers automatically in a crash. It argued that reliable air bag technology did not exist. Chrysler lost; the United States Court of Appeals for the Sixth Circuit decided that Congress fully intended to force producers to expand technological frontiers in order to meet stricter standards.[57]

---

*When in the middle of the crisis a Chrysler director, Tom Killefer, petitioned Federal Reserve Board Chairman Arthur Burns to loosen the money supply and thus ease the panic that was strangling Chrysler, Burns reproached him for "trying to politicize the Federal Reserve Board of the United States and turn this country into a Latin American banana republic." But the Fed did eventually underwrite the banks' refinancing of Chrysler Financial by promising to open its discount window to cover member banks' Chrysler loans.[55]

(Chrysler lost only the first round. Thirteen years later, after many more lawsuits and administrative reversals, the rule was still kept at bay.)

Chrysler was similarly unsuccessful in its attempt to shape the specifics of the antiemissions law. The amount of noxious substances a car spews out per mile can be moderated in one of two ways: Either the engine can generate less pollution in the first place, or the pollutants can be captured or transformed by some mechanism interposed between the engine and the atmosphere. Chrysler preferred the former solution. Retaining an edge in engineering, it was confident it could develop a more precisely tuned "lean-burn" engine that would generate less pollution without any additional devices. General Motors, on the other hand, was alarmed at the prospect of redesigning the engines for every one of its vast number of vehicles. An add-on device to cut emissions from unimproved engines would require no fundamental engineering change. Moreover, GM's network of parts divisions could doubtless make antipollution devices at a profit. GM won, and Chrysler lost: The 1970 Clean Air Act amendments were worded so as to force adoption of the catalytic converter, a mechanism that treated exhaust gases before they reached the tailpipe.[58]

But for the present the automakers confronted only minor compliance costs; Congress scheduled the biggest regulatory burden for the mid-1970's and beyond. Meanwhile, Chrysler was enjoying a sharp rebound in 1973. A combination of general recovery and a fall in imports—which *The Wall Street Journal* attributed to a domestic cost advantage stemming from President Richard Nixon's wage and price controls—led to record sales of American-made cars in 1972.[59] The buoyant car market, a boom in truck sales, and exceptionally good performances by its foreign subsidiaries boosted Chrysler's worldwide vehicle sales past the 3-million mark. Earnings surged to $220 million—three times the previous year's net and a triumphant turnaround after 1970's debacle. The two-year austerity program had cut overhead by several hundred million dollars. The product line was rationalized: Chrysler fielded 30 percent fewer types of car in 1973 than it had in 1971. The Plymouth Valiant/Dodge Dart line was selling briskly and making money. President Riccardo attributed much of the improvement to Chrysler's decision to leave the low-profit minicar market to Ford's Pinto, GM's Vega, AMC's Gremlin, and the growing flock of cheap imports. "Quite frankly," said Riccardo, "I think the day this company really turned around was the day we decided not to build that subcompact.

Chrysler no longer operates by knee-jerk reaction. It does not imitate everything competitors do."[60]

The one sour note was Chrysler's margin of profit on sales. It was up smartly from its level during the troubles of 1969–71, but at 2.3 percent (in 1972) it still left little slack if markets softened. Chairman Townsend, who was gradually passing control of the company to his protégé Riccardo, said, "We have to think in terms of 4 percent, 5 percent, 6 percent on sales. If GM and Ford can earn 7 percent, 8 percent, 9 percent on sales in good years, we can't be happy until we're there."[61] Ford's margin on sales in 1972 was 4.5 percent, and GM's was 7 percent (see Appendix A, Figure 2A).

Riccardo placed his bets on tightening up the core company in North America and consolidating its position in the profitable compact market rather than pursuing the trendy subcompact market or exotic technologies. Investors apparently approved. Chrysler's stock price had toppled to $16 in 1970, but by early 1973 it was trading at around $40. Townsend summarized the mood at the time: "The company is back where its future is assured. It has an organization, it has product planning, it has cost controls, it has new management. It is a different corporation from 1969–70."[62]

Chrysler's recovery continued into 1973, carried along by the liveliest auto market in American history. Beyond the general boom, though, the company's business strategy seemed eminently sound: turning out Dart and Valiant compacts as long as demand stayed strong, picking up some profits in well-picked segments of the big-car market, and leaving the profitless subcompacts alone. Chrysler earned record profits on record sales in the first quarter of 1973 and then broke those records in the second quarter. The board of directors boosted quarterly dividends from twenty-five cents a share to thirty-five cents. Townsend announced plans to resume work on the New Stanton assembly plant near Pittsburgh, where construction had been stalled since 1969. Chrysler prepared to float $150 million in new long-term debt, most of it earmarked for New Stanton.[63]

But in the second half of the year Chrysler's luck turned unpredictably and almost unimaginably bad. The launch of its restyled line of 1974 C-body cars—big, well-appointed Plymouth Furys, Dodge Monacos, and Chrysler Imperials—was delayed by a series of wildcat strikes in the hot summer of 1973 and a plague of parts shortages. Then, in September, the United Auto Workers chose Chrysler as the target for the 1973 contract renegotiation, and a strike shut down the company's assembly lines for nine days. Early in October, Chrysler warned that it would show a loss—small and temporary, but a loss nonetheless—for the third quarter. Two other worries cast a pall over Riccardo's near-term plans. First, some analysts feared that the record sales of 1973 had been in part "stolen" from future years. Customers could be buying in advance, anticipating that the stiffer regulatory standards the 1975 models had to meet would ratchet up sticker prices. By this scenario demand would contract sharply in a year or so. Second, Chrysler's long-term debt was brushing $800 million even before the new $150 million issue (see Appendix A, Figure 3A).

Then, two days after Chrysler had released the bad news about the third quarter and just before the refurbished big cars were shipped out to showrooms, Israel and Egypt went to war. The Arab members of the Organization of Petroleum Exporting Countries (OPEC) declared an oil embargo on the United States and other friends of Israel. The price and supply of gasoline instantly became American consumers' reigning concern. Car sales in the first half of 1974 were down nearly a fourth from 1973 levels. Small cars surged to capture fully half the market. And Chrysler had just sunk $450 million into restyling all its large cars.

5.

Anxious to make up for sickly sales of the 1974 models, Chrysler ran its factories full tilt to ready the 1975 line, featuring restyled intermediate cars. Anticipating resurgent demand once the fuel panic had passed, Riccardo and Eugene Cafiero, Chrysler's head of North American automotive operations, pegged 1975 new-car prices an average of $500 higher than the previous year. But the launch of the 1975 models was wrecked by continued economic turmoil. Inflation spiraled up to its highest level since the end of World War I. The big increase in OPEC oil prices had something to do with it. But there was also the end of price and wage controls and a worldwide pattern of bad crops. At the same time the United States suffered the worst recession of the postwar period. Unemployment crept upward; by May 1975, 9.2 percent of the work force would be jobless. Economists coined the ugly term "stagflation" for the bizarre concurrence of inflation and recession.

Consumers stayed away from auto showrooms or, if they bought, opted for subcompacts. Chrysler couldn't move its 1975 models. In November 1974 Riccardo met with Michigan's congressional delegation, urging it to press the Federal Reserve to provide special credit for buyers of 1975 model cars. (The idea got nowhere.)[64] In

December the cover of *Business Week* featured acres of unsold 1975 Chryslers in storage at the Michigan State Fairgrounds—some of the 360,000 new cars Chrysler couldn't unload. The company lost a record $74 million in the last quarter of 1974.

Lynn Townsend declared austerity. He ordered the assembly lines slowed down; they stopped running altogether in the last weeks of 1974. Tentative plans to close the Jefferson Avenue assembly plant were announced. (The plans were scrapped after the union, the city of Detroit, and Michigan's government objected vigorously.) Top executives took temporary pay cuts, and salaried workers saw vacations rescheduled. Late in 1974, Moody's Investors Service downgraded and then dropped altogether the rating on Chrysler Financial's commercial paper, forcing a switch to more expensive bank lending. (A short time later a new set of backup loan arrangements restored confidence in Chrysler Financial's solvency and renewed its access to the paper markets.) Chrysler's board voted to cancel quarterly dividends for the first time since 1938. Townsend's stated goal was now to restructure Chrysler into a leaner, more focused company that could better weather market downturns and break even by selling fewer than a million cars a year.[65] "Companies, like the Federal government, tend to pick up fat in good times," he explained. "When you hit a bump you try to take that out." But Chrysler shed more than fat. Construction work halted yet again at the New Stanton site. More than 30 percent of Chrysler's workers were laid off. Investment in tools and facilities fell 39 percent between 1973 and 1975; research and development spending fell 19 percent. More than 15,000 white-collar jobs were cut. And in an astonishing economy move for a company that still cherished a heritage of fine design, four out of every five engineers were fired or furloughed indefinitely.[66]

Near the end of 1974 Manufacturers Hanover, Chrysler's lead bank, orchestrated a consolidation of the company's tangled network of loan agreements into a single $455 million revolving credit arrangement. The arrangement—a revolver, in bankers' argot—was a contract between Chrysler and around 80 major American banks, each of which stood ready to lend the company specified sums on demand. The consolidated arrangement was tidier and more secure than the scatter of separate agreements it replaced, many of which were cemented by no formal contracts. (Chrysler also maintained $125 million in other credit lines with 115 smaller American banks and $200 million in foreign credits.) "The banks feel comfortable with Chrysler, at least for the short run," one banker noted at the time. "In the perspective of some of the other loans the banking industry is concerned with, Chrysler doesn't look so bad."[67]

Chrysler's 1975 troubles were national news. A lengthy feature article in *The New York Times* cast Chrysler as "a 50-year-old chronic invalid" but also as a patient that "always recovers from major surgery at the hands of its chairman, Lynn Townsend, nursed along by its lead banker, the Manufacturers Hanover Trust Company."[68] Some observers worried that this time the company's recovery might not be complete. One automotive industry consultant, John Z. DeLorean (a former head of General Motors' North American operations who was to gain a measure of notoriety in years to come), catalogued the troubles plaguing Chrysler, including "red ink on the bottom line, a prolonged decline in share of market, the cost of tooling new lines, the pressure of new competitive lines, the high cost of manufacturing in marginally efficient plants, quality, morale, dealer profits and morale, and so on." The challenge was daunting but not insurmountable, DeLorean advised. "The first step is the establishment of a viable product strategy." Chrysler should stop trying futilely to follow Ford and GM into every market segment and instead "establish a dynamic new strategy of product leadership within the entire organization. . . . The proper solution, the required strategy, is to create a distinctive and desirable product—and to price it profitably."[69] (DeLorean's advice on how to do this was imprecise.)

U.S. senators friendly to Chrysler's cause tried to nudge some public money toward the carmaker through an amendment to a 1975 tax bill. The proposal would have let Chrysler claim a refund from the federal government on taxes it had paid in profitable times as far as eight years earlier. The tax code gives firms some leeway to average out gains and losses over time, which can often result in retroactive changes in tax liability. A company that paid taxes in profitable years can claim some of it back in bad times. Normal carry-back rules let a company reach three years into the past to apply current losses to past profits. But the three-year limit gave Chrysler access only to taxes paid since 1972. It had used up $97 million of these available tax refunds to lessen its 1974 losses; it had only $18 million of potential refunds left for 1975. The extension provision, tailor-made for Chrysler, passed the Senate but was deleted in the House-Senate conference three days later.[70]

Stock analysts worried that Chrysler was loading up with too much debt. Its long-term borrowings were equivalent to 37 percent of stockholders' equity, compared with 24 percent for Ford and 7 percent for GM (see Appendix A, Figure 4A). Observers also alluded ominously to the possibility that the American auto market would fail to rebound promptly from its slump. Following each earlier crisis, a string of rich years, like the boom from 1971 to 1973, had nourished Chrysler's recovery.

Yet Lynn Townsend professed himself content. The financial consolidation of late 1974 had stabilized Chrysler's credit arrangements. He expected compact cars, not the puny subcompacts, to set the new standard in the American market. Chrysler had long excelled in this slice of the market, and a promising new line of upscale compacts—the Dodge Aspen and Plymouth Volaré—was being readied for launch. Chrysler would count on captive imports from Mitsubishi to keep its hand in the subcompact market while it called on the design experience of its foreign subsidiaries to develop, in good time, a subcompact it could make in the United States and sell at a profit.[71] In July 1975 the chairman declared success in his third campaign to revive Chrysler and abruptly resigned. John Riccardo, Townsend's protégé for more than a decade, assumed the chairmanship, and Eugene Cafiero moved up to the presidency. "Lynn tried to make it look as if he was passing the torch," one observer noted at the time. "In reality he was tossing a hot potato."[72]

6.

Almost as soon as he took over, John Riccardo assigned Cafiero to prepare a plan for focusing Chrysler's operations on the North American market. The first and most urgent problem was with the former Rootes Motor Company. The ensuing negotiations over the fate of Chrysler U.K. would be a taste of things to come.

Chrysler U.K. was the sorriest part of Chrysler's network of foreign subsidiaries. It was the feeblest of Britain's four car companies, with a market share fallen to 4 percent. It had lost money in six of the preceding nine years, and from mid-1974 to mid-1975 it had lost more than $70 million. Late in October 1975 Riccardo and Cafiero called a news conference to announce third-quarter losses for the company as a whole and to present their strategy for restoring profitability. In response to insistent questions from reporters, Riccardo mentioned Chrysler U.K. as a candidate for closure.

Riccardo had planned to give the bad news to Chrysler U.K. and the British government the next day. Instead, the subsidiary, which had been indignantly denying shutdown rumors, got the word from a union militant in Glasgow, who had learned by telephone from a New York reporter of Riccardo's remark at the news conference. A political donnybrook ensued. Closing Chrysler U.K. would idle

25,000 workers; another 25,000 jobs would be lost in supplier firms.[73] Unemployment had already reached painful levels in Britain. Worse, many of the jobs at stake were in poor and politically volatile Scotland. The prospect of 50,000 lost jobs was distinctly threatening to the Labour government.

Prime Minister Harold Wilson denounced Chrysler before Parliament, claiming that the company had "put a pistol to the government's head." The image stuck. English political cartoonists instantly cast John Riccardo as a menacing Italian mobster.[74] The "godfather" himself (as some British officials privately called Riccardo) flew to London in the first week of November. Politely, but altogether firmly, Riccardo laid out his position to Labour officials: The government was welcome to take over the subsidiary. Or Chrysler might be willing to manage a nationalized operation. It would pay up to $70 million to cover severance benefits to workers and other shutdown costs. But it would not stay in the car business in Britain. With that preamble, negotiations between Chrysler executives and Labour government officials began.

The talks were stalemated from the start. Chrysler was unwilling to stay; the government was unwilling to see it go. The deadlock lasted four weeks before two events inspired a new offer from the government. First, in a minor by-election in early December Labour candidates lost heavily and unexpectedly to Scottish Nationalists, heightening Labour's anxieties over the party's grip on restless Scotland and rendering the prospect of thousands of unemployed Scots even less palatable. (Earlier the Scottish members of the Cabinet had pledged to resign if Chrysler's Scotland plant was closed.) Second, the shah of Iran had expressed concern over his $200 million contract with Chrysler U.K. for parts and engines. Officials worried that default could threaten the rest of Britain's exports to Iran, worth $1 billion a year. "To put that at stake for a few lousy million quid would have been a grave error," said one minister.[75] Harold Lever, the economics minister, argued that it would cost the government twice as much to cope with the social fallout from a Chrysler U.K. failure as it would to prop up the company and prevent the failure.

Despite energetic opposition from some Labour officials, a plurality of ministers came to favor making Chrysler a better offer, and by the end of the year—in what one newspaper called the Wilson Cabinet's most difficult decision—a deal was struck. The government would put up around $300 million to make good Chrysler U.K.'s losses and guarantee its loans. The government would also share in any profits, becoming in effect a partner in Chrysler U.K. The union, while refusing to budge on wages, agreed to accept the loss of 8,000 jobs, or nearly 1 in 3. And Chrysler would stay in Britain, committing $135 million in investment to the British subsidiary.

One Conservative leader dismissed the deal as a politically motivated bailout: "Labour's whole future power base depends on fighting off Scottish nationalism. I don't doubt for one instant that the Chrysler rescue was a political, not economic, decision." Even some Labour members of Parliament saw the rescue as a stopgap. According to one, "I doubt very much if this is going to last more than a couple of years. Basically, we've got a holding operation that gets many people off the hook and gives us some breathing space."[76]

7.

Chrysler as a whole, meanwhile, was struggling to regain its footing after the worst year it had ever endured. Despite savage cuts in employment and investment, the company lost $260 million in 1975. By the start of 1976 the economy was beginning to bounce back. Shaken by surging unemployment, the Ford administration had engineered an expansionary tax cut, and the Federal Reserve boosted the money supply. The sputtering economy steadied. As the general recession subsided, Chrysler gradually recovered along with the rest of the industry. Losses slowed in the last quarter of 1975, and early in 1976 Chrysler started making money again. In the first quarter of 1976 it posted solid profits of $72 million, and Riccardo was hailed as the architect of a turnaround reminiscent of the rescues Lynn Townsend had pulled off in the 1960's. "Mr. Riccardo stepped up to the plate and hit some home runs" was how one stock analyst explained the upturn.[77] A feature article in *The New York Times* on March 3 celebrated the changing of the guard and Chrysler's new profitability:

> Instead of great gambles for great gains—the traditional Chrysler approach—the new management's goal is simply to make a good and steady profit. . . . Instead of trying costly competition in every segment of the automobile market with a full line, they plan to specialize, pick their spots carefully, and see if they can sell as many cars but in fewer segments. . . . Instead of building more plant capacity, integrating vertically, they plan to buy components from other auto makers and sell major components to competitors and thus keep Chrysler plants busier and more efficient. . . . Instead of developing new products from the ground up, they plan to draw on existing cars for new models, and spin off new cars from a few basic designs.[78]

Riccardo's strategy had three main components. First, he began selling off parts of Chrysler that weren't needed, didn't fit, or lost money. He unloaded the Airtemp division, the air-conditioning manufacturer Chrysler had owned for decades. He also sold Chrysler Realty's stake in the Big Sky resort in Montana. And after five years of stop-and-go construction he agreed to sell the unfinished New Stanton assembly plant to Volkswagen of America.

The second reform was tighter management. Comments from Chrysler managers highlighted his rigorous managerial style: "He was the first no-nonsense kind of guy Chrysler had"; "John doesn't like to have a problem lying around. He's very prone to push for a solution"; "The last thing you'll find around him is a yes-man. We're all a bunch of battered and beaten no-men."[79] The particular object of Riccardo's managerial zeal was getting control of the sales bank. He quickly ordered corporate inventories pared down and announced his intention to keep them lean. "When the market falls off again, we won't have a big inventory around our necks to weigh us down," he said.[80]

Third was a redefined product strategy. Riccardo sought to erase Chrysler's plebeian image and attract a more affluent clientele. The venerable Darts and Valiants, still making money, were not retired in 1975 as originally planned. They were kept on to meet the demand for a cheap, reliable compact while their intended replacements— the Aspen/Volaré line—were prettied up to catch the next richer slice of the market, broadening Chrysler's coverage. The luxury intermediates Córdoba and Challenger drew a new and better-off set of consumers into Chrysler showrooms. Americans used to well-appointed automobiles but worried about mileage turned to Chrysler as the only maker of smaller deluxe cars.[81] There was also a domestic subcompact in the works, scheduled for launch for the 1978 model year. But Riccardo was not expecting it to be a big seller. Indeed, he pointed to faltering sales of Ford's Pinto and GM's Vega to justify Chrysler's 1970 decision to drop its planned subcompact in favor of light trucks.*

Chrysler's position looked solid once more by the fall of 1976. The Aspen/Volaré line, now nearly a year old, appeared to be a triumph, restoring Chrysler's dominance of the compact market. The wagons were particularly successful, claiming the number one

---

*Throughout the 1970's, vans and trucks became more important to Chrysler. In 1972 the Dodge division invested $50 million in trucks—producing two new light trucks and restyling the rest of the line—and this investment led to a sharp sales increase. Two years later Chrysler introduced the four-wheel-drive Ramcharger and Trail Duster to compete with AMC's Jeep line. By 1977 the firm had 13 percent of the total U.S. truck market and 43 percent—the biggest share—of the submarket in vans.

and number three spots in their market segment. An extraordinary 63 percent of Aspen/Volaré wagon buyers were new Chrysler customers. Riccardo's strategy of luring car buyers away from the competition with the new luxury compacts seemed to be working. Now Chrysler could turn with some confidence to its longer-term product plan. Programs for restyling and downsizing existing lines and launching new ones called for nearly $3 billion by the end of the decade, yet Chrysler aimed to do it without adding to its billion dollars in long-term debt. Riccardo was anxious to root out any signs of backsliding. "We will be in trouble before our nearest competitor," he predicted. "So the industry is on a little upturn—let's not get complacent."[82] He pledged to continue cutting costs, fine-tuning inventories, and honing product lines so that "when the industry has another downturn we won't fall into the soup again."[83]

Analysts had worried that Chrysler would be too strapped for cash to finance its transition to smaller, cleaner cars. Its competitors were budgeting far more in capital spending for the 1976–80 period than it was: $15 billion for GM and $10 billion for Ford, compared with Chrysler's $3 billion. But early successes for Riccardo's strategy made the plan seem achievable. President Eugene Cafiero declared his confidence in the company's development program, despite a 1976 R&D budget only a fifth as big as GM's. "We have kept up with all the government requirements and have been very innovative in the electronic area. . . . Where the opposition has four or five people doing something, we have one at our company. But they feel this is a challenge and they have got enthusiasm. We have a very aggressive product program. . . . We've got the strategy now and we are going to maintain the continuity of our product program."[84] Anxious lest a sudden downturn land Chrysler "in the soup" again before the program was complete, Riccardo and Cafiero arranged for "war games"—simulations of what might happen under different assumptions about the auto market and the economy. But the strategy seemed sound even with a pessimistic scenario: If the next recession came as soon as 1978–79, Chrysler would still keep its footing since its long-delayed subcompact would be launched by then—subcompacts sell well in recessions—and since many of the new, more affluent customers it was attracting would be able to stay in the market even in a weak economy.

The accounts for 1976 were consistent with Riccardo and Cafiero's happy predictions for the new Chrysler: There were record profits for the year. Cost cutting, along with a 31 percent rise in the number of units sold—versus 22 percent for the industry as a whole—yielded earnings of $423 million. This was a stunning recovery from 1975's losses of $260 million. And the industry's prophet and chronicler, *Ward's Automotive Reports,* said in early 1977 that the industry was poised for the biggest surge in production and sales since before the Arab oil embargo of 1973.[85]

8.

Just as it seemed to be coming to terms with a fickle car market, Chrysler's management was challenged by that normally most placid group—the shareholders. Despite the record profits of 1976, Chrysler's stockholders were up in arms over erratic earnings, shrunken dividends, and generous bonuses for executives. Top salaries in Detroit were uniformly impressive and often bore only the faintest relationship to corporate performance. At the 1977 annual meeting a dissident shareholder group called the Stockholders Committee for the Preservation of Chrysler Corporation submitted several proposals to limit executive compensation. All the proposals lost, but two of them—one holding total bonuses to 50 percent of total dividends and one limiting stock options—claimed more than 20 percent of the votes cast. (Proposals that management opposes are typically judged symbolic successes if they get 3 or 4 percent of shareholders' votes.)[86]

The stirrings of shareholder revolt were a worrisome development for Riccardo and Cafiero, but a vastly more discomfiting trend was the sudden collapse of Chrysler's luxury compacts, the Dodge Aspen and Plymouth Volaré. The "war games" had not considered such a reversal. But the decimation of the engineering department in Townsend's 1974–75 austerity crusade, coupled with the design challenges new regulations imposed, turned out to have riddled the new compacts with technical flaws. (The line, successors to the splendidly reliable Darts and Valiants, accounted for about 40 percent of Chrysler's 1977 sales.) In November 1977 Chrysler recalled more than a million Aspens and Volarés to check for defects that could have caused brake failure. Two more recalls followed in the next month, one for engine stalling and one for bad hood latches. By the end of 1977, the odds were better than nine out of ten that any given Aspen or Volaré had been called in to remedy defects. Chrysler spent half a million dollars just to mail the recall notices.

No customers had complained of the brake problem that prompted the first recall. Engineers at Chrysler's proving grounds had found that a subtle design flaw threatened brake failure after 150,000 miles or so. Nor was the latch problem particularly grave. It involved the secondary latch, and only three failures had been reported by the time several hundred thousand Aspens and Volarés were on the road. The stalling was another matter. It was both serious—the cars lost power unpredictably—and mysterious to Chrysler engineers. The company spent millions of dollars replacing carburetors, but new units failed as often as old ones. It was not until after months of testing that engineers isolated the problem: A component in unleaded gasoline—the only fuel compatible with catalytic converters—was reacting with the plastic of a plunger valve, hardening the material and spoiling the seal. Chrysler quickly replaced all the plastic valves with rubber ones.[87] But it was too late to salvage Aspen/Volaré's reputation. The Center for Auto Safety bestowed its Lemon of the Year award on the line. (The same cars had won *Motor Trend*'s Car of the Year award a year and a half earlier.) *Consumer Reports* rated some versions "worse than average," others "much worse than average" on frequency of repair and reliability. The recalls, along with competition from new Ford and GM compacts in the 1978 model year, cut Aspen/Volaré sales by around a fifth; Chrysler slowed production and trimmed its labor rolls. Third-quarter earnings dropped to around half the 1976 level.

Late in 1977 Chrysler launched its American-made subcompacts. The Dodge Omni and Plymouth Horizon—called collectively Omnirison in Highland Park code—were solid little vehicles with German engines and transaxles (a transaxle takes the power from the engine to the wheels in a front-drive car), put together by men and robots at Chrysler's Belvidere assembly plant in Illinois. The line quickly won praise from dealers, the press, and energy-conscious consumers, and *Motor Trend* magazine awarded it the Car of the Year award for the 1978 model year. Omnirison sales—along with the marketing boost the new subcompacts gave the rest of Chrysler's products—pushed its market share up nearly a point and a half from late 1977 to early 1978.[88]

The early success of the Omnis and Horizons was a boon for Chrysler, but Riccardo had never expected to make much money on the subcompact. The firm's flagship car was still in the works. Code-named the K-car, it would be a fuel-efficient luxury compact to replace the ill-fated Aspen/Volaré line. Originally Riccardo had planned a more or less conventional rear-wheel-drive compact, but senior engineer Harold Sperlich had convinced him of the importance of shifting to front-wheel drive. Ford had fired Sperlich late in 1976 after twenty-five years in the firm and six years as a vice-president. Sperlich attributed his abrupt dismissal to his stubbornness in pushing for a major shift to front-wheel-drive cars.[89] Chrysler hired Sperlich in March 1977. By the end of the year he was named vice-president for product planning and design, and in his new position, he resumed his front-wheel-drive campaign. Running the power directly from the engine to the axle is somewhat more efficient in a narrow technical sense, but—at least as important—it eliminates the "hump" of the drive shaft to the rear axle and makes it easier to shrink cars without sacrificing comfort. The problem was that switching to front-wheel drive meant radical retooling. Not just engines and drive trains but a wide range of components that had been designed for rear-drive cars had to be changed. It would be very expensive—roughly $300 million more than had been budgeted for the new line.[90] Higher tooling costs raised the stakes; Chrysler was now even more vulnerable to a bungled product, bad timing, or another external shock. But the 10 percent increase in federal fuel economy regulations scheduled for 1981, coupled with good market prospects for an upscale but fuel-efficient car, persuaded Cafiero and Riccardo to take the plunge into front-wheel drive for the new compact. The bet was on.

A major new line was now in the works. But aside from the Omni/ Horizon, which did more for Chrysler's image than for its balance sheet, the near-term picture was unsettling. Inflation was increasing, pushing up Chrysler's costs and intimidating potential car buyers. A six-week strike cut truck production. A shortage of engineers and technicians—the legacy of cutbacks in 1974 and 1975—delayed the launch of the 1978 models. (Indeed, every new model launched after the fall of 1974 was between four and eight months late.)[91] All of Chrysler's foreign subsidiaries except Chrysler España filed either lower earnings or losses in 1977. Partly because of the late launch and a consequent drop in market share, Chrysler lost $50 million in the last quarter of 1977 (this was a much bigger loss than analysts had expected).[92] Earnings for the whole year were $163 million, down sharply from the record $423 million of 1976.

The whole auto industry had been on a roller coaster for more than a decade. Chrysler had the most harrowing ride since it spread its bets over a narrower range and had less of a cash cushion to buffer it from illiquidity. Earnings continued to zoom up and down with no solid trend. All that company executives could say for sure was that the highs were getting higher over time and the lows were getting lower (see Figure 2, opposite). (Inflation amplified the swings, but even in real terms Chrysler's earnings became much less stable.)

FIGURE 2
Chrysler's Net Earnings

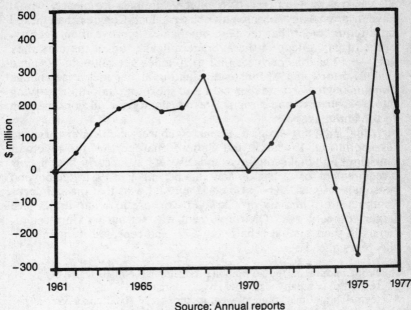

Source: Annual reports

Product development was still Chrysler's lifeline to the future, and Riccardo pressed ahead with an even more ambitious program than the $3 billion originally budgeted. Chrysler's 1977 report to its stockholders reviewed the short-run reasons for the year's poor results—the truck strike, the late launch, inflation, and poor sales— but explained that new investment was critical to the firm's long-term health, and not just because Chrysler had to keep up with its competitors. There was another reason: federal regulations. The safety and pollution control requirements that had been enacted years before were now taking hold. There was also a requirement that each automaker's products must average out to specified levels of fuel efficiency (see Appendix A, Figures 5A-1 and 5A-2). This last set of regulations had resulted from the public's continuing distrust of the oil companies. Two years before, President Gerald Ford had been ready to take price controls off oil, but the public protested. Congress had responded with a bill ordering the Federal Energy Administration to roll back the price of oil by more than $1 a barrel by February 1976. Since this measure clearly would have destroyed any incentive to conserve fuel, Congress had tacked on a requirement that the auto companies improve their fleet average of gas mileage—the average mileage for all the cars they sold—by 2 gallons per year first to 20 miles per gallon in 1980 and then 27.5 mpg in 1985. Instead of letting higher fuel prices nudge consumers toward smaller cars and more parsimonious driving habits, Congress had assigned responsibility for oil conservation to the automakers.

While endorsing the goals of energy conservation, safer cars, and less pollution, Riccardo and Cafiero charged that the levels of emissions and fuel economy standards set for the early 1980's, plus a requirement for air bags in new cars beginning in 1981, "go beyond reasonable limits." The problem, they said, was that the standards "impact more heavily on Chrysler Corporation than on its two larger competitors." Their argument was set out by Chrysler officials in their annual report for 1977 (and repeated frequently in the years ahead):

> Profit margins in the automobile industry have historically been related to company size. The larger company . . . has greater integration and marketing power; it can spread fixed costs over a greater volume of units; it can maximize the efficiency of its manufacturing processes; and it has lower cost access to capital markets. . . . The effect of these unreasonable standards in the best of times is to have the government further strengthen the competitive advantage of the largest manufacturer. During any drop in total volume, such as the industry is currently experiencing, or any loss of market penetration, such as Chrysler experienced in the fourth quarter of 1977, the impact of these government actions on a smaller company is especially serious. . . . We recognize that in the face of the unprecedented convergence of new government regulations, we are left with no choice but to proceed flat out with the most accelerated product program in our history. . . . Accordingly, we are proceeding with a massive five-year $7.5 billion program in North America to modernize our plants and bring new products to market. This is double the expenditures we have traditionally made in past years. . . . [O]ur operating results through the balance of the 1970's will continue to reflect the high costs of the programs we have undertaken, earnings will be depressed, and there will be a strain on our financial resources. After this period, the cumulative effect of the gains from improving sales, higher unit profitability, and progress in correcting or elim-

inating loss operations should offset the high costs of these programs.[93]

According to one commentary on Chrysler's massive modernization plan, "the attitude in the financial community and elsewhere seemed to be: Here comes Chrysler again, hungry for capital and peddling another one of those plans to save the company."[94] Capital spending indeed did rise sharply in 1977. The rise, however, was relative to the low level of 1974–76, when Townsend's last retrenchment had slashed outlays. Compared to earlier peaks in 1969 and 1973, the current investment push seemed less explosive (see Appendix A, Figure 6A). Indeed, when adjusted for inflation, 1977's capital spending was less than in many earlier years.

Chrysler's $7.5 billion retooling campaign was still a steep challenge, though, particularly for a company already carrying $1.2 billion in long-term debt. And the cars weren't selling. On April 26, 1978, Chrysler stunned analysts and shareholders by announcing it had lost $120 million in the first quarter of the year. A loss had been expected, but nothing like this. (A year earlier Chrysler had earned $75 million for the quarter on roughly the same gross revenues.) Riccardo, attributing the loss to retooling costs mandated by federal regulations, predicted Chrysler would break even for the year. Analysts were dubious.[95]

A week later, John J. Riccardo faced several hundred shareholders in a Chrysler training center in Center Line, Michigan, a suburb northeast of Detroit. He had an unenviable task before him: persuading the owners to authorize new stock issues to fund the first stage of the $7.5 billion modernization plan. The program for 1978 included modernizing or expanding eight plants, extending testing and engineering facilities, and building a second proving grounds, in Arizona. The audience was suspicious. Shareholders were intensely mindful of the $1.98 per share loss for the previous three months. (General Motors had recently reported first-quarter earnings of $870 million.)

Making his pitch for the new equity sale, Riccardo directed stockholders' attention to recent successes. The Omni/Horizon cars were selling splendidly. Sales and market share in March and April were up sharply over the dismal levels of January and February. Chrysler's long-troubled British subsidiary appeared to have been turned around, showing its first profitable quarter in more than three years, and Chrysler France had just introduced a successful new small car.[96] Riccardo urged shareholders to look beyond short-term losses associated with the shifting auto market and stressed that the company was "right on schedule with our $7.5 billion program to provide all new products and to modernize our manufacturing facilities. We intend to keep on that schedule, regardless of adverse pressures in the short term, because this program is absolutely vital to the long-term success of our company."[97]

The stockholders would finally approve the issue, but by an uncommonly small margin and only after three hours of stormy criticism of top management. Chrysler now had posted losses for two quarters running. Its reputation for quality had been hurt badly by the 1977 safety recalls. Its share of the market for cars and trucks, which had been 13.6 percent as recently as 1976, had fallen to 11.2 percent. The new issue of common stock would dilute current stockholders' ownership stake by a third. The preferred stock, moreover, would carry a guaranteed dividend of $2.50 a year; preferred owners would thus take precedence over common whenever Chrysler had too little money to distribute dividends to both. And now the shareholders were being asked to stake more resources to the firm's top management. This time they had to be persuaded to do so. "I can only tell you," Riccardo said, "we believe very seriously that we know how to run this company." The response, according to *The New York Times,* was "laughter and catcalls."[98] *Fortune* magazine, though, said, "The stockholders . . . should have been toasting Riccardo, not roasting him. They are sure to have a hair-raising ride during the next few years, but at least they have a chance now of reaching the end of that ride with their company in a sound and profitable position, a chance they plainly didn't have" before Riccardo and Cafiero crafted their recovery plan.[99]

Two days after the new issue had been approved—by a vote of 54 percent to 8 percent, with the rest abstaining—Chrysler recalled 1.2 million Aspens and Volarés for "precautionary repair" of a suspension component, the fourth recall in six months. The first 40,000 Omnirisons sold were also recalled because of a suspension problem. The strain on a shrunken engineering department, the legacy of the cutbacks three years earlier, was being felt in the market.

The new securities went on the market several weeks later. Six million shares of preferred stock (later raised to ten) were priced at $25 a share and carried a dividend of $2.75, for an uncommonly high yield of 11 percent. Along with each share of preferred stock came a warrant, or option to purchase half a share of common stock at a premium over the current price. The warrants would be valuable if Chrysler's common stock rose appreciably. The high dividend and the common stock sweetener were necessary to persuade investors to buy into what *The New York Times* termed "the biggest speculative offering of 1978.''[100] But the return apparently overcame investors' distaste for risk; Chrysler eventually raised more than $200 million on the stock market (see Appendix A, Figure 7A).

Second-quarter profits of $30.5 million were announced in late July 1978—better than a loss, but nothing like the kind of earnings stream needed to feed the new-product program. The urgent need for cash, rather than any long-term strategy, now set the pace of Chrysler's retreat to North American operations. Riccardo accelerated the campaign to sell the money-losing Australian and Brazilian subsidiaries to Mitsubishi and Volkswagen. (Chrysler had already sold its Turkish operations and three-fourths of its South African subsidiary.) But the big sell-off came in August. Peugeot-Citroën took over 85 percent ownership of Chrysler's French, British, and Spanish plants in exchange for $230 million in cash and Peugeot stock with a market value of $202 million—a price that gratified and surprised Chrysler executives.[101] Lynn Townsend's empire was no more.

The product plan Riccardo and Cafiero had assembled called for a major launch each year: new standard-size cars in late 1978, intermediates in 1979, compacts in 1980, and downsize vans and trucks in 1981.[102] But the series was off to a bad start. The restyled New Yorkers, Newports, and St. Regises were launched late and, as a result of production problems, stayed in short supply, stalling Riccardo's campaign to double Chrysler's share of the big-car market.[103] Despite an expanding U.S. auto market, Chrysler's sales were down for 1978 (see Appendix A, Figure 8A). Third-quarter losses reached a record $159 million. The company withdrew its earlier prediction of a profitable year: The last three quarters would net out to a loss, and the twenty-five-cent quarterly dividend, which had been maintained in the face of earlier losses, was cut to a dime until further notice.

On the day the dismal third-quarter results were revealed the Chrysler board of directors announced that it had decided on a new helmsman. Lee Iacocca, fifty-four years old, would become Chrysler's president and chief operating officer only months after he had been fired from the presidency of Ford. The board, including Iacocca, its newest member, agreed that Riccardo would stay on as its chairman and as Chrysler's chief executive officer. But Eugene Cafiero, offered the ceremonial post of vice-chairman, opted to resign. (A few months later Cafiero was recruited to be president and CEO of John Z. DeLorean's ill-fated enterprise to produce sports cars in Northern Ireland.)[104]

Lee Iacocca had been fired by Henry Ford after an extraordinary thirty-two-year career. Iacocca's peculiar genius was in coming up

with designs that hit the market with precision but could be produced at modest cost. The Mustang, which Ford had introduced
in the 1960's and was still making money on, was Iacocca's best-
known success. Some observers felt Ford was threatened by Iacocca's ambition, demonstrated competence, and popularity in the
firm, particularly among dealers. Ford himself, when Iacocca asked
the reason for his firing, replied, "Let's just say I don't like you."[105]
The Wall Street Journal hailed the appointment in a front-page feature. It characterized Iacocca as "one of the industry's best-known
and most successful executives" who "appears to possess just the
talents that Chrysler needs: He seems to have a canny sense of the
public's taste in cars, of how to create them with minimal investment, and of how to inspire dealers and marketing men to sell
them."[106] Most observers saw the hiring as distinctly good news
for Chrysler. Not all concurred; one Wall Street observer said Iacocca was "15 years behind in his conception of the auto industry,
oriented toward flash and not substance."[107]

Nobody denied Lee Iacocca was a superb salesman, though few
could guess just how crucial those talents soon would be. Within
a year the chairman's pitch for public help would be Chrysler's
only defense against bankruptcy.

II

BANKRUPTCY AND
BAILOUT

1.

In 1979 Chrysler's constituents, and the nation as a whole, would
choose between two fates for the firm: bankruptcy or bailout.
The choice was by no means novel. Each alternative had been
invoked for major American companies many times before and with
increasing frequency in the difficult decade of the 1970's. By the
time Chrysler's predicament became a public issue, the most astute
observers perceived that these two paths were beginning to converge. For large firms like Chrysler—which were linked by intricate
webs of reciprocal obligation to suppliers, dealers, labor unions,
financial institutions, and cities—there was coming to be ever less
difference between bankruptcy and bailout. A hybrid of the two
was emerging. The evolution that preceded the Chrysler rescue
suggested the form of America's response to the automaker's plight.

The bankruptcy system does much to shape what we mean by
the market. Bankruptcy law, an artifact of public policy, defines
the consequences of a collapse of contractual arrangements. It em-
bodies the principles we choose to govern our responses to economic failure.

Bankruptcy's origins are part of the broader evolution within capitalist societies from common law to formal commercial codes. The premises of early bankruptcy were not legalistic and even less derived from theoretical economics, but rather were moral: What retribution is due the malefactor who has failed in an economic undertaking and left obligations unfulfilled? In general, premodern deadbeats faced unpleasant fates. Under the Code of Hammurabi, the ancient Babylonians sold bankrupts, and often their families as well, into slavery.[1] Early Roman law let unsatisfied creditors literally divide the debtor's body.[2] This system was later refined to parcel out the debtor's estate, not his person, to creditors. In medieval Venice, merchants conducted their business from wooden benches arranged in the town square. If a merchant proved unable to deliver on a contract or repay a debt, creditors could rightfully vent their anger by breaking his bench, symbolically and practically putting him out of business. (The Italian for "broken bench" is *banca rotta,* giving us the term "bankrupt.") English law relied on debtors' prison; reforms in 1705 let the jailed bankrupt retain some of his clothing and personal effects.[3]

The English system was transplanted in America and retained after the Revolution. Unbridled speculation in government scrip, land, and corporate stock culminated in financial panics in 1791 and 1797, swelling the population of debtors' prisons. Inmates included Robert Morris, a financier of the Revolutionary Army and delegate to the Constitutional Convention. Another drafter of the Constitution, Supreme Court Justice James Wilson, would have joined Morris in a Pennsylvania debtors' prison had he not fled to North Carolina.[4] By 1830 Massachusetts, Maryland, New York, and Pennsylvania each reported jails containing three to five bankrupts for every regular criminal.[5] In the decade 1820–30, the Suffolk County Jail in Boston alone contained 11,818 imprisoned debtors out of a total population that never exceeded 63,000.[6]

The futility of locking people up until they could satisfy creditors was not lost on our predecessors. But rectification was not the goal; a display of society's opprobrium was. Punishment for economic failure doubtless deterred early Americans from commercial recklessness. But it had two other, less benign effects: First, it left creditors indefinitely and often permanently unrestored, and second, it tended to make the prudent shrink from any endeavor, however desirable, that required borrowed resources and held an appreciable risk of failure. The goals of rehabilitation for the bankrupt and recovery for the creditors only gradually arose to counterbalance the principles of punishment and deterrence. The earliest procedure for rehabilitating debtors appears in Deuteronomy 15:1–2: "At the end of every seven years thou shalt make a release. And this is the manner of the release: Every creditor that lendeth aught unto his neighbour shall release it; he shall not exact it of his neighbour, or his brother; because it is called the Lord's release." It would be some 3,000 years before the notion would find more general application.

The Constitution authorizes Congress to establish "uniform laws on the subject of bankruptcies throughout the United States."[7] But perhaps because Congress sensed no firm conceptual footing for a national bankruptcy code, it exercised this authority irregularly. During the nation's first century, federal bankruptcy laws were enacted and repealed three times; they were in force for a total of only fifteen years. The rest of the time each state applied its own codes. These varied radically and often discriminated against out-of-state creditors. At least up to the Panic of 1819 respectable opinion stood foursquare against liberalized federal bankruptcy laws, fearing windfalls for the profligate and the unscrupulous.[8]

But economic change forced new responses to business failure. America's economy was developing, becoming at once riskier and more dynamic. In a culture that required and applauded economic risk taking far more than did its European antecedents, the problem of accommodating the inevitable failures arose. Codes worked out in more static economies served poorly. An 1832 treatise described the "great and extensive" hazards of the marketplace, which beset "the undertakings of merchants, and so frequently plunge them into misfortune. . . . Instead of converting every thing they touch, like Midas, into gold, they find all their hopeful expectations disappointed, and themselves surrounded by one unbroken scene of widespread ruin and desolation."[9] The unsatisfactory aspects of tossing the unlucky entrepreneur behind bars became by degrees more apparent. Business failure, once regarded as reliable evidence of moral inadequacy, came to be seen as more frequently the regrettable but unwilled consequence of external forces.[10] Kentucky passed the first state law abolishing imprisonment for unpaid debt in 1821. New York and several other states followed within a decade.

Early reforms merely absolved the bankrupt of part of the moral odium formerly attaching to failure and set limits on the retribution creditors could exact. Codes for salvaging troubled enterprises developed only gradually. Bad times marked the end of the nineteenth century, and a wave of visibly unmerited commercial failures stirred up sentiment to make reorganization, rather than automatic liquidation, a goal of bankruptcy law. A young St. Louis lawyer named Jay L. Torrey drafted a bill that would allow bankrupt entrepreneurs, under certain circumstances, to stay in business and gradually pay off creditors from the proceeds of the continuing operations. Torrey urged his reform on Congress. "When a vessel is labouring at sea," he wrote, "nothing will more surely sink her than to leave untouched the broken masts and loose spars which every wave is using as a battering ram to pound her to pieces and carry her to the bottom. She can be saved only by cutting away the wreckage. That relief is what the absence of a bankruptcy law denies to the businessman overtaken by a storm of disaster."[11] The bankruptcy bill Torrey submitted in 1896 was signed into law by President William McKinley two years later. It has since been amended nearly a hundred times and underwent major revisions in 1938 and 1978, yet its original provisions endure as the framework of American policy and practice for troubled enterprises.[12]

The new code's most notable departure from previous law was shifting the presumption away from liquidation and toward some form of reorganization. Creditors' claims still drove the bankruptcy process. But the manner of and timing for serving those claims changed in at least three ways. First, it became easier to preserve parts, even most, of a bankrupt enterprise as a going concern. Creditors could thus be paid off gradually out of operating revenue, instead of immediately from the proceeds of selling off the business in whole or bit by bit. Second, there was to be a stipulated priority of claims. This ended the destructive race to the courthouse by creditors who feared that they must insist on immediate payment from a shaky debtor or risk seeing the firm crippled anyway by less patient lenders and the estate depleted. An orderly queue reduces the possibility that a viable enterprise may be killed by edgy creditors seizing key operating assets. It also makes the ultimate distribution fairer; in principle at least, a judge ensures that comparable claimants collect comparable sums. The third key aspect of the 1898 reform was that reorganization plans were made legally binding documents and creditors' veto power was limited. That is, once a majority of creditors agree to a given plan, it can be crammed down on recalcitrant minorities. Otherwise, each creditor would logically undertake to extort favorable terms by blocking any settlement but the one most favorable to him. With each claimant following this tactic, a workable accord would be elusive.

When the proceeds of liquidation are too meager to meet all

claims, or when a reorganized firm still cannot generate enough cash to pay all creditors fully and on schedule, rules govern who gets paid first. These rules generally respect the contracts that creditors entered with the firm before it failed. Secured creditors—lenders whose loans are backed by title to some tangible asset—come before unsecured creditors; gradations of security are many and minute. Bankruptcy courts generally preserve the order of these contractual relationships. This is both fair and efficient; if creditors and debtors have struck their deals with eyes open, the interest paid on each loan will be proportional to its risk. A loan that is backed by no collateral typically earns higher interest than a safer, secured loan. Senior creditors' priority in bankruptcy is thus no windfall. They have paid for their favored spot in the queue by accepting lower returns on their loans while the firm was healthy.

Yet these priorities are by no means absolute. The bankruptcy court can and does depart from contractual priority in order to preserve the earning power of an enterprise if it judges this to be the fairest way to balance competing claims. For example, if a senior creditor's debt is secured by a firm's main factory, a court might restrain the lender from exercising his right to seize this collateral if by so doing he would destroy the enterprise and leave other claimants stranded.

The bankruptcy code guides commercial behavior even when it is not technically invoked. Indeed, relatively few troubled firms actually file for bankruptcy. They reach accommodation with their creditors in the anteroom of bankruptcy, without the formal authority of a court. These workouts serve better than formal bankruptcy when they spare large legal expenses or when news of a formal bankruptcy filing would alarm suppliers or drive off customers, imperiling the enterprise's operations. Yet, significantly, the precise terms of an out-of-court workout generally mirror what would have occurred in bankruptcy. The parallel is not mysterious. Bankruptcy court is always waiting in the background. If several parties can force a shift to the courtroom, the stake each expects to collect under formal bankruptcy proceedings sets a floor under what he will accept in an informal workout. Bankruptcy law establishes a framework of minimum entitlements. At the same time, competition among claimants pushes each back toward that minimum. Pressure from other parties prevents any single claimant from doing much better than he could in bankruptcy; his right to insist on a formal filing prevents him from doing any worse.* The main

---

*When creditors are uncertain how they will fare under bankruptcy the game becomes more complicated, as we will show later.

difference is that with a workout, claimants have an extra pool of resources—the costs saved by staying out of court—to divide among themselves.

2.

The Torrey reform was the last fundamental change in bankruptcy law. For three-quarters of a century it served reasonably well, in part because formal bankruptcy was invoked primarily to manage the failure of small firms. In a preface to his 1963 study of corporate crisis, Richard Austin Smith observed that few major corporations ever became terminal cases: "Big enterprises are hard to kill." In the files of bankruptcy courts—the "morgues" of corporate enterprise—"most of the corpses . . . are infants, in size or life span, and whatever can be learned of their fatal malaise has precious little application to the middle-sized corporations on their way to becoming giants, or to the giants themselves, the huge complexes that characterize our industrial machine."[13] Sick big firms eventually got well, most Americans assumed, even if they were altered somewhat by the experience or a few reckless or incompetent managers were cashiered.

America's largest firms were highly visible national institutions. But the technical legal form of the giant industrial company—which differed in no important sense from that of the incorporated corner grocery—became ever less consonant with its actual economic and political status. Owners yielded management to hired professionals. Corporations juggled diverse and changeable lines of business, shifting resources from endeavor to endeavor entirely within the firm. In part because its mandate was so malleable, the giant corporation's life-span became indefinite. The biggest manufacturers attained a permanence that matched and sometimes exceeded the staying power of fair-size towns. Their social significance and political influence grew accordingly.

For large firms in the prosperous postwar era, failure became a matter of degree. Perhaps sales failed to rise in pace with the economy. Perhaps costs crept up. Perhaps rivals pulled ahead in efficiency, quality, or innovation. Fresh infusions of capital might be needed more frequently, even as the pace of expansion slowed. How were the giant firms to interpret these signals?

Economic theory is precise: An enterprise should dissolve at the point where the resources it commands produce less value than they would if put to other uses. Market prices—of the goods the firm produces and of the resources required to produce them—convey all the information required to identify that critical point. When the arithmetic of buying costs and selling prices turns sour, profits evaporate. The firm's constituents take this as the signal to withdraw, freeing resources for new endeavors.* But in practice cost and price signals are blurred by uncertainty. Does a drop in profits herald permanent decline, or is it merely the cue to change presidents or advertising themes? There are no distinct stages with economic health here, sickness there, decline and death beyond. Any definition of corporate failure rests on expectations about the future, and these expectations are colored by hopes and fears.

These market signals are particularly muted and muddled for large firms. Size and administrative complexity tend to distort information and disperse responsibility for reacting to the news. A second factor is diversification. As the number of separate enterprises bundled within a single firm increases, it becomes ever more difficult to say anything that is simultaneously simple and true about the viability of the corporation as a whole. By the last third of the twentieth century, most major American companies included both developing and moribund enterprises. Substantial parts of a firm could be jettisoned and new pieces acquired with no change in legal identity. Corporate crisis, failure, and renewal had become a more subtle matter than the drafters of the bankruptcy code had anticipated.

Major enterprises also had become radically different from small companies in a political and social sense. The goals and obligations of most small firms could be spelled out pretty completely on a single sheet of paper. But the top few hundred enterprises in America had evolved into dense networks of claims and commitments. Some of these rights and obligations were well defined and bound by contracts: Legal covenants guaranteed bondholders fixed rates of interest and the scheduled return of their principals; governments collected taxes on property, sales, and profits at legislated rates. But the web of commitments extended further, beyond formal con-

---

*"Managing better," the layman's commonsense prescription for commercial distress, is not part of the economists' pharmacopoeia. Resources, including managerial talent, are assumed to be well employed and priced with precision. Getting better management means getting better managers and paying more for them. This is the economist's basic scenario; there are also more refined versions, and the curious reader is directed to Richard M. Cyert and James March, *A Behavioral Theory of the Firm* (Englewood Cliffs, N.J.: Prentice-Hall, 1963), and Harvey Leibenstein, "Allocative Efficiency Versus X-Efficiency," *American Economic Review* (June 1966).

tracts. Employees built up firm-specific skills and put down roots in anticipation of long careers with a firm. City governments provided roads and sewers on the understanding that major companies would in turn stay to provide jobs and pay taxes. Many firms attracted retinues of smaller companies that set up shop in the area to supply customized goods and services. Constituents' strong dependence on these ties contrasted with their feeble legal status. Sometimes implicit duties and obligations were parallel extensions of contractual ties. But sometimes legal and practical roles diverged. For example, stockholders were legally entitled to set policy, while management only implemented. Yet the incapacity of dispersed stockholders to influence operations and the substantial sovereignty enjoyed by most large firms' managers are too widely known to require elaboration here. Analogously, managers were in principle entitled to fixed returns—the hired professional's pay—while owners held claim to all profits remaining after workers, managers, and creditors had been paid off. But managers endeavored to keep dividends constant to gratify investment analysts and let retained earnings rise and fall rather than the payout to stockholders. Executive compensation, conversely, came to depend to a greater extent on the corporation's current performance.

The major corporation became, in short, a *political* entity. This was true in two senses. First, dealings within the large firm—across divisions, among managers, between management and labor—were governed by political as much as or more than by economic relationships. Large-scale production required advance planning, planning required stability, and stability required meticulous internal accommodation among blocs of constituents. The big industrial firm was also political in its external relationships. In order to secure the long-term stability it required, it had to manage its environment. The means for doing this were unabashedly political. Major corporations came to depend on an accommodating government and society. On the local level firms required roads, bridges, sewers, and schools. On state and national levels accommodation took the forms of preferential purchases of major firms' goods, subsidized finance, tailored tax and accounting laws, and protection from foreign competition and domestic usurpers. The legitimacy accorded the firm's demands on the public, and the reciprocal public demands made of the firm, has risen and fallen with the ideological tides, though it never has been wholly washed away.

During the postwar period of economic stability and American industrial leadership these networks of claims became at once denser and more extensive. Large-scale production demanded stable configurations of human, financial, and physical resources. The phenomenal profitability of this style of production sustained these networks. During the late 1960's and early 1970's new kinds of obligations were imposed on the firm. The most notable new stricture was to cease using the environment as a free resource, but there were also mandates to promote actively the hiring and advancement of women, minorities, and the disadvantaged. These new commitments were layered on top of existing claims. But so long as the postwar prosperity lasted, affluence attenuated conflict among claimants. The large corporation seemed perfectly capable of accommodating simultaneously its obligations—contractual and implicit—to shareholders, creditors, managers, workers, local communities, and society at large.

3.

Starting somewhere around 1970, the sturdy economic foundation that had supported these webs of claims began to crumble. First, "oil shocks" in 1973 and 1979 raised the cost of almost every business, forced hurried industrial change, and precipitated a sharp increase in the United States' foreign obligations. Suddenly higher energy prices ravaged the old industrial states of the Northeast and Midwest and bestowed a windfall on the Sun Belt states, causing wrenching regional shifts. Inflationary pressures brewing since the mid-1960's were released by the shocks. These pressures and the convulsive policy efforts undertaken to contain them were to dominate American industry for more than a decade.

Second, the peculiar postwar preeminence by default that the United States had enjoyed began, ineluctably, to erode. Foreign competitors shattered by World War II completed their reconstruction and rejoined the world economy. Even more significant was the emergence of many countries that had never before been serious industrial powers. Foremost among these, of course, was Japan. But by 1970 South Korea, Brazil, Hong Kong, Taiwan, Singapore, the Philippines, Mexico, and several others were competing with American producers in some world markets. The diffusion of technology, the development of a global capital market, and improvements in the mechanics of shipping goods worldwide accelerated these countries' development into proficient competitors in one or several industries. American firms were feeling the pressure by the mid-1970's.

Third, technical change—in part forced by rising energy prices and heightened foreign competition—intensified the challenge to American manufacturers. Shrinking demand for some products, and dramatically altered processes for making others, put heavy strains on networks of roles and expectations built up in more placid times. In some cases, technical change forced firms to dedicate huge sums to research and retooling, in effect betting the company on a new product or technology.

American industry was ill-prepared for this more fluid, more dangerous world. Each major enterprise carried an extensive collection of constituents; each dependent group, anxious to preserve its status, was vigilant against challenges. Claimants dug in. They sought to immunize themselves against change by locking up their claims and passing risk on to other parties. Managers sought stability by acquiring other firms and resorted to intricate, economically sterile legal and financial dodges to put the best face possible on their performance.[14] Investors anxious to lock in a predictable rate of return deserted the equity markets in favor of notes, bonds, and indirect fixed-income investments.* Unionized labor demanded wages indexed to inflation along with normal raises. As each of its constituent groups sought to evade risk, the large firm's capacity to change atrophied. As external challenges intensified, the old patterns of organization became less able to accommodate all claims. And as claims became more jealously defended, rigidities increased. Ever greater pressures came to bear on ever more brittle organizations. Some of these structures began to crack. (We can be more precise about the timing of this evolution for the auto industry. The epochal shakeout of the 1950's gave way to the placid 1960's, and it was not until the Japanese challenge emerged midway through the 1970's that the comfortable oligopoly began to erode. As American automakers lost the ability to control their prices, the inflexible claims that had grown up during the good times threatened to bear them down. Chrysler, the weak sister of the Big Three, felt the heat the most.)

The distress of established firms with concentrated operations and well-defined constituencies inevitably became a political matter.

---

*New equity fell from an average of 5.4 percent of corporate funding in the 1951–55 period to 2 percent in the 1976–78 period. Debt, meanwhile, rose from 18.5 percent to 27.3 percent. American households bought more equity than they sold in every year from 1948 to 1957. From 1957 to 1978 they sold more than they bought each year, turning instead to direct and (especially) intermediate debt. These figures are from Benjamin Friedman, "Postwar Changes in the American Financial Markets," in *The American Economy in Transition*, Martin Feldstein, ed. (Chicago: University of Chicago Press, 1980), Table 1.5, pp. 23 and 38.

As the tumult of the 1970's took its toll, pressures began to build for measures to shield prospective victims. Congress responded along two tracks. First, it altered the rules of the game for faltering firms. By changing the bankruptcy laws, it strengthened the hands of those constituents who favored reorganization instead of liquidation. Second, in a number of instances—one involving a city instead of a firm—Congress brought a new class of constituents, with its own resources and goals, to join the bargaining at the table: the public at large.

4.

The first track was the 1978 reform of the bankruptcy code. Since the Torrey reform bill eight decades earlier, the law had presented troubled firms and their claimants with a choice: liquidation or reorganization. Detailed specifications of debtors' and creditors' rights governed which form the bankruptcy process would take. The 1978 revision, long pressed by trade associations and business groups, made it easier to preserve a company as a going concern, harder to force it to pay off claims immediately at the risk of permanent dissolution.

Chapter 11 of the bankruptcy code protects a troubled firm from the warrants of claimants, principally creditors, whose demands imperil continued operations. Congress amended Chapter 11 somewhat and, more important, made it easier for companies to choose this option over liquidation. Prior to 1978 a company could seek Chapter 11 protection only if it was insolvent (that is, if its total assets were less than its total liabilities) or if it was unable to pay maturing debt. The reform bill quietly deleted the insolvency test, thus broadening managers' discretion to take shelter behind bankruptcy laws. Previously a Chapter 11 filing was only an application, which the judge could accept or deny. After 1978 the presumption would be that management files in good faith, and few cases would be dismissed. Managers formerly anticipated having to step aside in favor of a court-appointed trustee if total unpaid debts exceeded $250,000. The 1978 reform let managers keep control of the company unless the judge explicitly found them incompetent or untrustworthy. Instead of presiding over meetings of creditors where claims are bargained out, judges would now leave most decisions— even major ones—to the existing managers. (The White Motor Company sold off most of its truckmaking business to Volvo while in Chapter 11, for example. Investment bankers for buyer and seller, not a judge, presided over this liquidation.)

The Bankruptcy Reform Act of 1978 took effect on October 1, 1979. Its liberalized provisions, coupled with the effects of sequential recessions, led to sharp increases both in the number of bankruptcies and in the percentage of firms choosing to reorganize under Chapter 11 rather than to liquidate (see Figure 3, below).

FIGURE 3
Bankruptcy Filings

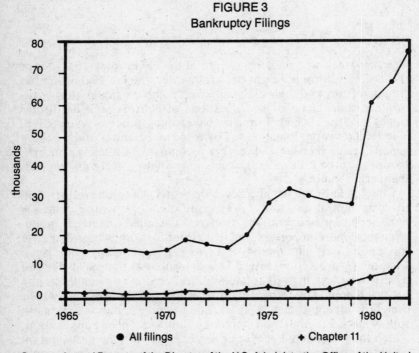

Source: *Annual Reports of the Director of the U.S. Administrative Office of the United States Courts, Tables of Bankruptcy Statistics.* Data for the year ended June 30, 1980, extrapolated from the last nine months of that period.

The 1978 reform strengthened the hand of management against lenders, labor, and other claimants. Congress endorsed the rationale that managers—as the custodians of the firm—come closest to a balanced position and are best placed to serve the interest of all the firm's constituents. The results at times have been startling:

HRT Industries, a Los Angeles-based retailer, filed for bankruptcy in November 1982. Chapter 11 let the company suspend payment for the bulging Christmas inventory it had ordered just before filing.[15] The managers of Wilson Foods, armed with powers the new bankruptcy code conferred, launched a successful offensive against the firm's labor union. A four-year contract signed while Wilson was a part of the LTV Corporation froze wages through 1985. Other firms in the troubled packing industry, however, had pressed the United Food and Commercial Workers to accept *lower* wages, and new competitors had opened nonunion plants. By early 1983 Wilson's labor costs were well above the industry average. Contending it could not stay in business without wage cuts, it filed for Chapter 11 protection. Within hours of filing Wilson had abrogated its labor contracts and cut wages in half. Continental Airlines, with labor costs nearly double the postderegulation industry average, employed similar tactics: It filed under Chapter 11, laid off two-thirds of its workers, and cut the pay of those remaining by up to 50 percent. Three days after filing Continental was back in business, though with less than a quarter of the flights it had operated before. Eastern Airlines, by threatening to follow the same route, brought its employees to the table to renegotiate wage claims. The Supreme Court conferred legitimacy on such tactics in early 1984, when it ruled that burdensome labor contracts could be abandoned.[16] By June of that year, labor had retaliated through the political process. Congress amended the bankruptcy laws to prohibit summary abrogation of labor contracts. The new provisions set up several steps that must be taken before a labor contract can be broken.*

Managers have also used Chapter 11 to parry lawsuits. In 1982 the Johns-Manville Corporation took refuge in Chapter 11. Its net worth was more than $1 billion. But damage claims from workers sickened by exposure to asbestos, one of Johns-Manville's products, could have eventually reached $2 billion, managers contended. Chapter 11 suspended these claims. By late 1984 the bankruptcy case was still pending, and no asbestosis claims had been paid. Revere Copper and Brass, which makes kitchen implements, entered Chapter 11 in 1982. Environmentalists had filed suit charging Revere with unlawfully polluting water around its Rome, New York, plant; the bankruptcy judge dismissed the suit. (Suits filed by government agencies cannot be stayed, but the

---

*Companies first have to bargain with unions over concessions. Then a bankruptcy judge has to determine if the unions refused the concessions without good reason, and if the firm faces financial collapse without a new agreement.

judge ruled that the environmental group's claim did not qualify.)

By the early 1980's, bankruptcy work had gained a certain glamour in legal circles. Prestigious New York law firms were building up their bankruptcy practices or acquiring specialized firms. The 1978 reforms both boosted the number of cases and made each case more lucrative. Previously, legal fees in bankruptcy cases were set under the economy principle—bankrupt firms, that is, should be billed at a lower rate than solvent ones for comparable legal work. After 1978 no such principle applied. Moreover, the lawyers and investment bankers who shepherd a firm through the bankruptcy process could step ahead of earlier constituents in their claims on the firm. Although Johns-Manville reported operating profits of $60 million in 1983, Chapter 11 protection denied damages to tort victims, interest to bondholders, and dividends to shareholders. But thirty-seven law firms collected a total of $25 million. The two investment banking houses involved in the case each collected monthly fees of $125,000.[17]

It is tempting to condemn as naked abuse the resort to Chapter 11 as a shield against labor unions or tort plaintiffs. But shifting bargaining power among the constituents that constitute the firm—and, specifically, strengthening defenses against immediate claims—were precisely the purpose of the 1978 reforms. Bankruptcy law sets the terms of bargaining. The new Chapter 11 was intended to bring all parties to a single bargaining table. Workers and tort victims join other classes of claimants in adjusting the goals and duties of the enterprise. Groups disadvantaged by this process—that is, by the loss of their right to demand their due unilaterally—are easy to identify: lenders and trade creditors, for example, or unionized workers with enough seniority to keep their jobs even if the firm shrinks drastically. But by preserving the enterprise and maintaining its ability to pay future claims, Chapter 11 has strengthened the positions of other, less identifiable constituents. The Johns-Manville case is again illuminating. Compensating current asbestosis victims fully would require that the company's assets be promptly turned into cash. But symptoms of the disease frequently appear decades after exposure. There are thousands of victims who will only gradually learn of their disease. If Johns-Manville were liquidated, there would be no firm left to sue for damages. Without Chapter 11 early claimants would be compensated fully, but late claimants not at all.

Most cases are less extreme, yet this episode helps illustrate how Chapter 11 tilts the bargaining table to favor preservation, even at the expense of valid claimants. The presumption is that constituents are in general best served by reorganization instead of by liquidation. This is not to say that the 1978 bankruptcy code struck the right balance among competing claims, but rather that there can be no objectively right or neutral balance. Bankruptcy law codifies choices about the kind of economy and the kind of society we want to have.

5.

New pressures on American firms forced institutional innovation. The first track of this evolution, as we have seen, was tilting the terms of the bankruptcy code in favor of reorganization and away from liquidation. The goal was to ensure that technical default on a partial obligation did not trigger liquidation, which might inefficiently and unfairly leave constituents stranded. The results have been mixed.

The second track of institutional evolution in the 1970's was a greater readiness to resort to direct public intervention to rescue failing endeavors. Such initiatives have carried the inelegant (and imperfectly descriptive) label of "bailout." Bailouts are by no means new responses to troubled firms.* During the Depression decade of the 1930's the federal government provided low-interest loans to failing enterprises through the Reconstruction Finance Corporation; the Small Business Administration continued the tradition after the RFC's demise. Nor was the border between bankruptcy and bailout always well delineated. Laws and judicial decisions had often invoked the "public interest" and tapped public resources to maintain the operations of bankrupt railroads, utilities, newspapers, and banks. But the turbulence of the 1970's precipitated several exceptionally visible public rescue missions. The first such episode began on June 21, 1970, with the collapse of the Penn Central Railroad.

Railroads had been declining for decades, particularly in the Northeast. Technology and demographics shifted in favor of other

---

*In his book *The Wheels of Commerce: Civilization and Capitalism 15th–18th Century*, Volume 2 (New York: Harper & Row, 1982), Fernand Braudel identifies a curious sixteenth-century precedent to modern bailouts. As certain Central European salt, copper, silver, iron, and lead mines were becoming depleted, the financiers managed to foist them off on the local princes, retaining for themselves the still-profitable businesses of refining and distribution.

forms of transportation. The government had some hand in this reversal: A 1961 Senate Commerce Committee report noted that between 1917 and 1960 the federal government had spent $20.7 billion on highways, $7.1 billion on waterways, $4.5 billion for aviation, and nothing on railroads.[18] In addition, regulations set freight tariffs on a strict dollars per mile basis. This hurt northeastern railroads, which did a disproportionate share of the switching and routing and helped railroads that mostly carried freight nonstop along straight lengths of track. By 1970 the rail labor force was only about half the size it had been in 1945. But in return for allowing job levels to fall, railroad unions had insisted upon strong work rules that protected members—especially senior members—against loss of income.

Two tottering firms, the Pennsylvania Railroad and the New York Central, joined together in 1968 in what was then the largest corporate merger in American business history. Suddenly Penn Central was the sixth-biggest firm in the country, with almost 100,000 employees, 118,000 stockholders, and 20,000 miles of working track in seventeen states. Most observers welcomed the merger. *Time* magazine honored its architect, Stuart Sanders, with a cover story and declared the formation of Penn Central to be "a victory for railroads across the country."[19]

In hindsight it is obvious that Penn Central was sick from the start. Wildly creative accounting concealed the trouble from the public and from the firm's unduly serene board of directors. In 1969 Penn Central lost $82.8 million. In 1970 its losses quadrupled, reaching a rate of a little more than $1 million a day. The value of its stock plummeted. By early June 1970 the company was visibly running out of cash. It was unable to roll over $75 million in commercial paper that came due that month. Penn Central's banks were willing to replace these now-dubious corporate IOUs with loans only if the federal government would guarantee repayment.

In Washington the temptation to oblige was enormous. Shippers and industries throughout the Northeast—as well as 100,000 workers—depended on the railroad. A Penn Central collapse might panic the commercial paper and stock markets and sour the business mood nationwide. Pointing to the potential for serious aftershocks from Penn Central's failure, Transportation Secretary John Volpe proposed that the government guarantee up to $200 million in loans to Penn Central; the railroad claimed this would cover its cash needs for up to six months. But ultimately the Nixon administration rejected the rescue proposal.

On a Sunday night in late June Penn Central went bankrupt. Its cash balance had fallen to $7 million. Current liabilities of $750 million swamped current assets of $280 million. In its fewer than 900 days of operation, the company had attained distinction as the most unprofitable private enterprise in history. Claims and commitments among 100,000 creditors, nearly that many employees, the constituents of 186 subsidiaries, and the customers and communities served by Penn Central were suddenly at risk.

There were also external stakes. Investors were already traumatized by the American invasion of Cambodia and by the abrupt deflation of several high-flying investment pools. Certain that the financial markets would react in panic to Penn Central's demise, the Federal Reserve moved to contain the chaos. A vice-president of the Federal Reserve Bank of New York called the top officers of the major New York banks at their homes that Sunday night, urging them to cover their corporate customers' credit requirements and assuring them that the Fed would accommodate the banks' cash needs. The next day the same message went out to other banks across the country. Catastrophe was averted, but at a cost: By dousing the kindling crisis with a flood of fresh liquidity, the Federal Reserve put new upward pressure on the inflation rate.

Penn Central came within Section 77 of the bankruptcy code, a special section for railroads in distress. This section, drafted during the Depression, required bankrupt railroads to keep trains running while a reorganization plan was prepared. When Section 77 was invoked for railroads shattered by a one-time trauma, it made sense to expect that financial reorganization would allow a speedy resumption of full service. The industry was different now. Competition from air and road transport meant that some of Penn Central's routes would never again be run at a profit. Keeping them going temporarily would call for more than protection against creditors; it would require large infusions of fresh resources. This is what the government eventually provided. In 1971 Congress created the National Railroad Passenger Corporation (Amtrak) to adopt the nation's entire intercity rail passenger service, including routes that the Penn Central was operating at huge losses.

Then, in 1976, following years of haggling over terms and plans, Congress took over the painfully unprofitable freight operations of Penn Central and five other bankrupt eastern railroads. The remains of these firms were swept together into a single entity, the Consolidated Rail Corporation, or Conrail, a quasi-governmental undertaking pledged to keep the freight trains running in the Northeast. Over the next five years taxpayers contributed several billion dollars to make good Conrail's operating losses and restore its dilapidated assets. The railroad labor unions, meanwhile, made only minor wage concessions. Few money-losing lines were abandoned since the communities they served objected to the prospect. Shippers continued to pay rates below the full cost of service.

Relieved of its railroad operations by the federal government, the Penn Central Corporation blossomed from bankruptcy in 1978 as a diversified conglomerate with assets in energy, entertainment, and real estate. The government paid it $2.1 billion for the money-losing railroad. In addition, the tax benefits it "inherited" from the railroad—roughly $1 billion worth of losses were carried forward—spared the new Penn Central from paying taxes on gains from its acquisitions.* By 1980 the company was making handsome profits. It paid off its $2 billion in debt. Its stock price climbed, and it established a new and much more successful role among America's top firms.

Conrail, meanwhile, was less prosperous. Losses mounted in 1979 and 1980, and in 1981 the Reagan administration announced it was looking for a buyer, even if selling Conrail meant sacrificing labor's income guarantees. Soon after the announcement some 15,000 members of the rail unions converged on Washington, D.C., where they marched from Union Station to the Capitol, periodically raising their voices in a mass impression of a train whistle. On the Capitol steps AFL-CIO President Lane Kirkland declared, to vigorous applause, "[I]f President Reagan's proposals are carried out . . . Conrail will be decimated. Thousands of workers will be thrown out of jobs. . . . We cannot let the future of our country be jeopardized by a misguided attempt to pinch pennies from the budget at the expense of economic prosperity and national security."[20] But as the recession abated, rail shipments took off, and with them Conrail's revenues. In 1983 it made more than $300 million; in 1984, around $500 million. Several groups bid to buy Conrail in 1984; the serious bids were in the range of $1 billion, only a little more than the cash Conrail had on hand. (Since 1976 buying and restoring Conrail's physical plant and making good its operating losses had cost American taxpayers some $7.6 billion.[21])

The reorganization created a few clear winners. Lawyers who worked on the bankruptcy billed $50 million over seven years. The firm that managed the reorganization of Penn Central's nonrail sub-

---

*In 1981 Congress amended the tax code to permit losses to be carried forward for fifteen years instead of five. This tripled Penn Central's planning horizon overnight. Two years later the Internal Revenue Service decided that Penn Central's loss account represented "operating" rather than "capital" losses; this gave the firm until 1993 to offset its new operating profits with old losses carried forward.

sidiaries and real estate holdings earned fees estimated to exceed
$20 million. Stockholders in the reincarnated Penn Central saw
shares climb gratifyingly. Most railway employees kept their jobs
until they retired with healthy pensions. This realignment of claims
relied on the government's readiness to assume the obligations that
other parties sloughed off. Penn Central's managers and their advisers gleaned from the wreckage a salvageable core, jettisoned the
rest of its operations, and let the public take care of the constituents—shippers, communities, and labor—whose claims had overburdened the old Penn Central.

The Lockheed Corporation had been one of the Pentagon's most
important suppliers through the 1960's. Its offerings included the
Trident ballistic missile for the Poseidon submarine, the Agena
spacecraft, and other technologically desirable hardware. But late
in the decade the company stumbled. It suffered a $500 million loss
stemming from cost overruns on four defense contracts, the most
significant of which was for the C-5A military transport plane. (The
company had agreed to produce 115 aircraft at a ceiling price of
$2.3 billion, but it delivered only 81 planes; its cost was $3.7 billion.)
Lockheed also underestimated the cost of research, development,
and production for a new passenger aircraft, the L-1011 Tristar.
Beyond its particular troubles, Lockheed suffered from the general
slump in government orders for aerospace equipment as the moon
race ended and the escalation in Vietnam slowed.

Its financial troubles worsened with the 1971 collapse of Rolls-
Royce, the venerable British firm that had contracted to supply the
RB-211 engines for the Tristar. The British government said that
it would rescue Rolls-Royce, but only if the U.S. government would
in turn guarantee up to $250 million of the new bank loans that
Lockheed said it needed to complete the Tristar project. U.S. banks
similarly refused to lend Lockheed additional funds unless the federal government guaranteed repayment. The loan guarantee issue
was joined.

Supporters of a Lockheed bailout warned of devastating job losses. An econometric model devised at the University of California
at Los Angeles predicted that 63,000 jobs would be lost if Lockheed
failed. While suppliers in twenty-five states would be affected, the
model predicted that losses would be concentrated in the distressed
aerospace industry and most heavily in California, where unemployment was already at 7 percent. The UCLA team also anticipated
extensive economic fallout if the Tristar program dissolved. Banks,
subcontractors, suppliers, and airlines—notably Trans World and

Eastern, which had already rendered progress payments for the new jet—would lose more than $1 billion. Shock waves would spread out to suppliers and other local firms, tipping more companies into bankruptcy. A further argument—traditionally so potent in American industrial policy making that its proponents feel little need to elaborate its logic—was that the loss of the large Pentagon contractor would have ominous implications for national defense. Lockheed's supporters also argued that some European countries financed their commercial aircraft companies; subsidizing Lockheed would only redress the balance, serving the cause of fairness as well as efficiency.

Opponents dismissed the horror stories as fantasies, and countered that the economy could accommodate Lockheed's failure with only very minor trauma. If the stumbling airplane division were to be nudged into bankruptcy, a reconfigured Lockheed could continue its missile and military aircraft operations. Alternatively, another defense contractor would acquire and operate Lockheed's assets. McDonnell Douglas in particular was well placed to adopt much of Lockheed's business, thus limiting employment losses and relieving worries related to defense production. Bailing out Lockheed not only was unnecessary, opponents argued, but would also establish a dreadful precedent, inviting other financially weak companies to seek government aid. Managers would take less care to stay solvent. Once in trouble, they would clamor for public help instead of undertaking the tough measures needed for recovery. *The New York Times,* among other journals, launched editorials against the loan guarantee:

> Lockheed's management is apparently confident that the company's financial obligations are so huge—especially to many banks and airlines—and the fallout of its collapse on subcontractors, its employees and stockholders, and the Pentagon, would be so great, that nothing could happen. . . . The public interest would be badly served if the Pentagon yielded to this bluff. Lockheed has demonstrated a degree of managerial inefficiency unusual even for defense contractors. Rather than rescue Lockheed's existing management, it would be better for the Government to let the company go under and, as was done in the case of Penn Central, reorganize in bankruptcy.[22]

The Lockheed issue fell to Congress's banking committees. As the atmosphere of claims, charges, and proposals thickened, Congress began consideration of the Nixon administration's Lockheed rescue bill. Senate Banking Committee Chairman John Sparkman

(D-Ala.) and Wright Patman (D-Texas), his counterpart in the House, had long favored establishing a national development bank that would finance firms in high-unemployment areas. At the height of the crisis, Federal Reserve Board Chairman Arthur Burns put a new spin on the debate. Burns's proposal, something of a hybrid between the targeted Lockheed bailout and the broader development bank idea, was to set up an emergency loan guarantee board authorized to guarantee up to $2 billion in bank loans. The board, composed of the chairman of the Federal Reserve Board, and the secretaries of the treasury and commerce, would select, under congressional oversight, which companies should get such aid. No single firm could receive more than $250 million in guaranteed loans. Assistance would be reserved for essentially sound firms suffering temporary trouble. The recipients would also have to be sufficiently large or sufficiently concentrated that failure would have "serious and adverse effects on the economy of the nation or a major region."[23] The Senate Banking Committee voted 10 to 5 to substitute a bill inspired by Burns's proposal for the administration's Lockheed bill.

The House Banking and Currency Committee held hearings shortly thereafter. But the House declined to follow the Senate's lead on a permanent loan guarantee institution. One central reason, according to a contemporary observer, was that "nobody could think of any company except a defense contractor who might be the next one. There are rumors that Grumman, Boeing, and some other aerospace businesses are teetering not too much farther from the brink than Lockheed," wrote Eileen Shanahan in *The New York Times*. "Thus one key ideological issue that has motivated members of Congress throughout the discussion of the Lockheed rescue plan has been their attitude toward the military-industrial complex."[24]

Once the House had rejected the Burns guarantee board initiative, attention returned to the more limited Lockheed legislation. The bill would establish the Emergency Loan Guarantee Board, to be chaired by the secretary of the treasury and to include the chairman of the Federal Reserve Board and the chairman of the Securities and Exchange Commission. The board's jurisdiction would formally extend to any qualifying firm, but the qualifications were drafted with care so as to exclude any firm but Lockheed. Before authorizing guarantees, the board would have to determine, first, that Lockheed could tap no other, more conventional source of credit; second, that federal intervention was needed to avert serious economic consequences; and finally, that Lockheed would in future both be able to repay the loans and be constrained to do so by the government's claim on its assets.[25] No more than $250 million in loan guarantees could be outstanding at any given time. The act barred dividends on common stock and restricted the repayment of unguaranteed debt. It directed the guarantee board to monitor Lockheed's accounts and empowered it, under certain circumstances, to force changes in Lockheed's management. To cover its risk, the federal government would take a priority claim on the firm's assets, shouldering aside other creditors in the event of bankruptcy and liquidation. The bill passed narrowly—by 49 to 48 in the Senate, 192 to 189 in the House—and President Nixon signed it into law on August 9, 1971.

The guarantees let Lockheed put its finances in order.* Lenders, reassured by federal backing for at least part of Lockheed's debt, agreed to restructure $400 million in unguaranteed credits. They temporarily cut their interest rate to 4 percent and stretched out maturities by two years. The banks also agreed to convert $75 million of debt into preferred stock and warrants—options to purchase common stock at a specified price. Lockheed's customers (the airlines) advanced $100 million in early payments for new jets.

Lockheed survived and eventually prospered. Its recovery was fueled by an improved economy, strong foreign sales, and rich government contracts. By the end of the decade it was out of the civilian airplane business altogether and was making all its money on military hardware. The company paid off the last of its guaranteed loans in 1977, a few months ahead of schedule, and replaced its government financing with a $100 million revolving credit agreement with its banks. By 1979 the warrants Lockheed had given its bankers to sweeten the restructuring had yielded a paper profit of $58 million. Lockheed ranked number five among the Fortune 500 in 1983 in total returns to investors over the previous ten years.[27]

New York City's financial troubles began in the early 1960's— though the booming economy hid the problem for years—when its annual revenues first began falling short of its rising operating expenses. The strain was rooted in problems shared to some degree by many other large American cities. The flight to the suburbs, led by the most affluent citizens, was draining tax dollars from city

---

*In June 1974, Textron, Inc., a major Lockheed competitor, arranged to provide Lockheed with enough equity capital to substitute for the public loan guarantees, in exchange for a large ownership stake. Under the terms of the deal—which investment banker Felix Rohatyn arranged—Textron's chief executive officer, G. William Miller, would assume control of Lockheed as well. The deal unraveled before it could be completed, but its principals later got their chances in the Chrysler deal.[26]

coffers. The disadvantaged poured in from overseas and from other parts of the country, pushing up the costs of social programs. Residents demanded higher levels of municipal services, including new hospitals and college facilities, and officials felt constrained to oblige. Well-organized municipal workers negotiated steady wage increases with rich pension and benefit packages attached.

Current municipal receipts could not cover all these claims. The city resorted to borrowing to cover its operating costs. Its debt burgeoned. The 1974–75 recession undercut sales and income tax revenues while it increased the demand for social services, intensifying the pressure. Ever more fanciful financial legerdemain dominated the city's fiscal practices.

By the middle of the decade New York City, with about 3 percent of the nation's population, accounted for around 30 percent of all tax-exempt borrowing in the United States. The debt became by degrees harder to sell, and by early 1975 there was essentially no market for New York City securities. In May Federal Reserve Board Chairman Arthur Burns warned that any bank lending money to the city could be sued by shareholders for violating standards of prudence. The city was stranded.

New York State arranged a short-term program to keep the city functioning. The legislature created the Municipal Assistance Corporation (MAC), which was to replace the city's short-term debt with its own long-term bonds. MAC securities were backed by levies on stock market transactions in Manhattan and by a special state sales tax collected only in New York City. The city, for its part, had to balance its operating budget within three years. A second round of state legislation in September established the Emergency Financial Control Board, endowed with nearly complete authority over the city's fiscal affairs.

The federal government first stepped in with the New York Seasonal Financing Act of 1975. One of the city's problems was that its revenues were out of sync with its spending; tax collection was episodic while operating costs were more or less constant. The Seasonal Financing Act provided up to $2.3 billion in short-term funds—loans of less than a year's maturity—to cover these liquidity gaps.

From 1975 to 1978 the city took drastic steps to contain its costs. The municipal work force dropped from 360,000 to 300,000. City workers' wages were frozen, and previously granted increases were deferred. Transit fares rose 44 percent. City colleges, traditionally free, began charging tuition. MAC initiated or monitored most of these changes and itself arranged $7 billion in financing over a period of several years. The cutbacks, along with MAC's assistance, the federal government's seasonal loans, and a fortified financial planning and accounting system, stabilized the city's fiscal situation somewhat; all seasonal loans were repaid on time. But the city remained in such precarious financial shape that no private investors were willing to buy its debt without federal loan guarantees. The city, its overseers, and its allies petitioned Congress for more long-term help.

The New York City Loan Guarantee Act of 1978 authorized the secretary of the treasury to guarantee up to $1.65 billion in New York City bonds. Some of the conditions were copied from the Lockheed bill: The secretary had to find that the guarantees were needed to keep the recipient solvent and that they would likely be repaid. (Unlike the case of Lockheed, the secretary was to act on his own, not as head of a board.) But there were other conditions, these less rooted in the Lockheed precedent. The city had to develop a financial recovery plan including concessions from its workers and commitments from New York State and private lenders. The plan had to culminate in a balanced budget by fiscal 1982. And New York had to submit to annual audits by an independent committee to ensure the plan was in force.

The bill, predictably, summoned controversy. Supporters invoked three general arguments. First, insolvency would mean a rise in unemployment and decay in urban services that the United States could not accept for its economic and cultural capital. Second, if New York were to default on even a part of its $30 billion debt, it would shake the hundreds of banks holding its securities and possibly undermine the municipal bond market, which sustained cities throughout America. Finally, there was vague but anxiety-provoking speculation on what bankruptcy for New York City—the world's densest financial and commercial nexus—might do to international confidence in the U.S. financial system, to the value of the dollar, even to the stability of the world economy. The case against aid was blunter: Bailing out New York would set a loathsome precedent, erode fiscal discipline in American cities, and unbind public-sector unions previously restrained by the fiscal limits of their municipal employers. Proponents prevailed: The legislation passed the Senate 53 to 27 and the House 247 to 155.

The rescue mission mounted by the state and federal governments, along with changes initiated by city officials, saved New York City from bankruptcy. The budget was balanced, albeit only by sharply cutting municipal services, especially in the outlying boroughs. The city sold small quantities of its own securities in

1981 and 1983 and reentered credit markets on a larger scale in 1983. By early 1984 it had paid off nearly a third of its guaranteed long-term debt and was gradually relaxing austerity measures.[28]

These rescues—Conrail, Lockheed, and New York—are less extraordinary in intent and result than they may seem. What distinguishes such programs from common American practice is not so much the fact of intervention as it is the openness of the means employed to avert failure. Direct financial help is only one form of governmental assistance. Bailouts are *visible* instances in which public policy shunts money to where it otherwise would not go. There are other, more covert ways to channel resources to an entity out of favor with the market, and these are the mechanisms that Americans by tradition prefer. Ours is an economy of tariffs, quotas, trade regulations, and excruciatingly complex tax preferences. Some of these measures are meant to benefit healthy firms but end by propping up sick ones; others are supposed to support troubled businesses but are preempted by the prosperous; others have no more specific purpose than somehow to further enterprise. These policies shape much of what we think of as the market. They set the slant of the economic terrain. We have examined specific bailouts not because they are more important than these other policies—they are not—but because they are uncommonly transparent and thus reveal many of the philosophical and economic underpinnings of our industrial politics.

6.

Many governmental projects to prevent economic decline or to moderate its pace occur below the federal level. State-administered development programs allocated to businesses almost $20 billion in 1981 by means of interest subsidies, quasi-official investment funds, and the like. This was only partly public money, and much of it was originally collected by the federal government even when it was controlled by the states. Nor was it all directed toward faltering firms. But many state-level initiatives have been intended to protect major employers against failure or—probably more commonly—to dissuade them from moving to where taxes are lower and labor and supplies cheaper, either elsewhere in this country or abroad.

One particularly striking development has been the rise in industrial development bond (IDB) financing over the past fifteen years. States and cities can raise money more cheaply than private firms because the interest from state and municipal bonds is exempt from federal tax; this tax subsidy tempts investors to buy public-sector debt even though it pays lower pretax interest rates. In an industrial development bond deal, a public agency in effect transfers this privilege to a private firm. For state and local development agencies IDBs are useful lures to attract or retain footloose firms. For companies the interest rate subsidy is welcome, even if it only rarely changes location decisions. The losers are federal taxpayers. Tax-exempt industrial financing means others must make up the estimated $3.5 billion in lost revenues that IDBs cost the Treasury each year.[29] Indeed, the loss is greater than it might seem. For every seventy-five cents an IDB-funded business saves, the federal Treasury forgoes $1; the extra twenty-five cents go not to the state development agency but to intermediaries like banks, lawyers, developers, and financial consultants.

In 1975 only a fifth of all tax-exempt financing was for private purposes; in 1984 the proportion was almost 70 percent. States and localities that lose jobs when firms are lured away by cheap financing have learned to match other bidders' subsidies, at the federal Treasury's expense. Twenty-five states had IDB programs in 1982 (up from thirteen in 1967), while in only two states did no local or county agencies issue IDBs.*[30] States and cities also have sought to draw in businesses through tax abatements. (The New York Job Incentive Board approved more than $1 billion in state income tax abatements between 1968 and 1981; New York City granted $300 million in property tax abatements between 1977 and 1981.[31]) In 1982 half the states provided working capital loans to businesses suffering fiscal distress.[32]

Two examples illustrate the politics of corporate rescues undertaken at the state level. They are not "typical"; business problems and government concerns, as well as the means of intervention open to public authorities, differ too much to allow any examples to be held up as representative. But they do convey some idea of what occurs at the state level as public and private entities respond to economic pressures.

The Hyster Company, headquartered in Portland, Oregon, makes forklift trucks used to shuttle loads of parts or inventory around

---

*In 1984 perceived abuses in the IDB codes, combined with a campaign to raise tax revenues, led Congress to cut back on IDB uses. The reforms limited all users in each state to a total of $200 million, or $150 per resident, whichever is higher.

factories and warehouses. Manufacturing firms need more or fewer forklifts in rough proportion to their own shipments, so the business is viciously cyclical. Japanese rivals, moreover, have been making steady inroads into the market. In 1979 Hyster sold $700 million worth of forklifts and earned net profits of $63 million; in 1982 sales fell by two-fifths. In September 1982 the company informed public officials in the five states and four nations where it built trucks that some Hyster plants would have to close. The governments were invited to bid to keep local jobs; operations would be retained wherever they were most generously subsidized. By February 1983 Hyster had collected $72.5 million in direct aid from various jurisdictions. The United Kingdom reportedly offered $20 million to ransom 1,500 jobs in Irvine, Scotland. Several American towns—including Kewanee, Illinois; Sulligent, Alabama; and Berea, Kentucky—surrendered a total of $18 million in direct grants and subsidized loans to attract or preserve around 2,000 jobs. In hard-pressed Portland a fifty-four-year-old Hyster plant was to close in 1985; Oregon's bid of a $20 million loan from the state employees' pension fund was insufficient. The biggest winner was Danville, Illinois. This city of 39,000—with an unemployment rate of 16 percent at the time—agreed to provide roughly $10 million in operating subsidies and training grants. The citizens of Danville, and the other American cities competing for Hyster facilities, were bidding primarily with federal tax dollars, not with revenues raised locally. Most of the money came from block grants. In addition to these funds, Danville's Independent Forklift Builders' Union made concessions totaling around $10,000 per employee over a three-year period. In return Hyster would keep its Danville plant in operation.

Yet long-term demand for forklifts was expected to grow only very slowly, even with recovery. Sales would continue to fluctuate violently. Toyota, one of Hyster's chief rivals, had distinct cost advantages from assembling its products in a single efficient complex at Nagoya. For all the effort, the future of Hyster jobs remained in doubt.[33]

Adams, Massachusetts, is a town of around 10,000 people in the picturesque but industrially stagnant Berkshires region. The area has never fully recovered from the exodus of the textile industry to southern states and to Asia. Adams itself is one of the poorest towns in Massachusetts. The Arnold Print Works, sited in an old brick building near the center of town, printed patterns on the fabrics made by the textile firms that had for one reason or another stayed in the region. The works had about 1,000 employees in 1970 and formed the hub of a web of regional suppliers and purchasers accounting for many more jobs. But the continuing decline of textiles in the Northeast progressively eroded Arnold's finances. By 1981—with a work force shrunken to 450—the company was unable to pay its bills and filed for bankruptcy under Chapter 11.

Adams residents and business leaders feared that the company would be liquidated, with the permanent loss of much needed jobs. Massachusetts's undersecretary for economic affairs, Richard Demers, concurred. He commissioned a study showing that closing the works would cost 891 jobs in Berkshire County. Personal income would be $16 million lower, and state and federal agencies would lose $3 million in taxes while paying $3 million in extra welfare claims.[34] Demers argued that Adams depended on the works' continued operations; if the town's industrial mainstay disappeared, he said, "you might as well take a shade and pull it down. That end of the state is shut down." Edward King, Massachusetts's governor, had won election on a conservative platform of tax cuts and less government intervention in the economy. But another election was approaching. Western Massachusetts would be an important electoral battleground; the governor's ideological resistance to intervention turned out to be surmountable.

King's predecessor, Michael Dukakis, had set up a quasi-public economic development agency, with $10 million in capital, to provide debt and equity finance for small business ventures in depressed areas. The Community Development Finance Corporation (CDFC) had been notably inactive since Governor King's election. But the Adams case seemed to meet its mandate precisely, and the CDFC swung into action. It offered $2 million in new debt and equity to pay off old creditors and buy out the shareholders. It bargained with local banks for additional loans of $650,000. It raised $150,000 in new equity from local businesses and citizens. It persuaded the state to defer for a year the company's $100,000 waste water treatment bill. It negotiated a $15,000 loan from the federal Department of Housing and Urban Development. When the Bank of Boston agreed to lend $750,000 if a guarantee covering 90 percent of the loan could be arranged, the CDFC sought help from the Small Business Administration in Washington. When the SBA balked, the CDFC turned for help to Massachusetts's congressional delegation, including Senators Edward Kennedy and Paul Tsongas and Congressman Silvio Conte. (Conte chaired the House committee responsible for the Small Business Administration's funding.) The loan guarantee eventually came through.

The company, renamed the Adams Print Works, was purchased on January 3, 1983, by the CDFC and local business and citizens' groups. After an extensive search the CDFC found a new chief executive for the firm. The new board of directors was composed of local residents and delegates from the CDFC. As of mid-1984 results of this initiative remained unclear. The firm had installed new and more efficient equipment. The economy had improved, orders had increased, and the prospects for the Adams Print Works seemed less grim. But labor relations were still strained. Labor had had no role in the rescue; state officials worried that involving workers invited leaks to the press. Some workers anticipated further subsidies if the firm stumbled again. (Since the restructuring, eight other firms in the Berkshires had applied to the CDFC for help.[35])

The Hyster and Adams Print Works cases—like New York, Lockheed, Conrail, and other, less direct rescues—summon three broad concerns.

First, how can we test the soundness of claims that a rescue is a matter of *public* interest? In almost any case of business or municipal distress—however inevitable or richly merited—one can find voices that claim with conviction that failure would be a national disaster and that both compassion and prudence call for a rescue. At the other extreme are those who challenge the legitimacy of any claim not based on formal contract and conclude that social costs need not enter the calculus. These disputes are invigorating and sometimes entertaining but rarely settle anything. The first task that arises in each case is evaluating—by some criteria—claims that the public interest mandates a rescue.

Second, what can governments *do* that other entities cannot? How do bailouts alter the allocation of sacrifice that would have prevailed under bankruptcy or in an out-of-court workout? One public-sector specialty is the most obvious: Governments can spread costs and risks thinly across a population of taxpayers. In the Conrail and Adams Print Works episodes the government kept marginal operations in business by taking on burdens that would otherwise have brought the enterprises down. The more interesting issue, though, is what governments can bring to a rescue besides simple subsidies. If a public agency commands some special competence that averts decline or smooths adjustment, it reduces or reallocates—instead of just passing on to the public—the costs of change. In the Lockheed case the government relieved private bankers of risk and hence subsidized the firm's borrowing. But at the same time it insisted on covenants that changed the rights and obligations of constituents. Managers' discretion was curbed as they underwent government monitoring. Banks sacrificed their first claim on Lockheed's assets in the event of liquidation. The New York City rescue took this principle of conditionality a step further. There, loan guarantees were part of a package that included substantial private concessions. The Chrysler rescue, as detailed later, would extend the principle further.

The third set of issues concerns not the means but the ends of intervention. What principles impel the government to alter the allocation of rights and obligations that otherwise would prevail? A corporation is a network of claims. Corporate distress occurs when the network becomes attenuated or entangled. The organization's capacity to create value falls short of what is needed to meet all claims. Normal reorganization, under formal bankruptcy or informal workout, amends these claims. The unworkable old deal is suspended, and a new one is struck. Some constituents accept delayed payments. Others trade assured returns—fixed-interest bonds, indexed wages—for benefits like stock options and profit-sharing plans that are contingent on the firm's future capacity to deliver. Other constituents are simply cut off from the corporation. Shrinking the organization is often the simplest way of bringing claims into line with the firm's ability to meet them. But an expanded public role adds a new dimension. If public agencies are to enter the negotiating arena, putting up taxpayers' resources as a bargaining chip, what ends should they aim to serve? How should new deals struck with the government as a player differ from other restructurings? The conditional bailout would inevitably involve more discretion, more debate, more legislative oversight—in short, more politics.

These three issues—the motivation, the means, and the goals of public rescues—will be examined at considerable length in the context of the Chrysler case. But first it is revealing to examine analogous episodes in two very different systems.

7.

The bailout is by no means unique to the United States. Two cases in other industrialized countries exemplify almost opposite positions on a continuum. At the one extreme is the use of public funds merely to preserve ill-working configurations of resources. At the other extreme is a highly selective intervention designed to cut the costs of adjusting to change. Both episodes concern auto companies: The fable of preservation is British Leyland; the fable of managed adjustment is Toyo Kogyo.

British Leyland (BL) was formed in 1968, when Harold Wilson's Labour government resolved to maintain a world-class British auto industry. It subsidized the merger of the two remaining British-owned companies, the British Motor Company and the Leyland Motor Company, into a single entity. But the two firms, themselves the products of more than thirty mergers over the years, remained fragmented. Several of the auto lines that now constituted BL had been bitter rivals for decades. As one industry observer described the enduring enmity, "The people at Longbridge [where Austins were made] wouldn't talk to the people at Cowley [the Morris plant], and the snobs at Jaguar wouldn't speak to any of them."[36]

The merger occurred only on paper. More than 200,000 employees were divided among 8 divisions, 17 unions, and 246 individual bargaining units. Thirty-odd different contracts had to be negotiated; most came up for renewal on their own schedules. Interunion rivalries were poisonous. Man-hours lost to work stoppages in 1972 were double the figure of two years previously. Yet, buoyed by rising sales resulting from liberalized tax and credit policies, BL managed to make money in the early 1970's, although its profit margins were embarrassingly thin.

Then came the first oil crisis, followed quickly by soaring inflation. BL's costs were dauntingly higher than British competitors Ford and Vauxhall; its quality was generally dismal. The Austin 1300 sedan became one of the few cars ever awarded a "silver lemon" by the West German Automobile Club, a distinction bestowed for "horrible" mechanical faults. At the time of the merger BL's share of the British market had been 45 percent. In 1974 it was 33 percent. Over the same period its share of the continental European market fell from 10 to 7 percent. British Leyland started losing money. In July 1974 BL's executives met with the firm's principal bankers—Barclays, Lloyds, Midland, and National Westminster—to arrange financing for $1.2 billion in new investment over the next six years. (BL had already borrowed $315 million.)

As negotiations continued, the company's cash position decayed. Losses for the year reached $46 million. With its shareholders' investment now valued at only $360 million BL's debt-to-equity ratio had reached a troubling 1:1. In September the banks decided not to extend new loans. BL calculated that it could pay its bills for only a few months longer. The firm's managers met in late November with BL's bankers and Anthony Wedgwood Benn, the Wilson government's secretary of state for industry. On December 6, 1974, Benn announced that the government would solicit Parliament's blessing for public aid to the company. He appointed a team

of business and labor representatives to assess BL's current predicament and its prospects for recovery and report back to Parliament. Sir Donald Ryder, an industrialist of sound reputation, directed the study.

The Ryder Report, which appeared four months later, blamed
British Leyland's troubles on inadequate investment, poor labor
relations, and an awkward organization. But it declared the enterprise to be worth saving: "Vehicle production is the kind of industry
which ought to remain an essential part of the UK's economic base.
We believe, therefore, that BL should remain a major vehicle producer, although this means that urgent action must be taken to remedy the weaknesses which at present prevent it from competing
effectively in world markets."[37] Roughly $6 billion would be re-
quired to "remedy the weaknesses"; the report called for the government to provide half this investment funding, while acquiring a
majority stake in the company. At the same time, the Ryder Report
proposed, BL should be split into four separate profit centers: one
for cars, one for trucks and buses, one for international sales, and
one for diverse endeavors. Finally, "industrial democracy" should
be encouraged so that BL could benefit from the ideas and enthusiasm of its work force.

On April 24, 1975, Prime Minister Harold Wilson unveiled to a
packed and somber House of Commons the government's plan to
rescue BL. "Vast amounts of public money are involved, representing one of the greatest single investments in manufacturing industry which any British Government has ever contemplated," he
said. But BL's importance to the national economy impelled action.[38] After an acrimonious debate Parliament consented to Wilson's proposal.

As the government became senior partner, British Leyland's
management was overhauled. The aging chairman, Lord Stokes,
was installed in the figurehead position of president, and a new
chairman was enlisted. The government quickly infused $425 million
of new equity capital into BL; the rest was to be provided in stages
as the firm met stipulated performance measures. The National Enterprise Board, a semiautonomous government agency headed by
Sir Donald Ryder, was to manage the program. This board joined
forces with BL's new management to transform the company.

Labor disputes intensified. Ryder's plan for industrial democracy
involved an intricate arrangement of plant committees, divisional
committees, and senior councils. But shop stewards, endowed with
impressive power by the old labor regime, feared that the new system would establish a rival channel of communication. They forced

a compromise: Worker members of the committees and councils had to be nominated by shop stewards. Other troubles surfaced. Middle managers felt excluded from the process. Senior executives spent much of their time dashing from meeting to meeting; there were 760 each week somewhere in the BL network. Confidential information leaked out to the press. Rank-and-file workers, unimpressed by the new labor structure, engaged in wildcat strikes: Toolsetters pressed for higher pay; electricians battled transport workers over job responsibilities; warehousemen protested overtime policies. Assembly lines shut down at the Triumph works over line speed, at Bathgate over pay, at the Coventry Jaguar plant over management's decision to install a new paint shop at Castle Bromwich, conceivably compromising Jaguar's independence.

British Leyland's labor productivity in 1977 was below what it had been in the crisis year of 1974. Strikes and work stoppages cut production by nearly a quarter. BL sold 785,000 vehicles in 1977; it had sold 1.2 million in 1973. Its share of the British automobile market slipped to 23 percent, putting it behind Ford. Losses reached $111 million in 1977. While the National Enterprise Board continued to make good these losses and to bankroll investment, the government was threatening to reconsider the Ryder plan. A turning point of sorts came in the fall of 1977, when Leslie Murphy took over from Ryder. One of Murphy's first acts was to dismiss BL's chief executive and its chairman. (The chairman's departure was doubtless hastened when a concealed tape recorder at a private dinner party captured for the media his assertion that "bribing wogs" was a "perfectly respectable" tactic for boosting foreign sales.[39]) The National Enterprise Board appointed Michael Edwardes to fill both positions.

Edwardes had a stellar reputation from his days as head of Chloride Group, Britain's largest battery maker. (He was also one of the first members of the National Enterprise Board.) Once in charge of BL, he quickly set out to prune it back to a profitable size. He offered workers bonuses of up to $3,000 to leave the firm voluntarily. At the same time he took a tough line with the unions. He closed the Speke plant in Liverpool, which had been plagued by work stoppages and poor workmanship. The closing idled 3,000 workers; Edwardes promised generous severance payments, contingent on a peaceful shutdown. When machinists at Scotland's Bathgate truck and tractor factory went out on strike, Edwardes retaliated with a $70 million cut in the plant's investment budget. Within two years the payroll fell to 165,000, around a 20 percent drop from its peak.

But the retrenchment exceeded Edwardes's plans. As Margaret Thatcher moved into 10 Downing Street in late 1979, BL's share of the British market dipped below 20 percent. Only 625,000 vehicles rolled off the lines that year, a cut of nearly half from the 1973 production level. With less than 2 percent of the international market BL was the world's smallest full-range automaker. Losses for the fiscal year ending in September were $242 million—double 1977's losses, four times those of 1974. This sorry performance, to be sure, was by no means exclusively the fault of British Leyland's management. Revenue from North Sea oil sales had strengthened the pound, making all British exports less attractive and drawing in competitive foreign products, including cars. At the same time, higher oil prices dampened demand for the big cars that earned the highest profits for BL.

The Labour government had invested more than $1 billion in British Leyland and lent it more than $500 million. Now it was the Tories' turn. During the election campaign Mrs. Thatcher had pledged continued funding for BL. But now Sir Keith Joseph, her secretary of state for industry, pronounced himself wary of continuing large subsidies. Labour leaders petitioned the secretary to continue government assistance. British Leyland's Chairman Edwardes argued that additional public investment was needed to launch new models and to encourage voluntary layoffs. Without further funding, he warned, BL would be forced into bankruptcy. He promised to resign if new funds were not forthcoming. Joseph relented: The Conservatives agreed to provide a further $660 million.

BL's performance was more dismal still in 1980. The auto industry was depressed worldwide, and BL's losses reached $1.2 billion on sales of $6.5 billion. A few months before its new models were due to reach showrooms the need for new cash became acute. Following a stormy Cabinet meeting in February 1981, Joseph announced that the government would pour another $1.2 billion into BL, prompting another minister to comment, "There's a job waiting for Sir Keith Joseph in Oxford Street [London's shopping district]. He's been practicing the role of Father Christmas."[40] But this final infusion of cash carried BL through the crunch. Its losses in 1981 were less than the year before, and by 1982 losses were limited to $275 million. A few divisions—notably Land-Rover and Jaguar —turned a profit in 1983, and the company as a whole almost broke even. BL was drastically leaner: Capacity was down to around half a million units; employment was down to 100,000. Productivity was much improved over the late 1970's, and the new models, the preparation of which had so painfully strained BL's budget, were hugely successful. The Metro quickly became Britain's most popular compact. The five-door Maestro was introduced by television footage of Mrs. Thatcher at the wheel, proudly cruising up and down Downing Street. In the end the company was saved. But approximately 100,000 jobs were lost, and sections of the Midlands were decimated.

Toyo Kogyo, based in Hiroshima, began in 1920 as a small manufacturer of cork. Its first automobile appeared in 1931; it was essentially a wagon hooked onto a motorcycle. During World War II the company made rifles, rock drills, and gauges for precision engineering instruments. (It subsequently dropped the rifles but kept on making the drills and gauges.) A small hill separating Toyo Kogyo's factory from Hiroshima proper shielded the firm and most of its 10,000 workers from the atomic bomb attack of August 1945.

Tsuneji Matsuda, the son of the firm's founder, became president in 1951 and strengthened Toyo Kogyo's line of trucks. The trucks were sold under the brand name Mazda, a contraction of Matsuda; by the end of the decade Toyo Kogyo had become one of Japan's leading truckmakers. But Matsuda was intent on marshaling Toyo Kogyo's engineering prowess to compete with much larger Toyota and Nissan in the car business. The company's first passenger car, a two-seater with a tiny sixteen-horsepower engine, was produced in 1961.

Soon after it had sold its first car, Toyo Kogyo changed banks, a portentous step in Japan. The Hiroshima Bank had previously been its lead banker. But now it needed a bigger financial backer and turned to the Sumitomo Bank, a large Osaka institution. The new alliance proved auspicious. Shozo Hotta, Sumitomo Bank's chairman, introduced Matsuda to West Germany's Konrad Adenauer, who in turn arranged for Toyo Kogyo to obtain from Audi-Wankel a license to make the rotary engine Audi engineers had just designed.

Toyo Kogyo became the world's first maker of rotary engine cars. The new Mazdas were wildly successful. Rotary engines were relatively free of pollution—a signal advantage as Japan progressively tightened its environmental laws in the early 1970's. They were snappy and responsive. And they were novel, a feature that enhanced their allure for many hardware-minded car buyers. Before its agreement with Audi-Wankel, Toyo Kogyo had made about 150,000 cars and trucks a year. By 1973 it was up to 740,000 vehicles and had become Japan's third-largest carmaker. Export sales, chiefly to the United States, were booming. Plans were under way to expand capacity to 1 million units a year, and the labor force had reached 37,000, almost 5 percent of the working population of Hiroshima Prefecture. Counting suppliers, 1 out of every 4 manufacturing workers in the prefecture was employed making Mazdas.

The first oil shock intervened. With all their virtues rotary engines had one flaw: They were sadly inefficient. Mazdas with rotary engines got only ten miles to the gallon in city driving. As oil prices shot up, Mazda sales plummeted. Shipments to the United States dropped by more than 43,000 cars in 1974, and Japanese sales also fell.

Kohei Matsuda, the third Toyo Kogyo president in the Matsuda dynasty, had by now taken over from his father. As sales shrank, his predictions remained sanguine. At a press conference late in 1974 Matsuda pledged that a redesigned rotary engine with 40 percent better fuel efficiency would be in production within a year. (It would, in fact, be six years before Toyo Kogyo's engineers achieved this feat.) Despite declining sales, he refused to cut production; by year end Toyo Kogyo was left with 126,000 unsold cars. The firm's financial performance was dismaying. It lost $75 million on revenues of $2 billion in 1974. Toyo Kogyo's debt load mounted, and by the end of the year it carried $1.5 billion in bank loans—four times shareholders' equity.

Sumitomo Bank officials urged Toyo Kogyo's president to curtail the expansion program and cut back production, but Matsuda resisted their suggestions. Toyo Kogyo's dealers from around Japan confided their worries about the firm to Sumitomo Bank officials. The dealers' lack of confidence, in combination with Matsuda's intransigence and the firm's rapidly deteriorating position, forced the bank's hand. In October 1974 two senior Sumitomo officers came to Hiroshima to help "strengthen the company's financing operations [and] prepare for a possible deterioration in the company's business," in the words of a Toyo Kogyo spokesman.[41] They took responsibility for two crucial tasks: financing the swollen inventories of unsold Mazdas in the United States and projecting the firm's performance for the next two years. The first two emissaries were soon joined by others; over the next two years the Sumitomo Bank and the Sumitomo Trust Company placed eleven of their top executives in key positions within Toyo Kogyo. Tsutomu Murai, Sumitomo's managing director, assumed an executive vice-president's position with a blunt explanation: "For now, we're an army of occupation. Active intervention is unavoidable."[42]

The Sumitomo team quickly relieved Kohei Matsuda of operating responsibilities and installed him in the role of chairman. (He retired from the firm at the end of 1977.) Two-thirds of Toyo Kogyo's section chiefs were shifted to new positions. Costs were cut back drastically: Production was curtailed. Expansion plans were dropped. The company sold off $54 million in stock and real estate, cut dividends by a fifth, and halted hiring for assembly work for four years. All employees made some degree of financial sacrifice: Directors' salaries were cut, and bonuses ended, for three years; top officers' pay was frozen; and the union accepted pay increases below what the other auto companies paid.

The production cuts meant Toyo Kogyo no longer needed a quarter of its work force: Around 10,000 employees were suddenly redundant. They were not laid off, however. The company's new managers devised a scheme for training production workers as car salesmen and assigning them to Mazda dealers to help sell surplus cars. About 5,000 employees, mostly from the shop floor, joined the program between 1975 and 1980. (Another 5,000 retired.) Each participating employee spent two years in sales, then returned to his factory job. Most of the temporary salesmen were assigned to Tokyo or Osaka, each several hundred miles from Hiroshima. The company paid their expenses, supplemented sales wages to bring total compensation up to factory levels, and housed them in company dormitories. Mazda dealers were delighted with the program. It is common in Japan to sell automobiles door to door; a bigger sales force means more sales. But the workers were less enthusiastic. Many found the transition from production to sales uncongenial. The program meant prolonged absence from family and friends. Hayato Ichihara, later president of the Toyo Kogyo union, explained why workers went along with the program: "We feared that if we didn't accept the proposal the company would demand we accept dismissals of workers in exchange for wage increases. And union members did understand that there were too many workers for the work that existed."[43]

As the austerity program stanched short-run losses, the new management team revised the firm's competitive strategy. Toyo Kogyo's emphasis on innovative engineering would henceforth be supplemented by a fortified sales organization and a relentless campaign to streamline manufacturing operations. The engineering stress was retained, though. New engineers were hired throughout the crunch. Investment funds were poured into the development of both piston and rotary cars. Between 1977 and 1980 Toyo Kogyo introduced ten new models, including the heralded fuel-efficient rotary.

The Sumitomo Bank financed much of this transition and arranged financing for the rest. The bank held about 16 percent of Toyo Kogyo's $1.6 billion debt load in 1976. The next year the lead bank raised its stake by $71 million, to a peak of $327 million. At one point, when the other sixty banks and insurance companies that had loans outstanding to Toyo Kogyo threatened to cut off credit, Ichiro Isoda, the Sumitomo executive in charge of the Toyo Kogyo account, took control. He summoned all lenders to a meeting at Sumitomo's Osaka headquarters and pledged that no matter what happened to Toyo Kogyo, the bank would "stand by the company to the end" and would soon infuse fresh funds. He appealed to the other lenders not to desert Toyo Kogyo. While only a few lenders came forth with additional loans, none demanded repayment of the loans then outstanding. (Ichiro Isoda later became president of the Sumitomo Bank.)

Sumitomo mustered its *keiretsu*—a network of companies sharing stock and debt ties, united by links to a common lead bank—to Toyo Kogyo's aid. Firms belonging to the *keiretsu* lent Toyo Kogyo money, bought most of the $54 million in land and securities the troubled car company had to sell, and picked up large numbers of Mazdas from its bloated inventories. Officers in Sumitomo branches throughout Japan were instructed to steer bank customers to Mazda dealers. Sumitomo also struck a deal with C. Itoh & Company, a trading company that did not belong to the *keiretsu:* The bank lent C. Itoh a large sum at attractive terms, and the trading company took over Toyo Kogyo's sales organization in the eastern United States, including its 10,000-car inventory. Finally, in 1979, Sumitomo engineered the Ford Motor Company's acquisition of 25 percent of Toyo Kogyo, a transaction that dramatically improved the firm's cash position.

Additional help came from the city of Hiroshima. Local business leaders formed *Kyoshin Kai* ("Home Heart Group") to promote Mazda sales in the region. The prefectural government in turn enacted a new, far stricter antipollution code that resulted, quite by design, in cutting in half the pollution tax on rotary-powered cars while increasing the levy on conventional models. These initiatives helped raise Toyo Kogyo's share of the regional market from 20 percent to 35 percent.

The national government's role in the rescue, while pervasive, was subtle and highly indirect. The Sumitomo Bank was made aware that Tokyo had a lively concern for Toyo Kogyo's future and that the central bank would make every effort to cooperate. Sumitomo depended on the central bank's lending window; in Japan, bank interest rates are pegged below market rates, so that there is always more demand for funds than supply. The government's concern therefore made a marked impression on Sumitomo and stiffened its resolve to preserve Toyo Kogyo. In addition, early in 1976, while the car company's fate remained much in doubt, the Ministry of International Trade and Industry (MITI) pronounced itself in favor of Toyo Kogyo's independent survival. Tomatsu Yoguro, vice-minister of MITI, said MITI would not look with favor on Toyota or Nissan's acquiring the troubled firm. "A two *keiretsu* concentration of the automobile industry is not desirable," he said. "I hope that Toyo Kogyo will remain an independent number 3." MITI also urged Toyo Kogyo's suppliers, such as Mitsubishi Steel, to continue their shipments on normal terms.[44] MITI and the Ministry of Finance encouraged major banking institutions to support Toyo Kogyo with additional credit, and in 1979 MITI expedited Ford's infusion of equity capital.

Toyo Kogyo's new models proved to be popular. Moreover, they were produced with exceptional efficiency. Since they all were based on the same platform, allowing different models to be made on the same line, the company could vary its output without shutting some lines down and running others overtime. This helped raise output from nineteen cars per worker per year in 1973 to forty-three cars in 1980. By 1980 Toyo Kogyo was making money; it sold more than 1 million vehicles, slipping past Chrysler to become the world's ninth-largest carmaker and reclaiming its number three spot in Japan. Its debt load had fallen sharply. The equity stake from Ford had cut its debt-to-equity ratio back to under 2:1. Export sales under the Mazda label continued to climb, while Ford began relying on Toyo Kogyo subcompacts and components. A Mazda was named "Import Car of the Year" by *Motor Trend* magazine in 1983, and sales were up to 1.2 million. The government's involvement had been extensive but not intrusive, and the rescue had engaged almost no political controversy or public trauma. There had been practically no layoffs. Shrinkage had been limited to regular attrition. Satoshi Yamada, head of Sumitomo's credit department and one of the "occupiers" at Toyo Kogyo, looked back in the fall of 1983 and summarized the nine years of restructuring: "It was a difficult period. Many people sacrificed. We didn't know how it would come out in the end. We are very pleased."[45]

In future years, both the Japanese and the British styles of corporate rescue figured in discussions of what the United States should do about its own crippled giants. In the Toyo Kogyo case, the costs of adjustment were spread enough to avoid placing a crippling burden on any single group, but not so thinly as to spare constituents the need to struggle to turn the firm around. The automaker was completely reorganized. The architects of the rescue had been Toyo Kogyo's bankers, suppliers, dealers, and employees and managers. Public help, from several layers of government, had been limited and discreet. British Leyland was a different matter. It had been less reorganized than pruned back to a tractable size. Despite the British government's highly visible efforts to promote recovery, the firm emerged as a much smaller version, only moderately different in nature from the crippled behemoth the state aimed to succor. No significant share of the costs of change had been borne by bankers, dealers, suppliers, or the employees who kept their jobs. In short, Toyo Kogyo's turnaround looked like a Japanese version of Chapter 11 reorganization, with the government standing in as coach and cheerleader. British Leyland's rescue was the classic bailout. The two episodes seemed to define the range of responses to imperiled carmakers.

Neither episode, Toyo Kogyo or British Leyland, represented the result of a calculated policy. Each was a largely improvisational response to crisis. A system often reveals its essence under pressure. Just as these cases displayed with uncommon clarity the alignments of interest, the procedural options for coordinated public and private action, and the tenor of industrial politics in Japan and Britain, so was corporate crisis about to cast light on the American system.

Late in 1978 Michael Edwardes in England was pressing his austerity campaign at British Leyland. In Tokyo the "army of occupation" from the Sumitomo Bank was arranging to sell a quarter of Toyo Kogyo to the Ford Motor Company. Back in Highland Park, Chrysler's John Riccardo and his new deputy, Lee Iacocca, were gradually realizing that their troubles were a good deal worse than anyone would have predicted a year or two earlier. Soon it would be Chrysler's turn.

III

THE CHOICE

1.

Public choices are seldom neatly posed. Indeed, it is rare that political problems are even well defined. A policy crisis typically consists of a vague sense that things cannot be left to proceed on their present course and an ambiguous imperative that *something* be done. But the data are incomplete and open to multiple interpretations. Causes are elusive, and the obvious options are unpalatable. The courses of action that come to mind often refer less to the problem at hand than to a previous endeavor that met with a measure of success. The powerful instinct to replicate what once worked comes into play, however slightly the earlier situation resembles the current one. Faced with a mandate to act but lacking any reliable guide to action, public officials—most of the time understandably and often wisely—play for time. They address the most pressing parts of the problem with the most plausible responses at hand and wait to engage the rest until they understand it better. More often than not it is through the incremental accretion of partial responses that a policy emerges. So it was to be with Chrysler.

Two weeks after Lee Iacocca had signed on as president in late 1978, Chrysler broke ground for its $160 million transaxle plant in

Richmond, Indiana. Two weeks after that a Chrysler official walked into the Indiana office of the Farmers Home Administration—a branch of the U.S. Department of Agriculture that helps fund rural development projects—and submitted an application for $250 million in federally guaranteed loans to build the Richmond plant. Chrysler's treasurer, William G. McGagh, told a reporter, "We'd be delighted to get any help that we can. . . . If we could find another provision we could fit into, we would."[1] But an FmHA official judged it to be "most unlikely that we would allocate almost 25 percent of our program to one company for one project in a single state."[2] This was the first of the probes and false steps that preceded the main event in Washington.

John Riccardo went to the White House early in December to meet with Stuart Eizenstat, President Jimmy Carter's chief domestic policy adviser. The Chrysler chairman lamented the twin plagues of a crumbling auto market and looming capital requirements. He held the government to blame for much of the strain on Chrysler's finances. Fully half the retooling scheduled for the next five years, he claimed, was due to government regulations. And he warned Eizenstat that despite his campaign of divestiture and consolidation, despite recent layoffs and the new equity sale, Chrysler might still fall short by a billion dollars in its capital needs for 1979 and 1980. To ensure that the fuel-efficient 1981 compacts would hit showrooms as scheduled, Chrysler needed relief from certain federal regulations. Riccardo wanted a two-year grace period, delaying the deadlines for stricter rules. Chrysler would still be in full compliance by 1982, but it would be able to pare its capital investment by 25 percent. The chairman stressed that he did not want a "Lockheed-type loan" from the government. The publicity surrounding such federal financial help would undercut sales and hurt Chrysler more than it helped.[3] Eizenstat listened attentively but made no promises, and John Riccardo went back to Detroit to finish out a bad year.

The Federal Reserve Bank of New York is the most important of the twelve regional banks that constitute the Federal Reserve System. Its bailiwick includes the Manhattan banks that influence the flow of much of the money in the United States. Because trouble for a major industrial firm eventually means trouble for at least some of the big money center banks, the New York Fed tries to be alert to early warnings of industrial distress. Late in 1978 Paul Volcker, then the head of the New York Fed, assigned a team of analysts in the bank's discount and credit department to prepare a detailed report on Chrysler and its financial subsidiary, Chrysler Financial.

In Washington, Deputy Treasury Secretary Robert Carswell, prompted by the White House, ordered a similar study. He handed the project to two civil service employees, Brian Freeman and Philip Loomis. Freeman, trained in both business and law, had taken a hand in parts of the Conrail, Lockheed, and New York City rescues. Loomis was a Wall Street veteran with extensive financial experience. Their assignment was to evaluate the seriousness of Chrysler's situation and to make a guess at the national consequences that should be expected if the firm went into bankruptcy. Freeman and Loomis were warned that the project was strictly confidential. Loomis later described the analysis as a frustrating chore. "There was scarcely a shred of financial-analysis talent in the government," he recalled. "Economists here, econometricians there, lawyers and bureaucrats as far as the eye can see, but nobody with the skill to interpret a balance sheet. It was very hush-hush, so we couldn't do the obvious thing and call up the industry analysts on the Street. They knew what we needed to know—what kind of predicament the company was in and how bad it was."[4] Neither Loomis nor Freeman could spend much time on the Chrysler issue; it was only one potential crisis to be monitored. Nor did they coordinate their efforts formally with the study of Chrysler under way at the New York Fed, although, as it happened, Freeman was acquainted with some members of the Fed team—they had worked together on the New York City rescue—and they compared notes. In all, Chrysler claimed little of the bureaucracy's time in the first half of 1979.

Chrysler's application for a $250 million loan guarantee from the Farmers Home Administration, to finish the Richmond transaxle plant, was shunted to a high-level policy group that had already been debating a similar request. The previous summer the American Motors Corporation had informally sought a $109 million loan guarantee from a comparable agency, the Commerce Department's Economic Development Administration. This request had prompted the Carter administration to establish a policy group charged with formulating guidelines on financial aid to industry. The Commerce Department—the representative of which chaired the group—supported a ceiling as high as $100 million for federal aid to any one company, a figure that would let it accommodate AMC with only modest adjustments. Treasury, the Office of Management and Budget, the Department of Agriculture (where the Farmers Home Administration resided), and the White House staff all favored a lower limit.

American Motors never filed a formal application, and in January 1979, citing "new circumstances and profitability," it withdrew its request.[5] But the policy group continued to work out its guidelines.

The more parsimonious faction prevailed, and with no immediate public announcement, a ceiling of $50 million was set on federal assistance to any single enterprise. Chrysler learned on February 2, 1979, that its request was out of bounds. On the same day, however, the White House announced that other forms of help for the firm were under study. Treasury Secretary W. Michael Blumenthal—trained as an economist and long familiar with the auto industry from his years as head of Bendix, a major Detroit supplier—surveyed Chrysler's financial documents and told an administration colleague, "They'll be back."[6] Meanwhile, the company said it would resubmit its application, scaled down by four-fifths, and seek further funding through "normal credit channels."[7]

Late in February Chrysler's financial performance for 1978 was announced. It had lost $205 million (see Figure 4, opposite). Moody's Investors Service, citing "recent adverse operating results," lowered its appraisal of Chrysler's debentures and short-term commercial paper as of April 13.[8] One week later the other major rating service, Standard & Poor's, downgraded Chrysler's senior debt and preferred stock. The rating firms' alarm signaled to the financial community that any future Chrysler securities should be considered risky propositions. In principle this meant that the auto company would have to pay steep interest rates on its borrowings, to compensate for the greater risk of default. In practice it meant that Chrysler would have a hard time selling any new securities unless the ratings improved. "Normal credit channels" were narrowing for Chrysler.

Government help was, at least for the present, unavailable. The credit markets were inhospitable. Chrysler was losing money every day, but it dared not slacken the pace of its capital-spending program lest it miss the growing market for compact cars. So in order to raise cash, Chrysler sold off more pieces. Peugeot-Citroën (which in 1978 had become Europe's biggest automaker at one stroke by acquiring Chrysler's manufacturing operations) bought Chrysler's European financial subsidiary for $80 million on the second day of 1979. Later in January Chrysler announced that it was selling a two-thirds stake in its Brazilian operations to Volkswagen for $50 million. On February 23 General Motors bought Chrysler's plants in Venezuela and Colombia. Mitsubishi signed on to buy a third of Chrysler Australia for $30 million early in March. Industry analysts generally commended the decision to jettison the marginal or money-losing foreign operations, but some noted that by shedding these assets—located in markets growing twice as fast as the American market—Chrysler might be surrendering its best hope for long-term growth.[9]

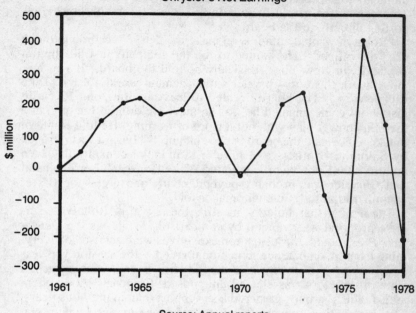

FIGURE 4
Chrysler's Net Earnings

Source: Annual reports

* * *

Chrysler's 1979 annual meeting—the first to put Lee Iacocca in front of the shareholders—was held in mid-May not in the Detroit area, as had previously been the invariant custom, but in Syracuse, New York, the location of Chrysler's New Process Gear division. The board of directors convened in a private session the evening before the stockholders' meeting. One item on the agenda was a report by Felix Rohatyn of the investment banking firm Lazard Frères. Rohatyn was best known for his role in the New York City rescue, when he had chaired the Municipal Assistance Corporation, which managed the city's austerity campaign. Chrysler had hired Lazard Frères to handle the sales of its foreign subsidiaries and had kept the firm on retainer to provide general financial advice. Rohatyn was scheduled to give the board of directors a more or less routine appraisal of Chrysler's current fiscal problems. But he departed from the program. Without consulting Riccardo or Iacocca in advance, Rohatyn proposed to the board that it appoint a special committee, with himself at its head, to renegotiate Chrysler's commitments to its workers, creditors, suppliers, and other constituents. This committee would have authority over top management, reporting directly to the board.

"Rohatyn wanted authority to make the deals," according to one Chrysler officer. "He wanted to run the company just like he ran Big MAC in New York. Basically he told the board, 'If you hire me to work this out, Chrysler's management works for me. Take it or leave it.' The board decided to leave it. But John Riccardo just about came unglued he was so mad. He'd hired the guy, and then this power play with not a word of warning. He told Rohatyn to take a hike, and the board backed him up."[10] Lazard was replaced by Salomon Brothers as Chrysler's financial consultants. Two months later Rohatyn privately told White House adviser Eizenstat that Chrysler was probably beyond saving and urged the Carter administration to let the automaker fold.[11]

The annual shareholders' meeting the day after Rohatyn's surprise proposal was tranquil by comparison. While, as the *Detroit Free Press* noted, "as usual, top executives were accused of everything from incompetence to personal greed," the session was less divisive than the stormy 1978 meeting had been.[12] Management's slate of directors was elected unopposed. Proposals by dissident stockholders' groups garnered less support than in previous years. The explanation, apparently, was confidence in Lee Iacocca. Iacocca took to the podium with three themes: First, he deplored the "wild fluctuation" in energy prices that was undercutting the market for big cars and trucks. Second, he promised to eliminate the sales bank, which at that time contained more than 100,000 vehicles worth $600 million. (It was costing Chrysler about $5 million a month just to cover the interest costs on the inventory.[13]) Third, he pledged recovery. "I have no illusions about our present situation," he said, "but I honestly believe that within a very short time the opportunities for Chrysler Corporation will be far greater than the problems."

One sign of Iacocca's ascendancy was the directors' decision, taken in a meeting immediately after the session with the shareholders, to appoint his old Ford compatriot Gar Laux as Chrysler's executive vice-president for sales and marketing. The directors also voted to continue the quarterly dividend of ten cents a share—arguably an optimistic gesture for a company that had lost more than any other Fortune 500 firm the previous year, had dropped $53.8 million the first quarter and was heading for an even worse second quarter, and was selling off assets to raise cash.

Early in June 1979 Chrysler treasurer William McGagh said that the company could weather a loss as large as another $200 million for the rest of 1979. "It's not very comfortable," he said, "but we can tolerate it."[14] The *Detroit Free Press* observed that while "almost nobody expects Chrysler to go bankrupt," the challenge of maintaining investment and keeping the company operating while losing money at such a rate called for "an imaginative approach." And Chrysler did embark upon some innovative methods of saving money. Instead of buying outright the expensive new tools it needed, for example, it arranged for finance companies technically to own the equipment and lease it to the automaker. This saved $100 million in 1979. The company worked out a similar arrangement for a $17 million addition to its transmission plant in Syracuse, New York. Rather than go to the market to cover its stock thrift plan for salaried employees, it dug into its own holdings of Chrysler stock, easing the strain on the annual cash flow by $40 million to $50 million (at the expense of existing shareholders). The Chrysler Financial Corporation set about raising another $100 million by selling overseas financing operations in Europe and Latin America.

Imaginative or not, these measures were not enough. Keeping the company afloat meant lightening the load. Chrysler started closing down plants.

2.

John and Horace Dodge had assembled their first automobile—a five-passenger $785 touring car—in a four-year-old factory in Hamtramck, which in 1914 was a northern suburb of Detroit. (Hamtramck today, though strictly speaking a separate town, is surrounded by Detroit and tightly linked to the larger city.) When Walter Chrysler bought the Dodge Brothers Company in 1928, the same factory had expanded into an ugly but powerfully productive complex called Dodge Main. The plant was one of the most appealing parts of the Dodge acquisition. As Walter Chrysler's company took over Dodge Main, Hamtramck had become a magnet for job-hungry Eastern European immigrants, especially Poles. "Dodge Main" was the first English term many immigrants learned.

"They brought their families, they all worked for Dodge Main, and they all bought Dodge products," Hamtramck's mayor (and a thirty-five-year Chrysler veteran), William Kozerski, reminisced. "The plant was Hamtramck's life." Hamtramck and Detroit workers—Poles at first, then later blacks lured from the South by auto industry wages—built some 14 million Dodges and Plymouths at the plant. For decades after it was officially rechristened the Chrysler Hamtramck Assembly Plant, it was called by no other name than Dodge Main. The town sponsored a five-day festival complete with floats, bands, and a beauty contest to celebrate the 1954 model year.[15] By the late seventies 5,000 hourly workers were assembling Aspens and Volarés at Hamtramck.

On May 29, 1979, Chrysler announced it was shutting Dodge Main down for good by the following summer. The official statement—released almost simultaneously to the workers, the city government, and the press—termed the closing "one of the essential steps that must be taken to reduce losses, to increase efficiency and productivity, and to establish a firm basis for continued operation as a healthy producer and employer." The sprawling 120-acre plant, built bit by bit over the decades, was by now obsolete and grossly inefficient; it cost almost $15 million just to heat the plant in 1978. Eight stories high in some parts, Dodge Main was out of sync with the era of automated, straight-line car assembly.

Labor leaders were irritated that Chrysler had announced the news with no advance consultation. Marc Stepp, the head of the United Auto Workers' Chrysler department, said that the company had refused as recently as a week previously to acknowledge rumors that the plant was slated for shutdown. Mayor Kozerski was also dismayed at the abruptness with which Chrysler announced that the plant, which amounted to 10 percent of the town's tax base, would be closed. "I thought at least they'd let us know earlier, not 15 minutes before the announcement was released to the press," he said.[16] Kamil S. Gulla, the proprietor of Mickey's Diner, across the street from Dodge Main, said, "If Chrysler goes, I go. I'm 100 percent dependent on the workers." The owner of a nearby hot dog stand, Al Trescone, warned, "This is going to close down the whole city of Hamtramck." Leo Garfield, manager of the G-Mart Men's and Boys' Clothing Store in Hamtramck, was unconsoled by assurances that some of Dodge Main's jobs would be transferred to other Chrysler assembly plants: "If you live here and work here, you shop here. But if you get a job 10 miles away, you shop somewhere else. The only thing that can help is somebody else comes in here."[17]

But among Dodge Main's workers the predominant attitude was a curious blend of shock and a hopeful incredulity. Clarence Dowdy noted that "the UAW contract expires in September. Every year the contract comes up they talk of closing this plant." Rachel Hale cited other times in her thirty-four years at the plant when talk of closing it had arisen. "I didn't believe it then," she said, "and I don't believe it now. We're still here, and we'll be here another 40 years." Darrell Warren told reporters, "When I was hired in, they told me the plant would probably close down within 90 days. That was 15 years ago. This plant saved Chrysler four years ago. They're putting in lots of big new machines and I can't believe that's just for one year."[18] In fact, the last car rolled off the line at Dodge Main within seven months, in the first week of January 1980.

For fifteen years Chrysler had been the main employer in Lyons, Michigan. Its trim plant there employed as many as 900 people from Lyons and the surrounding countryside. (The population of Lyons proper was about 800.) In the same month that the closing of Dodge Main was announced, a shutdown notice was posted at the Lyons trim plant. The doors closed in late July. John Devers, president of UAW Local 1424, had bitter words for the departing employer. Chrysler, he said, is "really not doing nothing. They're sticking right to the contract."[19] The "contract" was a negotiated provision that gave workers at any shut-down Chrysler facility first claim on openings at the company's other factories. The closest alternative jobs, though, would be fifty miles away, in Lansing or Grand Rapids; taking them would mean either long commutes or else pulling up stakes and leaving Lyons. But moving was an unappealing option for many Lyons residents. As Devers put it, "They're in hock real bad because we got paid real good and most people have nice homes." A Chrysler spokesman said, "The first thing we did was offer everyone a job. The second thing was we offered early retirement to everyone who was eligible. What else can we do?"[20]

The firm's whole work force was shrinking. In 1978 Chrysler employed more than 130,000 people in the United States. As the company made its pitch for public help, its payroll, including both hourly and salaried workers, was heading below 100,000 (see Appendix A, Figure 9A).

3.

Early in 1979, Wendell Larsen, Chrysler's vice-president for public affairs, flew to Washington, D.C., to hire a lobbyist. It was ever harder to dismiss the conclusion that some kind of government help—rescinding or delaying regulations or else special tax benefits—was going to be needed for Chrysler to survive in anything like its present form. But the approach had to be delicate. If the bid for assistance were not made discreetly—if the seriousness of Chrysler's trouble became public—panic could stampede the firm's constituents. Lenders might start refusing to honor lines of credit or even call in old loans; suppliers might tighten terms; dealers and employees with attractive alternatives might bolt from the fold. Larsen knew he needed the best. His contacts in the capital steered him to Tommy Boggs.

Thomas "Tommy" Hale Boggs, Jr., a partner in the firm of Patton, Boggs & Blow, had a formidable Washington pedigree. His father was the late Hale Boggs, a distinguished Louisiana congressman who seemed destined to be speaker of the House until his small plane crashed in Alaska in 1972. His mother, Lindy, succeeded her husband as the representative for Jefferson Parish and attained a measure of distinction on her own account. Tommy Boggs had set up shop as a Washington lawyer several years earlier and was considered a singularly talented lobbyist. His access and influence were unexceeded, and probably unmatched, among professional representatives. Boggs told Larsen that he would not take the Chrysler job sight unseen. He invited Larsen and Riccardo to spend a weekend at his retreat on the Maryland shore. They met and talked about Chrysler's financial bind and what it would take to get some kind of action in Washington. At the end of the weekend Boggs was convinced that Chrysler had a plausible case and that Riccardo was determined to see his turnaround plan through. Boggs took the job. Chrysler now had a professional—by many estimates the best in town—planning the moves in its Washington campaign.

John Riccardo came to the capital on June 22. Two of his main allies in the Senate were Donald Riegle of Michigan and Thomas Eagleton of Missouri. (There were major Chrysler operations in both Michigan and Missouri.) The two senators accompanied Riccardo and his aides to separate meetings with Treasury Secretary W. Michael Blumenthal and domestic policy chief Stuart Eizenstat. The Chrysler chairman and his Senate backers offered a range of options: Chrysler could be granted special terms for carrying forward past losses to offset future tax liabilities. It could be exempted from the rigid timetable for emissions control or granted a delay for meeting fuel economy regulations. Alternatively, the government could lift the $50 million limit set the previous January and channel credit to Chrysler either directly (through a federal loan) or indirectly (by guaranteeing new loans from banks or investors).

Eizenstat and Blumenthal promised to keep an "open mind" about granting relief to Chrysler. They agreed to launch a study of all the options, including special legislation and even direct federal aid (although an official termed this last option "very unlikely"). One participant from the administration side stressed that "all options are still open, including insolvency." Yet the tenor of the meetings—the willingness of senior officials to consider forms of support that had previously been ruled out of bounds—offered Riccardo at least some ground for optimism. (Earlier the same week the Department of Transportation had, in fact, lowered by eight-tenths of a mile per gallon the fuel economy standard for pickups and vans, a technical change that had the effect—and the intent—of sparing Chrysler substantial tooling costs. The Transportation Department declined broader or more fundamental changes in fuel economy standards, though.)[21]

Dow Jones & Company announced later that month that it was dropping Chrysler from the list of thirty firms that constituted its widely watched industrials index. This was the first major revision in the index in twenty years.[22]

Among Chrysler's bankers, unease was turning into a dull panic. In January 1979 a team from Chrysler's lead bank, Manufacturers Hanover Trust, had taken the unusual step of visiting the automaker's headquarters in Highland Park to review its finances. Two months later, when estimates of Chrysler's 1979 losses first approached $200 million, Riccardo had met with John McGillicuddy, the chairman of Manufacturers Hanover. The lead bank promptly put together a syndicate of more than 100 domestic banks that jointly agreed to lend Chrysler around $560 million on demand. Such credit agreements generally are arranged to back up issues of commercial paper.* Typically they are not used at all. When they *are* drawn down, it is not to finance major investments but rather to balance uneven flows of operating cash and keep the firm liquid. In April, when weak ratings expelled Chrysler from the commercial paper market, the company started drawing on this credit. Some members of the syndicate—particularly small local and regional banks—were startled that Chrysler was actually holding them to their agreement to lend.

"Sometimes we bankers are kind of dumb," one regional banker recalled in 1984. "We set up these standby credit facilities for

---

*Commercial paper is short-term, unsecured corporate debt which is sold in large denominations to institutional investors. It is usually a cheaper way to borrow money than either bank loans or longer-term notes and bonds. Only the biggest and best-rated firms command enough confidence among money managers to qualify for such financing.

Chrysler, all the time thinking they really weren't going to be used. They were just insurance. But insurance sometimes gets used. Hurricanes and disasters happen all the time. We really kidded ourselves on this. All of a sudden Chrysler's paper rating went away, and they started drawing down their lines of credit. The company calls up these little banks and said it actually wanted the money. A lot of small regional banks really thought this was just a backup. When they were asked to come through with the funds, that got their attention. 'What? You mean lend Chrysler money? A loan? We thought it was just a line of credit.' ''[23]

From April to June 1979 Chrysler borrowed $102 million from the syndicate. Near the end of June, as the bankers who had signed on to the revolving credit agreement grew more nervous about Chrysler's future, Riccardo invited them to Highland Park for a summary of the company's plans and an introduction to Lee Iacocca and the new financial officer whom Iacocca had lured away from Ford, Gerald Greenwald. The bankers were shown prototypes of the K-car and regaled with optimistic forecasts of the firm's long-term prospects. But Riccardo also warned the bankers that the cost of retooling for the K-car was straining the firm's cash resources and that more borrowing might be necessary. There were no detailed financial numbers and no comprehensive plan. Many of the creditors left feeling unsettled.

As Riccardo had warned, Chrysler's borrowings accelerated, and in July alone it drew down another $306 million from the revolving credit agreement.[24]

Treasury Secretary Blumenthal and his deputies were attending more closely to Chrysler's situation. But they were working in the dark; the government had little solid data on the company's troubles. The studies that had been assembled hastily at Treasury and the New York Fed the previous year contained too little information to make solid projections. The summary data that Chrysler had sent to the government that spring were equally feeble. Several Treasury officials—like the company's bankers—assumed that Chrysler was holding back more detailed numbers. The more troubling truth, they learned, was that the firm was sharing the best data it had.

Treasury's Brian Freeman grew increasingly frustrated trying to figure out Chrysler's status with the impressionistic data his team commanded. "The information was completely inadequate," he recalled. "Their business plan was sophomoric. So we had to go to the source."[25] He insisted that the company send him all relevant financial and operating data. Soon thereafter a truck rolled up to the Treasury Department and workmen carted bushels of documents to Freeman's office. Daunted by the task of sifting through the piles of information, Freeman borrowed three analysts from the New York Fed. They spent most of June poring through the files, trying to assemble a coherent picture of Chrysler's condition and its prospects.

At the end of the month the team of bureaucrats went to Highland Park for a reprise of the presentation Chrysler had staged for its banks. But the review of the firm's eroding cash position and preview of the K-car was no more detailed or comprehensive for the government officials than it had been for the bankers. Soon after returning from Detroit, Brian Freeman flew to New York with his immediate superior, Assistant Treasury Secretary Roger Altman, to confer with officers at Manufacturers Hanover on the likely extent of Chrysler's cash shortfall. The officials discovered, with growing unease, that the bankers knew no more than the government did.

Douglas Fraser, president of the United Auto Workers union, had a special link with the Carter administration, particularly with Vice President Walter Mondale, whom he had known and worked with for years. Fraser also had a special link with Chrysler. He had spent long years on the line at Chrysler plants before becoming a leader of the union. Fraser had been monitoring Chrysler's situation since the beginning of the year. As the company's predicament worsened through the summer of 1979, Fraser began taking a hand in forging a political strategy.

He met with Stuart Eizenstat on July 25. Fraser warned the President's adviser that Chrysler's loss for the second quarter alone would exceed $200 million and that full-year losses would likely be $600 million or more. Like Riccardo, he cast the challenge as a matter of staying in business long enough to bring the new compacts to market. But Fraser's preferred remedy was distinctly less conventional than the options Chrysler's management was proposing. The labor leader wanted the government to buy a big piece of Chrysler. He feared that new loans would increase to unsupportable levels Chrysler's already onerous debt load. Nor would an outright cash grant be appropriate. Partial state ownership would allow the public to share in Chrysler's profits, if it survived, not just in the risks of failure and default.[26] Professional staff members at Solidarity House, the union's headquarters in Detroit, had suggested earlier in the summer that a public stake in Chrysler would have several advantages for the union, "including greater public input in the company's affairs, worker control, and clearly spelled out worker protections. In fact, we could propose that there be a direct link between any government investment program and employee ownership."[27] Fraser and his staff were mindful of the political furor that would be created by any move toward partial public ownership, however, and some observers interpreted the union's proposal—which Fraser had issued publicly even before seeing Eizenstat—as a way of dramatizing Chrysler's predicament.[28] In any event, the proposal was equally unwelcome at the Carter White House and at Highland Park. Marc Stepp, of UAW's Chrysler department, only reluctantly abandoned the idea of a public equity stake: "That's what other industrialized nations do when this kind of thing comes up. But they weren't too keen on that idea. They didn't want the government owning a piece of them—that would be some kind of ism, I suppose. So that was that."[29]

John Riccardo summoned reporters to Chrysler's Highland Park headquarters on the last day of July 1979. The company had just revealed its second-quarter loss of $207 million—more red ink than the disastrous total for *all* of 1978. Riccardo was ready to announce, in public and explicitly, that Chrysler was doomed without government help. Regulation—if not the direst of the threats confronting Chrysler—was clearly the only one that Riccardo could hope to dispel by denouncing it. He read his prepared statement:

> We're working on the assumption that the Government will provide some way to offset the effects of regulation on this company. We have met in recent months with a number of people in the Administration, as well as key members of both the House and Senate. They are fully aware of the contributions of our company, our dealers, our suppliers and the 500,000 employees involved to our national economy. And they understand the importance of maintaining three full-line competitors in the automobile industry. There is a growing awareness in Washington that, because of the disproportionate burden which regulations place on Chrysler, they currently constitute a serious threat to competition. . . . We have also had expressions of support from key members of Congress for the tax relief we have chosen to pursue. With all of these signs of support, we feel justified in working on the assumption that some form of relief will be granted. We are not considering any alternative and we will not speculate on the likelihood of any alternative.[30]

The centerpiece of Chrysler's initial plea for help was a proposal to extend the tax laws. The proposal was unprecedented in its scale but more or less routine in its form. The tax code had long been considered the easiest port of access to public assistance for business. Most major firms maintained Washington offices and paid squads of representatives to monitor legislation and to lobby for seemingly minor and technical changes in the rules that could translate into many millions of dollars' difference in after-tax revenues. These changes were invisible to the public at large; the average American's ignorance of corporate tax law was close to complete. Yet the tax code powerfully affected the prospects for individual firms and the tilt of the economic terrain in America. Business lobbyists—with Chrysler's representative, Tommy Boggs, the best in the trade—labored to ensure that shifts in tax law would favor their clients. This was the heart of the business-government relationship in Washington.

Various tax provisions, introduced to encourage investment or simply to accommodate accounting conventions, already allowed companies to subtract a portion of their investment costs from their annual tax bill. In a normal, profitable year Chrysler would lop off a large fraction of its taxes by claiming investment credits, depreciation allowances, and other special deductions based on its investment spending. Now it was spewing out potential tax benefits through its massive new-product program. But since it had no profits, it had no tax bill to reduce. And while it could "bank" these tax benefits and use them to offset taxes in future years when it would presumably be making profits from the investment now under way, the company might not survive that long. So Chrysler proposed that the government give it $1 billion as an advance against these future tax benefits. The scheme was dubbed, in the exotic parlance of tax lobbying, a Secured and Refundable Tentative Adjustment. The "refundable" term suggested that Chrysler was getting nothing it didn't deserve; after the firm returned to profitability, it simply would "refund" to the government the "tentative adjustment" it had received in previous money-losing years.[31] With an eye to political image—and, internally, as a matter of pride on the part of Riccardo and other executives—the bid was carefully drafted to look as little like a handout as possible.

Riccardo said that the company would also request a two-year reprieve from environmental regulations. Under the proposal Chrysler submitted, it would not have to meet the 1980 emissions standards until 1982 or the 1981 standards until 1983. This could save the company $100 million to $300 million.[32]

Lee Iacocca held a separate press conference later that day to elaborate on Riccardo's blunt declaration that Chrysler was in deep trouble and needed public help to get out. It was mostly a matter of bad timing, he said. The cars Chrysler had weren't the cars Americans wanted to buy, and Chrysler did not yet have enough of what the public wanted. Production of the fuel-efficient Omnis and Horizons, which oil-starved consumers were clamoring for, was rigidly constrained: The four-cylinder engines under the Chrysler hoods were made by Volkswagen. But the contract with Volkswagen, worked out four years earlier, specified only 300,000 engines a year. The little engines were sought after all over the world, and Volkswagen was disinclined to expand the deal; there were no more engines to be had. Meanwhile, Chrysler's big eight-cylinder cars—the Grand Furys, Newports, and New Yorkers—and the ponderous vans and pickups were piling up, unsold. The collapse of the big-car market had frustrated Iacocca's ambition to eliminate the sales bank, and 80,000 large vehicles—a ninety-five-day supply—were sitting in inventory. And Chrysler was spending money on new equipment at the rate of $100 million a month. Iacocca told reporters that the firm's stash of cash and marketable securities was $252 million; a year earlier it had been $676 million. The automaker already had drawn down most of the short-term credit its banks had agreed to keep available.[33] Later that week Standard & Poor's downgraded Chrysler's debt securities from A-2 to B.

One of the most respected observers of the auto industry was Maryann Keller of the investment banking house Kidder, Peabody & Company. Commenting on Chrysler's second-quarter losses and Riccardo's bid for public help, Keller said, "Chrysler's only strategy appears to be to get to September 1980," when the K-cars would be unveiled. "The $1 billion in government aid . . . could tide the company over until the '81 models arrive. But Chrysler is telling everyone the new cars will make it profitable again, despite the fact the other auto companies aren't standing still. Ford will have its new replacement for the Pinto out by then and GM is introducing another front-wheel-drive line at the same time. . . . Chrysler probably can make a good case for government regulations getting it into the mess it's in today. My gut feeling is Chrysler is too big, too important, has too many employees and pays taxes in too many states for the government not to consider seriously the possibility of the company going out of business."[34]

4.

Political issues are often enmeshed in tangled skeins of cause and effect. Public goals are typically unclear or controversial. Thus the mere definition of a public problem, and the first depiction of the choices it poses, can be among the most decisive political acts. Chrysler's troubles were acknowledged by the Carter administration as a growing problem, but the precise nature of the problem and the range of solutions to which it might be amenable continued to elude the White House during the summer of 1979.

On July 26 the team of Treasury officials that had been assembling information on Chrysler briefed Stuart Eizenstat at the White House. In their view the practical choice facing the administration was to provide some form of government help—coupled with co-operation from Chrysler's bankers—or to let the firm slide into bankruptcy. But they worried that a formal bankruptcy filing—even as a reorganization under Chapter 11 —would destroy Chrysler as a car marketer, cost a great many jobs, and perhaps threaten the stability of the financial markets.[35] An auto company was based on confidence. Everyone connected with it, from bankers to suppliers to buyers, was betting on the firm's ability to come through on its promises. A declaration of bankruptcy would shatter confidence and signal the end.

A few days later Eizenstat held a larger meeting with delegates from several agencies, including the Commerce Department, the Department of Transportation, and the Council of Economic Advisers. In this group sentiment ran against special help for Chrysler. Even officials anxious to save the company from bankruptcy—out of concern for employment or for competition in the auto industry —insisted that before the government provided help, it should impose tough conditions on the automaker, including a requirement that Chrysler demonstrate how the new cash would restore it to health.[36]

Leaving aside the question of whether the government should help Chrysler, there was still no consensus on what type of subsidy would work. One thing the Treasury task force *had* concluded was that of all the possible instruments, Riccardo's tax scheme—by which Chrysler would get a cash advance on future tax refunds—was among the least appealing. "From the very beginning it just wasn't a starter," Robert Carswell later explained. Carswell had been deputy treasury secretary as Chrysler made its case. "It's

very expensive. You end up having to pass a statute that sets a
principle that other people then try to use, and you don't know
who they are. Individual tax relief statutes end up being a precedent
for other tax relief, and other people climb on board it as it goes
through Congress. . . . The second thing was that in tax statutes
it's traditionally been very difficult to design review procedures.
The notion is you give the tax relief and they're on their own; I
don't think anyone who looked at Chrysler was satisfied that we
could dare do that."[37]

Despite the distaste of Treasury officials for the notion, the tax
credit approach was by far Chrysler's preferred solution. "The loan
guarantee option was always there in the background, but Chrysler
didn't like it," according to lobbyist Tommy Boggs. "First, they
needed equity; more debt was the last thing they needed. Number
two, they didn't want to have to rework their loan structure, which
would involve renegotiating deals with all of their lenders. And
number three, they didn't want the government in there telling them
how to run their business. The tax idea seemed cleaner. Instead of
asking for money for nothing, they would just be getting an advance
on what they would eventually be entitled to anyway. It felt better.
So John Riccardo was hell-bent on tax credits."[38] From Chrysler's
standpoint the tax route offered another advantage: Legislation
would go through the Senate Finance Committee and the House
Ways and Means Committee. The chairmen of the two committees,
Senator Russell Long and Representative Al Ullman, were sympathetic to Chrysler's plight. Tommy Boggs had splendid relations
with both committees. And by midsummer Chrysler had already
invested considerable time lobbying the senators and congressmen
with the greatest political leverage on tax issues.

Over a few days in late July 1979 Jimmy Carter drastically overhauled his Cabinet. The attorney general and the heads of four departments—Treasury; Health, Education, and Welfare; Transportation; and Energy—quit or were fired. The turmoil distracted
attention from Chrysler's problems. Of more lasting significance
was the ouster of Michael Blumenthal, whom Chrysler officials
considered both sophisticated in his grasp of auto industry problems
and generally sympathetic. Blumenthal was replaced as treasury
secretary by G. William Miller, who had been chairman of the Federal Reserve Board. Before coming to government, Miller, a lawyer
by training, had been chairman and chief executive of Textron,
Inc., a major conglomerate. (He had also served on Conrail's board
of directors.) "We'd made the rounds of D.C. when we first came

out with the tax thing,'' recalled Wendell Larsen, who had coordinated Chrysler's Washington campaign. ''We stopped in at the
Fed to touch base with Miller. He said we were full of crap; there
was no way that it was going to work out like we proposed. He
was very negative. But we thought, screw Bill Miller, what can the
head of the Fed do to us?''[39] As head of the Treasury Bill Miller
could do a lot.

As he moved into his office in the Treasury Building next to the
White House, Miller retained his dim view of a tailor-made tax
subsidy for Chrysler. The new treasury secretary met with Jimmy
Carter on August 3 to argue against a special tax break for the
stumbling carmaker. ''Chrysler had been stirring up a good deal of
political support all over this town,'' Miller later recalled. ''They
were lobbying on the proposition that the government had caused
their problems. The way to correct it was to give them a refund,
an advance refund, of a billion dollars on future taxes, disguised
in terms like some kind of advance R&D or industrial transition
tax credit. There was a lot of momentum building up. Then I came
in—a newcomer, no ax to grind. My first proposition was that this
was absolutely unacceptable, and we should knock it down immediately. We shouldn't invite a situation where by being quiet,
the White House seemed to signal tolerance. So before the Congress
could build up any expectations, we had to knock that idea down:
'We're *not* going to have a tax-based solution; we're not going to
open up the tax books to this kind of thing, period.' The President
said, 'You're absolutely right—put it any way you like, we're not
going to do it.' ''[40]

But the Chrysler team, not yet convinced of the earnestness of
Treasury's opposition, continued for some time to press the advance
tax refund proposal. ''In the late summer we made one final push
for the tax thing,'' Larsen related. ''Doug Fraser warned us that
we were crazy, that it would never happen. We went to see everyone again. Stu Eizenstat was reasonably confident. He told us all
we had to do was get Bill Miller on board and it would work. Then
Miller just blew us right out of the water. He said, 'No, forget it,
no way, absolutely not, get it out of your head.' He was pretty
firm. He said, 'If you're going to get anything, it's going to be loan
guarantees, and even then you'll only get seven hundred fifty million
dollars, and it's going to be tough to pass, and even if it passes,
it's going to be so awful you'll wish you'd never brought the whole
thing up, and I hate you guys and wish you'd go away.' He was
vicious. But that was that.''[41]

It would be weeks before Chrysler would finally and publicly abandon the tax approach, but Miller essentially killed the option in August. Tommy Boggs observed, though, that Miller's position symbolized "a subtle change: In saying to us, 'Forget *this* solution,' the government was coming along with the idea that there should be *some* solution."[42] During the same meeting in which he killed the tax approach Miller tentatively endorsed the goal of some kind of action to keep Chrysler in business. This was no small success. Chrysler had installed itself on the public agenda.

The meetings at the White House grew more frequent. John Riccardo met once more with Eizenstat and Deputy Treasury Secretary Carswell on August 8. Riccardo withdrew Chrysler's earlier proposal for a two-year grace period for meeting environmental standards; even if Congress would grant it, the delay would save too little money to alter Chrysler's prospects much. He was ready to accept the loan guarantee alternative. The two government officials made it clear that they would expect some changes in Chrysler's operations as a quid pro quo. Riccardo countered that Chrysler had already changed: It had jettisoned its European operations and withdrawn into North America; it had fired Cafiero and hired Iacocca; it had closed plants, canceled dividends, limited management pay and benefits, and cut 7 percent of its white-collar workers, saving half a billion dollars in fixed costs; it had hired the investment banking firm of Salomon Brothers to help hunt down potential merger partners; and it was preparing to demand concessions from the UAW in negotiations scheduled for the fall. Chrysler already had the best fuel economy of the Big Three, Riccardo reminded the officials; the K-car, due in a year, would solidify this position. He reiterated—perhaps undiplomatically—that he considered the government in large part responsible for Chrysler's problems. He rejected the suggestion that Chrysler had been mismanaged or needed further reorganization. Bankruptcy was no solution. Simply filing under Chapter 11, he said, would panic suppliers, dealers, and customers and force Chrysler into liquidation.[43]

Coleman Young, the mayor of Detroit, met with Eizenstat later that day to urge a quick decision on help for Chrysler. Young, an early and powerful political ally of the Carter team, was anxious to get the White House on record in favor of rescuing Chrysler. The mayor had known of Chrysler's troubles since early 1979, when John Riccardo phoned to lobby him to pick Chrysler for a contract to supply the city with some 500 cars. "It seemed to me a little unusual for the CEO to be selling automobiles," the mayor recalled. "That alerted me to the seriousness of things."[44] Now Young wanted to be sure that Eizenstat appreciated Chrysler's predicament. He also wanted the White House to be clear about how very seriously Detroit's mayor took it. The banks were getting nervous, he warned; some signal that the government would come through was needed to keep Chrysler's existing loans in place. Young also suggested that if the White House were to accommodate Chrysler's plea for help, the United Auto Workers would be very gratified.[45]

Several officials, including Eizenstat and G. William Miller, met that same afternoon. Miller argued that if the public provided Chrysler with financial help, the government should have some voice in the firm's operations. Other officials agreed that at the very least the government should insist that the company submit an acceptable management plan.

Of all the ways to help Chrysler, a loan guarantee began to seem the most workable to the top officials of the Carter administration. Guarantees could be issued a few hundred million at a time. Each installment could be made conditional on satisfactory performance by the company and its constituents. There were precedents in the New York City and Lockheed rescues. The Treasury team that had been working on the problem for several months had come to the same conclusion. "Several of us had spent nearly a whole year of our lives on the New York rescue," recalled Roger Altman, who was assistant treasury secretary below Miller and Carswell and above Freeman and Loomis. "It's fair to say that we knew right away what the options were. The tax grant was out. There wasn't anything like enough cash flow in the regulatory relief issues. So we're talking about either nothing or a loan guarantee. Much of what we ended up doing was lifted right out of the New York City episode. We had gone through and developed the model there: loan guarantees as our lever for a much bigger package of total concessions. New York City served as the blueprint for Chrysler."[46]

After the White House meeting, Eizenstat explained to Jimmy Carter that a loan guarantee appeared to be the likeliest form of aid but that the company first had to come up with a plausible strategy for using the new cash to restore its long-term profitability. A few weeks later the President mentioned at a breakfast for the congressional leadership that the White House would support only a loan guarantee, not a tax subsidy.[47] And any formal administration proposal would have to await a credible Chrysler turnaround plan.

Early in September Treasury Secretary Miller warned that it might be weeks before the company and the Treasury could concur on a realistic package.[48]

5.

Gerald Greenwald had come to Chrysler in the spring of 1979 after
twenty-two years with Ford. (His last job had been as chief of
Ford's Venezuelan subsidiary.) Soon after arriving, he was named
a vice-president and controller. Greenwald was a finance man,
trained in economics and attuned to numbers. He was dismayed
by the weakness of Chrysler's formal financial controls. When the
Carter administration demanded a detailed plan of action before it
would support a rescue bill, that weakness became a serious threat
to Chrysler's bid for federal help. "You'd think that a company
the size of Chrysler would have had the discipline of an operating
plan," Greenwald later said. "It did not. There wasn't a clear vision
of how we were going past the next month, except in John Riccardo's head and a few others. I had only three or five weeks to
try to do the first Chrysler operating plan. I tried to reach for pieces
that were in the company at the time. There was a product plan,
and there was a cash plan, but it didn't match up against the product
plan."[49]

After weeks of frenzied drafting by Greenwald and his staff
—coached and hectored by Brian Freeman, who led Treasury's
delegation to Highland Park—a booklet, bound in plain white paper
and labeled "Analysis of Chrysler Corporation's Situation and Proposal for Governmental Assistance," was delivered to the Treasury
on September 15. The core of the document was a thirty-one-page
exposition of why Chrysler needed $1.2 billion in guaranteed credit,
why it felt justified in asking for it, and what it intended to do with
it.

The plan began by attributing most of Chrysler's problems to
three external factors: regulation, the gas crisis, and recession. The
central claim was that "the burden of regulations falls most heavily
on the smaller manufacturers, especially Chrysler, placing the
company at an increased competitive disadvantage."[50] The plan
cited several studies supporting its assertion that the disproportionate burden of meeting regulatory requirements threatened
Chrysler's strength and perhaps its survival. (Curious readers are
invited to read the summary of one of these studies, by H. C. Wainwright & Company, in Appendix B.) The second external factor
the plan indicted was the "turmoil created by the Iranian crisis—
the temporary shortage of crude oil, the failure of the U.S. Government's fuel allocation system, the sharp rise in oil and gasoline
prices, and the public's concern about gasoline availability," which
had "created the most abrupt change in buying patterns in auto-

motive history."[51] Demand for the little Omnis and Horizons leaped
as consumers grew more anxious about the price and availability
of gas, but Chrysler could make only 300,000 a year; there were
no more of the German engines to put into them. Meanwhile, the
old lines of big cars, trucks, vans, and recreational vehicles, which
were supposed to generate profits to finance the downsizing program, languished on the lots. Finally, the recently begun recession
now looked to be both more persistent and more damagingly concentrated on the auto industry than anyone had anticipated.

In response to these threats, Chrysler said it had already taken
action on six fronts. First, it had unloaded most of its overseas
assets—Chrysler Europe, the Venezuelan and Colombian operations, most of the Brazilian company, and a third of the Australian
subsidiary—and was arranging to sell its remaining stakes in Australia and Argentina. The Airtemp Commercial Products division
(the air-conditioning subsidiary Walter Chrysler had bought during
the Depression) and the Chrysler Realty Corporation had gone on
the block as well. Second, it had raised funds on its own through
the 1978 sale of $250 million in preferred stock and had extracted
from its banks the largest possible loans. Third, it had cut costs by
closing the Lyons Trim plant and phasing down operations at other
plants, by dropping 8,500 salaried workers during 1979, by cutting
salaries, and by scaling back advertising and tightening financial
controls. Fourth, it had postponed $230 million in contributions to
employee pension funds and saved $52 million a year by dropping
dividends on its common stock. Fifth, it was taking drastic steps
to eliminate the infamous sales bank that would cost it $55 million
in excess interest alone in 1979. Sixth, it was continuing the radical
management shake-up that had begun with Iacocca's appointment
as president and chief operating officer.[52]

In an extraordinary and doubtless painful move for a major manufacturer, Chrysler summarized its competitive strategy for the next
several years. Essentially, the company intended to concentrate
its limited resources on three (instead of five) "families" of cars:
the L-body Omnis and Horizons; the K-body line of front-drive
two- and four-door cars and wagons to replace the Aspen/Volaré;
and the X-body, due in 1984–85, a downsized standard line. It would
also upgrade one of its standard vehicles to target a segment of the
luxury market. By 1985 Chrysler would offer only fuel-efficient
front-wheel-drive cars, plus two lines of trucks and vans (one standard and one downsized) and the subcompact cars and trucks it
imported from Mitsubishi.

Anticipating comments and suggestions, the plan went to some length to explain why Chrysler had selected this strategy instead of limiting its offering to only small cars, or only standard cars, or only cars instead of trucks. Essentially, small cars meant small profits, but big cars alone could not meet the government's fuel economy standards, and Chrysler was good at making trucks and could reasonably anticipate selling them profitably.[53]

The Treasury officials were not happy with this strategy. It seemed quixotic for Chrysler to try to compete across the board with Ford and GM. The officials wanted Chrysler to narrow its planned product line. But Chrysler executives argued that the company needed an "integrated product strategy"—a full line of cars that would satisfy a broad range of consumers and give its dealers adequate scope for sales. Besides, the added cost was not all that significant. At Ford, Lee Iacocca had proved his genius at putting new "skin" on an old car to expand the product line cheaply. Now he was beginning to do the same at Chrysler. The program to upgrade one of Chrysler's middle-of-the-line cars to compete in the luxury market, for example, would cost less than $100 million. But at a late-summer meeting with Chrysler officials, Treasury Secretary Miller called Iacocca to task for what he saw as a reckless expenditure for a company pushing bankruptcy. "If he'd had his way, the secretary would have cut Chrysler back to making just small cars," was how Philip Loomis, a senior Treasury analyst, recalled the session. "He was determined not to let this foolish extension into the luxury market proceed. After letting the secretary go on for a while without saying anything, Iacocca suddenly jerked his glasses from his face and rapped them loudly against the table. He then made it clear—without being abusive but with clearly evident emotion—that it was his understanding it was the job of Chrysler's president to run the car company and the job of the secretary of the treasury to run the government's side; if the secretary didn't mind, he would decide which car programs were warranted. Miller gritted his teeth and went back to the question of loan guarantees."[54]

The plan also included a program of "variable margin improvements"—ranging from more careful purchasing practices to new option mixes to boost per unit revenues—meant to ensure that the K-car could be made and sold more profitably than its predecessors. The company predicted that this program would increase the profit margin on a 1981 K-car by $244 over a comparable 1980 Volaré. This could yield $105 million in extra profits for 1981 alone.[55]

The plan projected losses of almost $1.1 billion in 1979. However, 1980 would not be so bad (with losses limited to less than half a billion), and Chrysler predicted that as the K-car began to sell, the company would regain profitability. After-tax profits of almost $400 million was the estimate for 1981. Profits should climb smartly over the next five years, to come close to $1 billion in 1985. But to get there—or anywhere near this lofty figure—Chrysler had to stay in business and finish the K-car. This meant pouring money into retooling, even as it was losing a fortune every quarter on its current operations.

Chrysler was planning to invest $296 million in the face of a billion-plus 1979 operating loss. It predicted that after the firm had scraped together all possible sources of cash to cover the gap, there would still be a shortfall of $334 million. In 1980 operating losses would be smaller, but investment costs would be bigger, and there would be no new loans or any remaining cash to draw on; that year's financial gap would be $1.2 billion. The plan projected an operating profit in 1981, but investment costs would still exceed available funds. So not until 1984 would cash flow turn solidly positive. Chrysler projected a cumulative need for special funding of $1.6 billion by 1980 and $2.1 billion by 1982. The plan said $928 million of this could be covered by selling more corporate assets. But a gap of $1.2 billion would remain.

Chrysler stressed that its banks could not make good this gap since most of them had already lent the maximum that regulations, or bank policy, allowed to be risked on any one firm. Nor was it hopeful that it could merge with a larger company with the cash to cover Chrysler's shortfall. The same factors that brought it before the government for help made it an unappealing merger partner.[56] That left the public as the source of the $1.2 billion. The company pledged to enter into loan covenants to limit the public's risk and to pay guarantee fees to cover the government's costs. It predicted that all government-guaranteed debts would be repaid by the end of 1985.

Chrysler's plan embodied four crucial assumptions. The first was that automobile sales in the United States would bottom out in 1979. The U.S. car market, which had reached 11.1 million units in 1978 before falling to 10.4 million in 1979, would recover to 10.5 million in 1980, 11.1 million in 1981, and rise steadily to 11.9 million in 1985. Second, Chrysler's share of that market would rise from the 10.2 percent projected for 1979 and 1980 to 11.1 percent in 1981, 11.6 percent in 1982, on up to 12.4 percent in 1985.[57] (The plan rested on equally optimistic assumptions about the U.S. truck market and Chrysler's share of it.) Third, Chrysler's 30,000 suppliers would continue to sell it parts on the same credit terms even as the company's losses deepened. By selling Chrysler components on account, the suppliers in effect provided the company with an $800 million line of credit.[58] Finally, the banks would maintain and, as necessary, renew their $4.8 billion in loans to Chrysler and its financial subsidiary. (Around 100 banks had $1.6 billion in outstanding loans to Chrysler, the company that manufactured cars; an additional 300 or so had extended $3.2 billion in credit to Chrysler Financial, the company that lent money to dealers and to people who bought Chrysler cars.)[59]

6.

Numbers are more tractable than values. Numbers can be arrayed tidily in columns and charts. The eye can fix on bottom lines, and calculations invite crisp conclusions. Values are slippery. They are difficult to talk about with any precision. Discussing the ultimate ends of public policy makes many people uncomfortable and inspires many more to posture fruitlessly. Numbers sometimes can illuminate values: We can profitably use analysis to assess the ramifications of a given decision. But often numbers offer too easy a substitute. Analytical busyness can serve as a means for dodging the larger questions. Public officials too often are tempted to let the numbers do the work and surrender to analysts the job of deciding what is at stake.

Throughout 1979, as Chrysler's plight became more obvious and as policy makers struggled to develop a response, there appeared a raft of reports on the causes, extent, and import of the firm's distress. Chrysler commissioned its own appraisal in anticipation of the need to sell Washington on an assistance plan. Other studies were drafted by or for various government agencies. Most were prepared by private consulting firms. There was no coordination among the researchers, no mechanism for squaring assumptions or testing the models' sensitivity to different starting points. Some analyses were by intent objective; some sought more or less openly to make a case. These studies willy-nilly set the terms of debate on the Chrysler rescue. While they probably did not convert anyone who started out with strong views on the subject, they did shape public understanding of what was at stake. They informed congressional deliberations. Statistics cobbled up at consulting firms in Boston and New York would be cited, denounced, compared, and angrily flung one against the other in the media and on the floors of the House and Senate.

The studies were of necessity speculative. Nobody really knew what would happen if Chrysler failed or if the government endeavored to save it. The assumptions that drove the analyses were in most cases little better than guesses. Most of the reports were workmanlike jobs. Within the constraints imposed by haste, uncertainty, and the paucity of raw data they were useful appraisals. But these limitations were quickly forgotten as the studies were summarized, excerpted, and arrayed in debate. Tentative guesses hedged about with warnings were restated as hard facts. The numbers took on a life of their own in countless speeches and commentaries. (Several of the most influential studies are summarized in Appendix B.)

7.

By early fall 1979 the law firm of Patton, Boggs & Blow had a dozen lawyers working full time to "sell the company on a one-to-one basis" to every legislator.[60] But most of Tommy Boggs's connections were with Democrats, and there was little doubt that the other side of the aisle would have to be sold as well. So Chrysler also engaged the firm headed by William Timmons, a onetime aide to Presidents Ford and Nixon and a man skilled in gaining Republican sympathy for corporate causes. To round out the effort, Chrysler signed on two former Michigan congressmen, Garry Brown and James O'Hara, along with ex-Senator William Hathaway of Maine, to lobby their erstwhile colleagues. Others who would carry Chrysler's message to Congress included Howard Paster, once an aide to Democratic Senator Birch Bayh and now the United Auto Workers' legislative director, and Dorothy Brody, of the city of Detroit's intergovernmental affairs office. Wendell Larsen coordinated the campaign from Chrysler's Washington office. The entire lobbying team was soon meeting daily for strategy sessions.

In the Senate, predictably, Chrysler's cause was consigned to Michigan's senators, Donald Riegle and Carl Levin. They had been laying the groundwork for Chrysler legislation for months. Riegle— a onetime Harvard Business School student and former Republican congressman turned feisty liberal Democrat—had narrowly won a close, bitter race for the Senate in 1976. The United Auto Workers had been instrumental in his victory. In contrast with Riegle's reputation as something of a grandstander, Carl Levin was a quiet but strongly principled legislator, a Democrat who in his year in the

Senate had been viewed as earnest and diligent.* When Jimmy Carter came to Detroit in mid-July 1979 to address a convention of the Communications Workers of America, Riegle and Levin had shared a limousine with the President from the airport. The half hour drive downtown had sufficed for a basic briefing on Chrysler. Riegle later said, "It was obvious he wasn't intimately familiar with the situation. He was obviously preoccupied with Camp David and his road show. We were trying to get it higher on his list of priorities."[61] Now as the campaign began in earnest to lock in Carter's support and to draft and pass appropriate legislation, Riegle and Levin took an active hand in Chrysler's strategizing. By late summer Senator Thomas Eagleton of Missouri and James Blanchard, an ambitious young Michigan congressman, joined them in the lead.

They faced a skeptical Congress. By mid-September sentiment on the Hill was running against helping Chrysler. Many legislators still assumed that Chrysler's final proposal would be for tailored tax benefits, which one Democrat on the House Ways and Means Committee, Abner J. Mikva, of Wisconsin, termed "the goofiest and most offensive idea I've come across in some time."[62] One problem that the company's advocates faced was legislators' unfamiliarity with the specifics of Chrysler's situation. A second was their general distaste for highly visible bailouts after the Lockheed and, especially, Penn Central episodes; both had excited the scorn of columnists and editorial writers and fed public suspicions that Congress was lavishing tax money on well-connected special interests.

A third problem was Chrysler's chairman. Riccardo was well respected among those familiar with his stewardship. But now his company had to make its case to an extended audience that knew nearly nothing about the twisted roots of Chrysler's distress and assumed that dim-witted leadership was behind the problem. Brian Freeman, the Treasury official most familiar with the company, recalled, "Riccardo is basically a smart guy who got blamed for a situation that wasn't his fault. Without Riccardo the company would have tanked; it wouldn't have had a chance. He deserves a lot of credit he'll never get."[63] There are few knowledgeable observers— even among those who would have much preferred no public response—who see John Riccardo as the source of the problem. "Chrysler's trouble was rooted in an excess of marginal overseas investment and a weak product line," according to Tommy Boggs,

---

*Five years later, Lee Iacocca and Douglas Fraser were to serve as co-chairmen of Carl Levin's successful 1984 reelection campaign.

who came to know the chairman well during the early stages of the Washington campaign. "Riccardo solved both those problems, but it hadn't sunk in yet by the time he had to take it to Washington. And he was somewhat anathema on the Hill because he'd been up there for a year and a half preaching about how the stupid regulations were killing his company. He had irritated a lot of members. He had a credibility problem on the Hill."[64]

When a majority of legislators had to assent to a rescue, there was no room for the more subtle measures of corporate accountability. Wendell Larsen, formerly Chrysler's vice-president for public affairs and a longtime Riccardo confidant, told the story in 1984: "Congress wanted to hang somebody. They wanted an expression of guilt; they wanted contrition and punishment. So eventually, to get the loan guarantees, we did something that was very dramatic and very cynical: We helped John Riccardo see that the company would be better served if he resigned. Don Riegle came out to Detroit, had me arrange a meeting with Riccardo, and sat down across the desk from him, looking him in the eye, and told him that it would be tough to get anything through Congress with him still in charge. He told him face-to-face, and that took guts; the two have been friends ever since.

"So that Sunday," Larsen continued, "I went to Riccardo's house, and we worked it out. I'd written my master's thesis in English literature on scapegoat symbolism in Faulkner; that came in handy. I told John that Congress and the country weren't going to act until we'd staged a morality play, and I told him how he'd been cast: John Riccardo takes on himself all the sins of commission and omission, we drive him into the woods, and the company is pure again. At the end of the day we drafted his resignation statement. The script was for Riccardo to fall on his sword—a ritual ending, for Congress's benefit, to the dumb management that had got Chrysler in such trouble. The next morning we issued the statement, and Riccardo was gone. A few days later, when Iacocca testified again before Congress, we'd changed the story. Instead of going through the reasons we were in trouble, he basically said, 'We're guilty, we're sorry, the bad guys are all gone now, and we'll never do it again. Now please just give us the money.' "[65]

But even if Riccardo's stewardship had been laudable and his ouster a matter of symbolism, the symbol was far from empty. Chrysler had to change. Its managers and employees, its suppliers and dealers, its creditors and shareholders, and—in the first and most important instance—Congress had to be convinced that it was the start of a new era for the firm. On September 20 Chrysler's board of directors appointed Lee Iacocca chairman in Riccardo's stead. J. Paul Bergmoser, an old associate of Iacocca's at Ford who had been lured out of retirement to lend a hand at Chrysler, was moved up to president, and Gerald Greenwald was named executive vice-president for finance.

Battle lines were being drawn on Capitol Hill, even though no administration bill was yet ready for consideration. Once the tax credit plan had been scrapped in favor of loan guarantees, the forums for legislative action became the House and Senate Banking Committees, both chaired by Wisconsin Democrats. Representative Henry Reuss had declared himself opposed to a bailout, but he pledged not to bottle up a loan guarantee bill in his committee.*

The chairman of Senate Banking was another story. William Proxmire had a cherished reputation as the Senate's pinchpenny. In what was by 1979 a Washington institution he regularly selected for the Proxmire "Golden Fleece Award" what he considered the most wasteful government undertakings; aside from skewering scientists with silly-sounding research projects, Proxmire had exposed major Pentagon boondoggles. He had also fought an energetic rearguard action against the New York City bailout. Proxmire was disciplined, straightforward, self-righteous, and rather prickly. He was indignant at Chrysler's petition for federal help and early on cast himself as the chief opponent of a bailout. Throughout the debate Proxmire's argument was consistent: "If we provide loan guarantees to Chrysler, we will be saying, in effect, to every business in the country that it doesn't matter if you make bad management decisions, it doesn't matter if you no longer make products that enough people want to buy, it doesn't even matter if the federal government has no direct stake in your continued existence. None of this matters so long as you are big enough and can muster enough interest groups to fight your cause in Washington."[67] His solution: reorganization under Chapter 11. Proxmire outlined the logic on a televised panel discussion in mid-September. "When you go into bankruptcy," he said, "what the judge does is he says the creditors have to stand back for a while. You keep all your profitable operations going—Omni and Horizon would continue, the tank operation would continue, the Mexican operation would continue,

---

* Reuss was concerned that any help that did emerge from Congress require Chrysler to build energy-efficient vehicles —including mass transit equipment—instead of gas guzzlers. "If the U.S. is going to hazard three-quarters of a billion for a loan guarantee, it ought to be done on behalf of a company that is willing to provide employment and produce products that are needed," Reuss said.[66]

many of their other operations would continue, and their inefficient, highly costly operations would not. Also inefficient management would have to step aside. That's what happens. That's what's happened before. What's wrong with that? You're not going to lose any more jobs than you are under a reasonable kind of federal program that insists that they get rid of their high-cost operations."[68]

Another panelist on the same television program was Congressman James Blanchard of Michigan, a junior member of the House Banking Committee. Blanchard had been eagerly proffering his assistance ever since learning of Chrysler's troubles, but his advances had been spurned until the tax bid collapsed in late summer and action shifted to the banking committees. In that forum the ambitious young congressman could be distinctly useful, and by late summer he had emerged as Chrysler's champion in the House. He later recalled the television discussion with Proxmire. "I was barely settled in my seat when Proxmire started railing 'The fix is in!' Meaning, no matter how hard we martyred saints of the opposition work to prevent the loan guarantees, Chrysler is going to get away with bloody murder. Because they've got big union, big lobbyists, and big dealers behind them. He made it sound like we're all corrupt and dirty."[69] While concurring that "there's probably been some bad management" at Chrysler, Blanchard called the crisis essentially "a human problem." He added, "Thousands of people —semiskilled blacks—and they're not going to be able to leave Detroit to enter the insurance business in Dallas or the computer industry in Minneapolis. The fact is to let Chrysler fail in any sort of major way would be devastating."[70] Soon thereafter Blanchard announced that he would feel compelled to submit his own bill if the administration held off too long.

A House colleague of Blanchard's offered his own diagnosis of Chrysler's distress and a quite different solution. Most observers attributed the trouble either to bad management or to wrongheaded regulation. David Stockman, a Republican congressman from Michigan, blamed both. Chrysler's managers, he charged, had "bled its balance sheet with foreign acquisitions that produced more losses than new markets. Its domestic diversification efforts yielded a similarly large crop of lemons. Meanwhile, its domestic auto market share plummeted by 37 percent as it consistently got to the showroom with too little too late." The only competitive strength it had managed not to squander—selling recreational vehicles like vans and pickups—was undercut by government gasoline price and allocation rules, Stockman charged. Chrysler could still "turn the corner despite an accumulation of self-inflicted and policy-induced

wounds," but "the corner is blockaded by regulatory barriers."
Stockman charged that the regulatory burden that was weighing
Chrysler down "has little to do with legitimate public policy ob-
jectives."[71] He told the *Detroit News,* "If you bail Chrysler out
now, you're just bailing out the Environmental Protection Agency
and the Transportation Department regulations."[72] The solution:
Drop the air bag requirement, freeze emissions standards, and extend the timetable for fuel efficiency rules. But Neil Goldschmidt,
secretary-designate of transportation, dismissed the idea of targeted
regulatory relief, and an aide to the House Interstate Commerce
Committee, which would have jurisdiction over Stockman's proposal, said he doubted the idea "would get past the news conference
stage."[73] More to the point, nobody familiar with Chrysler's fortunes felt that even the most drastic regulatory relief would free
enough money to save the company.

8.

Treasury Secretary Miller was determined not to endorse any proposal until he got better information about Chrysler's plight. The
New York City rescue—considered by Treasury staffers the model
for a sound bailout program—had involved clear agreements on
sacrifices from constituents before any legislation was passed;
Treasury hoped to repeat the pattern. But in order to calculate what
levels of concessions would suffice, the government needed fairly
solid, fairly detailed projections of Chrysler's future earnings and
cash needs. Miller and his colleagues were contemptuous of the
financial forecasts they had received from Chrysler so far. Treasury
officials were coming to doubt that Chrysler even had the capacity
to plot its course. What numbers the company *had* produced seemed
wildly optimistic. "The big question was how much money they
needed," a key Senate aide later explained. "We had a feeling they
were lowballing it—and for a very good reason, from their perspective. They just needed money; they just wanted to keep going.
They would have taken five bucks to keep going five more seconds
if that's all they could get. They didn't seem inclined to take an
overall view of how much would be needed."[74]

Yet there was no group in Treasury—or anywhere else in the
government—that could independently appraise Chrysler's situation. Lacking in-house industrial expertise, Treasury had no choice
but to rent some. Late in September Assistant Treasury Secretary
Altman summoned several top accounting firms to bid for an unspecified "forecasting project." Two days after the audition Ernst

& Whinney was hired, and on October 7 a team of twenty-seven specialists descended on Highland Park to begin an exhaustive study of Chrysler's books. The Ernst & Whinney consultants immediately fanned out into six groups, each responsible for some narrow part of Chrysler's plan. Treasury Secretary Miller would make no promises until the study was complete. "One had to balance one's determination to implement this [loan guarantee] policy— which had been decided in early August as a principle—with one's need for credibility in order to make a big deal," he recalled. "You can't adopt a posture where you look too eager to hand out money."[75]

Blanchard and Riegle, both unwilling to wait any longer for the administration to take the lead, submitted almost identical bills to the House and Senate on October 17. Blanchard's Chrysler Corporation Emergency Credit Assistance Act would establish a three-member board—comprised of the secretaries of treasury, commerce, and labor—to provide loans or loan guarantees to Chrysler. Riegle's bill would allow only loan guarantees, not direct loans, and would require Chrysler, as a condition for assistance, to establish a $250 million employee stock ownership plan.*[76] Neither the Blanchard bill nor the Riegle bill set any ceiling on federal help. Both legislators noted pointedly that they would rather have lent their support to an administration bill, but they were anxious not to delay legislation into the next year. Their initiatives were intended to spur the White House to action. (Chrysler officials had warned them that if federal help did not come by early in 1980, it might as well not come at all.) Senate Majority Leader Robert Byrd and Speaker of the House Thomas "Tip" O'Neill agreed to clear time for Chrysler on the crowded agenda for the end of 1979.[77]

House hearings before the Banking Committee's Subcommittee on Economic Stabilization began the day after Blanchard submitted his bill. William Moorhead, the Pennsylvania Democrat who chaired the subcommittee, let Blanchard take the lead in lining up witnesses. Blanchard made little pretense of neutral fact-finding: The hearings would be choreographed sessions for raising Congress's consciousness about Chrysler's predicament and drumming up support. The star performers would be Lee Iacocca, Douglas Fraser, and Coleman Young.

Iacocca faced the subcommittee in a hearing room bright with

---

*Senator Russell Long (D-La.), the powerful chairman of the Senate Finance Committee, was an enthusiastic proponent of employee stock ownership plans and had made clear by midsummer that he would be much more inclined to look with favor on a Chrysler aid bill including such a plan.

the glare of television lights. "Quite frankly, I would rather not be here at all," he told the congressional panel. "I am a strong advocate of the free enterprise system. I grew up in it and slugged my way through it for over 33 years. I am sure you share my conviction that in the long run the answers to our problems are going to be found not in the halls of Congress, but in the marketplace. We intend to compete aggressively in the marketplace of the 1980's with new lines of more fuel-efficient cars and trucks. We will be profitable. And we will provide secure employment for those 140,000 men and women who are directly employed at Chrysler Corporation."[78] Iacocca urged the legislators to consider the "awesome total [of] well over 2 million Americans who would be severely impacted by the failure of this company," including the families of workers employed by Chrysler itself and its dealers and suppliers. (Iacocca's figure of 2 million potential victims of a Chrysler collapse represented the upper reaches of a range of estimates that varied bafflingly from very close to zero upward into the millions.)

Iacocca cited regulations as a central cause of Chrysler's trouble. Unlike Riccardo, however, he did not indignantly demand their removal but merely noted that the required retooling called for average spending of $160 million a month for two years "in good times and bad, in times of gasoline shortages, and in times of financial loss, or we will fail to meet the law. . . . Without questioning the goals of these programs, one can still say that they have been tremendously expensive, and especially so for Chrysler."[79]

Citing a study by Data Resources, Inc., of Lexington, Massachusetts (see Appendix B), Iacocca said that a Chrysler failure would cost taxpayers $10 billion in the first year. "As a businessman," he said, "I believe a loan guarantee of at least $750 million, at no cost to the taxpayer, is a far better investment than a government loss of $10 billion in reduced revenues and increased unemployment benefits."[80] Cast in those terms, Iacocca's argument invited no quick protest.

Bankruptcy was not an option, Iacocca stressed. "We're dying out there in Detroit with just the talk of it." Bankruptcy "would have a falling domino effect that could completely paralyze us in a few short weeks. . . . Any announcement of a bankruptcy proceeding would create a virtual halt—and I mean fast—in cash flow as customers do the only honorable thing and cancel orders, as suppliers demand payment for goods on a C.O.D. basis, and as dealers lose their ability to finance their own purchases from the factory."[81] Iacocca was predicting that Chrysler's constituents would not be able to distinguish between reorganization under Chapter 11 and liquidation. Chapter 11 would *look* like an end to the firm, and that appearance would conjure up its own reality. In an effort to win over or at least to neutralize legislators who opposed loan guarantees on ideological grounds, Iacocca argued that "this nation has long since established the precedent of loan guarantees, and with a good measure of success. Our request breaks no new ground. . . . Loan guarantees have gone to steel companies, to chemical companies, to airlines, to railroads, to ship builders, to farmers, to home builders, to small businessmen. In fact, according to the Office of Management and Budget, in 1980 federal loans and loan guarantees to private business and public programs will amount to $409 billion. . . . We should not argue precedent. We should argue causes, needs, and how the future looks."[82]

Douglas Fraser, the president of the UAW, testified the next day, along with Marc Stepp, head of the union's Chrysler department. Fraser seconded much of Iacocca's testimony and called on Congress to approve loan guarantees quickly: "The auto market is too volatile, monetary policy is too tight, and the uncertainty bred by postponing action too threatening to take a chance on delay."[83] The United Auto Workers were already doing their part, Fraser said. They had let Chrysler delay scheduled payments to the pension fund and might even consider a loan from the $800 million fund if the government guaranteed members' benefits. (Were the government to provide such a guarantee, the risk to the union would be nil. Fraser's offer, in this case, was less than recklessly generous.) But a loan from the union's strike fund, which some observers had suggested, would violate the UAW constitution.

The key issue, though, was wage concessions. The labor chief declined to speculate publicly on the outcome of new negotiations. But he promised that the workers would be ready to sacrifice if it turned out to be truly necessary. Fraser stressed that departing from the industry-wide pattern bargain by accepting less from one of the Big Three was "a very difficult thing for us to do. It defies 42 years of tradition. What it means is that Ford and Chrysler workers living side-by-side are going to be at two levels of wages and fringe benefits."[84]

The next day's witness was Detroit's mayor, Coleman Young. Detroit is a city where electronic billboards flash up-to-the-minute car production figures and where taxi drivers argue auto import policy with passion and detailed statistics. Chrysler was by far the biggest single employer in Detroit proper; the other auto companies had been easing out of the central city for decades. Dorothy Brody, an aide to Young, recalled the atmosphere in the mayor's office as Congress took up the legislation: "Our main concern was the fact that the plants here were old, and the fact that if you were going to cut your losses, the logical ones to cut would have been the Detroit plants."[85]

Young returned repeatedly to a study produced by the Department of Transportation's Cambridge, Massachusetts, research unit, the Transportation Systems Center (see Appendix B). The analysts at the center had estimated that a Chrysler shutdown would double Detroit unemployment to about 20 percent. This burden would fall disproportionately on blacks, who accounted for two-thirds of the Chrysler workers in Detroit. Young depicted for the legislators and the press the grim implications of Chrysler's failure for a city just emerging from near collapse. "[A]fter having suffered severe setbacks during the last recession," Mayor Young said, Detroit "is now in a period of renaissance. . . . There is a new spirit of hope and determination in our city. The city is rebuilding." But the slump then under way was sapping tax revenues, and the city government had already invoked an austerity plan. "Just a week ago we had to lay off approximately 100 employees, including policemen and firemen, sanitation workers—the second layoff in the last 12-month period. . . . We have cut to the bone." Under these circumstances a Chrysler failure, which Young estimated would cost the city about $30 million a year, "would literally bring Detroit to its knees. It could literally reverse the progress that this city has made through self-help to restore itself."[86]

Anxious to dispel the widespread assumption that Chrysler's troubles imperiled only Detroit, Young drew heavily on the Transportation Systems Center's estimates of the damage other American cities should expect. "In Delaware, the Wilmington-Newark area would lose 14,000 jobs and, again, have its rate of unemployment doubled," Detroit's mayor said. "In St. Louis, more than 25,000 jobs would be lost. . . . Metropolitan Syracuse would have its unemployment rate doubled, as would Huntsville, Alabama. Perhaps the hardest hit would be the smaller cities of Kokomo and New Castle in Indiana. In New Castle, one-third of all jobs— one-third!—might be lost. In Kokomo, 40 percent of all jobs would be affected by direct and secondary effects of a Chrysler shutdown. . . . And although economic theoreticians may be comforted by the fact that over the long term our economy would adjust, this is no comfort to those in so many of our cities who face the loss of a job. Because of age, some of those, as a matter of reality, will never be able to find a job again, or at least will never be able to find a job at anything close to comparable wage rates or in the places where they now live."[87] Young wrapped up with a pledge that Detroit would do what it could to keep Chrysler going and with a call for the federal government to "step up its share of the responsibility for saving this corporation, whose continued stability is in the interest of every person in this room."[88]

Young was one of President Carter's key political supporters. He had endorsed Carter early in the 1976 presidential campaign. Now, with less than a year before the 1980 election, Young was a valued Carter ally, calling on blacks and urban Americans to support the President as the candidate who best appreciated the needs of the nation's cities. As the *Detroit Free Press* observed, "Young would have difficulty repeating that claim unless Carter did all he could to avoid a Chrysler shutdown."[89] Following Young's testimony, Representative Stewart McKinney (R-Connecticut) said, "We spent a lot of time drafting a plan to rescue New York City from bankruptcy three years ago. I'd hate to have us have to do the same for the city of Detroit because we failed to tackle Chrysler's problems."[90] Young chaired the Urban Economics Committee of the U.S. Conference of Mayors, and his aide Dorothy Brody had been the conference's chief lobbyist during the New York loan guarantee campaign. The conference issued a strong statement urging federal help for Chrysler.

9.

The United Auto Workers cherished the reputation for integrity it had retained since the early postwar years, when Walter Reuther and his allies had built the union into a redoubtable force in the labor movement. It was among the best respected American unions. The UAW also had an enviable record of economic gains. The industry offered its blue-collar laborers one of the richest wage and benefit packages in America. Pattern bargaining, in which the union held each of the Big Three to the same wage demand, had proved a splendid tactic. The assurance that all firms would pay the same price for labor let managers grant generous increases with no fear of handing competitors a cost advantage. The dearth of serious foreign competition had long blunted consumer resistance to the resulting price increases. Every three years, when contracts came up for renewal, the union leadership targeted the firm most vulnerable to a strike and least inclined to parsimony. Negotiations with the target company set the scale the other companies would be required to match. In four decades the UAW had never granted any company a break from the industry-wide pattern.

Wage rates and benefits had been inflexible. In bad times the auto companies adjusted by laying off workers, not by cutting wages. By contract the most junior workers were the first to be idled and the last to be brought back when sales improved. Auto workers learned to accommodate to the ebb and flow of the car market. Younger workers tolerated periodic layoffs, anticipating steady work at high wages once they had accumulated the seniority to stay on the line even in slumps. Contractual promises also guaranteed them extra cash to supplement what they would collect in unemployment insurance during the interim. There had never been much support within the UAW for limiting wage demands in order to boost auto sales and increase the number of jobs. Even in the worst postwar recessions only a minority of auto workers had been laid off. Because of the seniority system, which limited management's discretion in choosing whom to idle, the majority of workers could be confident that they would keep their jobs. Thus most unionists had no stomach for wage restraint. Indeed, the antagonism between labor and management in most auto plants inspired even many junior workers to ignore economists' counsel on their own best interest and to insist on aggressive wage demands, notwithstanding the predictable result of longer and more frequent layoffs.

For all these reasons, Douglas Fraser's pledge to make concessions in Chrysler's favor was an extraordinary move for a United Auto Workers leader. In a sharp departure from the hallowed tradition of ever-rising wages, the same in each firm, the UAW reopened its contract with Chrysler in October 1979. The union negotiating team—led by Fraser, UAW Vice-President Stepp, and chief rank-and-file delegate Joseph Zappa—faced Chrysler managers across the table, but both sides knew that the real project was drafting a deal that would satisfy Washington.

On October 24 Fraser left the negotiations to attend a breakfast meeting with Stuart Eizenstat and Treasury Secretary Miller at Walter Mondale's house in Washington. Miller began the discussion with a pitch for President Jimmy Carter's reelection campaign. (Mondale was said to have been embarrassed by Miller's remark. The UAW so far had refused to endorse Carter for renomination in 1980 and was leaning toward Senator Edward Kennedy, his chief rival.)[91] Once the talk turned to Chrysler, Fraser emphasized how far the union had come already. He urged the officials to appreciate the wrenching departure from labor tradition involved in reopening the contract and sundering Big Three wage parity. Secretary Miller, incompletely impressed, complained that Chrysler had not yet submitted a viable plan, and he worried that a package of guaranteed loans would leave the company crippled by the burden of the debt. He still saw more merit in an infusion of equity—merger with another automaker, or acquisition by an oil company. Fraser countered that loan guarantees were the only real option the government commanded.[92] Miller insisted that the government should not be in any hurry to provide aid. The company should be required to cut its costs and squeeze sacrifices from constituents first. This prospect—both the open-ended conditions and the delay—dismayed the union leader. "We had a hell of an argument," Fraser recalled. "Miller was saying to me, 'You see that pear in the center of the table? You know, sometimes you shouldn't eat fruit unless it's ripe.' I said, 'On the other hand, if you let it lay there long enough, pretty soon it'll get rotten, it'll be all full of maggots. That's where we are now.' Miller was putting the pressure on us."[93] After the meeting Fraser flew back to Detroit to rejoin the contract negotiations. Mondale and Eizenstat anxiously tracked the talks by phone.

On October 25, following a marathon session in Highland Park, Chrysler and the union reached a deal. The pattern was shattered; the new Chrysler contract was leaner than the deal for Ford and GM workers. There was a wage concession, although not a straight cut: Each of the "kick-in" dates for scheduled wage increases throughout the three-year contract would be delayed by a few months. In a second concession Chrysler workers would get twenty days off with pay—"paid personal holidays"—while other auto workers would get twenty-six. Third, pension increases for Chrysler retirees would lag behind the industry pattern. For most of the contract, benefit improvements would be about 30 percent lower than they otherwise would have been, although they would increase faster near the end of the contract to reach parity with Ford and GM retirees by May 1982. Fourth, sickness and accident insurance benefits would be frozen until the third year.[94] These concessions would save Chrysler about $203 million over the course of the contract, compared to what a pattern deal would have cost. (Chrysler workers would retain the same cost of living adjustments as other auto workers, however, so that wages and benefits would rise with inflation.)

At the same time, Lee Iacocca promised to nominate Fraser for a seat on Chrysler's board of directors at their May 1980 meeting. (The company and the union differed over whether this represented a permanent labor seat on the board or a one-time invitation to Douglas Fraser.) This was the only one of several proposals for union participation in management that Chrysler accepted. But a number of other, more modest concessions were achieved. The company agreed to let 10 percent of the union pension fund be earmarked for "socially desirable investments," like residential mortgages in Chrysler communities or nonprofit nursing homes and day care centers. This concession, first pushed by Walter Reuther fifteen years earlier, was perhaps less significant than it seemed: Chrysler agreed only to join with the union in recommending such investments to the independent trustees who controlled the pension plans. Under federal law, such suggestions could not be binding.[95] The company would also endorse union petitions that the trustees *not* invest in up to five companies with operations in South Africa. Finally, workers aged fifty or older who were displaced by a plant closing would be eligible for special early pension benefits—a significant gain for the employees scheduled for joblessness when Dodge Main closed down.[96]

While the deal had no provisions for recovery—that is, for workers to recoup forgone wages and benefits if and when Chrysler regained profitability—it did ensure equality with Ford and GM workers by the end of the three-year contract. "Parity is the cornerstone of the agreement," Fraser told reporters at Chrysler's Highland Park headquarters. He emphasized the unprecedented pledge to seat a union leader on the board: "I sincerely believe the voice of the worker will be heard in the highest echelons of the Chrysler Corporation and the concerns of workers will be expressed there. This represents a tremendous step forward in labor-management relations in the United States. We think it gives workers an effective voice in their own destiny."[97] Later, in a press conference announcing the deal, Fraser said, "These actions make clear that the UAW has met its responsibilities in the broad effort to save Chrysler workers' jobs and restore the company to stability. The burden now rests on the Congress to act promptly to assist Chrysler, as well as on the banks, supplier companies, and others with a stake in this matter."[98] Jim Wright, the House majority leader, called the renegotiation "one of the most unselfish, public-spirited, forward-looking acts in the history of the American labor movement. If Chrysler's own workers are willing to make such concessions, surely the Congress cannot do less."[99]

But no UAW contract is official until the membership votes it in. The UAW's Marc Stepp said, "We are confident our members will ratify this agreement. They recognize that we were engaged in survival negotiations." Stepp's confidence notwithstanding, the UAW leadership spared no effort to explain the plan, and the urgency of the situation, to the rank and file. A statement by Fraser and Stepp was attached to a thick booklet detailing the tentative contract:

> For the first time in 42 years, we were faced with the stark reality that we would not be able to obtain the full auto pattern for Chrysler workers immediately. Instead, our principal goal had to be the preservation of Chrysler workers' jobs. Without the jobs, the best benefits in the world are meaningless. The corporation is in desperate straits. It is going to lose more than $1 billion in 1979—more than any other company has ever lost in the history of North America. It has been forced to sell off most of its overseas operations and some of its domestic operations. It has had to close plants. It has been severely downgraded by the credit rating services, to the point where it can no longer obtain credit. It has been forced to open its books to the U.S. government and its executives have been grilled by congressional committees. There is no way your bargaining committee would allow any deviation from the pattern if we were not convinced that Chrysler was "on the brink" and that concessions are necessary to save the jobs of Chrysler workers.[100]

The contract passed by a comfortable margin.

Six days after the labor deal had been struck, Chrysler made it even clearer how close to the brink it was by announcing third-quarter losses of $460 million. No company had ever lost so much in a single quarter.* Chrysler's working capital was down to $356 million—$250 million short of what its bankers required as a condition for keeping existing lines of credit open. The syndicate of American banks headed by Manufacturers Hanover granted a temporary exemption from the requirement.[102] But a group of Japanese banks that had been financing Chrysler's Mitsubishi imports pulled out of the arrangement, forcing Chrysler to pay cash for 12,000 imports every month until a new deal could be struck.[103]

10.

On October 17 Chrysler submitted its revised financial plan to the Treasury. The new plan differed from the old in three principal

---

* GM had lost $100 million for the quarter, while Ford showed a profit of $103 million; both were doing much worse than they had in the third quarter of 1978.[101]

respects. First, it was longer—nearly three times longer—and much more detailed. Extended scenarios, supported by graphs and tables, explained and elaborated upon the sales and market share projections that had been baldly asserted in the earlier plan. Second, it asked for less money. A month previously Secretary Miller, calling Chrysler's original $1.2 billion request "way out of line," had told the firm to come back with a loan guarantee figure of no more than $750 million. The number in this plan was exactly $750 million.[104] Curiously, though, Chrysler's estimated cash shortfall for the next three years was precisely the same as the prediction in the September plan, when the bid had been for $1.2 billion. The difference could be discerned only through a close reading of the category "asset dispositions, financial institutions, state and local government, and other." Earlier, when Chrysler still nurtured hopes for $1.2 billion from the federal government, this catchall list had been assumed to provide $450 million. But now that the government's contribution had been cut to $750 million, this category rose to $850 million. Similarly, the category "constituents and employee participation" had been $450 million and was now $500 million. In other words, the company had accommodated Miller's ceiling on loan guarantees by the unsubtle expedient of increasing—by half a billion dollars—its assumptions about what it could squeeze out of its other constituencies.[105] Third, in the new plan the company confessed some degree of unease about the direction in which the economy was moving. The plan still assumed that the looming recession would be a mild one, with the U.S. auto market rising in 1980 from the 1979 trough of 10.4 million, then recovering to 11.1 million in 1980 and resuming the historical upward trend.[106] But it obliquely conceded that things might not work out this way, citing "adverse trends in the economic environment [that] have occurred since the previous submission."[107]

The "adverse trends" that worried Chrysler were rooted in the drastic policy change that Federal Reserve Chairman Paul Volcker had launched suddenly ten days earlier. The Fed can control either interest rates or the money supply, but not both at the same time. If it wants to reduce interest rates to spur the economy, the money supply rises and inflation threatens. If it seeks to constrain the money supply to dampen price increases, interest rates tend to rise. In mid-October 1979, the Federal Reserve Board, under Volcker's leadership, opted to concentrate on limiting the money supply, which had been rising beyond the Fed's targets. No sharp change in goals was announced. But the Fed's priority was now to restrain inflation. Henceforth it would let interest rates move sharply upward. The policy change—termed Volcker's "Saturday night special" since it was made over the weekend, when markets were closed—was to badly shake financial markets and raise fears that the recession might be worse than anyone had expected in the early fall.[108] More to the point, the rapidly rising interest rates were to choke off sales of big-ticket items, like automobiles, which consumers had to take out loans to buy.

Although Representative Blanchard and Senator Riegle had committed themselves to going ahead on loan guarantee legislation with or without administration support, they were anxious to get the White House to follow. They had introduced their own bills mostly to spur the administration to a decision. By the last week of October Blanchard felt exposed, vulnerable, and unwilling to wait any longer for the White House to sign on. He laid siege to Stuart Eizenstat, repeating the urgency of having an administration bill by markup date, November 1. Douglas Fraser, meanwhile, was pressing Vice President Mondale on the same point. But Treasury's platoon of Ernst & Whinney accountants had not yet finished its study, and Secretary Miller was unwilling to endorse a bill until their appraisal was turned in and assimilated. November 1 was too soon.

Despite assurances from Eizenstat that the White House fully appreciated the need for haste, Blanchard was irate. On the night of October 30 he attended a dinner for Carter's reelection campaign. He decided against a subtle protest. "I charged through the doors of the Hyatt Regency like a bull at Pamplona and told every person I knew that the administration was flushing Detroit down the toilet and Carter didn't even know what was going on," Blanchard recalled. "I told everyone what a bastard Miller was, and pointed so he could see me. . . . Coleman Young shot me a glance that said, cool your jets, squirt. 'These guys are gonna kill us!' I told him. 'They've stabbed us in the back!' He told me to keep my shirt on and he'd see what he could do. They had seated Mayor Young right next to Carter. I could see him ranting and raving about something, and later I would learn that after the dinner, that very night, Carter ordered a meeting with Eizenstat and Miller."[109]

At that meeting Carter asked for the final options on Chrysler. Miller said there were two: Either let the automaker enter Chapter 11, or come through with loan guarantees. The President judged that Congress would likely act even if the White House held back. He made the call: Go with option two, a package of loan guarantees contingent on matching sacrifice from Chrysler's constituents.

Carter directed his aides to get commitments from Douglas Fraser and Coleman Young to back the package.*

The day Blanchard's bill was scheduled for committee markup—November 1—Eizenstat summoned Chrysler's congressional supporters, Treasury Secretary Miller and his aides, and the press to the White House for an announcement: The Carter administration was proposing to Congress a $1.5 billion package of guaranteed loans for the ailing automaker, conditioned on matching concessions from Chrysler's banks, suppliers, dealers, employees, and other levels of government. The fact that the administration was now formally backing loan guarantees for Chrysler caught few observers by surprise; the amount of the guarantees did. Treasury Secretary Miller had previously placed a ceiling of $750 million on any aid. But when Treasury's hired analysts—accountants from Ernst & Whinney and consultants from Booz, Allen & Hamilton—delivered to the Treasury their appraisal of Chrysler's funding needs, the cash gap came to "a big, truly awful number," as one aide recalled: "This was not welcome news to those of political sensibilities."[111] Indeed, the total was so daunting that top Treasury officials decided to shorten Chrysler's planning horizon, lopping off several potentially bad years, in order to make the rescue seem less futile. "We had solidly proved to any reasonable person's satisfaction that it was quite impossible for Chrysler to survive," one of the analysts ruefully remembered in 1984.[112]

The consultants' reports had inspired Treasury to double the ceiling on loan guarantees. The federal help, along with matching funds from private sources, constituted a package Miller termed "adequate and sufficient to accomplish the purpose."[113] Roger Altman later explained the decision to double the ante. "The real motivation was our knowing that the worst thing to do would be to put a Band-Aid on this and know when you're doing it that it's not going to solve anything," according to the former assistant secretary. "If we're going to cross the ideological and philosophical hurdle of getting into this situation, let's get into it in a way we can succeed."[114]

Miller took pains to point out that the administration's support was contingent on Chrysler's ability to raise matching funds from its various constituents. One Treasury official revealed that the administration had been delaying its formal support in hopes of

---

* In a separate session with White House aides Hamilton Jordan and Jody Powell later that night, Eizenstat and the President decided to ask Fraser to keep the United Auto Workers from campaigning for Senator Kennedy in the Iowa primary.[110]

having these commitments locked up in advance. "But the situation was deteriorating enough that it was important that we take action quickly if we wanted to still have a company to rescue," the aide said.[115] Miller set out to quash the notion that the administration's support was the political price of forestalling a UAW endorsement of Senator Kennedy for the Democratic presidential nomination. "This has been approached by us merely as a financial program," he told reporters. But another official, who declined to speak for attribution, said, "It's hard to argue with the fact that this is fundamentally a political decision. But it's really a case of politics and substance coming together. The failure of Chrysler would have a devastating impact on the Midwest. Is it substance or politics to decide to do something about it?"[116]

The way the issue came to be posed—a bailout or collapse—effectively dictated the administration's choice. There was little confidence in the new reorganization provisions of Chapter 11. Nobody seriously weighed the option of a workout outside bankruptcy. Nor was there any system in place to help Chrysler's constituents weather the company's failure. There were too many hostages for the administration to consider letting the automaker go.

Soon after the administration had unveiled its own loan guarantee bill, Congressman Blanchard said he would abandon his plan in favor of the Treasury's, and Speaker O'Neill promised that the House would take up the proposal before adjourning in December. Senator Riegle followed suit, submitting the administration's bill hours after Miller endorsed a rescue. "With fast action we can pass this legislation this year and save 600,000 jobs," Riegle told reporters.[117]

Senator William Proxmire tempered the "relief and glee" with which Chrysler officials and supporters greeted the administration announcement by assuring reporters that he intended to "see that the terms of the legislation reported are as tough and protective of the public interest as possible. They should insure maximum security for the Federal guarantees and maximum participation by the other parties involved."[118] Proxmire was chagrined that the administration bill, while stressing the principle of sacrifice by all parties and setting a $1.5 billion total goal, did not specify what would be expected from each group. He announced that his Senate Banking Committee would start hearings soon and continue them "until the many issues involved have been thoroughly explored and discussed." If he followed his customary form, Senator Proxmire would be very thorough indeed.

11.

Cynics suspect that politics is more or less a matter of arithmetic. Any well-organized group able to apply the needed degree of pressure to the needed number of legislators can have, within broad limits, any law it wants. This view is by no means wholly at odds with reality; the concerns of articulate and well-endowed interest groups indisputably matter in Congress. But America has not yet reached the point where pork-barrel logic predictably drives legislation. Principles still animate the process. Principles were not absent from the debate over saving Chrysler. The battle lines were drawn on an ideological plane, not simply according to the number of Chrysler workers and dealers in a lawmaker's district.

The House Banking Committee approved the administration bill, now called the Chrysler Loan Guarantee Act, and sent it to the full House on November 15. Meanwhile, the Senate Banking Committee was holding hearings. Chairman Proxmire had promised not to use his position to kill the bill, but he made no pledge to restrain his rhetoric. "We let 7000 companies fail last year; we didn't bail them out," Proxmire said in his opening statement. "Now we are being told that if a company is big enough we can't let it go under. . . . It is impossible to know how many businesses will not get loans they need because Chrysler gets a Federal guarantee, how many potential homebuyers will not get mortgages, how many cities will have trouble floating bond issues. It is impossible to calculate the cost in terms of lost efficiency in the economy."[119]

He lost no time in summoning Lee Iacocca to testify before the committee. Proxmire was notably less deferential to the auto executive than Moorhead, Blanchard, or the rest of the House panelists had been. "You are now asking the Government to risk $1.5 billion," he lectured Iacocca. "If it fails, the taxpayer takes a painful bath. If it succeeds, you will be a famous success and be made very, very wealthy."[120] Iacocca retained his composure under Proxmire's siege, but he sharply challenged the charge that not even federal help could avert huge job losses at Chrysler. "It has been said that even with loan guarantees, Chrysler Corporation will flee the cities, leaving thousands of people unemployed," Iacocca told the Senate panel. "This is not true. It *is* true that we have announced plans to close a few marginal older plants, but we will offset these actions with the expansion and modernization of other key plants."[121]

Proxmire assigned committee staffer Elinor Bachrach to round up other witnesses for the hearings. There was a premium on critics, to counter what Proxmire saw as a generally pro-Chrysler lineup on the House side. Bachrach found it frustratingly difficult to persuade well-known voices to go on record against the administration's bill. "There are lots of people around—influential people representing influential interests—who will tell you privately that they're absolutely opposed to some bill," she recounted in 1984. "They will complain about the stupid things Congress does, but will they come out in public and say that? Will they lend the weight of their opinion to the other side of the debate? No, they don't want to antagonize anybody."[122] Philip Caldwell, president of the Ford Motor Company, and Thomas Murphy of General Motors were among the invitees who declined to address Proxmire's committee. Both demurred on the ground it would be inappropriate to comment on legislation affecting a competitor.[123]

But there were other witnesses. Peter G. Peterson, secretary of commerce under Richard Nixon and head of the investment banking concern Lehman Brothers Kuhn Loeb, Inc., said that bankruptcy for Chrysler would be preferable to the noxious precedent a federal rescue would set.[124] (Lehman was one of the consultants Treasury had engaged to help it analyze Chrysler's predicament.) But if Congress was hell-bent on a bailout, government help should be limited and strictly contingent on sacrifice by interested parties. The "prospect of federal assistance in a substantial amount should provide a 'carrot' to induce these parties to participate," Peterson said.[125] He feared that Chrysler would become a cash sink, claiming ever larger swallows of federal funds. "There is clearly a grave danger that the ultimate costs of government assistance may escalate far beyond the initial projections," he warned, predicting, "Even then, the company still will not be cured."[126]

Yet Peterson was heartily supportive compared to Walter Wriston. The chairman of Citicorp, at that time America's largest bank and one of Chrysler's major creditors, doubted that additional loans to the automaker had "a reasonable chance" of being repaid. Risking the public's money would be a bad business move, he contended. But Wriston's main objection concerned principle and precedent. "There is no avoiding the fact that it is an attempt by the government to move economic resources to places where they would not otherwise go," he insisted. "Such distortions inevitably lead to less, not more, productivity—and therefore to fewer jobs, less return on investment, and fewer bona fide lending opportunities for banks and everyone else."[127]

James D. Davidson, chairman of the National Taxpayers Union, a nonprofit foundation dedicated to fiscal austerity, said the proposed loan guarantee exemplified "the worst kind of subsidy. It will increase the rigidity in our economy and send a signal to all large corporations that they need not control costs, because in the event they reach bankruptcy, which is the ultimate consequence, they will be bailed out by the taxpayer."[128] R. Heath Larry, president of the National Association of Manufacturers, offered the Senate committee a speech denouncing regulation and government meddling in general without coming down clearly on either side of the loan guarantee issue. David Padden, a board member of the business group the Council for a Competitive Economy, was less ambiguous. "Loan guarantees are necessarily a forced redistribution of wealth, as much so as direct loans or subsidies," he told the Senate panel. "By guaranteeing loans, the government will enable Chrysler to get credit that would have gone to someone else had the market been left free. Those without guarantees will pay more for credit, or will be pushed out of the market altogether." Meanwhile, another industry association, the Business Roundtable, issued a statement opposing loan guarantees: "Whatever the hardships of failure may be for the particular companies and individuals, the broad social and economic interests of the nation are best served by allowing this system to operate as freely and as fully as possible."[129] Iacocca immediately canceled Chrysler's membership in the Roundtable.

The witness most hostile to Chrysler was no laissez-faire curmudgeon, though, but consumer activist Ralph Nader. He said that "Chrysler's problems flow from a two-decade pattern of mismanagement which includes an over-extension of the company worldwide, the production of too many of the wrong kind of vehicles at the wrong time and the production of too few of their better-selling vehicles at the right time."[130] Nader submitted a twenty-five-page package of consumer complaints about Chrysler cars. He called for requiring Chrysler, as a condition of federal help, to manufacture only safe and fuel-efficient cars and mass transit equipment. "If you are going to guarantee anything, guarantee a product that has multiple social, humane, and economic purposes to it. Don't guarantee a mismanaged company so that the executives can proceed with the public's guarantee and further their own tired managerial practices and policies."[131] (Nader precipitated an exceptionally nasty exchange with Republican Senator Jake Garn of Utah when he claimed that the recent automobile accident that had killed Garn's wife may have been survivable in the kind of car Nader wanted to compel Chrysler to produce.)

Senator Lowell Weicker, a generally liberal Connecticut Republican, joined Nader in a populist philippic against big-business bail-outs. "How do you think they feel in the Naugatuck Valley of Con-necticut, where literally hundreds of small businesses have gone under over the years? Those businesses tried their best; but they couldn't make it. However, they didn't have the army of high-priced lawyers and executives pleading their case in the halls of Congress. So now they are out of business."[132]

Most senators saw the choice facing Congress to be between en-during either the unseemliness of federal intervention or the social costs that would inevitably attend Chrysler's collapse. One excep-tion, who envisaged other alternatives, was Democratic Senator Adlai Stevenson III of Illinois. "The proposed fix for Chrysler unites all of the worst facets of government meddling in industry's fortunes," he argued in a committee session. "It is a shortsighted reaction to economic necessities with political expediencies. It is thin on constructive ideas; it leaves critical questions about the long-term future of hundreds and thousands of workers in the auto industry unarticulated and unanswered. . . . A real exercise of governmental responsibility to workers would be to provide ex-tensive retraining and relocation costs, and to locate new jobs. . . . At issue is not whether the government acts, but how to act intel-ligently. The British have made support for geriatric industries into a national habit and, led by the labor unions, have dragged their economy into a spiral of decline. The Japanese have met it no less extensively, but have achieved dramatically different outcomes [through] their quiet steps to wean labor and capital away from declining industries and into the future. I believe we should go the way of the Japanese, not the British, but by means of our own American making."[133]

12.

Stevenson's bid to shift the focus of concern from the company itself to its imperiled workers and communities failed to alter the debate. The alternatives had been posed as either bankruptcy—which experts agreed would in this case likely mean liquidation since a reorganization under Chapter 11 would be *seen* as a collapse of the firm and create a fatal crisis of confidence—or a bailout. Most senators were by now resigned, or reassured, that there would be some kind of Chrysler rescue. Saving the company to save jobs was a potent political argument. Even those who in principle would have preferred a more direct approach to the jobs problem embedded within the Chrysler problem saw no practicable alternative to keeping the firm in business. Almost from the start the legislative project was defined as building a better bailout.

The administration bill required private money from Chrysler's constituents—workers, bankers, stockholders, suppliers, and dealers—to match public money dollar for dollar. It did not specify how much each group would give but simply stipulated that $1.5 billion in concessions had to come from somewhere. Some senators were concerned that unless responsibility for private contributions was assigned share by share, each constituent group would hold back in hope the other groups would come through with most of the money. No group would have any incentive to sacrifice more than it stood to lose if Chrysler went bankrupt. Indeed, by diminishing the likelihood that the company would be liquidated, the government would make these constituents less willing to sacrifice. Thus public funds could perversely shrink the total pool of resources available to Chrysler or leave the taxpayer exposed to huge losses.

Proxmire and his aides and allies were anxious to find ways to *increase* private parties' readiness to contribute. They had small confidence in the executive branch's competence or will to extract such concessions. So they determined to fix requirements in the legislation itself. The Senate Banking Committee summoned representatives of Chrysler's constituent groups to find out how much of the burden each might be induced to bear.

Chrysler owed nearly $5 billion to banks scattered from Arkansas to Iran. Two-thirds of this sum, however, was in loans to the Chrysler Financial Corporation, a "captive" finance company. The links between the parent and the finance company were ambiguous. Chrysler Financial's central mission was to provide credit to Chrysler dealers and buyers, but the finance company was not technically a part of the car company. And Chrysler Financial was in distinctly better shape than the parent. Around two-thirds of the financial company's loans were from American banks, with the rest mostly from European lenders. None of this debt was legally secured, but the company was well managed, and its assets were sound and to a great extent liquid. Essentially Chrysler Financial borrowed from banks and investors and passed the money on as loans to finance car sales. There was little reason to suppose that the dealers and consumers would fail to repay them. So its creditors felt only limited anxiety.[134]

The parent was a different matter. Lending to Chrysler itself amounted to $1.6 billion (see Figure 5, opposite). This included the

FIGURE 5
Chrysler's Debt, End of 1979

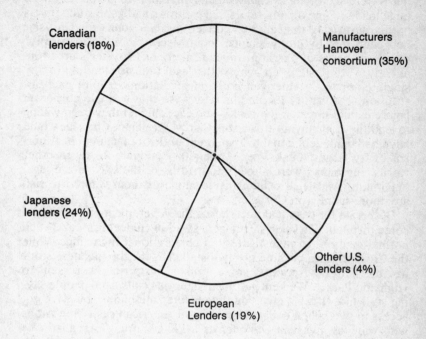

Canadian lenders (18%)

Manufacturers Hanover consortium (35%)

Japanese lenders (24%)

Other U.S. lenders (4%)

European Lenders (19%)

$567 million credit agreement with a consortium of U.S. banks led by Manufacturers Hanover (MH); $72 million in other American lines of credit; $305 million in short-term credits and other loans from European banks; a $400 million account with a consortium of Japanese banks for financing Mitsubishi imports; and $290 million in loans to Chrysler Canada from various Canadian banks.[135]

Many of these loans carried covenants binding Chrysler to minimum standards of fiscal soundness. As a legal matter, if the automaker failed to live up to these covenants, the lenders could demand full payment immediately. Cross-default clauses in the covenants meant that one such demand would trigger others and quickly bring the firm down. As the Senate took up the rescue bill, Chrysler already was in flagrant violation of many of these covenants—like the $600 million minimum on working capital

—and was poised for performance a good deal worse in the near future. In well-appointed offices throughout the world, lending officers were squirming as chairmen and directors wondered how such huge loans to one of America's biggest firms had gone sour. It was hardly surprising that queries concerning *new* loans for Chrysler had been met by stony silence, polite lectures on fiduciary prudence, or hoots of derision. Indeed, many of Chrysler's creditors already were pushing up against the legal limit for lending to any single company. (American banking regulations require each institution to diversify its lending widely so that a single corporate failure cannot threaten the bank's solvency.*) Had they been willing to lend the company as little as another $400 million, Chrysler would have had bank debt equal to 10 percent of the total capital of America's fifty largest banks (see Appendix A, Figure 10A). In other words, the banks were already four-fifths of the way to the legal maximum. And legal ceilings aside, none of them wanted to risk any more money on Chrysler.

Desperate for cash and uncertain if the government money would come through, Chrysler's managers swallowed decorum, and even normal caution, to investigate less conventional financing. While the Chrysler saga became firmly installed as the top business story in American newspapers, some unusual proposals were sent to Highland Park. "We kept getting mysterious calls from people saying stuff like 'I can't give you details over the phone, but I've got access to two billion dollars in cold, hard American cash from Arabs who want to invest in Chrysler as a PR gesture,' " recalled one Chrysler officer. "We chased every one of them down. One of them, the most intriguing, was from James Schlesinger, the former secretary of defense, as the middleman in a deal that was supposed to involve money from the shah of Iran, who was then in Mexico. Billions of dollars! Schlesinger's aide contacted [Chrysler officer] Harold Sperlich, who went to Lee [Iacocca], and they dashed off to Washington to meet with Schlesinger and these Arab-looking guys. The moneymen wanted a letter of authorization and a fee of something like two percent, in advance. We checked it out—a wild-goose chase. Totally phony. They'd fooled the former secretary of frigging defense of the United States of America. Con men, like the hundred other contacts. But we followed up every one of them, we were that desperate."[137]

Chrysler had abandoned hope of getting new loans and was grap-

---

*At the time, national banks could not lend any company more than 10 percent of their capital.[136] Most state-chartered banks faced comparable restrictions.

pling instead with the stomach-twisting problem of preventing one or more major creditors from bolting from the herd and starting a stampede. "We were trying to persuade the banks to sweat it out with us," recalled chief finance officer Gerald Greenwald. "They weren't ready to put up one more dime. We said, 'At least don't pull out on us; we're going for the loan guarantees.' I think it was only because they figured they had nothing to lose—they might as well wait a couple more months and see what happened—that they didn't just pull out on us. They really didn't believe we could get a loan guarantee act. . . . It was only about September or October that we got smart enough to just shove the door closed and say, 'We're not paying anybody a dime. If any of you wants to be known forever as the bank that brought Chrysler down, you take us to court.' "[138] It was a grim standoff: The banks brandished their rights under bankruptcy law, while Chrysler raised the shield of public opinion and tried to pacify creditors with the plea that their best shot at getting their money back was letting the firm live to carry out its turnaround plan. Then the Senate announced it would expect the bankers to come through with fresh money.

In testimony before the House subcommittee Walter Wriston, chairman of Citicorp, had dismissed with contempt the notion of new loans for Chrysler and advised Congress to do the same. Wriston's tone was all his own, but the views were shared by many bankers, who feared that a loan guarantee program would pile new claims on Chrysler ahead of existing lenders without succeeding in saving the company. Now John McGillicuddy, chairman of Manufacturers Hanover, was fielding questions from the Senate on the same issue. It was a delicate position. "Manny Hanny" had been Chrysler's lead bank for years, and McGillicuddy devoutly hoped Congress would approve a rescue bill. But McGillicuddy the supporter made essentially the same response as had Wriston the opponent: He would approve no more unguaranteed loans to Chrysler. Legal standards of fiduciary responsibility to the bank's shareholders and depositors prevented additional loans unless there was a firm expectation of repayment. Nobody could reasonably claim such an expectation of Chrysler in the fall of 1979. Nor could Manny Hanny pledge to soften terms on existing loans or consider converting some loans to equity. Proxmire, with grim satisfaction, called the banker's testimony "devastating evidence" against the administration plan.[139] McGillicuddy protested that the government was not bound by the body of traditions and laws that forced an extreme caution on bankers. "I don't think that it is inconsistent for me to say that the plan has a reasonable chance for success and yet say that we as a bank will not advance additional funds," he told the Senate panel.[140]

The Senate committee next turned its attention to Chrysler's unionized workers, a major constituency by any measure. Wages and benefits were one of the largest categories of claims on Chrysler. Out of every dollar Chrysler took in, thirty-one cents went to its workers.[141] (Most of the rest went to suppliers.) The unionized employees, moreover, had perhaps the strongest stake in keeping Chrysler in business. The best alternative employment available in Detroit, or Rockford, Illinois, or Kokomo, Indiana, was likely to be a good deal less lucrative than a job with Chrysler. Total compensation at Chrysler was sharply higher than the manufacturing average. If the company failed, its workers would be worse off than any other constituent group. The banks, for example, would have to declare losses and write off part of their loan portfolios, and some of their lending officers would have to live with blots on their records. But many of Chrysler's blue-collar workers would be suddenly, substantially, and by all odds permanently poorer.

Less than three weeks after having negotiated a new contract with Chrysler, Douglas Fraser and Marc Stepp were called before the Senate to testify. The union leaders' stance was simple: Labor had already anted up. Chrysler workers did not compare their lot with some abstract manufacturing average but with that of their neighbors working for Ford and GM. By that standard, they were $203 million worse off than they had been as of mid-October. It was now somebody else's turn to sacrifice.

But the union's position was suddenly under very effective fire from an unexpected quarter: Alfred Kahn, chairman of the Carter administration's Council on Wage and Price Stability. Testifying on the heels of the labor leaders, the former Cornell economics professor pointed out that the deal struck between UAW and Chrysler bargainers on October 25—while indeed saving the firm $203 million relative to Ford and GM wage and benefit scales—would still cost the company $1.3 billion more than the old wage and benefit levels would have over the three years of the contract. "I'm supposed to be the adviser to the President on inflation," Kahn said. "The Chrysler episode is the story of inflation, writ small."[142]

Kahn's specific figure for the cost of the October contract—$1.3 billion—was not entirely accurate since it failed to account for the shrinkage of Chrysler's work force.[143] But it summoned wider attention to UAW pay scales. Worse, from Fraser's perspective, it invited a comparison with the $1.5 billion in aid the administration proposed, a quick calculation, and the conclusion that the guaranteed loans Chrysler wanted would do little more than cover the wage increase the union had just negotiated. It seemed as if taxpayers were being asked to hand over money to Chrysler's well-paid employees. Kahn's arithmetic galvanized the senators on the Banking Committee to demand additional sacrifices from labor.

Faced with the insistence that labor do more to save Chrysler, Fraser did not flatly rule out further concessions. But he stressed that the October contract had already been negotiated "with one eye on Congress . . . because we knew Congress would not act favorably on the loan guarantee idea if Chrysler workers did not make a sacrifice." He pointed out that the average Chrysler employee, over the course of the contract, would make the "not insignificant sacrifice" of around $2,000 in wages, benefits, and forgone days off relative to the industry pattern. Referring to Kahn as "the court jester of the Carter Administration," Fraser suggested that he "should stop shooting off his mouth. He's a dangerous man when he's on the loose and ought to be locked up for a couple of weeks."[144]

Carter administration officials, while declining to incarcerate Dr. Kahn, did move to distance him from the White House. Treasury Secretary Miller told reporters, "Fred extrapolated his charter a bit and began to move from Administration view to personal view. . . . In our system of government, where not every participant has been schooled in communications within government, there's bound to be instances where we mix up personal views with Administration views. We try to minimize these because they confuse people."[145] Kahn himself, while still insisting that the contract was too rich, labeled the demand that the UAW contribute more as his own personal opinion and said, "[T]here is uncertainty as to what the Administration view is. What the Administration view is will appear as we go through the process."[146]

Chrysler's stockholders constituted a third constituency. Just over half of the company's 66 million shares were held directly by the public and were in the hands of about 185,000 people. (Brokers, estates and trusts, pension and mutual funds, and Chrysler's own employee thrift program controlled the rest.)[147] The average individual stockholder held roughly 180 shares; their combined value had fallen from about $3,600 two years earlier to about $1,200 as the Senate panel met (see Appendix A, Figure 11A). These stockholders in some ways had an even clearer stake in the firm's survival than its employees had. If Chrysler were liquidated in bankruptcy, its stock might very well be worthless, while workers would find some other jobs eventually. On the other hand, the typical shareholder was far from wholly dependent on his Chrysler holdings. Few, if any, investors owned *only* Chrysler stock, and most were comfortably installed in the top income brackets.

Senator John Heinz of Pennsylvania—himself a very wealthy man as the heir to the H. J. Heinz fortune—felt it was only fair to ask Chrysler's stockholders to contribute to the rescue. A Harvard M.B.A. who prized his financial sophistication, Heinz knew that Chrysler's stock, now languishing between $5 and $10 a share, would shoot up if the firm recovered. If workers should sacrifice wages, banks grant concessions, and the government guarantee new debt, why shouldn't the stockholders be expected to do their bit? It would clearly be impractical to ask each stockholder to ante up in proportion to his stake; the owners were too many and too scattered. But Heinz proposed a simpler method: Chrysler should issue new stock. This would bring the company new money at the expense of existing shareholders, whose ownership claims would be diluted. If Chrysler were to double the shares outstanding, each share would in principle be worth half what it otherwise would be. And the money investors were willing to pay for these new shares should reduce the company's need for government help by an equal amount. Heinz warned Treasury Secretary Miller that unless the administration required Chrysler to issue new shares, "you are going to create . . . an incredible windfall for Lord knows who. The stock will go from $7 to $20 or $30."[148]

But Miller claimed it simply couldn't be done: "I do not believe that as an independent underwriting of equity, a significant amount of money can be raised by selling stock."[149] Lee Iacocca agreed with Miller. Chrysler's recent losses had so eroded confidence in the company that nobody wanted to buy its shares. "We have no possibility of raising money in the private sector on an equity basis today, because we lost $1 billion this year," Iacocca said. "They handle us like we have leprosy."[150] James Wolfensohn of Salomon Brothers, Chrysler's investment banker, told the senators that "the shareholder body to whom we would be seeking to address our request for funds is not a wealthy group and has already taken quite a beating." Proxmire, who liked Heinz's idea, pressed Wolfensohn to estimate how much money Chrysler could raise by selling stock. Uncomfortably and reluctantly, he guessed that *if* guaranteed loans were part of the package, Chrysler could sell $50 million in stock at a price of $2 to $3 a share, less than half the current price.*[151]

A fourth constituency that might be tapped for funds consisted of the cities and states in which Chrysler was a principal employer. Coleman Young, the mayor of Detroit, was queried by the Senate panel on what the city could offer Chrysler. Young pronounced himself eager to help but explained that Detroit was in no position to make major financial contributions. He said that Detroit already gave the company $3 million a year in tax abatements. Questions about further contributions elicited from the mayor a somewhat elusive plan for building a new assembly plant for Chrysler.[153] Early in November the *Detroit News* had reported that Young was considering a scheme to merge city money with federal and private funds to put up a new $100 million assembly plant. Two days later Young's press secretary, James Graham, had denied there were any such plans: "We are not going to build Chrysler a plant. The Mayor was talking about what we could do to help Chrysler. He was talking about all kinds of options. He went too far. He began over-speaking himself."[154] But the idea had resurfaced within a week. At a November 13 press conference in Detroit, Young had suggested offering Chrysler a deal that John DeLorean's fledgling sports car company had spurned in favor of a better offer from Northern Ireland: Detroit would float municipal bonds, apply the proceeds to building a new assembly plant, then lease the plant to Chrysler and use the lease money to make the bond payments.[155] Now, when Young mentioned the plan at the Senate hearings, the senators were skeptical that it would work or that the scheme would represent much of a concession from Detroit. (The real cost of such tax-exempt bonds would fall on the Treasury.) Chrysler executives themselves doubted that a new assembly plant could be built for anywhere near the sums Young cited. In any event the company was then shutting down operations at a rapid clip and hardly needed a new plant.[156]

Several senators became convinced during the hearings that the administration bill was too lax. They felt that it called for too little

---

* Treasury's Brian Freeman later said, "Sure you could sell some. But as you set the price of each new chunk low enough to find buyers, you're bringing it down lower and lower. You could easily raise a hundred million dollars selling new equity. You could probably raise two hundred million dollars, maybe three hundred million dollars, maybe more. But you couldn't raise enough to solve the problem."[152]

in private concessions. More important, they were concerned that the failure to assign each constituent group responsibility for a fixed share of the total was a tactical error. If the guaranteed loans were issued—or even simply promised—before Chrysler's dependents had committed themselves, each might assume that the pressure was off or that another group would come up with most of the money. More detail had to be built into the rescue bill.

Senator Richard Lugar pressed this theme with Douglas Fraser. "I do not see a prospect that the Chrysler Corporation is going to continue without there being a very substantial renegotiation," the Indiana Republican warned. "I don't see any way the banks can take the position they have taken that they are already as far as they want to go with these loans. . . . The Chrysler management and board can see no particular value in new equity and the sale of stock, albeit at bargain basement prices. . . . Can you offer any thoughts as a practical negotiator as to how the parties who are involved in this might come together, and who might convene them? . . . I am simply troubled by the fact that the right people are not talking to each other at this point, and the time is seeping out on all this."[157]

Fraser was keenly sensitive to the widespread instinct to look to the UAW contract as the most obvious source of further cash. But he agreed with Lugar that each of Chrysler's constituent groups feared it would be stuck with an unfair part of the burden and shunned responsibility for saving the firm. Fraser told of a recent conversation he had with Lee Iacocca, in which Iacocca had shared the frustration of trying to forge a deal among groups that distrusted one another. "[He] can't get a grip on this because he goes to the banks and they say, 'What are the dealers going to do? What is the union going to do?' And then you go to the dealers and they say, 'What are the banks going to do?' And everyone is just running in circles."[158] As each group dodged responsibility for saving the firm, Chrysler was edged closer to either insolvency or abject dependence on the public.

In the last days of November 1979, the Senate Banking Committee set to work on a new loan guarantee bill featuring stiffer and much more specific requirements for sacrifices from Chrysler's constituents. Two senators took the lead: Lugar and Paul Tsongas, a Democrat from Massachusetts. In their careers to date the two had staked out positions near opposite ends of the ideological spectrum, inspiring Proxmire to dub them the committee's "wide receivers." As is customary, the senators delegated much of the actual drafting to Banking Committee staffers. "After the hearings and before the markup," Proxmire aide Elinor Bachrach later recalled, "a bunch of staff who had been working on the issue from the Banking Committee sat down and tried to put together a bill that had some specificity and had some teeth in it. There was strong feeling that we had to nail down the financial package. There had to be some indication of how much would come from each, and it had to add up to a particular amount. There was some flexibility for shifting dollars around, but it had to come from somewhere in that coalition."[159] Nor was it only Banking Committee staffers who contributed language. Brian Freeman, the Treasury bureaucrat who had tracked Chrysler since late in 1978, had developed specific ideas on how best to allocate the burden. He was not reluctant to share these opinions with the Senate staff. Many of Freeman's suggestions found their way into the draft legislation. What emerged from the staff was a package that cut guaranteed loans by $250 million (to $1.25 billion) while nearly doubling the requirement for outside funding (from $1.5 billion to $2.75 billion). Total assistance to Chrysler—from public and private sources—would come to $4 billion. Most important, no government guarantees would be issued until Chrysler had "legally binding" commitments from its constituents.

The draft Senate bill spelled out these constituent contributions in detail. U.S. banks would have to come up with $400 million in new loans and $100 million in concessions on existing loans; foreign banks, $150 million in new loans; Chrysler would have to sell additional assets totaling $300 million; $30 million would come from a new stock issue; and $250 million from state and local governments.

But most of the extra money—$1.32 billion of it—would come from a three-year freeze on wages. Two provisions softened this requirement somewhat. The freeze would be reviewed in the third year; if by then the company had gained enough financial slack, wages could be increased. More significant, the company would grant its employees a major equity stake: Workers would be issued $250 million in new shares. Pressure had been building for weeks to include an employee stock ownership plan in the package. Chairman Russell Long of the Senate Finance Committee had been promoting such plans since 1973. Under the plan, a company puts shares of its stock into a fund that holds them in trust for employees. Workers can claim or sell the shares only when they leave the firm. Long had authored tax legislation that made it advantageous for firms to fund such plans; he was an enthusiastic believer that "by making more working Americans dividend-receiving capitalists they will begin to feel more a part of the system and will begin to think and act as owners.''[160] When the Senate began considering aid for Chrysler, Long had warned that he would lend his support only if the legislation included an employee stock ownership plan, and he hinted that he could persuade many of his colleagues to the same conviction. Such a plan would be a positive spur to Chrysler's recovery, he said, adding, ''Give the workers a share in the company and they'll work like little beavers.''[161]

A second major departure from the administration bill concerned the structure of the agency that would be set up to run the rescue. The original proposal had vested all authority with the secretary of the treasury. But the Senate wanted a composite administrative board that would have a measure of independence from the White House. The new proposal added the comptroller general (the head of the General Accounting Office, a congressional agency that monitors how the executive branch implements laws and spends appropriations) and the chairman of the Federal Reserve Board. The comptroller general, Elmer Staats, was expected to be a no-nonsense overseer. According to Senate Banking Committee staff chief Kenneth McLean, ''The Chrysler lobby was deathly afraid of the General Accounting Office. What they wanted was either something run by Treasury without the GAO or something with enough other administration people that GAO would always be outvoted.''[162] The other board member, Paul Volcker, the current chairman of the Federal Reserve Board, had impressed Proxmire as sufficiently tough-minded to let Chrysler fold if it failed to meet Congress's conditions.

The Lugar-Tsongas version of the loan guarantee bill also required that Chrysler and its lenders recognize the federal government as senior creditor. If the company ended up in bankruptcy, in other words, the government would have first claim on the money raised by selling off its assets. Other creditors would be paid only after the government's loss had been made good. (There was one exception: After a Treasury official had warned that banks would never consider offering new loans without security, a clause letting the government waive its senior claim in favor of private sources of fresh money was added.[163])

The Banking Committee approved the Lugar-Tsongas bill by a 10 to 5 margin and sent it on to the full Senate.* The wage freeze clause sparked an instant and lively reaction. It would require the

---

* *The New York Times* commented on the proceedings: ''The committee's session at times had an almost carnival-like atmosphere as lobbyists for the measure darted in and out of the committee room and clustered with senators and their aides to plot strategy and indulge in political backslapping.''[164]

UAW to reopen its contract with Chrysler—an unprecedented legislative imperative. Howard Paster, the United Auto Workers' chief lobbyist, learned that the Banking Committee had sent the Lugar-Tsongas version of the bill to the Senate floor when James Blanchard called him at home. "My people can't live with that," the lobbyist told the legislator. "Let's face it, Jim—we're finished."[165] Paster's public response, issued the next day, was feistier: "This proposal is punitive, discriminatory, and outrageous." He pledged to do what he could to remove the freeze on the Senate floor.[166] But as the Senate's tougher version took shape, pressure to demand more concessions from constituents, including labor, was also growing on the House side. Harold Sawyer, a Michigan Republican, charged that the administration's plan amounted to "subsidizing that wage increase. That'll send a message to every labor union in the United States that they can demand government backing to cover wage increases."[167] A staffer on a key House committee said, "There is considerable feeling around here that if the bill contains a wage freeze, it will clear the House by a good margin. If it's not there, passage would be in doubt."[168]

13.

Bills to rescue Chrysler went to both houses of Congress on December 6, 1979. At the insistence of the Republican minority on the House Banking Committee, the House's bill was sent to the floor with no limits on the number or type of amendments that could be proposed. "It's definitely going to be a long siege," predicted James Blanchard, who had hoped for a quick, clean bill. "I just hope we don't design tailfins and set salary scales."[169]

Chrysler's meticulously orchestrated lobbying campaign swelled to a crescendo as the House and Senate went to work. Lists of every Chrysler plant, dealership, or supplier were fed into computers and recombined by congressional district. The district printouts let the Chrysler lobby sketch detailed scenarios on the town-by-town impact of a Chrysler failure: so many hourly workers, so many dealership jobs, so many suppliers with annual sales to Chrysler down to the penny.*

---

* To cite one example, the list of Chrysler suppliers produced for Congressman Elwood H. Hillis, Republican of the Fifth District of Indiana, ran to three and a quarter single-spaced pages and included the names of 436 companies in Hillis's district whose sales to Chrysler totaled $29.52 million for the year. Among them was Leek's Radiator Repair Shop, in Kokomo, with $90 in Chrysler business. Occasionally there were slipups. One congressman complained that the "suppliers" that were supposed to be located in his district were just newspapers that some Chrysler office received.

Chrysler lobbyist Garry Brown, the former Republican congressman from Kalamazoo, had planted himself on the hearing room dais to offer suggestions as his erstwhile colleagues on the House Banking Committee worked out their version. Now—along with James O'Hara, the other former Michigan congressman in on the lobbying—Brown helped monitor and interpret moves in the House at large.[170] Victor Gotbaum, head of New York City's largest municipal union, was recruited by the UAW to garner support from the New York delegation. Mayor Coleman Young came to lobby, invoking the statistic that 1 percent of all black America's income came from Chrysler.[171] Governors of states that would be hurt by a Chrysler collapse, notably Otis Bowen of Indiana, labored to bring their delegations around.[172] Wendell Larsen—Chrysler's vice-president for public affairs, head of the company's lobbying effort, and an active leader in the Lutheran Church—arranged to preach the sermon one Sunday at Detroit's largest black church. "I talked about jobs and human dignity and all that kind of stuff. They loved it. We had prayer meetings, bake sales, everything," he recalled.[173] The Reverend Arthur L. Gooden of the United House of Jeremiah Church in Detroit used his weekly Sunday morning radio show to launch a drive for signatures on "Save Chrysler" petitions. Church members fanned out to shopping malls and grocery stores around Detroit, collecting signatures. A delegation of ministers brought the sheaves of paper to Senator Riegle's Washington office; they stayed on to lobby.[174]

Joseph Ventura, the head of the Italian American Foundation, invited the members of the House Italian-American caucus for coffee and doughnuts and a speech by Lee Iacocca. "I walked in with [New Jersey Representative] Pete Rodino," Iacocca recalled, "and he says, 'I want you to talk to my pal here.' The Italian caucus—thirty-one Italians—voted as a straight bloc. Screw the Republican or Democratic party lines; they voted the Italian party. It was because I'm Italian, I guess. You used everything in the book. You pulled out all the stops. There is nothing seedy about that. That's democracy in action, really."[175]

"He was marvelous," according to Ventura. "He answered all the members' questions and after the meeting, several of them told him they would rethink their positions." The Italian-Americans could count themselves honored; Iacocca, desperately busy in Detroit trying to keep Chrysler alive, did little lobbying in person.[176]

Jimmy Carter stepped in directly to persuade fellow Georgian Senator Sam Nunn to look kindly on the guarantee plan; Nunn reversed his stand and voted for the bill. Gloria Steinem was brought in to work on Senator Robert Packwood. The UAW thought the feminist leader might succeed in gaining Packwood's support where other advocates had failed. (She failed, too.)[177]

But the most important lobbying forces were three: Chrysler's dealers, the team of in-house and hired professionals, and the United Auto Workers.

Chrysler financial officer Gerald Greenwald recalled, "We try to pick community leaders as dealers. They tend to be people who are politically active or just generally active. You send a big bunch of dealers to see their congressmen in Washington, and it's amazing what they can accomplish. One of our managers from the Washington sales office got a call from Detroit asking, 'Can you help us out with some hotel rooms and some cars?' The sales guy said, 'Sure, how many do you need?' The answer was eighteen hundred hotel rooms and I don't know how many cars. This was the dealers coming in en masse. By the time they arrived, each had a list of who he should see, what the key issue was, and what political buttons to push."[178] The dealers mustered early each morning in a hotel ballroom for a briefing by Wendell Larsen. After an update and a pep talk they fanned out to knock on doors all over Capitol Hill, armed with talking points and protocol tips. The dealers converged again in the evening to report commitments, incipient conversions, and continued resistance. Chrysler's Washington staffers scrambled to find answers to the questions the dealers brought back from legislators and by the next morning would usually have detailed responses prepared. "I had 20 dealers in my office last week," Les Aspin of Wisconsin said. "They're hunting in packs."[179]

The United Auto Workers Union was well set up for lobbying. Its chief Washington representative was Howard Paster, a master both at behind-the-scenes strategizing and at one-on-one persuasion. According to the labor lobbyist—who later accepted a job with Timmons & Company, Chrysler's voice among the Republicans—the joint campaign by labor and management, dealers and suppliers, and elected champions of both parties generated remarkably little friction. He attributed this to the recognition, on the part of Chrysler and its other constituents, that the UAW was the real source of political strength in the coalition: "The fact is that most of the votes that were cast for the act were cast because of the union. I don't mean the company didn't pull some votes, but it was easier for a conservative Republican to tell a corporate lobbyist, 'I can't go with this' than for a liberal to tell a worker, 'I won't vote to save your job.' "[180] While union and Detroit lobbyists, organized by Tommy Boggs, worked on liberals and Democrats, William Timmons mobilized a campaign to sway a crucial faction of Republicans and conservatives. In the campaign for conservative votes, the lobbyists took the tack that the government had caused Chrysler's trouble with burdensome regulations, so helping it recover was not a bailout but only fair restitution.

On December 13 the Chrysler coalition in the House abandoned the administration bill in favor of a $3.33 billion financial package crafted by William Moorhead and Stewart McKinney. The two houses' bills were converging. Like the Senate bill, the new House bill included specific concessions from Chrysler's constituents. But it called for significantly less sacrifice from Chrysler's workers— $400 million in wage concessions, buffered by $150 million in Chrysler stock for workers—and around $1.4 billion from other groups.* All told, the new bill was slightly tougher than the administration's version, and it won some converts in the House. Harold Sawyer, the Michigan Republican, said the Moorhead-McKinney bill "just makes me gag, whereas the original bill made me throw up."[182] He became a supporter.

The House debated the Chrysler bill in several separate sessions from December 13 to December 18. Proponents, led by Blanchard and Moorhead, had honed the basic case for the bill into an unvarying litany. The first issue, and by far the most fervently invoked, was jobs. The printouts that the Chrysler team had prepared, listing Chrysler employees, suppliers, and dealers in each congressional district, were cited again and again, along with the national totals, the concentration of jobs in Detroit and other major urban areas, and the preponderance of blacks among the workers whose jobs were at risk. The second argument concerned the cost to the government of a Chrysler failure. Many proponents mentioned the drain on the Pension Benefit Guarantee Corporation (the government agency that would step in to honor Chrysler's pension obligations in the event of a bankruptcy); the rise in unemployment compensation, welfare, and food stamp budgets; and the fall in personal and corporate taxes. Some legislators cited the wider impact of a Chrysler failure on the national economy. The total public cost was estimated, variously, as between $3 billion and $15 billion. Lee Iacocca later credited these two issues—jobs and the direct public cost of a Chrysler failure—with bringing Congress along. "Those two nailed them to the wall. All the rest was just periphery. But

---

* Other features of the Moorhead-McKinney bill: The loan guarantee program would be administered by a five-member board instead of by Treasury alone. In another move toward compromise with the Senate bill, the Moorhead-McKinney substitute would allow the government to subordinate its claim on Chrysler's assets—but in this version, only to state governments and to suppliers with claims against Chrysler of less than $100,000. Moorhead characterized the substitute as deliberately "mean and nasty" to give potential future applicants pause before seeking federal help.[181]

those two arguments, to the House of Representatives, had great meaning."[183]

Other arguments were raised to cement support: Aid for Chrysler, far from betraying a pristine legacy of nonintervention, followed a well-established American tradition of targeted government help. A Chrysler failure would seriously imperil the nation's balance of trade as Japanese cars replaced Chrysler compacts. The nation would lose the fuel-efficient luxury model, the K-car, that Chrysler was preparing to launch in less than a year. Competition within the U.S. automobile industry would slacken.

Opponents—because they were less organized or simply because reasons to object to any legislative initiative broadly tend to be more diverse than reasons to endorse it—covered a somewhat wider range of rhetoric. The most common argument raised against the rescue in the House debate was that Chrysler had been badly managed and that in the name of efficiency and of fairness, bad management should fail. While some dismissed loan guarantees as futile, others condemned them as unfair. Various representatives, according to their inclination, attacked the bill as a boondoggle for big business or big labor. Several congressmen took up the theme that Chrysler's troubles signaled real economic problems but that saving the company itself was not the best remedy.

Dozens of changes were proposed as the legislation took shape. Some representatives, at times profoundly misinformed on the facts of the matter, simply sought to score political points. An issue involving big business, labor, regulations, local politicians, and federal bureaucrats offered an irresistible opportunity for oratory. Any legislator could find in the case his favorite demon to excoriate. Fortney Stark, a San Francisco Democrat, launched a salvo of amendments that would bar Chrysler from buying foreign or non-union parts or equipment or investing overseas; from using rebates as a marketing tool; from spending any money in areas with below average joblessness. He also wanted to require Chrysler to favor small-business and minority-owned contractors; to hire 50 percent women for all jobs and to hire only women and minorities for management jobs until the proportion of black and female executives matched the national population proportions; and to use only second-class airline tickets. Finally, Stark would require Chrysler by law to increase its market share by 1 percent a year.[184] James Weaver, an Oregon Democrat, proposed limiting management salaries and benefits to what a top-level civil service worker earned.[185] Ohio Republican Chalmers Wylie wanted to prevent the loan guarantees from being used in any way that would benefit foreigners.

Two amendments, proposed on the last day of House debate,

dealt more directly with the essence of the bill. House Whip John Brademas of Indiana called for a section requiring nonunion employees to make sacrifices worth $100 million. This would make the average concession per worker about the same for union and nonunion employees. The bid was very popular, even among opponents of the overall bill, and quickly passed. Fortney Stark praised Brademas's amendment: "It is picking one more louse off the turkey."[186]

The second major proposal came from Dan Quayle, an Indiana Republican. Near the end of the debate he called for tossing out the revised House bill and substituting a version of the Senate bill, requiring that unionized workers contribute $900 million instead of $400 million.[187] Moorhead spoke out against Quayle's initiative: "I believe this amendment pushes the union to the brink and quite possibly over it. . . . These workers are not millionaires. They have to pay the mortgage and the grocery bill and they are squeezed right now. I am concerned that if we force them through this amendment to take a severe cut in their living standards they are likely to say the hell with it and take their chances on finding a job elsewhere. Many of them will not find such jobs, of course. But we are dealing with psychology here." The proposed Quayle substitute was rejected.[188]

The issue was brought to a vote in the House on the evening of December 18. Representative William Stanton, another Ohio Republican, complained that the House debate "never hit on the precedent we're establishing here" and made a last-minute bid to send the bill back to committee; his motion was defeated.[189] As the representatives prepared to vote, Speaker Tip O'Neill took the floor to speak on his own behalf—an unusual event in the House. He offered Congress his memories of the Great Depression, grim anecdotes of the days of joblessness and public relief when "the dignity of people was destroyed." The speaker told of a recent talk with Treasury Secretary Miller: "I said, Bill, give me the accurate figures on how many people will lose their jobs. He said the best we can determine is somewhere between 360,000 people up to as high as 700,000. . . . I understand in the Commonwealth of Massachusetts we will lose 5,600 jobs. I understand in the State of Connecticut they will lose 8,000 jobs. That is how recessions start. That is how depressions start. You know, the fellow has a nice little home, a fellow who has been working for Chrysler, or somebody that supplies Chrysler, in a job for 25 to 30 years. All of a sudden he has lost his job. The neighbors were going to buy a new car, or they were going to buy a stereo, or they were going to buy a refrigerator. Then they saw that the next-door neighbor had lost his job, so they tightened their belts and they did not buy some product along the line. Then it spreads, and it spreads, and it spreads. . . . I look at this issue and I think of the bleak days of October 1929, 50 years ago, when I was a kid and The Crash came. We did not realize then that 10 years of the deepest national depression had commenced. By laying off 700,000 people—and that is what a Chrysler collapse could do—we would start a chain reaction. And believe me, we would not be able to dig ourselves out for the next half-a-dozen years. I speak as Tip O'Neill, who has been through it a long time, who has seen the ups and downs of this country. I say to you as an American—the right, the solid thing to do is to think of the future of this country."[190]

At seven-thirty that evening the Moorhead-McKinney bill, with no essential changes, passed the House by a vote of 271 to 136.

The Senate bill was still much tougher. The size of the sacrifices required of Chrysler's constituents was one difference. But there was a further complication: The Senate version required binding commitments of concessions from other constituents before the automaker could collect any guaranteed funds. Nobody was entirely sure what qualified as a binding commitment, but company officials worried that the tedious process of locking up each sacrifice in advance could consume valuable time. And Chrysler was short on time. Iacocca dispatched Wendell Larsen to the Treasury Department with orders to enlist the administration's support in the campaign to excise from the Senate bill the daunting binding commitment language. The Chrysler team was anxious to substitute language that would let it get guaranteed loans as soon as the bill was signed.

Soon after alerting Treasury to the peril of delaying the funds, Larsen got a telephone call from a distressed assistant secretary, Roger Altman. Chrysler's most recent projections showed it would run out of cash by mid-January. Altman said that the news that Chrysler would fail early in 1980 without fresh cash could radically affect its stock price. He told Larsen he was required by law to disclose that information to the public. Larsen was stunned. "I called Lee and told him the world would soon know that Chrysler was going to die in a few weeks because Roger Altman got scared by some lawyer," Larsen related. "Lee said, 'It can't happen or we're dead. Go stop him.' So I rushed over to Altman's office at Treasury, pushed in past his secretary, and we argued and argued. I couldn't talk him out of it. Finally, I just said, 'Roger, I've worked too hard to see you destroy this company with one press release.' " As Larsen has told the tale, he planted himself in Altman's office and swore to gun down anybody going out the door with a statement to the press.[191] The threat was probably less than wholly credible, but no release was sent that day. While the news leaked out by mid-December, there was time for Iacocca to prepare himself and stage a press conference. The deteriorating economy was shrinking the auto market, he told reporters. Consumer worries about the firm's survival were cutting into Chrysler's share of the market. And the company's aggressive promotion programs were squeezing margins on the cars Chrysler did manage to sell. "The current softness in the economy and in the car market are eating a cash drain at Chrysler, and interim funding will be necessary in January," Iacocca said. "Only prompt action in the legislature will provide enough time to put in place a program of interim financing."[192] Congress was due to adjourn in four days.

The Senate, like the House, engaged the Chrysler issue with a blend of grand principle and picayune detail. The upper chamber dwelt at more length on the technical arcana of Chrysler's operating plans. Several senators entered a lively dispute over how much a Chrysler Imperial weighed, for example, and how many of them the company could realistically expect to sell five years into the future.

From the start of the debate on December 18 Senator Riegle was curiously voluble. He rebutted with meticulous detail every attack on Chrysler's plan. He warned that the Senate still expected too much sacrifice from the UAW. He chided Proxmire over the latter's record of support for laws aiding Wisconsin-based American Motors. And at each opportunity he summoned up once again, at painful length, the arguments for keeping Chrysler in business. As the session wore on, it became apparent Riegle was stalling. His allies were puzzled; Proxmire, Lugar, and Heinz were annoyed. Gradually the rationale was revealed: The House was at the moment finishing debate on its bill, which required only $400 million from the UAW. If the House moved first, it could anchor the labor sacrifice at a lower number.

Chrysler's Gerald Greenwald was parked in Senator Eagleton's office with Tom Korologos, a senior partner in Timmons & Company and a former Nixon staffer. Greenwald, an auto manager for all his career, was inexperienced in the workings of the Congress, but he knew he was in the presence of a professional as he watched Korologos's performance. "All I could think of was that he was playing chess," Greenwald said four years later. "He'd be on the phone with his counterpart in the House every fifteen minutes. When the Senate was getting ahead of where they should be relative to the House, he sent out the word: 'Slow them up, they're going too fast.' He called Riegle and told him he had to filibuster and hold up the vote.''[193]

Riegle took the cue and held the floor for three hours. As Speaker O'Neill was making his speech in the House to soften up the lower chamber for a final vote, Senate Majority Leader Robert Byrd called a brief recess and summoned Proxmire, Lugar, Riegle, and several other senators into his office. They emerged with a deal: The vote would be postponed until the next day. When debate resumed—under a rule limiting each speech to five minutes—Senators Thomas Eagleton, William Roth, and Joseph Biden offered another version, cutting the union's concession down to $400 million, to match the House bill. Roth said the lower number was needed to have a workable package.

Proxmire denounced the change. The $203 million concession in the October contract already covered more than half of the $400 million. "What the Eagleton-Roth amendment provides is an added $197 million contribution, but the employees get $250 million in stock at today's depressed market. That is $50 million more than they gave up." The deal, Proxmire said, lined up too little money for Chrysler and inflicted too little pain to deter future aid requests.[194] Lugar urged the Senate to defeat the amendment, contending that "the only argument that can be made in favor of the $400 million is that it is the only figure the UAW will accept."[195] At the very least, said Lugar, the Senate should vote a higher figure than the House in order to leave some room for bargaining in conference. But the amendment's supporters stressed that even Chrysler's managers preferred the lower figure. Carl Levin posed the issue thus: "You can either require more funds in this bill and doom it in the real world, or you can get less, still a substantial sacrifice, and give the bill a chance—a good chance—to succeed."[196]

The Eagleton-Roth-Biden amendment passed 54 to 43. Chrysler's supporters were jubilant. With the labor sacrifice numbers the same in both versions, differences from the House bill were minor; a conference bill could be prepared, passed, and signed expeditiously. It looked as if the Chrysler Loan Guarantee Act would become law with a day or two to spare before Congress recessed.

Lowell Weicker dispelled the air of triumph. "I assure the Senators that I and many others on this side of the floor now feel it is the worst of all worlds," he warned. "I suspect there would be no great difficulty in assuring that debate will be thorough, very thorough." In short, he would block a quick passage by using the venerable Senate prerogative of the filibuster. And as Chrysler's cash evaporated, it had to be a quick bill or none at all. Riegle said later, "We got the message very quickly." Robert Byrd summoned Riegle, Tsongas, Lugar, Eagleton, Biden, Roth, and Proxmire to his office, where they were joined by Douglas Fraser, to work out a compromise. They settled on a labor contribution of $525 million. Biden reassured Howard Paster that it would be brought lower in the House-Senate conference. (The compromise also raised the loan guarantee figure from $1.25 billion to $1.5 billion, matching the House bill; added a $150 million pay cut for nonunion employees; and set the employee stock ownership plan figure at $175 million.) Weicker was persuaded to forswear filibustering.

The compromise passed 69 to 28. But even at this late stage in the legislative process, the Senate bill was almost scuttled by the unresolved issue of interim financing. Carl Levin, prompted by Chrysler's repeated warnings that the company could not keep going while a complex package of concessions was worked out, proposed a stopgap plan. Levin's amendment would let the Chrysler Loan Guarantee Board issue $500 million of the $1.5 billion immediately "if necessary to preserve the Corporation" until the long-term aid package could be assembled.[197] Levin called such interim financing "the common sense thing to do." It would relieve the desperate pressure on the loan board, he said, and give it time to structure the best possible deal. Proxmire vigorously objected to the amendment: "The Federal Government would have $500 million on the line when no one else had put up a penny—nothing. . . . We would have the Federal Government—which means the taxpayer—first in, last out, always on the line and begging for crumbs from the other parties—which are the ones who have the real stake in Chrysler's survival."[198]

"If the money wasn't nailed down from the start," Senate aide Elinor Bachrach later explained, "then if things went badly—and there was every reason to believe they might—the other parties would just walk away and leave the federal government holding the bag."[199] The absolute prohibition against federal help before private sacrifice was crucial to Proxmire and his aides; the bridging loans would violate that principle. Weicker seconded Proxmire's judgment and volunteered to act on it. Calling the bridging loan bid "the wickedest part of the proposal," he again threatened to filibuster, and he did hold the bill hostage for two precious hours. "This is not an investment," Weicker said. "This is a holdup, a rip-off, a picking of the pocket."[200] And Senator Barry Goldwater called the bill "probably the biggest mistake that the Congress has ever made in its history. I think future historians will register this as the beginning of the end of the free market system in America."[201]

Levin and Riegle took the bad news to Chrysler financial chief Gerald Greenwald. "They told me, 'Pick your poison,' " Greenwald recalled. "We could either have no act at all, or an act without interim financing. I took about three minutes to call Lee on the phone and told them to do what they had to do."[202] As supporters staged a tactical retreat, Levin's bridge loan amendment lost 33 to 64.

There was one more major skirmish. John Heinz, long concerned that Chrysler's shareholders were getting a free ride, had for days been at work on a stock dilution plan. Now, as the bill moved toward a vote, he presented his plan to the Senate. Chrysler would have to issue 1.04 new shares for each share already outstanding to a board of trust made up of the Loan Guarantee Board and four outside finance experts. The shareholders would surrender their stake in the company as the price of federal assistance. The board of trust would then sell off its holdings on the stock market "as it in its sole discretion determines to be appropriate," using the proceeds to pay down the guaranteed loans. The rationale of Heinz's proposal was both to infuse equity capital into Chrysler to balance its debt burden and to "make the terms of aid stringent enough to discourage similar requests. . . . Should Congress pass this aid package in its present form, I fear that I would see the shareholders and the board of directors congratulating each other. And why should they not do so? [They] have gotten the Federal Government to handle Chrysler's labor negotiations for the next few years. They have gotten the Treasury Department and the U.S. Congress to reschedule their debt. . . . They have even gotten the Government to hire management and financial consultants."[203] The amendment won 50 to 45; shortly thereafter the Senate passed the Chrysler Loan Guarantee Act 53 to 44 and sent it on to the House-Senate conference. Tsongas predicted that forging a compromise in conference would be fairly easy: "We'll be OK, assuming we all know how to divide by two."[204]

The result was much as Tsongas planned, but the process of getting there was less placid than he had anticipated. The House and Senate conferees met the next morning for what turned out to be a seven-hour session. They at first considered closing the conference to the public in order to speed the proceedings but decided on a simpler method: They met in the speaker's private dining room, one of the smallest rooms in the Capitol. Once the six senators and six representatives, aides, and a skeleton crew of lobbyists were arranged around the conference table, there was room for only three reporters. Most of the lobbyists and journalists had to wait outside. One member of the press, Judith Miller of *The New York Times*, had covered the emerging Chrysler story for months and was outraged at what she saw as a subterfuge to fix the final terms without the press looking on. After getting clearance from her editors, she wrote a pungent letter of complaint on *Times* stationery, which she sent in to key conferees. Uncomfortable with the prospect of a hostile senior *Times* reporter, the conferees moved the proceedings to the much larger House Banking Committee Room. As the press poured in, so did the full complement of Chrysler lobbyists. Wendell Larsen later recalled, "Without Judith Miller we wouldn't have had a workable bill."[205]

Senator Heinz's arrangement for extracting sacrifice from Chrysler's shareholders by diluting the stock, which corresponded to nothing in the House bill, was dealt with summarily. Congressman Henry Reuss of Wisconsin derided the plan as a "welfare program for investment bankers," and it disappeared from the bill. (A comparable but less onerous provision involving stock warrants was introduced later by the Treasury officials who administered the act. See page 254.)

The bill that emerged from the House-Senate conference drew more from the Senate's version of the organizational system for carrying out the act, but the concessions to be demanded of Chrysler's constituents were simple compromises between the two versions. Before the government issued any guarantees, Chrysler would have to get binding commitments from the other constituents. (But there was an ambiguity; at another point in the bill the language specified merely "adequate assurances.") The guarantees would be authorized by a Loan Guarantee Board made up of the secretary of the treasury, the chairman of the Federal Reserve, and the comptroller general; the secretaries of transportation and labor would be nonvoting members. The loan board could, at its discretion, guarantee interest as well as principal—a change that could boost the government's liability by $225 million.[206] It could also grant other lenders equal seniority to the government on up to $400 million in credit. (The House version had required government priority on all debt; the Senate version had let the board waive seniority on an unspecified portion.)

The conference bill was sent to the House late on the evening of December 20, 1979. After less than an hour of debate —featuring Representative Richard Kelly's lamentation that "we squander our hope for prosperity and security in the cause of short-term political advantage''—the Chrysler Loan Guarantee Act passed the House by a vote of 241 to 124, with 67 legislators not voting.[207]

In the Senate, Proxmire assured his colleagues that the bill prohibited interim financing and included strict Senate language to guard against substituting what he termed "funny money" for the concessions demanded. "The bill says that nothing can be counted as part of the non-federally guaranteed assistance required unless it materially contributes to meeting the corporation's financing needs."[208] Senator Russell Long told the Senate that in his three decades in Congress he'd never seen a vote changed after eleven at night; he begged aspiring orators to let the bill come quickly to a vote. But William Armstrong of Colorado, giving Long his regrets, launched a long speech denouncing not so much the substance of the bill as the process by which it had been worked out. He pointed to the working copy of the bill, littered with layers of changes, as evidence that the act was being pushed through with unseemly haste. He called for the draft, with its "chicken scratchings and underlining," to be photocopied and distributed as an object lesson in how not to legislate. "There are occasions when, in the rush to make decisions, we really do not know what we are doing," Armstrong lamented.[209] But eventually he relented. The bill came to a vote and, well after midnight, passed 43 to 34.

Lee Iacocca, interviewed the next day in Detroit, praised the compromise as "tough, but a strong bill that will provide the financing needed to return Chrysler to profitability."[210] Other parties were less anodyne. One Chrysler official, flying out of Washington after the conference, declined the flight attendant's offer of a sandwich. "I explained that I'd just seen a law being made, and it had killed my appetite."[211] Howard Paster of the UAW protested that the bill was "unfair, rough medicine that forces workers to accept a disproportionate share of the contributions required to save the company."[212] Howard Symons of Ralph Nader's Congress Watch, who had lobbied against any guarantee act, warned that the bill would not save the failing firm and Chrysler would be back for a "second dose of federal aid."[213]

Less than two weeks later, in a subdued White House ceremony, Jimmy Carter signed the Chrysler Loan Guarantee Act of 1979 while Douglas Fraser and Lee Iacocca looked on. "The hard part starts now," Iacocca said.[214]

IV

THE DEAL

1.

W e thought the deal was doable, but we thought also that it would test the wills of the parties involved," Elinor Bachrach later explained. She had been one of the Senate aides who insisted on rigidly conditional government help. "We wanted them to make meaningful contributions, not just paper contributions and empty gestures. We wanted them to be locked in if the deal went through. If they really wanted Chrysler to survive, they'd make it work; if they only wanted it if the federal government took on most of the risk, then the deal would come apart. This was exactly our intent."[1]

The act mandated a much more subtle thing than a simple financial rescue: It called for a new deal among the various constituencies that made up the Chrysler Corporation. If they could reach an accommodation among themselves—if, that is, they could agree to scale back or defer their claims on the faltering company or tie their claims to its future performance—the government would join the deal by guaranteeing up to $1.5 billion in Chrysler debt. Once the other parties had come through, the guaranteed loans would shorten the odds for a successful restructuring. But if Chrysler's constituents failed to reach a new deal, the government's ante, far too small in itself to save the firm, would be withheld. The rescue was a hybrid—not exactly a reorganization under bankruptcy but not a classic bailout either.

This strict condition might seem a reckless extra burden to put on a company that already faced a formidable task of renewal and renegotiation. But in many ways it strengthened Chrysler's hand. Bargaining power, as economist Thomas Schelling has explained, can be enhanced by convincing opponents that one *cannot* retreat from a favorable position. The advantage sometimes goes to the bargainer who can first commit himself credibly to a take-it-or-leave-it offer. In his seminal *The Strategy of Conflict* Schelling writes:

> In bargaining, the commitment is a device to leave the last clear chance to decide the outcome with the other party, in a manner that he fully appreciates; it is to relinquish further initiative, having rigged the incentives so that the other party must choose in one's favor. . . . If one carries explosives visibly on his person, in a manner that makes destruction obviously inevitable for himself and for any assailant, he may deter assault much more than if he retained any control over the explosives.[2]

The government's well-publicized pledge to withhold guarantees unless the other parties contributed their shares functioned, in a rough way, like the explosives in Schelling's analogy. Chrysler's fate was manifestly out of its own hands. It *could not* release a constituent from the obligation to contribute. If any group balked at its allotted share of sacrifice, the entire rescue would abort. Chrysler would explode. The blame would go to any party refusing to do its bit. Congress insisted on a deal that would ensure Chrysler stayed in business to pay off the loans. The firm either would be restructured to survive for the long haul or would promptly go out of business. Any new deal would be distinctly favorable for Chrysler, or there would be no deal at all. The government's intransigence let Chrysler tell its constituents, "Take it or leave it," and be believed. The catch, of course, was that some key constituent might be unable to fulfill its role or might find it more palatable to let Chrysler fail, and accept some responsibility for the failure, than to endure the sacrifice the act required.

The act specified eight sources, aside from government-guaranteed loans, for the money to turn Chrysler around. First, unionized workers would have to render concessions worth $462.5 million.[3] The $203 million in sacrifice in the UAW's October contract would be counted toward this total. Second, nonunion workers would have to give up $125 million. Third, Chrysler's U.S.-based banks and other creditors would have to contribute $500 million, 80 percent in the form of new loans and 20 percent in the form of "concessions with respect to outstanding debt."[4] Fourth, foreign creditors would have to contribute $150 million, all in new loans. Fifth, Chrysler would have to raise $300 million by selling off assets.[5] Sixth, state, local, and other governments would supply $250 million. Seventh, suppliers and dealers would have to contribute $180 million. Finally, Chrysler would have to sell $50 million in new stock. The act simultaneously forbade Chrysler to pay dividends on existing common or preferred stock as long as guaranteed loans were outstanding (see Figure 6, opposite). The requirements were rigorously detailed, specifying not just the amount but, in many cases, the form of assistance expected from various parties. Yet the act's specificity was oddly undercut by a vague phrase indicating that the Loan Guarantee Board, which was to administer the rescue, could "as necessary, modify the amounts of assistance required to be provided by any of the categories" except labor, so long as the total amount of concessions came through.[6] This clause would prove to be crucial.

The Loan Guarantee Board would be headed by the secretary of the treasury and include the chairman of the Federal Reserve and the comptroller general, with the secretaries of labor and transportation as nonvoting members. The board would hire a staff to which it could delegate day-to-day administration. For most matters, the staff would run the program, reporting up through the ranks of the Treasury Department.

Chrysler would have the first move. Gerald Greenwald hurriedly organized the firm's managers into twenty-two task forces, each responsible for surmounting some specific hurdle. One was charged with negotiating concessions from unionized workers; another, from white-collar employees. One dealt with lenders. Another lobbied for loans from state and local governments. There were groups working on asset sales, relations with Peugeot and Mitsubishi, and extracting concessions, including stock purchases, from dealers and suppliers. "Our greatest fear was that our constituents wouldn't go with us, and there we'd be: Congress would have passed the law, and then we couldn't qualify," Greenwald recalled. Chrysler had no organization for working out the terms of such a deal. (Nor, for that matter, had any other major American firm.) Simply developing a bargaining structure encompassing all constituent groups would challenge the ingenuity of the company and the government. "It was like trying to plan the invasion of Normandy in sixty days," Greenwald said.[7] Chrysler had first to draft its version of the deal,

FIGURE 6
Concessions Required by Act: $2 Billion

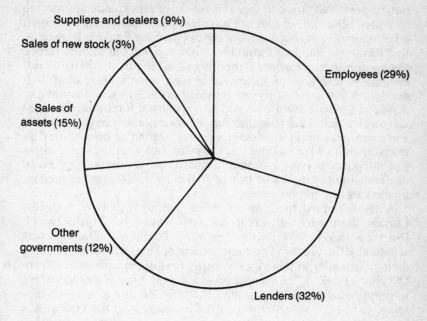

Suppliers and dealers (9%)

Sales of new stock (3%)

Employees (29%)

Sales of assets (15%)

Other governments (12%)

Lenders (32%)

then to get the government's provisional blessing, then to persuade each constituent group to pledge its share, and lastly to get final loan board approval and legal commitments from constituents before any guaranteed loans would come through. There was no time to spare.

Chrysler was skidding from one cash crisis to another through the early months of 1980. Several times the company was legally bound to come up with large chunks of money by a certain day to meet obligations or else stand in default. These came to be known around the firm as D-days, for "drop-dead" days. One after the other Chrysler was forced to renegotiate or unilaterally to break contracts and covenants simply to stay in business.

In mid-January Chrysler's board of directors gave tentative approval to a special "insider" debt issue; the firm hoped to raise up to $250 million by selling subordinated convertible debentures to

its dealers, suppliers, and others with a stake in the company.*
Before the act passed, Chrysler had been planning to sell $250 mil-
lion in preferred stock to these members of its extended corporate
"family." But the act blocked payment of dividends for as long as
government-guaranteed loans were outstanding, making it unlikely
that dealers or suppliers would be willing to buy the shares. Hence
the switch to convertible debentures—a technically distinct but
roughly similar type of security that pays interest instead of dividends.[8] When and if Chrysler regained profitability and could pay
dividends, the debentures could be exchanged for stock. The pro-
spectus carried a warning that the securities, with fairly low yields
and a junior claim on the issuer's assets, should be bought only by
investors with a special stake in Chrysler. (As it turned out, dealers
and suppliers bought less than a quarter of the issue, and many
dealers—in bankruptcy or nearly so themselves—later reneged on
pledges to buy the debentures.)

A more immediate form of relief was provided by Peugeot-
Citroën, the French auto company partly owned by Chrysler, which
lent the stricken American automaker $100 million. The loan was
secured by Chrysler's 15 percent holding of Peugeot stock. (Waiving
their prior claim to this stock was the first major concession from
Chrysler's banks.) The company bought more time in a cruder way:
It simply stopped paying around $150 million due to several Jap-
anese banks for short-term export financing. And on Valentine's
Day 1980 major suppliers—who had already suspended collection
of $100 million in bills during January—agreed to wait until April
to collect $150 million due in the first quarter.

The act required the largest concessions from Chrysler's banks
and unionized workers. Labor would deliver its share far sooner
than the banks and with considerably less trauma.

2.

Chrysler's request was a radical departure from normal labor relations, particularly in a basic manufacturing industry. Organized
labor had shown no eagerness to modify scheduled wage increases,
even for troubled firms. The reason had to do with the structure
of union decision making. Changes in contracts, like new contracts,

---

*"Subordinated" means "junior to other debt"; "convertible" means that under certain
conditions the bonds could be traded in for common stock. Such securities are relatively
risky and normally carry a premium interest rate. These did not.

have to be ratified by all organized workers. But union rules—for the United Auto Workers and other labor groups—specify that any layoffs must occur in reverse order of seniority, with the youngest going first. Typically, when a troubled firm seeks wage concessions from its organized work force, the workers assume that even in a steep downturn only a fraction will be laid off. Most—the more senior—will keep their jobs. The majority is safe, and therefore disinclined to vote to cut its pay. This time it was different. Without specified labor concessions, the overall deal would collapse, and Chrysler almost certainly would file for bankruptcy. Even if many of its plants someday resumed operation, there was no guarantee that senior workers would be the first to be rehired. Firms that bought Chrysler's assets at liquidation might resist union representation or reject UAW work rules. And even if seniority rules prevailed within plants, all the workers from a permanently shut factory could find themselves on the street. The question was whether skeptical employees would believe this and how they would respond.

Douglas Fraser shook hands with Chrysler vice-president William O'Brien on the fourth day of 1980, and bargaining began on the new contract. To meet the terms of the Loan Guarantee Act, Chrysler workers had to give up $259.5 million beyond the October concessions, to bring the total to $462.5 million. (Aside from the 75,900 UAW members currently on the payroll, this included about 4,200 workers in two electrical unions, the Plant Guard Workers, Allied Industrial Workers, and Die Sinkers unions.) Like the $203 million in concessions in the fall, this round had to follow the UAW constitution. The elected Chrysler Council appointed a bargaining committee including rank-and-file members, council head Marc Stepp, and Fraser. Once the committee had struck a deal with the company—and this time with the government as well—it had to be endorsed first by the Chrysler Council and then by the membership in all Chrysler plants. The first day's session was subdued. (Before getting down to serious negotiating, the bargainers had to wait for a roomful of accountants and actuaries to calculate how each possible concession would translate out into dollars.[9])

The burden on U.S. members was suddenly increased when Chrysler's 14,000 Canadian workers announced on the second day of the talks that they would not participate in any renegotiation. Canadian auto workers are more militant, by tradition, than their counterparts in the United States. In this case their recalcitrance also stemmed from national pride: They were loath to submit to conditions imposed by the U.S. Congress. When the Canadian

UAW members opted out, the share of the labor ante each U.S. employee had to bear rose proportionately. The company promised, in response to UAW demands, that "in view of the non-participation of the Canadian employees . . . the savings generated by the concessions of employees of U.S. plants should only be expended . . . in the United States."[10]

After only two days of talks a tentative deal was struck. First, the annual pay increases specified in the industry-wide pattern contract, already delayed for several months each year by the terms of the October revisions in Chrysler's contract, would be delayed further. This new delay would save Chrysler $36 million over the life of the contract. (At the time the average pay at Chrysler was $9.52 an hour plus benefits.)[11] But a bigger saving was to be in "paid personal holidays." The industry pattern had granted each worker twenty-six days off over the course of the contract. Chrysler workers already had agreed to give up six of these. "The membership hated to give PPH up," one UAW official said. "They called them happy days. We scheduled it so nobody's paid personal holiday would fall during his vacation or a regular holiday. Everybody got their fair share of Mondays and Fridays. The computer program to do the schedule at each plant was a monster."[12] But paid holidays obviously were costly to the company. And union officials, forced to make new concessions, would rather sacrifice some holidays than tamper further with wage increases or cost of living adjustments. So they agreed that Chrysler workers would give up seventeen more paid personal holidays, bringing their total down to three for the contract. This concession would save the company $201 million. Added to the delay in wage increases ($36 million), and the $203 million in concessions negotiated in October, the total would cover the UAW's share of the sacrifices the act mandated.[13] The pact preserved cost of living allowances and benefits, however, and provided for full parity with Ford and GM workers by the end of the agreement. From the union leaders' perspective, it seemed the best possible version of what inevitably would be a bad deal.

At the same time Chrysler pledged to set up an employee stock ownership plan worth at least $162.5 million, as the act required. The company would pay stock into a special fund in four annual installments of around $40 million each. The actual number of shares in each installment would be based on the market price at the time— the lower the price, the more shares would go in that year. The work force as a whole would hold title to the stock; each employee's claim on the fund would be based on his length of time with the firm. Once the stock had been paid in, the employees would benefit from any rise in its value. But any individual worker could collect his own portion only when he retired, resigned, or died (in which case the proceeds would go to his estate).

The 250-member Chrysler Council approved the contract, with only 5 dissenters, on January 9, 1980, and dispatched it to the seventy-five Chrysler locals for ratification. Douglas Fraser, Marc Stepp, and Joseph Zappa sent a letter to all Chrysler UAW members laying out the terms of the new contract and urging ratification, warning "unless the modified contracts are ratified, Chrysler will be gone and so will Chrysler workers' jobs."[14]

Within three weeks the contract was approved by more than 75 percent of the workers voting, a larger margin than the October deal had commanded. One UAW official explained: "The debate in Congress over federal aid and all the publicity convinced them. They voted to save their jobs."[15] A shop steward from Jefferson Avenue Assembly, an urban Detroit plant that voted heavily for the concessions, reflected later on the renegotiation. "Most of the people don't trust the corporation," said Bill Daniels. "Once the government got involved in it, that showed a lot of people that this was serious. They trusted the government more than they did the corporation. They didn't want to make concessions that weren't needed, and they didn't want to make the concessions and then see Chrysler go bankrupt anyway. Once the government took over, it made sense to go along."[16] Workers at only three plants—tank factories in Lima and Warren, Ohio, and the thriving New Process Gear division—voted to reject the deal. The reason these three went the other way was not hard to infer. The tank operation and New Process were distinctly more profitable than the rest of Chrysler. Their workers knew that these plants would almost surely be purchased and operated by other firms in the event of a Chrysler bankruptcy. There was no real threat of joblessness, and thus little reason to grant wage concessions.[17]

Soon after ratification came the anticipated but still sobering announcement of Chrysler's final 1979 accounts: The company had lost $1.1 billion, more than any other firm had ever lost in a year (see Figure 7, page 168).

3.

Chrysler now had to persuade its bankers to come up with $650 million, most of it in new loans. ("New" loans were defined in the act as credit in excess of what was available to Chrysler on October

FIGURE 7
Chrysler's Net Earnings

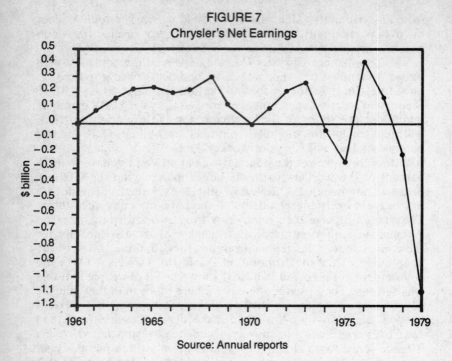

Source: Annual reports

17, 1979, the date of the final pre-act financing plan.) But there were at least five obstacles to extracting such concessions from the banks. First was the simple fact that Chrysler had several hundred bankers to sell on any final deal. This would grossly complicate the process of locking up any agreement. Second, there were radical differences among the banks. Some were based in the United States; some were foreign-owned but with American branches and staffs; some were foreign-owned and -based. Two-thirds of Chrysler's domestic bank debt was held by New York money center institutions, and another quarter by Chicago and Detroit regional banks. But the biggest category, measured by the number of separate creditors, was small local banks. There were dozens of these, each holding a small chunk of Chrysler debt.[18] The forms of their loans to Chrysler also varied wildly by terms, length, and security. Some banks—102 of them—were part of the credit syndicate organized by Manufacturers Hanover, and others were outside the deal. Indeed, some of the creditors were not banks at all; two insurance companies, Prudential and Aetna, were among Chrysler's biggest lenders. No bank was likely to be dragged down along with Chrysler if the automaker failed, but some would have damaging losses to swallow.*

Third, the term in the act "loans to Chrysler" covered not only different types of loans but also loans to several different entities. The Chrysler Corporation itself—the company that made the cars—owed $1.6 billion, including the $567.5 million revolving credit with a consortium of 102 U.S. banks, $72 million in other lines of credit, a total of $305 million in Eurodollar credit arrangements and term loans, and a letter of credit deal for $400 million with a group of Japanese banks.[20] The Chrysler Financial Corporation—the subsidiary that lent money to dealers and customers to buy the cars—owed twice as much, $3.2 billion. There were also loans to Chrysler Overseas Capital—a remnant of Townsend's overseas empire—and $290 million in loans from Canadian banks to Chrysler Canada.

Fourth, there was nearly perfect confusion over just what a bank concession would look like and how different possible restructuring plans would stack up against the congressional target. A loan is almost infinitely transmutable. Subtle differences in language can mean radically different payment obligations and sharply change the value of a bank's asset. Loan terms that to the uninitiated sound completely different, on the other hand, may work out to be so nearly identical that the differences are irrelevant. What a banker considered a concession, therefore, might not pass muster with the loan board or the Congress; what looked like a concession might be valueless to Chrysler. To complicate matters even further, the act flatly called for new loans, but the banks were having none of it. In September 1979 federal bank examiners had rated bank loans to Chrysler as "doubtful." Prudent banking practice requires that at least half the value of doubtful loans be written off as losses on the bank's balance sheet. This meant that the banks had to reduce reported earnings, the short-term financial score cards bank officers groom with such devotion. Now the same creditors confronted the outlandish proposition that they should make new loans to Chrysler and immediately write them off by half. As one observer put it, "Either Chrysler would have to force the banks unwillingly into a

---

*The seven most vulnerable, as measured by loans to Chrysler as a percent of total 1979 earnings: Bankers Trust (15.6 percent), Chemical Bank (10.3 percent), Manufacturers Hanover (9.5 percent), First Chicago (8.1 percent), Charter New York (7.5 percent), Crocker National (6.7 percent), and Continental Illinois (5.7 percent).[19]

new aid package, or the Carter Administration and Chrysler would have to reinterpret the will of Congress to make it fit the demands of the banks."[21] In the end it was to be a little of each.

Fifth, there were hard feelings and suspicion of bad faith all around. The banks distrusted Chrysler. The regional banks distrusted the New York money center banks. The foreign banks distrusted the American banks. And many of the lenders distrusted lead bank Manufacturers Hanover, which was widely seen as "soft on Chrysler."[22] Back in early August 1979, when Chrysler Financial had been expelled from the commercial paper market and forced to rely on bank loans, a dozen or so New York banks had wrested control of this transition from Manufacturers Hanover in what the *American Banker* called "the industry's first successful coup d'état. . . . The bank was uncomfortably close to the company, and this made its proposals suspect." The previous chairman of Manufacturers Hanover sat on Chrysler's board, and Lynn Townsend had been a Manufacturers Hanover director while heading Chrysler, fortifying a long-standing commercial connection that had led other banks to look to Manufacturers Hanover for guidance on matters concerning the automaker. The representative from Britain's Barclays Bank was blunt: "They were asleep at the switch. They should have been sounding the red alert earlier."[23] One Detroit banker spread the blame more widely. Since Chrysler, along with the other auto companies, had long relied primarily on retained earnings, its links with bankers were relatively weak. "Not many of us have the expertise we really need" to evaluate problem loans at a car company, he said.[24]

Whatever the cause, suspicion turned into frank hostility when Chrysler's finances came unraveled. Relations started to sour in the summer of 1979, according to one banker, "when we had to roll Chrysler Financial lines of credit into a revolver loan to replace the commercial paper they couldn't sell. We were preparing for an orderly meeting of about 25 banks in New York when we picked up the paper to see John Riccardo quoted as saying the company couldn't survive without government aid. Needless to say, his timing was very dumb."[25] Most of the bankers were unimpressed by the Chrysler Loan Guarantee Act. Quite a few were convinced Chrysler was going to fail anyway and feared that the government's involvement would only drain away assets that might otherwise go to private-sector claimants at liquidation. A senior officer of one of the insurance companies with large loans to Chrysler said, "That plan they presented to Congress may have been good enough for them, but not for us. We want to see much more detailed numbers."[26] The bankers were dismayed by the sketchiness of Chrysler's plans, and many were baffled by the terms of the act. They were uncertain what to expect from the government and what the government expected of them. Bankers are not noted for the grace with which they accommodate uncertainty.

There was animosity among the banks themselves. Early in the crisis a group of Canadian banks seized the Chrysler deposits they held and applied the funds against the firm's unpaid debts, a move known as a setoff. This outraged the American banks, which could legally have taken similar action, though at the risk of killing Chrysler. The Canadian setoff was to be a touchy issue throughout the dealing. Another source of friction, according to one lender, was that "the European banks don't see why they should go out of their way to help Chrysler since the company no longer has its European operations. Also, they're in for 100 percent of their commitment already. The U.S. banks were able to freeze their revolver."[27] (This last comment refers to the $567.5 million revolving credit arrangement. Chrysler had drawn down only about three-fourths of it before the consortium of domestic lenders, spooked by the company's crumbling finances, halted new disbursements. European lenders had not been so nimble.) The American banks, meanwhile, resented the fact that the guarantee act called for them to provide two-thirds of the concessions when they held only one-third of Chrysler's debt.[28] And small banks, some of which Chrysler owed less than $100,000, argued that the company could pay them off in full without even noticing the cash drain and clamored to be exempted from the debt restructuring.

In short, Chrysler's creditors lacked enthusiasm for the kind of brutal negotiating that would be required to restructure its debt. There was no institution to organize bargaining or any tested pattern for such an organization. Many bankers were resigned to seeing Chrysler liquidated, collecting what they could, and writing off the rest. Chrysler had to change their minds. It had to persuade them either that saving the company offered more benefits than they anticipated or that letting it die would be more painful than the bankers feared.

One factor that let many creditors contemplate without sharp anxiety the prospect of Chrysler's demise was this: By far the largest chunk of loans was to the Chrysler Financial Corporation, and the financial subsidiary was in much better shape than the manufacturing parent. Chrysler Financial had been run conservatively and well. Its main business, moreover, was the more predictable one of making secured loans to car buyers and dealers. Creditors with most or all of their loans to the financial subsidiary could face a Chrysler bankruptcy relatively serenely. In Senate testimony in November, John McGillicuddy of Manufacturers Hanover had explained the banks' limited resolve to save Chrysler: "Our expectations in terms of Chrysler Financial are substantially better than they are with respect to Chrysler Corporation. We would expect that essentially all of our outstanding debt under Chrysler Financial Corporation will be recovered."[29]

The expectation was to prove wrong. "People tend to believe what they see on paper," Leonard Rosen, the banks' chief counsel, later explained. "Corporations are always looking for new ways to borrow money. Captive finance companies [like Chrysler Financial] simply were a vehicle to get more credit. They looked like separate entities on paper, and institutions who lent money wanted to believe that they were separate entities. But in many ways they were a fiction. All the papers may have been in order. But no one had reviewed the legal documents and the actual operations of these entities from the creditors' rights perspective. No one had asked the critical question: What would really happen in the event of bankruptcy?"[30]

As the banks prepared their responses to the requirements of the Loan Guarantee Act, Chrysler's Greenwald was preparing a surprise for the finance company's creditors. "I was having a hell of a time getting the banks to even sit down and talk with me," he recalled, "when I got a call from Senator Don Riegle. He told me that at a hearing he'd met a guy named Ron Trost. He said, 'The guy's really interesting. He's got some neat ideas, and he may be able to help you.' Trost and I talked. The more I listened, the more fascinated I got. His premise was that the banks believed they could take a bankruptcy in Chrysler and lose roughly a billion dollars, but they would preserve their three billion dollars that was tied up in the finance company because the finance company was supported by receivables. Ron's view was that there was enough in the new bankruptcy code that would suggest that the two of them—Chrysler and its finance company—would get commingled and dumped all together."[31]

Greenwald invited J. Ronald Trost, one of the lawyers who had drafted the 1978 bankruptcy law, to come to Detroit, where he was introduced to Robert Stevens Miller, Jr., Chrysler's assistant controller and a former aide to Greenwald when both had been with

Ford Venezuela. Steve Miller, an affable, acute, and exceptionally well-liked finance man, quickly found his life dominated by Chrysler's debt restructuring. Trost's bankruptcy expertise and Steve Miller's grasp of Chrysler's finances were merged within three days into a formidable strategy, and on December 23, 1979, two days after Congress had passed the Loan Guarantee Act, Greenwald called a meeting of the banks.

The message to the bankers was summarized in a compact "Memorandum on Liquidation Scenario":

> The prevailing view among the banks is probably that their loss would be up to three-quarters of the loans to Chrysler Corporation, while full and prompt payment would be made on their loans to Chrysler Financial. This view appears to be·incorrect. We believe that the bankruptcy of Chrysler Corporation would necessarily result in a similar proceeding at Chrysler Financial. Even if there proved to be sufficient assets to pay all claims, the impact of the law governing interest accumulation during the post-bankruptcy period (6% rate) could reduce the present value of the loans by as much as one-half during extended [bankruptcy court] proceedings. There is, in addition, some risk that the assets would prove insufficient to meet all claims. . . . We believe this information is vital to assist the banks in reaching their decisions whether to support Chrysler with new loans so as to avoid bankruptcy.[32]

Trost briefly laid out the logic of his memo. The bankers had expected to sustain heavy losses on their loans to the part of Chrysler that manufactured cars. This expectation would be fulfilled, Trost began. The value of the Chrysler Corporation's assets in bankruptcy would be somewhere between $1.1 billion and $3.5 billion. Claims against that estate could total $5.6 billion to $6.7 billion. At best, then, the banks would recover sixty-five cents on the dollar and maybe as little as sixteen cents. And adjusting for the time the loans would be tied up in court collecting only low interest could bring the recovery rate down to a dime on the dollar. Meanwhile, at Chrysler Financial, where the bulk of the loans were, gross recovery probably would be no less than eighty-five cents on the dollar. But—and here was the unexpected rub—a five-year bankruptcy proceeding would erode the value of these claims to less than seventy-five cents on the dollar. Nobody would get paid until all claims had been sorted out, during which time the loans locked up would by law earn only 6 percent interest. This was well below the rate lenders could collect on the money if they had it in hand, even below the rate of inflation.[33] And it was far from certain that the finance company's assets would be sufficient to cover all the valid claims against it. One potentially heavy claim could come from the government's Pension Benefit Guarantee Corporation. If Chrysler went under and defaulted on its employee pension plan, this agency might have to step in to cover around $1 billion in Chrysler's pension commitments. To recoup that loss, the law gave the pension agency first claim on much of Chrysler's assets, possibly including those of Chrysler Financial.

As Trost blandly finished his presentation, Greenwald remembered, "You could see the bankers' jaws just dropping. They turned to Rosen, their own bankruptcy expert, and said, 'You'd better study this for us.' He more or less said, 'I don't have to study it— he's right.' "[34] James Wolfensohn, the Salomon Brothers partner who was Chrysler's chief financial consultant, recalled, "It was like an atomic bomb had gone off. It was a revelation to them. They saw at least six years of litigation and uncertainty."[35] It was suddenly a new game. The bankers were on the hook, and now Chrysler could try to make a deal. "The reason we spent the time and effort was to protect our exposure in Chrysler Financial," an executive at one major regional bank confirmed. "That's where the big bucks were. If we'd had to charge that off, that would have hurt."[36]

The core of Chrysler's team for negotiating with the banks was Steve Miller; Wolfensohn, the head of Salomon Brothers' corporate finance department, who had been working with Chrysler since July; and William Matteson, a lawyer with the firm of Debevoise, Plimpton, Lyons & Gates. In January the team settled into a grueling schedule: Monday in Washington, conferring with the Loan Guarantee Board staff; Tuesday through Thursday in New York, negotiating with the banks and their lawyers; Friday and the weekend in Detroit, coordinating with the other task forces engineering Chrysler's recovery.[37]

On the other side of the bargaining table, representatives of the fifteen largest U.S. bank lenders coalesced into a loose steering committee that by the end of January had become a de facto negotiating group for all the banks. The leadership role of the large American banks was ambiguous. They commanded a measure of influence with Chrysler's smaller lenders since the major money center banks that organize credit syndicates can exclude from these profitable deals any small banks with a reputation for uncooperativeness. But the steering group had no formal authority to commit the smaller creditors. There was no legal obstacle to rebellion on the part of any lender.

Many bankers, indeed, were firmly inclined to take what money they could and run. Nor was this pessimism about Chrysler's prospects limited to the small banks. When the steering committee first met, according to a participant, "not a single banker of the fifteen in the room believed that Chrysler would survive, even with government aid. There was simply no confidence in the company. They participated at first because they thought they were doing a public service, and they were afraid of bad publicity."[38] Leonard Rosen, the lawyer who had been retained to advise the bankers on their dealings with the company, gradually assumed stewardship of the group.

The central principle driving the discussion was the imperative of universal participation in the new deal. Each creditor would have to make concessions in strict proportion to its share in Chrysler's debt. If any more flexible formula were followed, scores of banks would submit compelling reasons why they should be spared their full share of sacrifice. The burden on those remaining would increase, intensifying the incentive to beg off. Any chance for a workable deal would evaporate.

The first application of the all-in rule concerned Chrysler's foreign creditors. The European and Japanese banks never joined the steering committee, nor, until late in the process, did they set up their own group. According to one observer, the overseas bankers "fantasized that the U.S. banks would come to consider Chrysler's plight a matter of national honor" and take on the full burden themselves.[39] But far from buying out the foreigners, the U.S. banks insisted on bringing them in deeper. Instead of carrying less than a quarter of the concession burden, as the act required, the U.S. banks held that their foreign counterparts should sacrifice in rigid proportion to their loans to Chrysler. (This roughly doubled the burden Congress had assigned to the foreign banks.)

The "Group of Fifteen" split into four subcommittees to work out different angles on the restructuring. Chrysler itself, abandoning the tradition of auto companies' closemouthedness with creditors, opened its books wide. "It was like letting someone walk into the vaults," said one stunned banker.[40] This atypical frankness could not undermine Chrysler's bargaining position for the simple reason that the company had little leverage to lose. "The management at Chrysler knew that the leverage they had negotiating with the unions and the banks was really the government's leverage," a loan board staffer recalled.[41] "They were eunuchs" was one creditor's blunter summary.[42] What power the company had derived from weakness rather than strength. It had to hew more or less closely—nobody knew just how closely—to the terms Congress laid down, which limited what it could offer (and, more to the point, what the banks could ask) without breaching the conditions of the act and propelling Chrysler into bankruptcy.

The Chrysler team's opening pitch was for the banks to leave in place for four years their loans to both the manufacturing company and the finance company, while charging a token 1 percent interest rate. Not unexpectedly this offer was instantly rejected. The banks refused to grant any concessions on Chrysler Financial debt. Indeed, they wanted the finance company to be sold off so that their loans to it would be quarantined from the ailing parent company. They also categorically refused to make new loans to Chrysler. The banks were willing to discuss only four options: They might forgive some of the principal on the $1.5 billion in loans to Chrysler proper; they might forgo all or part of the interest due on these loans; they might extend maturities on (or roll over) part of the debt; or they might grant delays on interest payments.

The bankers' bargaining position rested on a slippery reading of the act. The legislation required that domestic and foreign banks contribute a total of $650 million. Yet it remained far from clear how this sum was to be measured. The act defined the baseline as loans outstanding or committed as of mid-October 1979, when Chrysler's revised financing plan had been submitted. But since then U.S. banks had reduced their exposure to Chrysler by $159 million (the frozen revolver) and Canadian banks by $68 million (the Canadian setoff). The banks argued that any new loans should count against their contribution, even if the new loans still fell short of their previous exposure.

Just as the baseline for measuring the principal was ambiguous, so, too, was the baseline for calculating interest rates. "The requirements were sufficiently loose that the banks could continue to try and maneuver," Chrysler's Gerald Greenwald later explained. "For example, they might say, 'The current interest rate isn't what we were charging you; things are different now, and for any company like yours the current interest rate would be seventeen percent. So we'll take it down to twelve percent, or fifteen or whatever, and we'll commit to do that for the next ten years, so the difference in interest rates is our concession.' Any of them that began to have a ring of reality we'd take to the Treasury Department to see if they might buy it."[43] One banker acknowledged that these financial games reflected creditors' cynicism about the whole enterprise. The banks simply doubted the solidity of other constituents' sacrifices and felt no imperative to give up any more than they had to. "There was a strong feeling that the employees had really taken the government for a ride," the banker said. "Their sacrifice was not salary; it was days off and vacation time. They contributed, OK, no doubt about that. But when they talked about how they were bleeding and threw some big fancy number at us, we looked at it, and it wasn't what it looked like. So when the government said they wanted so many million from us, we said, 'Sure, whatever you want.' You sit down and make some assumptions: Assume that interest rates are going to be eighteen percent; if you only charge twelve, there's six percent times the principal for a concession. That's not enough? OK, then assume the interest rate's going to be nineteen percent. You could do about anything you wanted."[44]

Chrysler had publicly pledged that by the end of March it would meet the conditions for getting guaranteed loans. Congress already was scheduling hearings to review the terms of the final deal. But after nearly three months of negotiating with its flock of creditors there was nothing like a firm plan in sight. Chrysler's Steve Miller recalled the tension in notes he wrote a few months later: "As the end of March drew near I became increasingly concerned that we were never going to finish the negotiations. We still had several major issues with the U.S. banks [and] we were basically nowhere with all the other lending groups including the smaller U.S. banks, the insurance companies, and the European and Canadian bank lenders. Down in Washington the members of Congress who had worked so hard to pass the legislation were starting to get itchy and wondering why we didn't yet have the restructuring deal done." Miller invited around forty-five bankers, representing each main category of lenders, to meet at Chrysler's New York office on March 27, 1980. The first of the congressional hearings to review the final deal was scheduled for four days later. "My appeal to the attendees was fairly simple," wrote Miller. "I said that together we represented more than $3 billion in loans to Chrysler and more than 100,000 Chrysler jobs. Together we had the power to avert a disaster for the American economy, but we needed a real spirit of cooperation. Our time was running out. If we could not do a deal as businessmen then it would get out of our control and into the hands of politicians."

Miller opened this round with a concession: He yielded on the banks' demand that the company issue them stock warrants in return for their concessions on loan terms. Chrysler would grant the lenders 12 million warrants, or rights to buy its stock for a specified price at any time until 1990. The warrants' strike price was $13 a share, far above the stock's value at the time. This meant that the warrants would be worthless unless Chrysler turned around sharply before 1990. The bankers accepted the warrants but with no great enthusiasm. Prudential and Aetna, two major insurance companies, carried long-term loans to Chrysler at relatively low interest rates. They had been frustrated in an earlier bid for interest rate parity with the other creditors, and now, in recompense, they were allocated a disproportionate share of the warrants. (Later the loan board required Chrysler to issue 18 million warrants to the government, on similar grounds. The total of 30 million warrants, if turned into common stock, would represent ownership of about a third of the company.) "With that we got down to business," Miller recalled. "Over a period of three days the various parties hammered their fists on the table and called each other names. We replayed all the old battles." In one of these "old battles" a proposal by the European banks was rejected without ceremony by other creditors. The rebuffed Europeans prepared to quit the sessions as a hopeless cause, necessitating frantic conciliation by the Chrysler team.

The outside world intruded on Chrysler's closeted negotiations on the second day of the meetings, when the Hunt brothers' speculative bubble burst and the silver market collapsed. The whole financial community was badly rattled, and Chrysler's bankers were in no state of mind to strike a deal. The disruption was hard on frayed nerves. Steve Miller and the rest of Chrysler's team grew ever more anxious that an agreement would continue to elude them as the company's cash ran out and bankruptcy loomed as the only option. When Chrysler was compelled to cancel the March 31 meeting it had scheduled to submit the final package to the Senate Banking Committee, a headline in *The New York Times* ominously announced CHRYSLER MISSES DEADLINE FOR BANK AID.[45] On Friday, March 28, the bankers broke for the weekend, arranging to resume on Tuesday, April 1.

The night before the whole crowd reconvened a small group of bankers—representing Manufacturers Hanover, two other American banks, and five foreign banks—met for dinner at the Waldorf-Astoria and tried to work out informally a deal that the European banks might be able to accept. Over rounds of drinks the bargain took shape. Around $30 million of concessions by the European banks would be shifted from flat interest reductions to interest deferrals, and the Europeans would get paid in cash for the interest on the deferred interest instead of, in turn, deferring it. (Bankers are capable of talking like this without blinking.) The most sanguine of the conferees toasted the new deal with $200 champagne while the more nervous worried whether the rest of the banks could be persuaded to accept it the next day.[46]

But before this Waldorf Agreement could be unveiled at the morning's meeting, a somber Steve Miller faced the assembled bankers with an announcement: The night before, Chrysler's board of directors, forced to face the grim reality of a crumbling economy, rising interest rates, and the failure to strike a deal with the banks, had decided to file for bankruptcy; the formalities had been taken earlier that morning. Miller kept a straight face for several moments of stunned silence before pointing out that it was April Fool's Day. "It's a joke," he told the bankers. They were not amused. "It wasn't very damned funny," one said. "We believed him."[47] The invigorating shudder Miller's little joke had provoked, and the framework of the Waldorf Agreement, combined to inspire serious negotiations. The logjam broke that day, and a deal took form. On April 2 the business pages featured news of the tentative deal, and Greenwald announced that "significant progress has been made in negotiations with lenders on a general outline of their contributions toward a proposed financial restructuring."[48] There would not, however, be any new loans; instead, Chrysler would enjoy easier terms on loans already outstanding. A report to Congress by the guarantee board staff noted that "Chrysler's plan has not proposed, and the banks have thus far declined to provide, additional cash."[49]

What participants would remember as the Park Avenue Marathon got under way on April 9. The broad principles worked out on April 2 had to be translated into precise legal prose. It was a lawyer's saturnalia, involving 150 attorneys and financial representatives who ensconced themselves for three days in cramped law offices. Gordon Areen, the head of Chrysler Financial, was struck by the stamina of the lawyers as they conferred, disputed, drafted, cited, and amended the documents. "They kept it up all night long. At 2 or 3 A.M. you might see one of them drop off to sleep, but in an hour he would be back at work."[50] The completed draft was shipped off to Washington for the approval of the loan board. At the same time, the bankers who had devised the deal fanned out to try to sell it to their compatriots around the world.

The tentative deal looked like this: Creditors would grant about

$150 million in stretched-out maturities and would wait until after 1983 to collect about $400 million in accumulated interest. They would also forgive $100 million in interest flat out.[51] As for Chrysler Financial's loans, there were three provisions, together constituting a happy package for the banks. First, lenders would roll over the finance company's $3 billion in debt, relieving Chrysler of the burden of principal repayments for four years. Second, Chrysler would pay the banks market interest, pegged to the prime rate, on these loans. Third, Chrysler would undertake to sell a controlling interest in the finance company—thus insulating the loans from the feeble parent—and, sale or not, would give the banks full security on the loans. "We had to give the store away on Chrysler, but we saved our ass on Chrysler Financial," one banker said.[52] Another explained, "Not only did we not have to charge off any principal on Chrysler Financial, [but] we kept getting a market rate of interest on it. That struck close to home with us bankers—on the biggest part of our debt we're still making some money."[53] The *American Banker*'s correspondent called it a "sweetheart deal" for the banks.[54] Loan board director Brian Freeman shared this appraisal: "The most offensive part of this whole thing was letting the banks secure their interest in Chrysler Financial. What this did was put the banks ahead of the government if the whole thing went under."[55] But Freeman's objections were overruled. The government had already accepted the prospect that the finance company would be sold off. Securing its debt accomplished roughly the same purpose—insulating its creditors from a Chrysler collapse—and thus was adjudged no major concession. The Chrysler Financial security provision stood.

But when Steve Miller went to Washington to confer with the loan board staff, he found a more fundamental anxiety about the deal: It would give Chrysler a reprieve from the dangerous short-run drain on its cash but would do little to lighten the automaker's long-term indebtedness. The government team feared that Chrysler could remain a feeble company, with a chronically heavy debt service drain, continually in danger of sliding into bankruptcy and defaulting on the government-guaranteed notes. The staff had visions of nursing Chrysler through the four years of concession only to have it collapse under the weight of the deferred obligations as they suddenly came due. The remedy: First, Chrysler's creditors would have to extend the concessions beyond 1983, and second, they would have to forgive a big chunk of debt outright and convert the debt claim into equity. The loan board also insisted on striking a fail-safe clause that would have let the banks throw Chrysler into bankruptcy if the firm seemed on the verge of collapse. "Chrysler wasn't asking for enough from the banks," a Federal Reserve official recalled. "The government had to stand behind it to give it some backbone."[56] A Treasury official said the proposed revisions would "give Chrysler a chance to find itself after the 1983 period."[57] The changes were indisputably favorable for Chrysler. The question was whether the banks would ever buy them.

The Treasury Department seized an active role in the negotiations. In mid-April Chrysler executives, representatives of the creditors, and legal counsel for all concerned converged on Washington to begin eight days of negotiations with the government. Most of the business people settled in at the Madison Hotel, which became headquarters for Chrysler and its creditors during the "Siege of Washington," as Steve Miller titled the episode. It opened with a meeting in the Treasury's ornate Cash Room. Miller and Gordon Areen (the head of the Chrysler Financial Corporation), surrounded by half a hundred bankers and lawyers, faced a government team led by Assistant Treasury Secretary Roger Altman and Treasury's General Counsel Robert Mundheim.

The sessions began in stalemate. The government demanded that the banks trade $750 million in debt for Chrysler equity and make some provision for funding Chrysler and its finance company beyond 1983. The banks, in turn, held firm: The package of interest concessions, interest deferrals, and maturity extensions negotiated in New York was as far as they would go. Chrysler had little choice but to stand aside and hope the bankers and the bureaucrats could reach an accommodation before it was too late. *The Wall Street Journal* cited insiders' anxiety that the differences between the government and the creditors could harden into a standoff, with "each side waiting to see who blinks first," while Chrysler's money ran out.[58]

But the bankers were being worn down. At the same time they were negotiating over Chrysler, they were petitioning Congress, the Federal Reserve Board, and the Treasury Department for a more favorable regime of banking regulations. The two sets of negotiations inevitably intermingled. Lee Iacocca later said, "Bill Miller was the big ally here—saying, 'Let's not be so easy on these guys. Let's be tough as hell. Let me run that interference.' So he was the lead dog on that." The banks would not have agreed to more concessions for Chrysler, according to Iacocca, "unless you had Miller pushing and calling those guys and implying that somehow the government would get their ass someday. . . . I went to that House Banking Committee, where those same bankers would come back to for all kinds of banking rule changes and regulations, and we threatened the bastards. But you have to have the cooperation of the federal government to do that. If I had threatened them, they'd say, 'Show me your troops.' "[59] One lender cited the efficacy of a session with several legislators who made certain the bankers understood that "if we wanted the bank reform legislation being considered by Congress, we had better be flexible on Chrysler."[60]

The creditors finally agreed to accept Treasury's goal of longer-term concessions, but with a twist: The banks calculated that if they kept deferring the interest due on Chrysler's debt and in turn deferred the interest due on that deferred interest, the total would reach $750 million by the mid-1980's. At that point they would (under certain stipulated conditions) convert this accumulated debt into equity, thereby satisfying the government's demand without sacrificing any principal.[61] It was a deft accounting ploy. The bankers had been far from certain that they would ever collect on the deferred notes anyway, so it was no great sacrifice to pledge, provisionally, to turn them into equity. And by keeping the principal intact, they could avoid worse damage to their earnings reports.

Would the loan board buy it? It would.* The "Siege of Washington" was over; Chrysler and its creditors decamped from the Madison. The next tasks were to line up the remaining concessions, passing loan board inspection, and then to formalize the deal by getting all the parties to sign on. All this had to happen quickly if Chrysler was to get its guaranteed financing while there was still a chance it could do some good.

4.

By the time the tentative bank deal was hammered out in mid-April, Moody's Investors Service had dropped Chrysler debentures to the next to last grade on its seven-level scale and had downgraded the preferred stock and Chrysler Financial bonds as well. "Chrysler's sales are being affected by recent economic developments which may not be alleviated in the near future," Moody's explained.[62] One government source calculated that Chrysler was spending

---

*The deal in essence stipulated that the banks would grant Chrysler the option to convert its deferred interest into preferred stock anytime after 1983, so long as the company's cash flow and K-car sales met minimum conditions. The banks also agreed to keep open into the 1980's their lines of credit to the Chrysler Financial Corporation, thereby ensuring financing for Chrysler sales.

$5 million to $8 million more than it had been taking in every day from early March onward.[63] The company refused to discuss its finances, but one executive acknowledged to *The Wall Street Journal* that firm officials kept an anxious eye on daily cash reports: "We keep measuring our financial pulse to reassure ourselves there is still some life left."[64] Some suppliers, who had been "financing" Chrysler by accepting late payment without filing suit, were beginning to balk. The staff of the Loan Guarantee Board issued a gloomy report warning that "recent sharp increases in interest rates, reduced credit availability, and uncertainty over the state of the economy [have] complicated the situation by impairing prospects for future sales while increasing Chrysler's and its dealers' operating and financing costs."[65]

On the last day of April, a few hours before the company was due to run out of cash, a long-promised loan of $150 million from the state of Michigan was delivered to Chrysler's account at the National Bank of Detroit.[66] The loan, with a fifteen-year maturity and a 15.5 percent interest rate, was secured by Chrysler's new four-cylinder-engine plant in Trenton, Michigan. It had been delayed by difficulties in getting Chrysler's banks, which had held first claim to the Trenton plant in the event of liquidation, to surrender their priority to the state, as well as by a last-minute move by the state treasurer to hold back more than half of the loan until the federal government authorized the entire guarantee package. (The state treasurer relented, but only after a six-hour meeting between Chrysler and state officials.) Lee Iacocca was relieved that money had started to move. "For eight months we've had commitments and assurances," he told reporters, "but I haven't seen a buck of hard cash until today."[67] At about the same time Mitsubishi agreed to buy Chrysler's remaining interest in its Australian subsidiary, contributing $57.6 million to the company's cash flow.

A set of grim statistics on the auto industry was released on May 6. Fuel shortage anxiety, recession, high interest rates, and competition from imports were putting the industry in the worst slump since the Arab oil embargo. Automobile sales in April 1980 were down 31 percent from the year before. Chrysler and Ford were each about 42 percent down; GM was off by 27 percent. Even imports were selling almost 10 percent slower than they had been a year before (see Appendix A, Figure 12A). The high interest rates were taking their toll on dealers. Chrysler's dealers, typically smaller operations than Ford or GM outlets, were hit the hardest. Nearly 160 of them closed in the first quarter of 1980.[68] (By the end of the year there would be about 3,800 dealers, or 1,000 fewer than there had been two years earlier.) On the day the industry statistics hit the news, Chrysler announced that it had lost $449 million in the first quarter of 1980 and warned, in the bluntest terms to date, that bankruptcy was an immediate possibility if the loan board did not soon authorize guarantees.[69]

The next day Lee Iacocca flew to Washington for what he assumed would be the announcement that the company, its constituents, and the government had reached an agreement. He waited in an anteroom of the Federal Reserve Building as Treasury Secretary G. William Miller, Federal Reserve Board Chairman Paul Volcker, and Comptroller General Elmer Staats met for four hours inside. But it didn't happen that day. The treasury secretary emerged to tell reporters, "We have made considerable progress. But we seem to have one matter that we need a little more information on."[70] The "one matter" was Canada's continuing reluctance to commit itself to an aid plan as the Loan Guarantee Act required.

Even though Chrysler Canada, with 14,000 employees, was that nation's seventh-largest company, Canadian officials were loath to seem too pliant in the face of American demands. North of the border, patriotism is commonly equated with a refusal to be dominated by the United States. The Canadian minister of industry, trade, and commerce was Herb Gray, a member of Parliament from Windsor, Ontario (the site of most Chrysler Canada jobs). Gray held a fervent determination to strike the best deal possible for Canada. He argued that "Chrysler's problems in Canada aren't of its own making. It never had the autonomy to decide on its own product mix."[71] As a condition for loan guarantees and grants, Gray had insisted on investment pledges, on earmarking the guaranteed loans for specific retooling projects in Canada, and on some kind of job guarantee for Chrysler's Canadian workers. Chrysler had agreed to meet most of these terms. Now the holdup was with the provincial government of Ontario, which demanded additional job guarantees from Chrysler. Prime Minister Pierre Trudeau told the House of Commons, "We bent to the superior wisdom of the Ontario government," which thought "a better deal can be reached" with Chrysler.[72] Lee Iacocca was firmly set against any additional concessions to the Canadians: "We can't guarantee jobs to anybody. The market is lousy. We're still hemorrhaging with losses."[73] United Auto Workers' chief Douglas Fraser endorsed the Canadians' insistence on job security in principle but not this particular manifestation: "That's a lesson for our system. That shows you the difference in sensitivity. Hell, I didn't blame them. The only objection I had was they were going too far, at the expense of American workers."[74] But Chrysler had to strike a deal with Canada to satisfy the Loan Guarantee Board and its banks; negotiations continued.

When the loan board meeting broke up without a decision for want of a commitment from Canada, Iacocca and Greenwald flew to Toronto and holed up in the Harbor Castle Hotel with Gray and Lawrence Grossman, Ontario's minister of industry and tourism. They bargained through the night on Ontario's role, and by seven the next morning, a Saturday, they had worked out an agreement: Chrysler would site a $20 million research and development center in the province, and the provincial government would put up a $10 million grant to help fund it.[75] The deal with Grossman cleared the way for the overall Canadian aid package: Canada would provide guarantees on $170 million in loans. (This was less than a quarter of what Chrysler had requested.) Chrysler pledged for its part to retool and invest in Canada and agreed that its Canadian work force would remain at least 9 percent as large as its U.S. work force in 1980 and 1981 and at least 11 percent as large thereafter.[76] The Canadian loan guarantees did nothing to ease Chrysler's immediate cash crunch. They could be used only after 1982, when the investments in Canada they would fund were scheduled to get under way. (In the event, they were never used.)

The settlement with Canada, in turn, cleared the way for loan board approval of the overall deal. Late in the day on Saturday, May 10, 1980, Secretary of the Treasury Miller called reporters into the Treasury Department's press room to announce that the Loan Guarantee Board had unanimously, if guardedly, approved Chrysler's plan.* In return for putting its full faith and credit behind

---

*Here are the terms of the plan the board approved: Lenders would extend the maturity dates on $154 million in loans, forgive $181 million in interest, and defer $345 million in interest (this totals $680 million—a figure Chrysler had been using—but the government valued the package at $642 million). After 1983 Chrysler would have the option—if its cash flow improved and the K-car sold well—of giving the banks an equivalent value in preferred stock instead of paying deferred interest. Union employees would sacrifice $462.5 million, and nonunion benefits would be cut by $125 million. In addition, $418 million in pension fund deferrals would be valued at $342 million (given Pension Benefit Guarantee Corporation claims). The board counted $628 million in asset sales, based on "reasonable assurances" of $171 million from real estate sales, $250 million for a chunk of Chrysler Financial, and $100 million as an asset sale for the stock-secured loan from Peugeot, plus $106 million from subsidiaries in Brazil, Argentina, and Australia. Michigan lent Chrysler $150 million, and Delaware and Indiana were listed for loans of $5 million and $32 million. Canada would contribute $170 million in loan guarantees after 1982. Finally, the $78 million in convertible debentures sold to dealers and suppliers counted as $63 million, for a total private aid package of $2.6 billion.[77]

new Chrysler debt, the government would collect a fee of 1 percent a year on all outstanding guaranteed loans, would hold claim to Chrysler assets worth at least $2.4 billion at liquidation, and would hold 18 million warrants—based on the authorized maximum of $1.5 billion in guarantees—to buy Chrysler stock at a price of $13 a share anytime up to the end of 1990. The first $500 million might be available within fifteen days. Only one major condition remained to be fulfilled: The tentative deal with Chrysler's banks to restructure $4.4 billion in Chrysler and Chrysler Financial debt had to be finally approved by the creditors.[78]

The government would buy the deal if all the constituents would. Now Chrysler had to make it official.

5.

The day after the loan board had conditionally approved Chrysler's plan, Senator William Proxmire declared his suspicion that the deal failed to meet the terms of the act. He summoned Deputy Treasury Secretary Robert Carswell to appear before the Senate Banking Committee. "The plan is put together with mirrors and magnifying glasses," Proxmire said. Senator Jake Garn added, "It is obvious that the requirements for Federal assistance have not been fully met." Carswell vigorously defended the loan board's actions without denying that the deal departed from some of the provisions Congress had drafted. "The choice came down to exercising the right to modify the terms" of the act, he said, "or letting Chrysler go under. The board chose the right to modify, on the assumption that Congress wanted to see Chrysler saved."[79]

Proxmire doubtless could have made a determined effort to block the guarantees. But he limited himself, as he had since John Riccardo first raised the issue of federal aid, to getting his opposition on record and trying to tighten the terms of the deal. It was a tactic meant to remind the loan board of Proxmire's continuing scrutiny—to stiffen its backbone in dealing with Chrysler and its constituents—but not to scuttle the deal.

The real problem now was trying to get all 400 creditors to sign on. One major obstacle was the European bankers, who were aggrieved with the tentative agreement. The Europeans had been less organized and consequently less influential than the American creditors in the negotiations that had produced the restructuring plan. They thus felt no obligation to adhere to it. They were particularly unhappy with the new provision that the Treasury staff had demanded, allowing Chrysler to convert accumulated deferred interest into preferred stock after 1983. The prospect of owning a large stake in a feeble U.S. manufacturer with no European operations was distinctly unappealing.

Chrysler's Steve Miller, accompanied by James Wolfensohn of Salomon Brothers, left Detroit in mid-May for what turned out to be a ten-day ten-city campaign to bring the European lenders around. The federal government sent reinforcements to a meeting with about thirty creditors in Amsterdam. Treasury's Roger Altman flew in to impress upon the Europeans the importance the Carter administration placed on Chrysler's survival. Steve Miller followed Altman onto the podium with a four-point pitch: First, the deal was a good one for the European banks, promising them a better rate of recovery than they would get in bankruptcy. Second, in a world of integrated capital markets "any disaster caused by the bankruptcy of Chrysler could spill over to Europe."

Miller's third argument was that there could be "political repercussions" if Chrysler's failure could be blamed on the European banks. (One source close to the negotiations put the point less delicately: "Foreign banks cannot demand the right to do business here and compete equally with domestic institutions if they are unwilling to share equal responsibility for a restructuring of this importance to the nation's economy."[80]) Steve Miller later recalled with gratitude the leverage the government connection afforded: "We had friends in Washington—senators and representatives—who had no qualms at all about calling [the European lenders] and threatening to make adverse legislation affecting their interests as foreign bankers trying to do business here. They'd say, 'Now, you can't put one of our major industrial companies under. You'd better never come back to America.'"[81] Treasury's Brian Freeman, meanwhile, was busy mustering the executive branch's resources. "Treasury has all these economic attachés," he explained. "I sent telegrams to all the attachés in countries where the banks were causing trouble, saying, 'We're trying to put the Chrysler deal together, and X bank is not cooperating. See what you can do.'"[82]

Steve Miller's fourth argument with the European bankers came in a form that clinched the case with a recalcitrant lender over and over in the next few weeks: Chrysler was bound by the language that the Loan Guarantee Board had approved. There simply was no provision for softening terms in special cases. The Treasury Department would tolerate nothing short of unanimous participation.

The government had endorsed the all-in rule, transforming it from principle to policy. "It seemed to me that the only way to make it work," Treasury Secretary Miller recalled, "was to push the idea that everybody was in it together. Once you breach that principle, then all kinds of other classes of creditors come forward and say, 'We're different too, take care of us.' We just took the line that everybody had to be in it together. As soon as you break ranks, it all comes tumbling down."[83]

"It would have been extremely divisive to let anyone out, because everyone had a story," one participant in the negotiation concurred. It was not just the European banks; it was everyone. "There were some real sad stories. Some Japanese banks had thought they had just been doing routine letters of credit for shipping Mitsubishi cars. They had no idea they had become exposed."[84] A bank in Spain had issued a small ninety-day loan to the company and was indignant that it was expected to join in the same long-term restructuring plan as all the other lenders. Among the hundreds of banks there were dozens of compelling reasons to claim special terms. But the government and leading bankers held fast to the all-in rule. "There were no special deals," a principal bank negotiator said. "We all— all the banks—felt it would be much more difficult to do a deal at all if side deals were done, because everybody would be either suspicious or else standing there with their hands out, waiting for a better deal. If we were going to get a deal at all, it had to be just straight for everyone, plain vanilla. And it was. It was the biggest deal of its kind ever to be done plain vanilla."[85]

When Steve Miller spoke before the assembled bankers, "I told them what was the honest fact, that there was no plan to take care of them. Either we were going to get every single bank to sign, or we were going to go bankrupt." Miller followed up on the mass meeting in Amsterdam with bank-by-bank visits. He invoked the honor of the international financial community. He vowed to remember good turns in his future career. And he urged adamant lenders to consider what it would be like to bear forever the reputation of the bank that killed Chrysler.

On Wednesday, May 28, 1980 (nearly two months after most people had expected the deal to be locked up), representatives of Chrysler's banks—European, Canadian, Japanese, and domestic— converged on Washington to fine-tune the restructuring. The Treasury Department had called the session and issued an open invitation to any banks troubled with the tentative deal. Treasury Secretary Miller opened with a speech reiterating that the loan guarantees were strictly contingent on a successful restructuring encompassing all the lenders. After his speech the bankers and the bureaucrats got down to business. The session was to last three days. Government officials, especially Robert Mundheim, Treasury's general counsel, did most of the deal making.

The Canadian banks had negotiated a separate agreement with Chrysler Canada, featuring more favorable interest rates, better security, and a shorter interval before they could start collecting on their loans; they obviously did not want to adopt the harsher terms now of the Chrysler plan. After two tense days of entreaties from Treasury officials, the Canadian bankers reluctantly agreed to sign on with the rest of the creditors. (But the Canadians were still too indignant to shake hands with their U.S. counterparts when the agreement was clinched.)[86] The major European bankers gained a modest concession in return for pledging to stay in the deal beyond 1983, if necessary; Chrysler would open "compensating balances" in their U.S. branches. This sweetener meant that the Europeans would have more cash on hand and a somewhat larger presence in U.S. capital markets. Perhaps most important, it let the delegates return to Paris, Brussels, and Frankfurt with the satisfying news that they finally had pried a concession from the Americans.

"Miraculously, at six o'clock in the evening on Friday, the thirtieth of May," Steve Miller recalled, "we got to the point where all the groups could stand in one room and say that we had the basis for an agreement." But the "groups" were still only clusters of creditors with comparable goals, and the group representatives who signed on at this meeting had no real authority to bind all the banks they represented. Every lender had to sign on the dotted line.

A central office was set up at Manufacturers Hanover to keep track of the campaign. There was a "war room" on the walls of which were listed every bank and up-to-date details of individual negotiations. There was background information on each lender— what a participant called "the details of what turned them on and what turned them off." Teams of bankers manned telephones to persuade creditors around the world to accept the deal. In the days after the deal had been endorsed in Washington, bank after bank signed on. And more and more attention came to bear on those still uncommitted.

Several kinds of pressure were applied, openly or implicitly, in what came to be called a "search and destroy" campaign against holdout banks. Each bank was made to understand that continued resistance could gain it a reputation as a "bad actor," which would likely keep it out of future syndicated credits. Chrysler suppliers were enlisted to spread the word that their future choice of where to take their banking business would depend in part on each candidate's record on the Chrysler deal. Messages like these were extremely muted. Cordiality lubricates the banking business, and the subtlest of signals carried the message with no need for heavy-handed ultimatums.

Another kind of pressure—still mostly implicit—came from the government. Bankers worried that opposing the deal would invite eventual retribution, in some ill-defined but surely unpleasant form, from bank regulators at Treasury or the Federal Reserve Board. Government officials made little effort to allay these fears. Again, there were no express threats of regulatory retaliation, but the bankers' acute sensitivity to their relationship with the regulators doubtless helped shift some holdouts' position. Federal Reserve Board Chairman Volcker refused to intercede directly; Treasury Secretary Miller limited his involvement to the few most intransigent banks. Others were less restrained. Steve Miller was in Washington to brief several senators and representatives on the holdout bank problem when one legislator startled him by asking eagerly, "Who do you want us to get?"[87]

But the subtlest sort of pressure was by all accounts the strongest. No bank wanted to be known as the one that had killed Chrysler. It was an acute awareness of public opinion, rather than ultimatums from businessmen or public officials, that compelled assent. The First Security Bank of Salt Lake City was one of the last twenty or so banks to sign on. An officer explained, "I don't think we got calls from suppliers or other lenders. If we did, they were not important to our decision. Although the bank had objections, we did not want to be known as the bank that threw 600,000 Americans out of work."[88] The Michigan National Bank dropped its resistance in large part because of press features highlighting the potential for irony if a major Michigan bank brought Chrysler down. As Chrysler's cash dwindled, and as more and more lenders capitulated, each remaining holdout faced a greater risk of becoming the bank that wrecked the deal. The president of one of the last holdouts, Peoples Trust Bank of Fort Wayne, Indiana, protested, "I can't believe that this credit has been structured so that one or two tiny banks could throw Chrysler into bankruptcy. I find the whole thing incredible."[89] Yet that is precisely how the deal was structured.

In early June Chrysler ran out of cash. The company had little choice but to stop paying its suppliers until the guaranteed loans came through. Chrysler was pushing its luck here. Any one of its 20,000 suppliers could have forced it into bankruptcy by insisting on payment, and many of them could have shut down the company by the simpler means of ceasing to ship crucial parts. Since January the automaker had been pressing its major suppliers to hold off collecting on their invoices. Many bills remained unpaid, from Goodyear Tires' $5 million January tab to Lustro Steel Products' $25,000 invoice. The most cooperative suppliers, not surprisingly, were those who sold their wares almost exclusively to Chrysler. They knew full well that a Chrysler bankruptcy would hurt them the most.[90] A total of $75 million had been deferred in January alone; by April Chrysler had negotiated delays on $125 million of invoices.[91] But now, in June, the cutoff was across the board and unilateral. Nobody knew how long the suppliers would put up with it. Some, with bills of their own coming due and facing the grim alternative of borrowing at steep interest rates, had already insisted that Chrysler settle its account. The pressure was mounting to lock up the restructuring plan and get the guaranteed loans. But a few banks still wouldn't sign on.

Rockford, Illinois, was the site of the Belvidere assembly plant where Chrysler made its popular Omnis and Horizons. It was also the home of the American National Bank and Trust Company, ranked number 579 among U.S. commercial banks. American National had lent Chrysler Financial $525,000. Now its president, David W. Knapp, wanted the money back. Let the big banks that had negotiated the deal restructure their loans to Chrysler; American National wanted out. "We're just not interested in it and haven't been from the start, since they began proposing this last fall," Knapp said. "Their crystal ball tells them this solves Chrysler's problems. Mine doesn't. The decision and control rests with the large banks. That's rightfully so. But I just don't want to be part of a group of 350 lenders all bound by the same terms. . . . We've had calls from Chrysler, from suppliers, asking that we be reasonable. We have had calls from other banks, and I just told them we're not interested in getting in the agreement. I'm sure I'll get more phone calls."[92]

Chrysler could have paid American National its half million, or the crowd of bigger banks could have bought the loans and let the Rockford bank and other small holdouts off the hook. But once any bank had been paid off, others would inevitably demand to be bought out, too. The restructuring deal would speedily come undone. To preserve the agreement, every single bank would have to be brought aboard. Chrysler and the Treasury Department launched a grim crusade to win over American National and the handful of other hard-core holdouts.

By mid-June eleven U.S. banks and nine foreign banks had still refused to join the plan. Among them they represented $56 million in loans—only a little more than 1 percent of the total debt to be reworked. But any one of them could derail the deal. The Loan Guarantee Board had to cancel the June 18 meeting at which it was to have finally authorized the guarantees, rescheduling the session for the following day. "The recalcitrants are under tremendous pressure," Iacocca said in a press conference called to explain the delay. "We've got task forces working on them." Chrysler's chief said all the lenders should be lined up within a day.[93]

Yet as tension mounted in Washington and Highland Park, the loan board meeting had to be postponed again. By June 17 a number of holdouts, including the Banque Bruxelles Lambert in Belgium, had signed on. But several others were still left. One of them was American National of Rockford. Steve Miller flew to this small city midway between Chicago and Madison, Wisconsin, to meet with bank president David Knapp. After the meeting, Knapp told reporters, "[O]ur position has not changed. I told them I was sympathetic with their problem, but I still have some basic problems with the agreement."[94] Steve Miller's statement to the reporters was equally blunt: Chrysler was out of money. American National was one of the last holdouts. If American National stalled much longer, the deal would likely fall through, and Chrysler would go bankrupt.

Press reports on the standoff galvanized Rockford's Chrysler workers. The next day pickets surrounded the bank. Depositors rushed to pull their money out. The state of Illinois notified American National that it would withdraw $7 million in deposits. Calls came into the bank from Treasury Secretary Miller, Senator Charles Percy, and—by one account—President Jimmy Carter.[95] Anonymous bomb threats were phoned in. Finally, bowing to what he called "a certain divisiveness in the community," Knapp agreed to join the restructuring plan.[96]

It was late in the day on June 19. Chrysler had not paid any of its suppliers for more than a week. There were only two more banks to bring along: the Deutsche Genossenschaftsbank (referred to, for obvious reasons, as the DG Bank) and the Twin City Bank in North Little Rock, Arkansas. The DG Bank, based in Frankfurt, had seized $8 million passing through its system on its way to Chrysler from Volkswagen in mid-May. Such setoffs were common, but only

DG still refused to return the money and join the credit. A team of lenders flew to Germany to lobby DG's management in person, while Chrysler executives and Treasury Department officials cajoled by telephone. Manufacturers Hanover President John McGillicuddy traced one of the bank's executives to Hong Kong and promptly tracked him down for a long-distance telephone pitch for the deal. This coalition of persuasive powers—added to an explicit threat from Chrysler to bring a noisy and unpleasant lawsuit against the bank if DG's setoff killed the deal—brought the bank along at the last minute.[97] North Little Rock's Twin City Bank had lent Chrysler $78,000. Its officers flatly refused to believe Steve Miller when he insisted that its recalcitrance would block $1.5 billion in guaranteed loans. In the middle of their meeting Treasury Secretary Miller telephoned the president of the Twin City Bank to confirm Steve Miller's story and to exercise what one Treasury official called "a little friendly persuasion." The Arkansas bankers were duly impressed and called in the press to record a ceremonial handshake with Steve Miller.[98] The last dotted line was signed. Once the formalities were finished, the Chrysler Loan Guarantee Act could go into effect.

The Loan Guarantee Act had been signed into law by President Carter in early January. Chrysler's employees—blue-collar and white-collar, union and nonunion—had pledged their share of the deal by the end of that month. But it had taken nearly six months more of bargaining to bring the lenders along. The ordeal had claimed considerable resources—financial, political, and human. "The Chrysler restructuring was the scene to make that year in Washington and New York," a company official recalled.[99] Banking is a decorous and only occasionally arduous field of endeavor. Striking a new deal with hundreds of wary lenders meant pushing ponderous lending institutions out of procedural tracks they normally traveled, and this involved a staggering amount of organizational work. Bureaucrats, consultants, lawyers, financiers, and Chrysler managers labored together in unfamiliar ways at an unaccustomed pace. All the participants in this financial drama would have stories of nights spent working through to dawn, weeks of shuttling frantically from Washington to New York to Detroit, months without a day's break, crises managed in late-night sessions in hotel bars and coffee shops. They later told these tales with relish. For dozens, maybe hundreds, of America's most talented and ambitious professionals the Chrysler deal was the climax of their careers. Years later mementos still adorned their offices: press clippings; framed copies of key documents; a coffee shop place mat covered with scribbled figures that became the framework of a deal; poems and gifts evoking inside jokes exchanged in celebrations of crucial agreements. Reputations were established. Bonds were formed. And in the trauma and confusion of the Chrysler restructuring, subtle changes were wrought in some of the American economy's core institutions.

6.

Before it could guarantee any loans to Chrysler, the loan board had to make two separate and partly discordant findings: that Chrysler could not meet regular standards of creditworthiness but that it would be able to repay the guaranteed loans.* It was possible, in principle, simultaneously to satisfy these two conditions only because the act endowed the loan board with powers that were similar to, but stronger than, those granted to new lenders in a regular bankruptcy. First, and most important, the act specified that if the turnaround failed and Chrysler went into bankruptcy, "the debts due to the United States shall be satisfied first." Other creditors, even those with secured loans, would be pushed lower in the priority of their claims on Chrysler's assets. The loan board could waive the U.S. government's senior claim only in favor of loans from state and local governments, certain small debts to suppliers, and up to $400 million in new commercial loans.[101] Second, Chrysler had to get board approval to enter into any contract worth $10 million or more or to sell any asset worth $5 million or more.[102] Third, the company would prepare operating and financing plans and submit them for board approval as long as guaranteed loans were outstanding.[103] The act also required Chrysler to pay the U.S. government for any special costs and risk it incurred. Congress set a minimum guarantee fee of at least half a percent to cover administrative expenses. But more significant was a mandate for the board to "ensure that the government is compensated for the risk assumed in making guarantees" either through additional fees or through some mechanism whereby the government "contingent upon the financial success of the Corporation would participate in gains."[104]

*Technically the board had to sign findings, drafted by Treasury staff, that "credit is not otherwise available to the Corporation under reasonable terms or conditions" and at the same time that "the prospective earning power of the Corporation, together with the character and value of the security pledged, furnishes reasonable assurance of repayment."[100]

As is typical with complex legislation, most of the subtleties of interpretation and implementation fell to the staff. Only at relatively lowly levels of the bureaucracy do administrators have the time to iron out the details of how statutes are actually to work. The fundamental issues filter up to senior bureaucrats and political appointees. But the routine processes of enforcement—the countless mundane judgments that add up to give legislative mandates their practical force—are left to people who do their jobs unencumbered by any large political view but often with a finely honed sense of the possible.

Brian Freeman directed the small staff of the Loan Guarantee Board. He was a man of passionate cynicism, prodigious ego, and a gleefully blunt style. His admirers, of whom there were many, described him as "abrasive but . . ." His critics—fewer but still numerous—described him as "brillant but . . ." Freeman entered government service armed with a law degree and an M.B.A.; by the time of the Chrysler crisis he was indisputably the federal government's most seasoned bailout veteran, at the age of thirty-three. After brief sojourns in academia and with a Wall Street law firm he had joined the civil service to work on Conrail for the Treasury Department and had stayed on to participate in some aspect of each major federal bailout of the 1970's. (It was not the first time that talent had been drawn to government by the exhilarating challenge of a crisis.) Freeman had formed opinions in the process and was determined to apply them to Chrysler. "The government is traditionally easy pickings," he explained several years later. "There's nobody in the government who knows how to set these things up, so most of the time it's easy to milk the feds. I had seen it—Conrail, Lockheed—and I was aghast. My role, as a representative of the government, was to block that from happening here."[105] Freeman had helped write the administration's original loan guarantee bill and shepherded it through the gauntlet of amendments and extensions in Congress, at times advising Chrysler lobbyists and Proxmire staffers simultaneously. Once it had been passed, he staked out control over its implementation. He had little competition for taking the lead in day-to-day dealings with Chrysler. "This thing was a real tar baby. Nobody wanted to touch it. I thought it would be fun, I wanted to do it, it had to get done somehow, so they let me have it."[106]

Although he was far down in the Treasury hierarchy—formally reporting to Assistant Secretary Roger Altman and Deputy Treasury Secretary Robert Carswell—Freeman took the lead in filling in the details for the broad (and sometimes opaque) conditions Congress had written into law. A Chrysler official who worked closely with Freeman recalled, "He was supermotivated to make this thing work. He put in enormous hours, immense personal effort. I have no idea what his goal was—whether he thought he was in line for secretary of something, or a big Wall Street job, or just, like the mountain climber, because it was there to do. But I couldn't fault him for any lack of energy."[107] A company financial officer said, "I've been with him, and we'd be talking about an issue, and when it would get to the point where we needed a judgment, he'd get up and charge in to check it out with Secretary Miller. . . . He was a major contributor to our forward motion."[108] Wendell Larsen later called Freeman "the only guy in the government who knew everything that was going on. . . . He's as prickly as they come, but he's a straight shooter."[109]

Freeman's colleagues had comparable observations. "Brian made things happen without much in the way of formal authority," said a Federal Reserve official who worked with him. "He wasn't a principal; technically he was fairly junior. Carswell and Altman were appointed officials, confirmed by the Senate. They had official standing; Brian didn't. He lacked the authority to *make* people do what he wanted, but he didn't want to play that game anyway. He used the Chinese water torture approach. He just kept at you. He'd call people at all hours—late at night, weekends—pushing them on a point. People would tell him to get lost, but it didn't faze him. He held on like a bulldog. He kept on pushing and pulling and arguing and bullying. He could be extremely hard to take—coming at you without warning, always running around the ceiling at a million miles an hour, about as lacking in tact as you can be. But you knew he was working harder than anyone, so his pushiness was easier to take."[110]

There were other assessments as well, though. "It's true that there's not much that eventually happened that Brian hadn't thought of early on," said one knowledgeable observer. "But he thought of so much that didn't happen as well. If you spew out enough ideas—without testing or judging—you can claim to have thought of everything first."[111] Freeman could get so caught up in the legal and financial details, according to associates, that he risked missing the basic rationale for the program. He also at times alarmed his colleagues, who would arrive in the morning to find Freeman still at work from the night before, glassy-eyed and woozy; he once showed up for an early meeting wearing his vest inside out. But all concur that Brian Freeman was the draftsman for the program's crucial early phase.

Freeman pasted together a staff with some experience in law and public finance. Two analysts from the New York Fed had come down in January to help get things under way while Freeman auditioned candidates for the staff and tried to scrounge office space, desks, and secretarial help. Two veterans of the Conrail program were among the first staff members hired. (One of them recalls that his first task was helping to lug desks into the cramped offices in a Treasury annex while Freeman badgered administrators to install some telephones.) Two Treasury lawyers managed the huge chore of drafting the legal prose required to solidify the deals. Two junior analysts with financial backgrounds completed the staff; there were never more than eight. Most of the actual monitoring work was done by the accounting firm of Ernst & Whinney, which retained an office full of analysts at Chrysler headquarters, and by specialized offices at the Federal Reserve and the General Accounting Office.

Soon these bureaucrats were working with consultants, lawyers, and mid-level Chrysler executives to craft the covenants that were to govern the guarantee program. Their efforts were devoted to first developing and then enforcing an elaborate document called the "Agreement to Guarantee," which would bind Chrysler as soon as the first guaranteed loans were issued. The agreement, which when completed had the heft of a mid-size city's telephone directory, was carefully designed to link the government into Chrysler's planning process. It forced the loan board to be involved; it forced the company to involve them. The agreement included ten major sections, eighty specific covenants, fifteen exhibits, and around a hundred pages of assorted definitions, lists, and schedules. It was dubbed the fat pack by government and company negotiators. Attorneys from the law firm of Cahill, Gordon & Reindel helped draft the text, and many staffers contributed language to some covenant or codicil, but Brian Freeman dominated the process. "He was brilliant, but he'd play these awful intellectual games with us," one Chrysler executive remembered. "He'd say, 'Somewhere in there is something you're going to hate. Your job: Find it.'"[112] Nobody else so fully understood the minute details of the agreement or could navigate with as much confidence through the hundreds of pages of dense legal prose. "Brian had his notions as to how this thing should be done," according to another Chrysler manager. "You couldn't really argue with him. I'd say, 'Come on, why do you want to put *this* covenant in? We're going to have a terrible time living with this.' He'd say, 'Fine—if it's a problem, get a waiver.' His idea—and I guess it came out of his experience with Conrail—

is that he was going to write the agreements in a way that made the loan board active. They were going to have *something to do.* He was going to put in all these covenants that would require them to act; through that process they would be informed as to what was going on. . . . You couldn't argue him out of anything because he had an answer to everything, the same answer: 'Get a waiver if it turns out to be a problem.' "[113]

The seemingly interminable and almost impenetrable prose of the agreement stated and supported one fundamental goal: safeguarding the government's stake. Freeman and his allies were determined to prevent the government from becoming "easy pickings." To this end Chrysler was required to submit to Treasury Department oversight of the most detailed sort, to pledge essentially all its assets as collateral to the government, and to agree to myriad conditions ensuring that default on the guaranteed loans—or even a significant risk of default—would carry such unpleasant consequences for the firm that its managers would vigorously seek to avoid it.

Treasury oversight would center on the operating and financing plans Chrysler was required to file with the loan board. This review process fixed the form of the relationship between public and private officials. "They had to produce a plan each year," Brian Freeman later explained. "And we had to find it satisfactory. It had to make sense, and it had to have backups and contingency plans. In Conrail they would run out of money and just say, 'Well, that's too bad. Guess you'd better give us some more money.' I didn't want that to happen here. I wanted to hold management accountable for their actions. I focused on four or five elements that had to improve. This improvement was what the government was buying with its money. We asked management to set goals on each of these elements, and then we held them to the goals. If they missed, they had to explain it to us. They found this prospect embarrassing, and they hustled to reach the targets."[114]

A formal "Memorandum of Operating and Financing Plan Procedures and Requirements" spelled out in merciless detail Chrysler's obligation to keep the government apprised of its actions, predictions, and strategies. Plans were to be delivered, critiqued, revised, approved, and updated on a stipulated schedule. The list of documents Chrysler would have to send to the government was itself around twenty pages long. Michael Driggs, Freeman's deputy and later his successor as loan board staff director, recalled the daunting scope of the procedures memo. "The paper was so overwhelming that it wasn't until October 1980, months after the first drawdown, that we finally wrapped up the negotiations with Chrysler about what information they had to give us and were supposed to have been giving us since May," Driggs said. "We never used most of it, and it was horrendous to keep track of. But the failure of Chrysler to provide one of those documents was technically a breach of their covenant. Every time they were three days late with a copy of a press release or something, there was a big flap, because in principle the one point-two billion dollars in guaranteed loans were immediately callable. That's how rigid it was."[115]

The small loan board staff relied on its own private consultants—accountants Ernst & Whinney; lawyers Cahill, Gordon & Reindel—and also on Salomon Brothers and Booz, Allen & Hamilton, two concerns that technically worked for Chrysler but had specific duties, laid out in the procedures memo, to support the government's oversight effort. The chief of Booz, Allen's Chrysler team later recalled his firm's singular role. "We and Salomon had high credibility," Cyrus Friedheim said, "and we were looked to by the government to tell them whether whatever Chrysler came up with was viable or not viable. They [Chrysler's managers] didn't like it worth a damn sometimes. And on the other side, we tried to counsel and coach the company on elements of the plan. Sometimes it was counseling and coaching, that is. Sometimes it was battling them down to the floor."[116] The company found itself negotiating out its business strategy in iterative rounds with managers, bureaucrats, and consultants. "We used the operating plans as a means of communication among us and Treasury and our consultants and their consultants," Gerald Greenwald recalled. "They'd say, 'You're going to be short a billion and a half dollars, and we're not going to OK the guarantees until you tell us where you're going to get the money,' and we'd say, 'All right, we'll cut our capital spending some more.' And they might say, 'Bullshit, you do that and you lose even more market share.' And we'd go through that process until we worked it out. Frankly, even then, we were trying to make it as painless as possible for ourselves, focused on just getting that next guarantee, and they were trying to make it a little tough on us."[117]

Treasury scrutiny served a second function beyond limiting the government's risk: irritating Chrysler executives. A measure of annoyance was designed into the process as a spur to Chrysler to pay back the loans and a deterrent to other firms contemplating comparable bids for public help. The reporting requirements were deliberately onerous, requiring Chrysler to set up a new office solely to deal with the paper flow to and from the government. And there was also a personal element, as Treasury Secretary G. William Miller later explained. "Iacocca had to come see me every month and report," the secretary said. "They'd bring slides and things in just like a board of directors meeting. He hated it. He didn't want to report to me. I took it as if I were his chairman. . . . I told him, 'One thing I'll do that will end up as a benefit to you is make you hate the government so badly that the idea of getting them off your back will motivate you to make this a success.' "[118] Reporting *up* to anyone was a galling proposition for the head of an auto company.

The act required that the government take a security interest in Chrysler in return for its loan guarantees but left open what kind or how much collateral to claim. The General Accounting Office was responsible for valuing Chrysler's assets, with assistance from Ernst & Whinney and a private appraisal firm. The book value of the assets came to about $6.6 billion. But a good part of this was in the form of specialized plants and tools; if they had to be sold off in a forced liquidation, in the middle of an industry-wide slump, they would bring nowhere near book value. The best estimate of how much Chrysler's assets would actually sell for was around $2 billion.[119] If the loan board had simply laid claim to specific assets as collateral for the guaranteed loans, based on book value, it might be unable to recoup all the government's loss should Chrysler default. The solution: The government's collateral would be *all* of Chrysler's assets. "Why take anything less than everything?" Brian Freeman reasoned. "Why run around doing valuations when by rights you can claim it all?"[120] Donald Hammond, one of the first board staffers, recalled, "Chrysler said, 'Take collateral on a one-to-one ratio like normal people.' Treasury decided to put a lien on everything."[121] Chrysler officials were not particularly pleased with what came to be called Treasury's "belt-plus-suspenders" approach but felt they were in no position to protest. They also believed the loan board staff to be under pressure from Congress to minimize the government's risk. "If they had accepted a pledge of less than all the assets," according to Pierre Gagnier, the Chrysler manager responsible for collateral valuation, "the Proxmires of this world would have killed them."[122]

The first claim on all the assets of the automaker made the government's involvement in Chrysler's restructuring a radically less risky enterprise than it would have been for private investors. This became a central argument in the company's continuing attempts to assure Congress (and the public) of the wisdom of the deal. "We'd tell congressmen about the K-car and all that," a former

Chrysler officer said in 1984, "and they'd say, 'If you're such a hot proposition, why do you have to come to us? Go tell it to the private sector.' It was a good question. There were two reasons. First, bankers live by formulas, and our balance sheet stunk. The other thing is that we couldn't offer private lenders first claim to Chrysler's assets for collateral. What we could do with the government, what the legislation let us do, was to screw the banks and pledge all our assets to the government."[123]

Yet the government could collect its claim only if Chrysler were liquidated in bankruptcy. A scenario haunted the loan board: Suppose that after the company had collected the guaranteed loans, its managers simply refused to meet the restrictive terms of the Agreement to Guarantee and the procedures memo? Or, even worse, suppose Chrysler regained profitability but opted not to honor its guaranteed loans, requiring the government to pay off investors? Would the loan board then exercise its right to throw Chrysler into bankruptcy, sell off the assets, and pocket the proceeds? "What if we'd decided, 'We've got the money now—don't call us, government, we'll call you,'" Chrysler's Pierre Gagnier said several years later. "The only options [for the board] would have been to let it go and feel bad about it or pull the plug. Break them? Throw a hundred thousand people out of work? But . . . wait, we can't do that—the whole purpose of the act was to keep those people working. What's another sanction? Kick the management out. That's a sanction that will work, as opposed to the draconian one of throwing everyone out on the street."[124] So the loan board concocted yet another condition: It required that each Chrysler director sign a pledge that if the company substantially failed to meet loan board conditions, the director would vote to increase the size of Chrysler's board and fill the majority of its seats with loan board appointees.* In other words, if the government felt Chrysler was reneging on its side of the deal, the loan board "had the ability to kick the management out by taking a majority position on the board and saying, 'Lee, we're tired of you, out you go.' They could have had themselves a car company."[126]

---

*The condition stipulated that in the event of "material and adverse difference between the projections set forth in the Operating and Financing Plan . . . and the results actually achieved . . . and the Company shall fail to submit to the Board . . . modifications [and] corrective actions" the director would vote "to cause the size of the Chrysler Board to be promptly increased and cause persons specified by the [Loan Guarantee] Board to be promptly nominated and elected as directors of the Company so that a majority of the Chrysler Board consists of persons so specified."[125]

7.

The last step was the formal closing of the financial side of the deal. An underwriting syndicate headed by Salomon Brothers was ready to offer investors the first $500 million in guaranteed notes as soon as each of the major parties to the restructuring affirmed its assent. On June 23, 1980, mountains of documents were assembled, some in Europe and Japan, others in offices scattered throughout Manhattan, but most in the law offices of Chrysler and the bankers' steering committee, both in the Westvaco Building on Park Avenue. Lawyers, Chrysler executives, government officials, and journalists converged to seal the agreement, culminating the process that had begun with John Riccardo's bid for a quiet tax subsidy the previous August. After months of frenzied negotiating there was nothing standing between Chrysler and the money but formalities. Then the Westvaco Building caught fire.

A blaze that broke out on the twentieth floor sent smoke billowing up through stairwells and chased out the lawyers and officials presiding over the preparations for the closing. As squads of firemen battled flame and fumes and shattering glass littered the street, the Chrysler team fought back panic. The note sale that would bring the guaranteed funds to the corporate treasury was set for the next day. Chrysler's trade creditors were near the breaking point. The underwriting syndicate assembled to sell the guaranteed notes could easily come unraveled if the closing were delayed. Even if the documents survived, the building, damaged by smoke and water, could be shut down for days.

In the confusion of the crowd thronging Park Avenue to watch the fire fighters, a knot of lawyers and Chrysler executives assembled, conferred, and decamped to a nearby restaurant. There Steve Miller, James Wolfensohn of Salomon Brothers, and William Matteson of Debevoise decided the risks of delay were too great. They badgered the police and firemen for permission to go back into the building and, in the early-morning hours, led a rescue team into the smoky offices to retrieve the documents. They hurriedly stuffed the precious papers into boxes, walked them down twenty flights of stairs, and trundled the boxes along the street in commandeered mail carts. A train of executives pushing loads of boxes filed up Park Avenue, still blocked by fire engines, to the Citicorp Building six blocks away, where they dumped the documents at the law offices of Shearman & Sterling. One Chrysler executive who arrived in the middle of the rescue mission said, "It was quite a sight, all that pricey legal talent wheeling mail carts filled with documents up Park Avenue."[127] Senator Donald Riegle, who had arrived with his young son in tow to witness the closing ceremony, could not contain his exuberance: "The fire shows that not even acts of God can stop the Chrysler recovery."[128]

The lawyers worked through the night to reassemble the papers for the closing, and the next morning telephone hookups were arranged to Toronto, Paris, Washington, and sites around the city. The roll was called. Each group of creditors, the Loan Guarantee Board, and Chrysler formally assented to the agreement, and a few minutes after noon on June 24, 1980, the deal was closed.

The underwriting syndicate immediately put $500 million of ten-year Chrysler notes up for sale. The notes carried a 10.35 percent yield, three-quarters of a percent higher than U.S. government securities of the same maturity, and could be called—that is, paid off early at Chrysler's option—after three years. The offering circular warned that Chrysler "is faced with pressing financial problems which have significantly weakened its financial condition." But the warning was more or less pro forma; the attorney general had declared the guarantee of Chrysler's debt to be "a legal, valid, and binding undertaking of the United States of America." Few investors were put off by the weakness of the issuing company. Drawn by a yield *The New York Times* called "a rare rate of return for top-quality ten-year notes," some 30,000 investors bought up most of the half billion issue the first day.[129]

Lee Iacocca appeared before the news cameras in a ceremony he termed "the completion of the most complex financial restructuring program in history." He said, "Against all the odds, against the criticism of our detractors, against the basic complexity of a program involving five governments on three continents, and against the pressure of time, a team of highly dedicated people has completed the requirements of this loan guarantee. They will never receive the credit they deserve. They have worked seven days a week, often around the clock, giving up time with their families, for one purpose—to protect the jobs of 600,000 American workers who build American cars for American buyers. . . . On behalf of more than half a million Americans, I want to say thank you for one of the outstanding performances by any group of businessmen and government officials in the history of our country. . . . This is a great day for America."[130] Wolfensohn of Salomon Brothers and Iacocca posed for pictures as the investment banker handed the auto executive an oversize mockup of a check for $500 million.

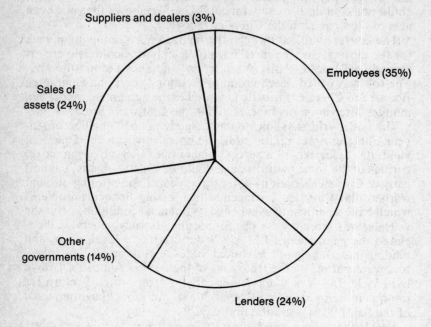

FIGURE 8
Concessions Agreed by July:
$2.6 Billion

Suppliers and dealers (3%)

Employees (35%)

Sales of
assets (24%)

Other
governments (14%)

Lenders (24%)

Steve Miller, meanwhile, deposited a very real $500 million in
Chrysler's account at Manufacturers Hanover, and the company
started paying its suppliers again.

The deal had not come cheap. Just printing the restructuring
agreements cost $2 million. Salomon Brothers collected $3.25 million of the $500 million guaranteed issue as an underwriting fee;
Merrill Lynch, First Boston, and other investment banks selling
the notes also had to be paid.* Chrysler had run up between
$4 million and $5 million in legal expenses with Debevoise. Booz,
Allen was drawing $100,000 a month for its services. The lobbying
campaign of late 1979 had cost $300,000 for the time of Tommy

*Underwriters and investment bankers earn their fees by bearing some of the risk of bringing
notes to market and some of the expenses of selling the debt. In this instance, with the
federal government backing the securities, there was a good deal less risk—and a less difficult
selling job—than underwriters normally confront. Salomon Brothers *had* committed considerable resources to provide general financial advice for Chrysler, however.

Boggs and his associates and $90,000 for William Timmons's firm.[131] (Chrysler estimated in 1984 that its legal, banking, and other fees for the guarantee program totaled $67 million, exclusive of interest on the loans and payments to the goverment.)[132] The subtler costs had yet to be measured. But it was clear that the terms of the act, the deals that had to be struck to get the guarantees, and the brutal reality of the auto market and the economy at large in mid-1980 all meant that Chrysler would become a very different sort of company.

V

THE CRUNCH

1.

The frantic race to lock up the financial deal overshadowed the quiet disintegration of Chrysler itself. On the day Salomon Brothers offered the market half a billion dollars in guaranteed Chrysler notes, the firm was well into a grim campaign to reduce its costs by cutting employment. Chrysler was shrinking. Forty percent of the company's production workers had been laid off. Four plant closings had been announced or completed: Lyons Trim in Lyons, Michigan; Dodge Main assembly in Hamtramck; the Fostoria, Ohio, foundry; and a stamping complex on the edge of Detroit.[1] As the last of the recalcitrant banks were being rounded up, Chrysler announced that it would be closing its V-8 engine plant in Windsor, Ontario; the St. Louis, Missouri, truck assembly plant; and the Lynch Road assembly plant in Detroit.[2] White-collar jobs had been cut by a third. But Chrysler still had to sell 2.6 million vehicles a year to cover its costs. It was not going to come close to that in 1980.[3] One senior executive predicted, "There will be further skinnying down. The future product plans require fewer people to carry out."[4] And a loan board staff official said, "On paper, they've closed and opened just about every plant they have.

It's very definite that plants will be closed. But I wouldn't venture a guess on which ones. Today's plans might be out the window tomorrow."[5]

It was not just Chrysler that was contracting. Pressure from Japanese imports conspired with collapsing overall sales to savage the domestic auto industry in the early 1980's. The anti-inflation policy that Federal Reserve Board Chairman Paul Volcker had launched in October 1979 raised the prime rate to stifling levels by the end of the year. In many states usury codes made it impossible to make auto loans without either losing money or breaking the law. The credit control program imposed in January had pushed rates down but at the cost of squeezing off auto loans. Around the time Chrysler's loan guarantees were finally approved, Secretary of Transportation Neil Goldschmidt distributed an internal Carter administration study which concluded that the U.S. auto industry "has been caught in a major demand shift for which it was not prepared. That shift, plus a credit squeeze and the onset of a recession, have caused the bottom to fall out of the automobile and truck markets. The short-term outlook is not bright, even if an easing of credit availability were to produce some rebound in sales."[6]

More than 250,000 U.S. auto workers, including 137,000 from GM, 69,000 from Ford, and 41,300 from Chrysler, were laid off by mid-1980. In Detroit, where 1 of every 3 manufacturing jobs depended on the auto industry, unemployment was 14.6 percent by July 1980. In some cities like Flint, Michigan, and Anderson, Indiana, where carmaking accounted for more than half of all manufacturing jobs, unemployment reached more than 20 percent. Chrysler's cutbacks were by far the largest in relation to the company's size but still were dwarfed by the proportionately less drastic layoffs at General Motors[7] (see Appendix A, Figure 13A).

Detroit felt most painfully the effects of the retrenchment. Chrysler's oldest and least efficient plants were clustered densely in the Detroit area. Early in 1978, 81,700 of the area's residents had worked for Chrysler. By the time the lawyers, bankers, and consultants had locked up the financial restructuring, its Detroit payroll had fallen to 47,200. City officials were anxious that Chrysler's consolidation not disproportionately burden Detroit. Mayor Coleman Young said, "Detroit and Michigan must fight to be able to provide facilities Chrysler needs in order to guarantee that as Chrysler retrenches, a majority of the jobs that are now in this area remain in this area."[8] But the company executives insisted that neither the $150 million loan from Michigan nor the help Detroit had promised bound the firm to the city. They reasoned that other states that had also pledged assistance, as well as the Canadian and Ontario governments, were just as anxious to maintain jobs, and the ax had to come down somewhere. (Industry watchers in Detroit recalled how Lee Iacocca, when he was president of Ford, had shrewdly played states and nations off against each other, bidding up the enticements they offered Ford to locate factories within their jurisdictions.)

Chrysler was betting it all on the K-car. Even while facing bankruptcy, it had staked $150 million readying two assembly plants—Jefferson Avenue in Detroit and the Newark, Delaware, factory—to make the front-wheel-drive compacts. It had retooled the Trenton engine plant to turn out the 2.2-liter four-cylinder engines that would go under the hoods, at a cost of $300 million, and had sunk $120 million into equipping Kokomo Transmission to make transaxles.[9] If the new car sold as well as Chrysler hoped—at a rate of half a million in the 1981 model year—employment at Jefferson Avenue could reach 5,000. This would nearly double Jefferson's head count and provide enough new jobs to absorb many of the 3,200 workers who had been laid off when Dodge Main shut down.

But as the summer of 1980 wore on, the auto market continued to crumble. Mid-July sales of all cars were down 27 percent from 1979 for the most sluggish sales pace since 1960, and Chrysler was doing worse than average with a 34 percent sales drop for the year. Industry experts were beginning to predict the worst might not be over. Reflecting the malaise in the U.S. auto industry, each of the big three fell in *Fortune* magazine's ranking of the world's fifty biggest manufacturers—GM from first to second, Ford from fourth to fifth, and Chrysler from fourteenth to fortieth place.[10]

As the first lot of guaranteed notes went on sale late in June, it was obvious that more money would be needed almost at once. Indeed, the company, its financial advisers, and the loan board staff were already at work on an application for a second chunk of the available $1.5 billion even before the first drawdown was approved. Chrysler submitted revised operating and financing plans to the board on July 10, 1980, and promptly requested a second drawdown of $300 million. This would bring the total to $800 million, halfway to the ceiling on guarantees. The decision this time, while still favorable, was a "much closer and more marginal judgment" than the first. Total U.S. auto sales in general and the demand for Chrysler products in particular had shrunk far more than had been assumed in Chrysler's restructuring plan. The loan board staff estimated that Chrysler's losses for 1980 would reach $1.2 billion—more than half again as high as the consensus prediction a few months earlier.[11] Moreover, the legislation had stipulated that the amount of guaranteed loans outstanding be no greater than private concessions already delivered. But by late July the total of "non-Federal assistance" stood at $800.6 million, clearing the legislative minimum by the barest margin. And about half this sum was attributable to asset sales and pension fund deferrals, the most dubious categories of aid.*

Again Congress had fifteen days to review the approval; again there was some resistance for the record but no serious threat to the new drawdown, and on July 31, 1980, an additional $300 million in notes was quietly put on the market by Salomon Brothers. The terms of the new issue reflected lenders' increased nervousness about Chrysler's prospects. It carried an interest rate of 11.4 percent, or 125 basis points above Treasury debt with a similar maturity, compared with a premium of only 76 basis points on the first $500 million in guaranteed notes (100 basis points equal 1 percentage point).

In the course of arranging the second drawdown, Chrysler informed the loan board that its consultants Booz, Allen & Hamilton had warned that both the size of the auto market and Chrysler's share of it looked likely to fall even further below the assumptions on which the company had based its plans. According to Booz, Allen, Chrysler would have to shrink still more: "In our judgment the high level of these risks makes it essential . . . that the restructuring plan be in place and ready to be implemented by September 1." The next day Chrysler announced plans to cut its white-collar work force once again by more than a fifth—5,400 out of 27,000—on top of the nearly 10,000 white-collar employees who had lost their jobs since late 1978.[13] And the search continued for ways to buy parts cheaper than Chrysler's aging plants could make them. By September 1980 nine manufacturing facilities would be closed and twenty-three of Chrysler's forty-four remaining plants would be targeted for sale or shutdown.[14] (Some of these operations were later saved.) Chrysler's then-president J. Paul Bergmoser summarized the strategy: "We're continuing to review our entire man-

---

*Asset sales amounted to partial liquidation, not to external assistance. Pension fund deferrals delayed rather than reduced claims on the firms and transferred risk to a federal agency that guaranteed pensions.[12]

ufacturing operation to find other ways to reduce overhead. If a plant is obsolete, or if the parts and pieces it produces are no longer needed, we will either convert the plant to new technology or we will dispose of it. That is the only way we can survive. We have to modernize, and we have to be efficient, or we won't make it in today's market."[15]

Soon after he had joined the Chrysler board of directors in mid-May, United Auto Workers head Douglas Fraser had said he would propose a special board committee to explore options for averting plant closings or reviving shut-down plants. "I don't know what the chances are for reactivating those plants, but I don't think the Chrysler Corporation can afford to turn its back on those facilities," Fraser said.[16] His proposal was approved at the July board meeting, and by the end of the month the Chrysler Plant Utilization and Human Resources Committee was established. "I'm not quite sure I know all the things we could do," Fraser told reporters, "but now directors of the company are going to be discussing things they never talked about before. I think we've brought home the point of the human misery involved in plant closings. . . . The committee won't decide when a plant is to be closed or which plant will be closed, but once that decision is made then we can move on it before it possibly becomes irreversible as has been the situation in the past."[17]

The committee intended not to lobby against plant closings (Fraser concurred with Chrysler's managers that the firm could survive only by shrinking), but rather to allow labor and management a chance to share information and look for ways to lessen the pain of retrenchment. Fraser predicted that the committee would explore options such as finding new internal uses for plants slated for shutdown, soliciting contract work from other firms, or even helping workers buy up the facilities.[18] "As soon as a study was undertaken, we knew about it," Fraser later explained. "As soon as they were even thinking about closing down a plant, we'd talk to the local union people to see if we could save that money some other way, see if there could be things we could do to make that plant more viable economically."[19] In the months to come, several plants were salvaged or shutdowns delayed. One widely celebrated example was the Detroit Trim plant, which was saved after workers agreed to fundamental work rule changes.

But more often the economics were insurmountable. Thomas Miner, Chrysler's labor relations chief, remembered a session with worker delegates after Chrysler had announced that it would close

Detroit's Huber Avenue Foundry. "We simply didn't need the foundry capacity anymore," Miner explained. "We had another large foundry in Indianapolis, and we were going to be downsizing our engines. . . . So we had one foundry redundant. The union's position was 'Well, you *have* to keep it open.' And we said, 'We can't afford to.' And they said, 'Well, you know, we need the jobs. Can't you go out and find more casting business on the outside?' We said, 'There is no more casting business on the outside. Ford is closing its casting center in Flat Rock. Everybody is closing up gray-iron foundries. Family-owned foundries are closing up around the country. The gray-iron business is practically going down the chute, and we're part of that. We have no chance of picking up any more business.' So then the discussions turned to acceptance of the facts of life and then: 'Well, what's going to happen to our people?' Then you could start to be a little bit positive. We had an agreement on how we could work people from closed plants into existing plants with their full seniority. . . . But we were in a drastic recession in this industry. It wasn't just Chrysler that was in trouble. The whole industry was in trouble, so it was the worst possible time to be trying to place people in jobs, because everybody else was laying off. Nobody was hiring. A lot of them went down to the Southwest and the Sun Belt; some went to Florida."[20]

The days of massive layoffs and plant closings are burned into the memories of the company and union people who endured them. One executive was at the time the manager of the Chrysler complex that had been the major employer in New Castle, Indiana. "It was a terrible bloodletting," he recounted late in 1983. "We had to do things around here that you wouldn't do to your dog. You'd go away at night sick to your stomach. . . . It got so I couldn't go to the store or the bank. One day I had to go into town for something, and a woman recognized me in the parking lot, ran up to me, and put her arms around me crying, crying for me to hire her husband back at the plant. And I couldn't do anything at all. That kind of thing was the worst. That, and the phone calls I'd always get at home Friday nights, after the bars closed. Then it was the men crying themselves."[21]

Marc Stepp, head of the UAW's Chrysler department, was distressed that even after the federal loan guarantees had come through, Chrysler continued closing plants and laying off workers. In October 1980 he made public his suspicion that the government not only was failing to block these cutbacks but was actually promoting them: "We believe—we have no proof—that the Loan

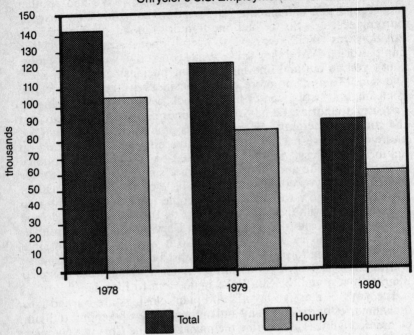

FIGURE 9
Chrysler's U.S. Employment

Source: Chrysler *Fact Book*

Guarantee Board staff is putting undue pressure on Chrysler Corporation to strip down its operations."[22] Treasury Secretary Miller quickly denied the claim, insisting that the board's "sole objective" was to ensure that Chrysler hewed to a "sound financial and operative plan."

Yet the matter was more complicated than this. The government's central concern, stipulated in the legislation and embodied in countless rules issued by the loan board, was to keep Chrysler in business. If this required shrinking the firm down to a viable core, the public officials administering the program took it as their duty to accept such shrinkage, indeed to insist on it. The irony of canceling jobs in order to preserve the firm in order to carry out the act Congress had passed in order to save jobs did not impress the bureaucrats caught up in the tension and excitement of the rescue.

Michael Driggs of the loan board staff later explained, "Chrysler did not take any cost-cutting actions voluntarily. It was a major battle, on a personal level, between [Treasury Secretary] Miller and Lee Iacocca, every time. In a time when the market was going to hell, Chrysler was still coming in with plans to increase capital spending. The government had to convince Iacocca to take responsibility for the company's survival. To do this, somebody in charge had to have the balls to walk away if we had to, and that was Bill Miller."[23] Miller himself recalled, "The truth is Lee [Iacocca] didn't want a downsized company when we started this; we had to fight for it. We weren't on the same wavelength. The first proposal he gave me I just slid it back to him across the table and said, 'You haven't thrown off any ballast yet. When the ship starts to sink, the first thing you do is get rid of ballast.' People who are nervous Nellies say you can save jobs by pumping money in. But you don't save jobs, that's foolish—you aren't going to make any more cars."[24]

"My game was getting resources for the company," explained staff director Brian Freeman. "There was no point in having this program if you weren't going to get them enough of a cushion to keep going." But to get that cushion, it was more or less a matter of arithmetic that Chrysler had to shrink. "It was clear they had to pare back," Freeman said. "We required them to have a business plan assuring viability. For that they had to get rid of people and close down plants. . . . Everybody isn't going to keep their jobs. You work it down to a viable base; society is better off keeping X percent of the jobs and providing social support programs for the rest. I didn't sit there telling them to close down plants. But to the extent it was needed to keep the company viable, it was part of the requirement for a reasonable business plan."[25] Lachlan Seward, a later director of the board staff, concurred that the government was the linchpin of Chrysler's austerity campaign, not because Miller's team knew better than Iacocca's team what had to be done but because the bureaucrats, as outside agents, could more readily impose pain on the social entity of the Chrysler Corporation. "There were some very painful things that had to happen, and everybody knew it but didn't want to do it," according to Seward. "That's where we made the difference. We were the big bad government. Chrysler could say to its workers, its suppliers, its bankers, 'Look, you know we wouldn't do this to you if it was just us, but the government says we have to.' It can be worth a lot to have somebody to blame. It takes some of the sting out."[26]

On July 29, 1980, Indiana became the third state (after Michigan and Delaware) to come through with money for Chrysler, when it finalized a $29 million loan secured by a mortgage on the Kokomo Transmission plant. (Chrysler officials had wooed Indiana legislators with a preview of the K-car and a reception at which, in a gesture of midwestern solidarity, only wine and cheese produced in Indiana were served.) But there were no immediate prospects that the four other states—New York, Missouri, Ohio, and Illinois—would soon fulfill their aid pledges.

Two days later, at the end of July, Chrysler quietly revealed that it had set another loss record: Its deficit for the second quarter alone was $536 million. (For a sense of scale, consider that in its best full *year* ever, the firm had earned $436 million.) Falling sales and a steady cash drain from retooling projects had pushed total losses for the first half of the year to almost twice the level that Chrysler's plan of the previous December had predicted for all of 1980. But the company still had hopes of keeping the year's deficit to under $1 billion. If all went well, the K-car would generate $250 million in profits during the last quarter. According to Harvey Heinbach, a Merrill Lynch auto analyst, "[T]he crucial issue is going to be the fourth quarter. . . . That is when some of the questions about Chrysler's ability to survive without more Federal help are going to be answered. . . . The public is concerned about whether the company is going to make it. That's why Iacocca's fighting so hard to restore the company's image."[27]

2.

The dilemma was excruciating. Only if people were confident about Chrysler's future would they buy its cars, but only a good stretch of healthy sales could build that confidence. And every front-page story about Chrysler's dealings with the government renewed the public's doubts about the automaker's future.

Along with the daunting industrial and organizational task of the restructuring, the financial negotiations, and the brutal job cuts, Chrysler was simultaneously engaged in a high-stakes public relations campaign. Jerry H. Pyle, Chrysler's vice-president for sales, said, "[I]t's tough when you're the subject of the longest-running joke Johnny Carson ever had."[28] Lee Iacocca's marketing flair was indispensable as he strode confidently through television commercials, selling not so much Chrysler cars as the company itself. There were other, less visible efforts as well. One concerned police cars, traditionally a small but lucrative Chrysler niche. California was the largest market for police cars and set the standard that many other state police departments followed. In 1980 California announced it would no longer buy Chrysler products. The state's explanation: The cars couldn't go fast enough. "They were the same cars we'd been sending for years," Wendell Larsen recalled. "We'd never had a single complaint about speed. It's just that when you're all over the news as a famous stupid company, people figure if you're all that dumb, your cars must be slow, too. So we had to prove our cars were fit to be driven by California state policemen."[29] Larsen flew out to California, met with Chrysler dealers and legislators, and staged a speed demonstration that reassured the police and preserved the contract.

Lee Iacocca drove the first K-car off the line at the Jefferson Avenue assembly plant in a late September ceremony that included Douglas Fraser, Senators Donald Riegle and Carl Levin, Congressman James Blanchard, and Mayor Coleman Young. But the formal unveiling was slated, perhaps appropriately, to take place in Washington, D.C. Surrounded by reporters and camera crews, Iacocca took time out to bemoan the damage that Japanese imports were inflicting on the U.S. auto industry. But he quickly turned to the business at hand: a boisterous celebration of Chrysler's still-precarious survival. "It's been a long road back," Iacocca said. "And not everybody is ready to say we're totally out of the woods yet. But those of us who are closest to the action can sense the turnaround. You'll see it today. I think the public senses it. They're lining up to order our cars, and for all the right reasons. I believe Americans love an underdog, especially when it's willing to take on the big guys and fight its way back. I believe they want to help an American company turn itself around."[30]

Chrysler's third-quarter financial results were released on October 29. The company had lost $490 million—much more than it could sustain for many additional quarters, but less, in any event, than it had lost in the second quarter. Chrysler's share of the auto market was down to 8.6 percent now; it had been 10.4 percent one year before, and the turnaround plan of October 1979 had assumed it would be nearing 11 percent.[31] Yet Lee Iacocca remained optimistic. "Assuming moderation in interest rates, a modest upturn in the economy, and some improvement in the current rate of truck sales," he said, "Chrysler should report a profit in the fourth quarter."[32] Auto analyst Maryann Keller was unpersuaded. "Hardly anybody believes Chrysler anymore," she told *The Wall Street Journal*. "Too many statements and projections in the past have turned out to be dead wrong. It's going to take more than hot air to get people to believe Chrysler now is a healthy company. They're going to have to back it up with some real progress."[33]

A team of Chrysler employees had taken to staying after work and dialing American households at random to find out how people were feeling about the firm. By November Chrysler's image was perceptibly improving. But a third of all new-car buyers still thought the company was destined for bankruptcy. This expectation could quickly cause its own fulfillment. Chrysler counterattacked by letting reporters and bankers examine prototypes of cars slated for production five or more years out—models that in other companies, and in Chrysler during normal times, would be reserved for the eyes of a select few insiders. Gar Laux, Chrysler's new vice-chairman, explained, "[I]f we can show people we've already got new models in line for 1985, maybe they'll realize we're serious when we say this company is going to be around. . . . People won't even come into your showrooms if they think you're about to go out of business."[34]

By the end of November Lee Iacocca's hope for a profitable fourth quarter was manifestly unachievable. The K-car had indeed drawn customers into showrooms. But unprecedented interest rates had stifled sales (see Appendix A, Figure 14A). Worse still, Chrysler had committed what turned out to be a strategic blunder at a time when its margin for error was perilously close to nil. The fumble concerned option loading—how many extras like power steering, white wall tires, and deluxe trim went onto the first K-cars sent to dealers. The base price for an unadorned K-car was set at $5,880— slightly lower than the prices of its main domestic competition, General Motors' X-car—and Chrysler's K-car offered better fuel economy. Filling showrooms with cheap basic models would likely win Chrysler a healthy share of the market, but selling stripped-down cars was no way to bring in the cash it needed to stay in business. Profits on options could match or exceed the profit margin on the car itself. So Chrysler's managers took a gamble: They loaded the first shipments of K-cars to the bulwarks with options. They lost the toss. Prospective customers had been hearing for months about the new economy cars that the company was readying. But when they visited showrooms, they encountered only option-rich Aries and Reliants bearing $8,000 to $9,000 stickers; a dismayingly large proportion of the shoppers left without buying.[35] Chrysler's projections called for the K-car to seize 25 percent of the compact market. From launch through the end of November it averaged 11 percent.[36]

High interest rates, along with lingering doubts about Chrysler's viability, were even cutting into star subcompact Omni and Horizon sales, forcing a slowdown and layoffs at the Belvidere plant for the first time in three years. Meanwhile, Chrysler still had an inventory of more than 100,000 unsold 1980 models. Iacocca announced a program of rebates and dealer incentives—uncommon for the height of the fall selling season—and the assembly lines began to turn out stripped-down $7,000 K-cars to capture the economy market. But there was little Chrysler could do about a prime rate in the high teens.

3.

November 1980 witnessed another event: Jimmy Carter's loss to Ronald Reagan. Reagan had declared his support for the Chrysler program on the campaign trail, recanting earlier denunciations. But many among his staff still viewed the effort with undiluted scorn. The Chrysler rescue was anathema to the free-market doctrine of the incoming administration.

After the election, but before the new administration took over, outgoing Treasury Secretary Miller warned Iacocca that if he expected ever to need any more of the $700 million in loan guarantees authorized but not yet used, he had better ask for them before Ronald Reagan's team took charge. Iacocca was reluctant; he had learned that each application for a drawdown of guaranteed loans generated news stories that seemed to hurt Chrysler almost as much as the loans helped. He later expressed regret at not asking for the authorized maximum in the first drawdown. "Once you've gone through all the pain of being a beggar, then don't get scientific," he said in 1983. "Take the money and run. Because we were selling a brand-name product, and every time we started the clock running for the debate on the next drawdown, our sales would drop from ten percent of the market to eight. We paid through the nose in lost sales."[37] The process of meeting conditions and collecting concessions had been so grueling, and the publicity surrounding the process so disastrous for Chrysler's image, that Iacocca fervently hoped to get along without any more guaranteed loans. But by the end of the month it was clear that such hopes were futile. Interest rates were choking sales; debt service and retooling costs remained high. After a meeting with Treasury Secretary Miller on December 1, Iacocca announced that the company would be applying for a further installment of guaranteed loans. "When they decided they wanted it," one loan board official recalled, "they wanted all of it, and they wanted it all right away."[38]

But the loan board would not be so accommodating. "The whole reorganization had to go in stages," G. William Miller later explained. "You could not get the whole lump of sacrifice in the beginning; they wouldn't believe it was needed. And you had to give enough to keep them alive. So you'd only get some sacrifice the first time. And you hold back the bait. This was like playing poker."[39] It was not simply strategy that led the government to extract the remaining concessions in chunks. The election was now over. Political concerns that might earlier have inspired officials to a certain delicacy were no longer relevant. As one close participant said, "Miller was no longer thinking he had to be careful so he could be a senator or something. He was going back to the private sector and was worried about how he'd look to the corporate types. He wanted to fix Chrysler before he left."[40] Whatever motives they attribute to the principals, observers agree that this time the loan board resolved to go beyond the letter of the Loan Guarantee Act. It was less than six months since the first restructuring, and it looked as if the company were going to have to go through it all again.

Early in December 1980, Iacocca and Greenwald met for two hours with all three loan board members and with senior board staffers. The excutives made the case for a prompt drawdown without drastic changes in Chrysler's current operating and financing plans. The board demurred. Chrysler would once again have to find additional help on its own before the board could attest to the firm's viability and authorize more money. "Whether we were going to go to the union, or a supplier, or merge, or get a rich uncle to come up with the money, or an Arab—all they said was, you have to come up with a viable plan," Iacocca told the press. "The pieces have to come together, or the mosaic will fall right off the wall."[41]

The next day Iacocca met with Chrysler's board of directors to explain the government's position and to get approval for a deep cut in the product development program. There had been about $8.3 billion in spending planned for 1981 to 1985; the new plan cut

$1.9 billion. This meant dropping the subcompact scheduled to replace the Omni/Horizon in 1985, delaying two upscale K-car derivatives, and deferring investments in front-wheel-drive component capacity.[42] "We have got to attack everything and we have got to do it quickly. When we have a total, integrated plan we will go in for [loan] board approval."[43] Iacocca pronounced himself confident that the loan board would approve new guarantees: "If you go back and look at the original plan before Congress, I said we wanted $1.2 billion. They said, 'We may have some bad times ahead—take $1.5 billion.' It's the worst depression in history, it's the highest interest rates in history, this is the bad time."[44]

During a break between briefings, in the Treasury lunchroom, Treasury Secretary Miller told Iacocca that only a wage freeze could yield the kind of cash Chrysler would need to cement its recovery. Iacocca protested that the United Auto Workers would never consent to a freeze. Wages that rose in pace with productivity, tightly indexed to inflation, were the cherished product of decades of union struggle. Indeed, the freeze proposal in the original Lugar-Tsongas version of the Loan Guarantee Act had provoked some unionists to speak of abandoning the rescue campaign. But Miller reminded Iacocca that the board could approve more guarantees only if Chrysler's long-term status seemed secure. He insisted that stringent wage restraint would be necessary to make such a finding. "Besides," he told Iacocca, "if you manage to negotiate a freeze, they'll set up a statue of you in front of the U.S. Chamber of Commerce building."[45] In December Iacocca jolted the United Auto Workers with a phrase that entered Detroit folklore: "It's freeze time, boys. I've got plenty of jobs at seventeen dollars an hour; I don't have any at twenty. Do you want 'em?"[46]

The freeze demand sent a shudder through union leaders nationwide, as UAW officials at Solidarity House scrambled to frame a response. Meanwhile, the financial news emanating from Highland Park was more detailed and worse in almost every respect: Far from turning a profit, Chrysler's dismal October and November sales would likely result in a fourth-quarter loss of $200 million or more. The automaker now predicted it would lose $1.7 billion for the year—more than any American company, in any industry, had ever lost. The next round of loan guarantees would have to come through by January. Otherwise, Iacocca said, "There would be no future. Eventually, we'd run out of money."[47]

The 250 members of the United Auto Workers' Chrysler Council met on December 22 to consider Iacocca's request for a twenty-

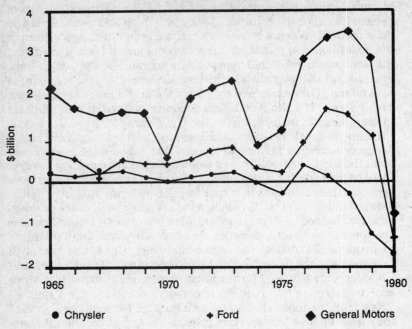

FIGURE 10
Automakers' Net Earnings

Source: Company reports

one-month pay freeze. The unionists were in no mood to make casual promises. "I don't believe they realistically expect me to ask for Iacocca's piece of paper so I can sign it," Douglas Fraser said.[48] The council was keenly aware of resistance within the union to further concessions, particularly if other parties escaped—or appeared to escape—this bitter new round of cuts. "Let 'em go under," said one senior worker. "Let 'em fold. I gave up too much already."[49] Despite vigorous opposition, the council did vote to reopen the contract, although it emphasized that any further concessions "are a response to the requirements of the Government decision makers rather than the demands of management."[50]

Marc Stepp, head of the union's Chrysler department, warned that conditions would be attached to any concessions. First, Chrysler's management, which workers had long considered top-heavy, would have to share in the sacrifice; the union would demand "enforceable procedures to control the number . . . and compensation" of nonunion employees. Second, the council said its bargainers would have to review Chrysler's situation directly with the loan board "in detail, including discussions with the Secretary of Treasury or other qualified representatives. . . . U.A.W. members will do what is necessary to meet the requirement of the Loan Guarantee Act, but we must know what is true necessity rather than merely a management goal."[51] The government quickly complied with the second condition. Treasury Secretary Miller invited the council's bargaining committee of around a dozen delegates to Washington. He installed the delegates, mostly burly veterans of decades on the shop floor, in an elegant Treasury conference room for a slide presentation on Chrysler's financial situation. Michael Driggs (who had taken over as loan board staff director after Brian Freeman returned to private endeavors) stood at the screen with a pointer as the secretary of the treasury interpreted graphs showing how current losses were "cannibalizing" product development programs and jeopardizing Chrysler's future. The union delegates were impressed. Few had ever before been offered a look at the details of Chrysler's plans. And to a team of longtime auto workers, the logic of wage concessions to free up funds for investment was compelling.[52]

A late December feature in *The New York Times* noted that shareholders' equity in Chrysler at the start of 1980 was $1.82 billion. If, as predicted, Chrysler posted a loss of $1.7 billion for the year and continued losing money into the first quarter of 1981, its assets would soon fall below its liabilities. One banker said, "Chrysler doesn't turn into a pumpkin when it goes from $1 of net worth to minus $1. But it is no good for a company to show a negative net worth." The symbolism would be all the more unwelcome to the loan board. *The Times* suggested that even though there was no requirement that Chrysler maintain a positive net worth, "companies with more debts than assets are not considered very viable."[53] "It makes it difficult for a loan board to make a finding of viability if the company is a technical bankrupt," Chrysler's Pierre Gagnier related. "So we had to have equity, and the only way to get it was to convert the bank debt to an equity instrument."[54]

Chrysler was preparing a proposal for its creditors that would improve the balance sheet bind by shrinking the debt load and raising equity, all at one stroke. Under the new plan, the company's creditors would convert about half of their debt into preferred stock. This conversion would do much to improve Chrysler's alarming debt ratio. But beyond beautifying the balance sheet, it would save the firm $100 million in accrued interest that otherwise would have to be counted against earnings.* Curiously, even though the earlier workout involved $900 million in debt while this deal would cover at least $1.3 billion, banking sources predicted that this second restructuring would be more tranquil than the first. Two points inspired this expectation. First, the players had learned from the previous deal. They now knew more about Chrysler; they were already organized into committees; they knew the government was serious in its insistence on unanimous participation. Second, there were fewer banks to deal with. Neither Chrysler nor the government intended to ask Chrysler Financial's creditors for new concessions. Had such a demand been made, the finance company's lenders now had no motive to comply since their debt had been secured as part of the first restructuring. Around the middle of December Steve Miller—now Chrysler's treasurer—once again began negotiations with the banks and the government.

4.

G. William Miller, the outgoing treasury secretary, took charge of the Chrysler program in the waning days of the Carter administration. At a six-hour meeting among the loan board, Chrysler officials, bank delegates, and the bargaining committee of the UAW's Chrysler Council, he warned that the government would—at most—grant another $400 million of loan guarantees. The government-backed money, moreover, once again would be only the cap on substantial private concessions. In a separate session the secretary told the press that Chrysler's most recent plan would not do. Its debt load was still crippling. Its cash cushion was so thin that the

---

*As part of the deal, Chrysler would double the fraction of accrued interest it paid in cash instead of in the form of deferred interest notes, or IOUs, so that the flow of money to the banks remained constant. From the banks' perspective, the problem with this plan was that it would reduce their stake—giving the banks a lower priority in bankruptcy—in the event that Chrysler eventually folded. That is, if the company's assets were liquidated in bankruptcy, preferred stockholders would get paid off ahead of common stockholders, but behind others to whom it owed money, like its suppliers. And of course, all creditors stood in line behind the government.

rocky K-car launch, which would have been a regrettable but not extraordinary setback for a stronger company, would very likely kill Chrysler in the absence of further assistance. The best option, Miller thought, would be for Chrysler to merge with another auto company to build a "world car" that could be made and sold in several countries. The last $300 million in guarantee authority was being held in reserve, at Miller's insistence, to help lure a merger partner.

Secretary Miller later detailed his frustrated hopes for a merger that would solve Chrysler's chronic weakness once and for all. "I sent [Salomon partner] Jim Wolfensohn all over the world, looking for somebody ready to give an infusion of capital," he said in 1984. "I told them it would be a steal—somebody could get control of a twelve-billion-dollar company with a few hundred million dollars. It might have been Peugeot; it might have been Mitsubishi; it might even have been Ford. But we never got any takers. In the dark days, people don't expect a turnaround, and after the turnaround it's too late. There were also problems with the company. Even when they're about to go down the tubes, they weren't motivated to become a subsidiary of somebody else. That would have taken a lot of pressure on our part."[55] At least one expert was skeptical about the merger option. David Healy, the auto analyst for Drexel Burnham Lambert, Inc., said, "Chrysler is still a giant operation from the standpoint of one of the foreign auto makers. If a Peugeot or Volkswagen or Datsun or Toyota wanted to enlarge its presence in the U.S. market it would make more sense for them to maybe buy a plant or two rather than take on something as big as Chrysler." Best of all, from the potential acquirer's perspective, would be to wait for Chrysler to disintegrate and then to pick up the best pieces without taking on its debt and pension liability.[56]

The treasury secretary also called for further concessions from Chrysler's constituents. He wanted suppliers to freeze prices for a year and drop them 5 percent for the first quarter, maintaining normal deliveries all the while. The biggest item, as before, was labor's contribution. Beyond the freeze Iacocca had already asked for, Miller wanted the UAW to commit itself not to try to quickly catch up to the industry pattern wage once the contract expired in September 1982. Douglas Fraser bridled at this demand: "We can't go beyond the current agreement. We have no right to. I don't believe that's within the purview of the loan board; I believe Miller is stepping beyond his legal mandate." The treasury secretary eventually prevailed upon a very reluctant Fraser to file with the loan board a letter affirming that the union would take Chrysler's special financial condition into account in negotiations even beyond the current contract.[57]

Secretary Miller was less specific about the banks' concessions, stipulating only that more was required. After the January 6 sessions at the Treasury Building, Chrysler's Steve Miller met Leonard Rosen, the bankers' chief counsel, and William C. Langley of Manufacturers Hanover at Washington's National Airport. While waiting for the shuttle to New York, they discussed Chrysler's debt situation over hot dogs in the snack bar. Steve Miller proposed that the banks forgive half the debt outright in exchange for security on the other half. The banks had long sought security; Chrysler had balked at granting it for fear that its suppliers would stop shipping if they stood after the government *and* the banks in claims on its assets. But now there was little alternative. Steve Miller returned to the Treasury with Salomon's James Wolfensohn to see if the loan board would buy some variant of this new concept. Through such sessions the deal continued to take shape.

By the second week in January 1981, Chrysler's suppliers were carrying a total of $200 million in delayed payments. Most of the suppliers had consented to the 5 percent price cut for the first quarter and a freeze for the rest of the year.[58] But some balked. Borg-Warner refused to cut prices and began withdrawing as a supplier, although it did not cease shipments already arranged or take Chrysler to court as it, or any other supplier, could have done.[59] Steve Miller recalled that when recalcitrant suppliers—principally the oil companies that provided lubricants and gasoline to fill up the tanks of new Chrysler cars—threatened to stop delivery, "the only thing I could threaten them with was to say, you know, 'You're going to cut me off? Tomorrow? Really? OK—do you mind if I go to my office? I've got a call from Bill Miller, secretary of the treasury, who'd like to know the names of anybody cutting me off.' "[60]

Steve Miller and James Wolfensohn came to the Treasury on Saturday, January 10, 1981, for what was to be a ten-hour meeting with the loan board and around a dozen bankers. "The government got very direct," Charles Struve, one of Steve Miller's deputies, remembered. "They played hardball toward the end of these sessions. They set deadlines. . . . You have to recognize that none of the representatives of the banking community were anointed with leadership capability. There were all sorts of different breeds of banks out there. The company tried to take the lead, but it was limited in its bargaining power."[61] Treasury Secretary Miller presided. (He had acquired a button proclaiming "No More Mr. Nice Guy," which he now wore prominently on his lapel.) He proposed terms, criticized bank proposals, thrashed out the financial details that would fix the size of the bankers' sacrifice. At one point a banker pulled aside a senior loan board staffer to say that he and many of his colleagues felt distinctly uncomfortable negotiating with the secretary of the treasury. "That's what he wants," replied the aide. "That's why he's here."[62]

At lunch in the Washington Hotel coffee shop that day the treasury secretary summarized the proposed restructuring in a diagram doodled on a place mat. The new deal was a refinement of the debt liquidation scheme that Steve Miller, Rosen, and Langley had discussed over airport hot dogs a few days earlier: Half the bank debt would be converted into preferred stock, and Chrysler would have the option of canceling the other half for thirty cents on the dollar. Immediate cash—even if it amounted to only fifteen cents for each dollar of original debt—was a gratifying prospect for the banks; the preferred stock was not. One lender asked if the preferred stock could be delivered "prepasted, double-rolled, and in a choice of colors" suitable for papering his kitchen.[63]

Yet despite the distaste lenders felt for the swap, the deal went through. One of the financial consultants who sat in on the deal emphasized the bankers' extreme reluctance to antagonize senior officials who, in other forums, so powerfully shape the environment for their industry. "The magic in this workout was nothing that we did or the company did; it was really the government," said David Schulte of Salomon Brothers. "There came a day in Washington when Bill Miller was solving the Iranian repatriation and asset-hostage question in one room and trying to button up the Chrysler thing in the other room, and he had very little time left in the administration, and the company was flat-out broke and needed the money, and then Bill Miller and Paul Volcker did a number on the American banks. They got them in a big conference room and then—not concurrently but kind of in a Mutt and Jeff fashion, Bill Miller being the nice guy and Paul Volcker being the heavy—worked them over. . . . You have to keep in mind that this was the secretary of treasury and the chairman of the Fed talking to banks—they're *the regulators,* and they called the tune. . . . Miller explained all about why the government cared about Chrysler and all about why this program existed, and he did it as a gentleman, in a soft way, and made no threats. . . . Volcker was wonderful. He came in in corduroy pants and a plaid shirt and a tweed jacket and one of his foul stogies, and he said, 'Here's the way I see it. You want me to pop four hundred million dollars to see if we can save this company, but you don't want to do anything. No deal.' He said, 'You want me to put up; then you put up. Because if I don't see that you've got the confidence to put something up, I'm not going to play; for me it's real simple.' So spake the chairman of the Federal Reserve, controller of the discount window. And by the end of the day there was a deal."[64]

Of the firm's $1.3 billion in debt, $680 million would be turned into preferred stock with a face value of $1.1 billion. The other $620 million would be paid off at thirty cents on the dollar. But once again the deal was only tentative. It had to be sold to all the creditors. The banks, moreover, were only one of the groups that had to endorse this second, tougher restructuring; labor had to be brought along, too. And time was running out for the Carter administration, for Treasury Secretary Miller, and for Chrysler.

5.

The logistics of negotiations among suppliers, lenders, workers, managers, and officials were getting increasingly complicated as inauguration day loomed. To keep two sets of key players in proximity to a third, Chrysler and the UAW moved their negotiations to Washington's Mayflower Hotel. This third concession demand— larger by far than the sacrifices of October 1979 or January 1980— was the most divisive for the union leadership. Some unionists, concerned that capitulation here would cripple the UAW in other negotiations, urged a hard line. But Fraser insisted on a settlement. There were murmurs—muted, though; Fraser was a well-liked leader—that board membership had tainted Fraser. But his determination to save the firm flowed in large part from his awareness that Chrysler's retirees, some of them old comrades from his days on the assembly line, would be worse off if the company ceased to exist. "When I was meeting with my colleagues," Fraser later recalled, "arguing and caucusing around the clock, you get to the point where you wonder, 'Would we be better off, would the country be better off, if we just let it go?' The thing that deterred me more than anything else was those forty-six thousand retirees. I'd think of them and have to say, 'I can't do it.' And we didn't do it. . . . If we'd turned our back on it then, it would have been gone."[*][65]

In sessions with company and Treasury officials, and with the press as well, Fraser protested that labor was bearing an unfair share of the cost of keeping Chrysler alive. He warned that the union would insist on sharing significantly in the benefits if the company returned to profitabilty. The union insisted on a profit-sharing plan as a quid pro quo for further pay cuts, and negotiations proceeded on the form of the plan.

While company and union bargainers continued talks at the Mayflower, Iacocca and Fraser met with the members of the loan board on Monday, January 12. The sessions had to be one on one. Ralph Nader had filed a lawsuit under the "Government in the Sunshine Act." The pending suit argued that loan board meetings had to be open to the public. Since there were only three members of the loan board, any two of them constituted a "meeting," and formal records had to be kept and published. But it was very close to impossible to conduct serious negotiations if every bargaining position, feint, and tentative compromise had to be taken down for public review. Bargainers would worry more about how their tactical proposals would sound when quoted—even out of context— to their constituents. Dealing would give way to posturing. So they avoided convening a quorum. Fraser met with Miller in the morning, Staats in the early afternoon, and Volcker in the evening. Iacocca and his lieutenants, as well as players in the creditors' negotiations, endured roughly the same shuffle.[66]

Douglas Fraser was a veteran of many grueling negotiations over the decades, but the January 1981 sessions in Washington were brutal by any standards. Emerging from a meeting, a grim-faced Fraser told reporters that the details of the talks with the government were too sensitive to discuss, beyond the basic fact that the union was determined to do better than the flat freeze Iacocca wanted. Fraser struggled to incorporate some provision for recovery—for wages to rise again if Chrysler's performance improved— into the concession package. But Paul Volcker was adamant: Judging Chrysler viable would require at least a freeze for the whole contract. "I was trying to get him to see they didn't have to cut us back so far to keep Chrysler in business," Fraser recalled. "But he said, 'Look, I don't mind calling white gray or black gray, but

---

*Although Chrysler retirees would not have been simply stranded if Chrysler had gone bankrupt—basic pensions were guaranteed by the government—they would have been worse off in terms of pension increases and benefits.

I'm not going to call black white or white black. It's just plain not
enough. You've got to do more.' He drove a goddamn hard, hard,
hard bargain."[67]

Volcker was eager to eliminate indexed wage increases not just
as a means of improving Chrysler's prospects but, more important
from his perspective, as part of a general wage-restraint policy that
he hoped would curb inflation. "It was clear the debt had to be
restructured and the equity swap had to happen," a loan board
staffer recalled in 1984, "but what caught Volcker's attention was
the need to do something on the labor side. Inflation was still running extraordinarily high at this point. Volcker got intrigued with
the idea of taking the COLA [cost of living adjustment] out of the
labor contract. Even though he remained skeptical about the program as a whole, he became convinced that changing the labor contract was something very significant, not only for Chrysler but as
a more general precedent. And as it turned out, when you saw what
happened at Ford and GM a little later, he was right. What started
at Chrysler turned into something that broke the back of the built-
in cost increases."[68]

The day after Fraser's series of meetings with the loan board,
Treasury Secretary Miller called a press conference: "The Board
does not feel that the plan presented by Chrysler is adequate. It
needs to be improved, needs to be tuned up, certain gaps need to
be filled." Miller said he had just met with the UAW negotiators
and set a deadline: "By tomorrow, we've got to have their best
shot. If we don't have a plan the Board will buy, the Board will
not approve it and it would have to go over to the new Secretary."[69]

Fraser responded to the treasury secretary's announcement with
palpable chagrin: "Apparently what is desired is not only a wage
freeze but an absolute cut." The loan board was asking the union
to give up a $1.15 an hour cost of living adjustment, a pension in-
crease that had taken effect on January 1, a new hearing aid benefit,
and scheduled improvements in the vision care program.[70] "I told
the Secretary that we will try to get as close as we can to the $673
million, if that's an accurate figure," said Fraser. "It depends on
the attitude of the company and whether or not there's enough time
to negotiate a profit-sharing agreement. I told Secretary Miller there
was a serious question in my mind that you could sell the design
of the program that was given to us to the membership of the
union."[71] But Fraser and the rest of the UAW team bargained with
their Chrysler counterparts all through the night, and in the morning
they had a deal ready for the loan board.

Fraser managed to preserve $51 million in scheduled pension

benefits that Chrysler and the loan board had sought to cut. But the new deal still included $622 million in new concessions. (UAW concessions required as conditions for the first $800 million in loan guarantees had totaled $447 million.) Scheduled wage increases, which the previous deal had only delayed, were now to be dropped. The three remaining paid personal holidays would be lost; Canadian workers, who had stayed out of the January 1980 round, would give up the sixteen days off they had retained earlier. But for labor the bitterest part of the deal was abandoning the hard-won rule of indexed pay. Wages would no longer be raised in pace with inflation. Making the freeze retroactive to the first of the year meant an immediate pay cut of $1.15 an hour. By the time the contract ended in September 1982 Chrysler would be paying around $3 less per hour than Ford and General Motors.

Marc Stepp, the head of the UAW's Chrysler department, retained several years later a lively resentment of the deal itself and the way it had been reached. "They would not give Chrysler that loan unless we gave up COLA," he said in 1984. "So we did, as of March 1, 1981. This was a dollar and fifteen cents an hour, forty-six dollars a week. . . . Volcker put our ass in a sling. He's a hard man. He stripped us. Volcker was the last holdout. He was concerned about his credibility, and he figured it would be bad for his reputation to look like he was giving anybody any easy money. Chrysler never put those demands on us. It was the government. It wasn't negotiating; it was just the government saying, 'Here's what you've got to do.' "[72] Added to the earlier concessions, the new cut meant that the typical Chrysler worker was giving up the equivalent of roughly $14,500 over the life of the contract. (Abandoning COLA counted for half of this, and sacrificing the paid personal holidays was another quarter.)

In return, Chrysler promised to set up a profit-sharing plan for the workers. This would go well beyond the employee stock ownership plan arranged the previous January. Workers now would share in profits directly, rather than indirectly through a rising stock price. Any gains, moreover, would be paid out on a regular schedule, not held until retirement or death. But the loan board declined to bless the agreement.

Douglas Fraser remembered the loan board's summoning Iacocca and him to report on the terms of their new deal. "We'd been up all night negotiating, and it was about ten, eleven o'clock in the morning," Fraser recalled in 1983. "We'd just worked out a profit-sharing plan as part of the package. But Volcker said, 'It's too rich. I want you to go back to your committee and tell them that you can't have a profit-sharing plan of that size.' I told him to go screw himself, I'm not going back to that committee. I'd brought them along as far as they were going to go, and I knew it.''[73] Marc Stepp, who was at Fraser's side throughout the session, recalled, ''We negotiated a very lucrative profit-sharing plan. We figured that was the way to get our reward out of it. If it worked, if Chrysler made a profit, we got some of it. The company said that was fair enough. But the government just flat rejected it. They said it was too rich and that it lasted too long; they said it was too much of a burden on the company. They let us keep the plan, but we had to shorten the time it ran for. That was the government's decision. The corporation wasn't the enemy on that one; it was the damn loan board.''[74] Paul Volcker wanted the profit-sharing plan to terminate by September 1982, when the current contract would be up for renewal; otherwise, he argued, it would undermine Chrysler's bargaining leverage in the next round of contract negotiations. But the union objected that Chrysler was unlikely to make any profits before 1983, if it ever would. The final compromise: The profit-sharing plan would run to the end of 1983.

Chrysler granted its workers three further concessions. First, it would suspend, at least for the life of the contract, plans to close five small plants that employed 3,800 people in the Detroit area. Second, it would regularly provide the union with ''financial and operating data in the form and content'' that the board of directors received.[75] Finally, it would offer workers an ''opportunity to constructively input ideas into the decision-making process prior to implementation of decisions which might adversely affect their job security.''[76] But at no time did the union seriously propose to tie the wage freeze to Chrysler's willingness to preserve jobs or to offer even greater short-run concessions for more job security. Marc Stepp later insisted that no such deal could have been struck: ''You just can't get job security. There are only so many auto jobs around, and we were heading into a recession.''[77] Only after several years, and a brutal shrinkage of the American automobile labor force, would union leaders engage in the trade-off between wage rates and job levels. For now, limiting the financial concessions—which UAW leaders feared Ford and General Motors might also demand— was the principal goal.

Once the union and Chrysler had reached an agreement, the loan board met to consider it formally. Lee Iacocca and Douglas Fraser waited in separate rooms in the Treasury Building. Four hours later they were summoned to the fourth floor for an announcement: The deal would do.[78] Iacocca said of the final package, ''It's a super deal and the union made big sacrifices.'' Fraser was less enthusiastic, calling the deal "the worst economic settlement we ever made. But the alternative is worse: no more jobs for Chrysler workers."[79]

It came down to the last day of the Carter administration. After working all night on the tortuous financial agreements required to resolve the Iranian hostage crisis, the outgoing treasury secretary called an 8:00 A.M. loan board meeting to give formal approval to the new Chrysler deal. The new concessions included in the January 14 plan varied strikingly in form and timing. Some obligations were simply delayed; others were canceled or deferred indefinitely; others were transmuted into radically redefined shares in Chrysler's future.* One way of measuring the concessions—probably the most valid—is to compare estimated claims on Chrysler's cash before the revised plan and after. The new deal cut Chrysler's cash needs by just over $1 billion in 1981. Almost two-thirds of those savings represented lower capital spending and other cuts in product programs. Roughly a quarter was from employee concessions. Supplier concessions and white-collar cuts each yielded well under 10 percent of the savings. (In fact, the planned debt restructuring actually *increased* Chrysler's 1981 cash drain by around $110 million as the company spent more to buy back long-term debt than it saved on interest concessions.) In 1982 about half of the $1.15 billion savings would be attributable to product program cuts, 42 percent from employee sacrifice, around 3 percent from shrinking the salaried payroll, and less than 2 percent from the effects of the debt restructuring. In the years after 1982, the January 14 plan projected about $2.2 billion in total savings. This is when the effects of eliminating long-term debt would kick in; around two-thirds of the savings from here on would come from the debt restructuring, a quarter from product program cancellations and deferrals, and most of the rest from cutting back the white-collar staff (see Figure 11, page 232).[80]

Secretary Miller spent his last seventy-two hours as treasury chief hammering out the financial quid pro quos for the release of the

---

*The deal required, first, that Chrysler's workers must ratify a concession package that would cut wages by $1.15 hourly on March 1 and freeze them until September 1982, as well as freeze certain pension and other benefits. Second, Chrysler's lenders must convert half of their holdings of Chrysler debt into preferred stock and accept repayment on the other half at a rate of thirty cents on the dollar. Third, suppliers must lock themselves into price breaks of $36 million and promise a further $36 million. Fourth, Canada must agree to a smaller investment package—by 40 percent—than it had previously negotiated with Chrysler. Fifth, a largely symbolic but nonetheless irksome sacrifice: Chrysler must sell its company airplanes.

FIGURE 11

Cash Savings from the January 1981 Deal

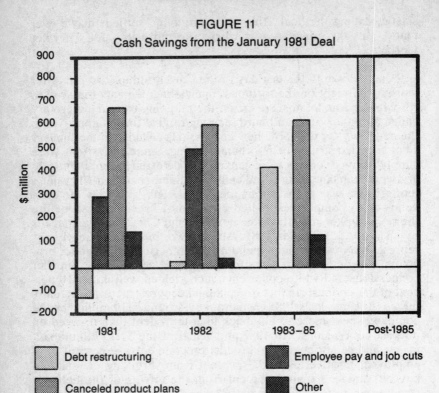

Debt restructuring

Canceled product plans

Employee pay and job cuts

Other

Source: October 1981 Loan Board Report to Congress

American hostages in Iran as well as the second Chrysler restructuring. He emerged from his office on inauguration morning, haggard and sleep-starved, to reveal to the press the basic terms of both deals. "It becomes my lot in the last days of the Administration to deal with two of the most complex issues in the memory of living people," he said as his tenure came to a close. In a transition briefing Miller told his successor, Donald Regan, that Chrysler had consumed a third of his time for a year and a half.[81]

Shortly after the outgoing treasury secretary had declared that the deal would do, the Chrysler Council of UAW local delegates moved it closer to completion by tentatively approving the union's share of the new concessions. There was opposition from a few of the Canadian leaders. Delegates from the two tank plants argued that they should be exempt from the cuts since that part of Chrysler remained profitable.[82] But enough of the council approved the package to send it on to the membership.

Rank-and-file Chrysler workers, in turn, began voting on the concessions on January 29. Dissident unionists attacked the cuts as excessive and Chrysler's concessions to its workers as token. The promise of strengthening labor's hand in management—or, as the agreement put it, to offer an "opportunity to constructively input ideas"—was derided as "a big suggestion box."[83] One UAW official, briefing workers at Local 869 in Warren, Michigan, conceded that the profit-sharing and worker participation provisions Chrysler offered in exchange for a wage freeze "don't amount to a hill of beans." But he added, "Those of you who don't want to take the wage cut, go out and find another job. No one's stopping you from leaving this organization."[84] Wages at Chrysler, even frozen, were distinctly better than other options open in the Detroit area and indeed in most of manufacturing.

Yet a wave of close votes, and a few rejections, in the first two days of balloting sparked serious concern among union leaders. A survey by the *Detroit News* on the first day showed a slim majority of locals voting against ratification.[85] The opposition was coming from four sources: Chrysler Defense workers, who resented accepting pay cuts when the firm was making money on its tank contracts; workers at modern plants that would almost surely stay in operation even if Chrysler failed; skilled tradesmen confident they could find work elsewhere, and—at least according to some sources—permanently laid-off workers who cast negative ballots to vent their frustration.[86] But later returns went more heavily in favor of the deal, and a surge of support came from white-collar locals. When employees of the big Mack Avenue stamping plant in Detroit approved the contract by comfortable margins late in the day on January 30, Douglas Fraser said, "That does it. We'll make it."[87] The final tally was nearly three to two in favor of the contract.[88]

Union leaders, anxious to forestall attempts by the other auto companies to extract comparable concessions, stressed the singular nature of Chrysler's predicament. "We did what we did at Chrysler because it was on the brink of bankruptcy," Marc Stepp said. "Let me hasten to add quite clearly and quite loudly: If any corporation thinks they can find this as an open opportunity to take advantage of the UAW members and the goals they have made down through the years, they've got a shocking surprise coming."[89] The issue was unlikely to be so quickly put to rest, however. The wage freeze saved Chrysler an estimated $800 on each car, taking it from far behind to well ahead of Ford and GM on production costs. Douglas Fraser acknowledged, "The philosophical question is how long the union can say we're going to give a competitive edge to Chrysler."[90]

6.

As before, the last hurdle between Chrysler and the final round of guaranteed loans was getting all its lenders to sign on to the deal. This time Chrysler Financial's debt was not at issue, so there were only 150 bankers to bring along. In the first week of the Reagan administration Steve Miller met with bankers in New York, Chicago, and Amsterdam, explaining the new package. The bankers' dominant concerns were how big the dimes-on-the-dollar cash payout would be and how soon they would get the money. Their disdain for the preferred stock, the other part of the deal, was close to complete.

Unlike the first restructuring, this time there was organized opposition among the lenders. About thirty banks, rallying behind Citibank, refused to sign the new agreement. "They ganged up on us, led by Citibank," Steve Miller recounted. "Their attitude was that Chrysler was a hopeless case. 'Why should we see an additional four hundred million dollars of government claims on those assets come in ahead of whatever is left of our claims? This whole loan guarantee business is an abortion; let's just get it over with.' "[91] The bankers felt it was time for Chapter 11. "Walter Wriston [the chairman of Citibank] called [Treasury Secretary Donald] Regan and said, 'I'm going to do the country a favor through this euthanasia.' "[92]

Chrysler probed Citibank and discovered that its executives would swallow their principled objection to the deal if the partial cash payout were made mandatory—rather than an option Chrysler could take or drop—and if more of it came up front rather than being stretched over several quarters. Chrysler was willing to comply. But Paul Volcker denounced with spirit and finality the prospect of seeing government-guaranteed money flowing directly to the banks, as would be the result of the Citibank change. He would approve no restructuring that involved a major payout at the closing. At one point, two Citibank officials sought from the new treasury secretary a pledge that if Citibank signed on to the deal, the Reagan administration would do whatever was necessary to ensure Chrysler's survival. "This Regan did not want to do," according to a key Treasury official. "He just said, 'Look, I want this deal done, and I want it done now.' The bank negotiator just checked his watch, looked at his partner, and said, 'The next shuttle leaves in twenty minutes; we can just catch it if we leave now.' And they did. It got like that sometimes."[93] Chrysler stepped up its efforts to structure a deal that both the loan board and the Citibank faction could accept. A few days before the deadline Regan and Volcker, for their part, consented to a compromise: A bit more than a quarter of the cash would go to the banks at a decent interval after the closing.

But on February 23 Roger Mehle, the new assistant secretary for domestic finance, learned that Citibank still refused to sign on. Mehle, himself no enthusiast of the Chrysler program, prepared a press release announcing that the conditions could not be met. The loan board meeting set for February 27 was canceled, and with it the $400 million drawdown and, by most estimates, Chrysler's hopes for survival. A horrified Steve Miller read the press statement at the Treasury a few hours before it was due to be released. Miller immediately launched a frenzied campaign of telephone negotiations with Citibank and Assistant Secretary Mehle and managed to concoct a compromise five minutes before the press was to receive word that there would be no loan guarantee. (Paul Volcker was instrumental in saving the deal.) Lee Iacocca announced the agreement from Florida, where George Steinbrenner had invited him to watch the Yankees at spring training: "It all came together Monday. It's real good news."[94]

The banks had been the last hurdle. On February 27, 1981, the loan board approved the issue of an additional $400 million in guaranteed notes. Chrysler's underwriters, led by Salomon Brothers, already had the notes printed, priced, and ready for sale. They hit the market a few minutes after Treasury Secretary Regan announced final loan board approval. The ten-year notes were priced to yield 15.13 percent and could be called—paid off ahead of schedule—anytime after three years. The yield was high for guaranteed debt with such a maturity. But few investors considered these to be ten-year notes. Many experts anticipated the notes would be paid off early: Either Chrysler would call them, or—much more likely—the firm would go under and the government would redeem them. One portfolio manager explained, "Since we really do not know the maturity of the issue, we wanted a yield that was higher than those available in the money markets for either two-and-a-half-year or ten-year notes."[95] The market had so little confidence in Chrysler that its old, unguaranteed bonds were trading at forty-one cents on the dollar, much more of a discount than their low-interest payments would warrant. Michael Milken of the securities firm of Drexel Burnham Lambert, Inc., said that the bonds wouldn't fall much farther if Chrysler filed for bankruptcy; failure was already seen as so likely that the contingency was built into the price of its securities.[96]

Once underwriting fees and discounts had been subtracted, Chrysler got $389 million from the $400 million in notes. Most of it was spoken for before it was raised. Suppliers had been holding around $350 million in past-due bills.[97]

The only direct confrontation between Iacocca and Donald Regan, the new treasury secretary, was over the smallest but most contentious of the requirements G. William Miller had earlier imposed: making Chrysler sell its airplanes.

The issue had first surfaced in 1980, when the loan board staff began dissecting Chrysler's operating plans in search of potential economies. "Out at the small airport near the good suburbs of Detroit is where each car company has a hangar," a former loan board staffer explained. "What kind of jet they have waiting in the hangar means a lot to auto executives."[98] Staff director Brian Freeman had made it a personal crusade to pare back or eliminate Chrysler's fleet of airplanes. "I thought it was unseemly for the government to be subsidizing these traditional perks," Freeman said in 1984. "It was also costly. And it also seemed like a good incentive to rub management's face in it. That encourages them to be more productive, to try to get free of this system. So I told them they didn't need them. They didn't make sense. If Lee wanted to fly, he could fly commercial, or he could get his own plane."[99] Freeman had tried without success in the summer of 1980 to persuade the treasury secretary to cut the airplanes.

The issue lay dormant until late in the year, when Treasury Secretary Miller and board staffer Michael Mates were flying to Detroit to confer with Chrysler executives. As they lunched on packets of peanuts in the back of a commercial airliner, Mates summoned for Miller the image of Chrysler's chairman luxuriating in his corporate jet. This time the treasury secretary concurred and saw to it that as a condition for the third drawdown Chrysler had to sell off its fleet. To make sure that the government's resolve did not flag under the Reagan administration, Brian Freeman exploited his links with a well-placed reporter. "I told him about the airplanes, and he wrote an article," Freeman recalled. "It had everything. The day it came out I got a message from [G. William] Miller saying he liked my story, and I started getting pissed-off calls from the company; they knew where it came from."[100]

Chrysler's Wendell Larsen had a different perspective. Mary Iacocca, the chairman's wife of nearly three decades, was in Florida struggling with the severe diabetes that was to conquer her within a few years. Most of Iacocca's trips that the government deemed wasteful were "to see Mary at the hospital when the doctors said she was in trouble, or to pick up his daughter at her college in Vermont so she could go down with him," Larsen said in 1984, after he had left Chrysler. "On one of these trips Lee stopped off for an hour on the way back to see George Steinbrenner, down there for spring training with the Yankees. A sports photographer snapped a picture of the two of them at the dugout. The next day that picture was in *The Washington Post*, and when Bill Miller saw it, he went wild and swore he'd make us get rid of the airplanes. What people forget is that if you didn't do that—if you don't keep the chairman functioning—you couldn't run the company. We all did the same thing. The kind of time we were putting in, we used the planes—we used anything we could—to grab a little slack to keep our lives in order. . . . That's the kind of thing that pissed the government guys off. So they grounded us."[101]

"Iacocca thought that this was really doing him in," recalled Michael Driggs, the second board staff director. "He came at us directly; he called congressmen; he even called the White House. That was the only serious political pressure we ever faced."[102] But despite the howling from Highland Park, Donald Regan stuck to the terms of Miller's deal. The Reagan administration—reluctant to get involved in the loan guarantee program at all—would not reopen the conditions imposed January 19. Chrysler had to sell off the planes.

The day the third infusion of government-backed money arrived, Chrysler reported its 1980 financial results: The loss was $1.71 billion—an unprecedented financial catastrophe, but no worse than had been expected. (The loss for the final three months, $235 million, was the smallest deficit for any quarter of 1980.) The year 1980 had been by far the worst in history for the U.S. auto industry. General Motors, breaking a string of profitable years that had run unbroken from 1921, lost $763 million in 1980. Ford lost $1.5 billion, almost matching Chrysler's record.

VI

CHRYSLER REDUX

1.

Donald Regan, Miller's replacement as treasury secretary, adopted a posture of *laisser-aller* on the Chrysler rescue. The Reagan administration would not seek to dismantle the program. But no official above the deputy assistant level would devote much time to it, and most of the loan board's functions were soon delegated to civil service staffers. Briefing the press after the February loan board meeting that locked up the $400 million in guaranteed loans, Secretary Regan made it clear that despite the $300 million in guarantee authority remaining, the new administration was not eager to supervise yet another drawdown. "We will have to pause, if Chrysler ever does come back for that $300 million," he warned, "in order to study the situation a lot more closely than we have for this particular one. The decision on this one was made by the last administration. All we had to do on this one was to see that the conditions that had been set down on January 19 had actually been met. On the next one we'll go into much more study."[1] That was in early 1981. There would not be another loan board meeting until the summer of 1983.[2]

In the eyes of most observers outside Chrysler's executive offices, hopes for the firm's long-term survival hinged on merger with a stronger company. The Salomon Brothers team was still seeking suitors. Speculation centered on firms that were already associated with Chrysler, principally Mitsubishi—by then the source of several of Chrysler's subcompacts—and Peugeot, which had bought most of Chrysler Europe. But analyst Arvid Jouppi doubted that either a French or a Japanese connection was in the cards. "Had there been a reason to create a business partnership it already would have happened. It's like the girl next door; they've known each other for years."[3] Another analyst, David Healy, commented, "I find it hard to conceive of Chrysler going on much longer. Whether any of these companies would want to merge with Chrysler now is open to question." Healy, who anticipated a fairly prompt bankruptcy filing from Highland Park, reasoned, "Why take all of Chrysler if they can get the parts they want" at liquidation?[4]

One scenario that had long been in the background was merger with an American car company. Rumors had been circulating for months about negotiations with Ford, but many observers were still startled when in mid-April 1981 Ford headquarters released a statement: "As a result of an approach to Ford by intermediaries acting on behalf of Chrysler, the Ford Motor Company's board of directors considered a possible merger or other similar arrangement with Chrysler." Ford rejected the advance as "not being in the best interest of Ford or its stockholders."[5] Despite some speculation that the proposal had been largely pro forma, to satisfy Treasury pressure to seek a merger, Chrysler's bid was apparently serious. "I felt that Ford in North America was in deep shit, and so were we," Iacocca explained in 1983. "The Japanese and GM were ending up with it all. . . . We put together a paper to them to consider the benefits of merger. I asked people—[Peter] Rodino [chairman of the House Judiciary Committee] and others on the Senate Judiciary Committee—'What about it? Under the failing firm doctrine [of the antitrust laws], what do you think?' So they said, 'Yeah, I imagine that the odds are pretty good that we'd let you and Ford merge. This would be unthinkable in any other period in our history or maybe in the future.' So we thought, well, if that hurdle was pretty well cleared, what did we have to offer and what did they have? We had a front-wheel-drive program, and they had nothing; they were three years late. Their strengths were our weaknesses and vice versa. I said, you know, if we could merge this in some way and build power trains and do like GM, put different grilles on, Alfred Sloan would turn over in his grave because we'd have four divisions against his five. They would wake up the next morning and pass out because we would just have become a General Motors with one stroke of the pen."[6]

But Ford wasn't interested. Many Detroit observers felt that the personal animosity between Henry Ford and Lee Iacocca was what made the union impossible. A Chrysler official, anxious to dampen press attention to the spurned proposal, said, "There is no deal with Ford and there are no deals on the front burner; the only difference between this and other inquiries we have made is that Ford felt constrained to put out a press release."[7]

On July 22 Chrysler messengers delivered bottles of black ink to the congressmen who had championed the Loan Guarantee Act: Chrysler actually had made money in the second quarter of 1981. It was only a speck of black ink—$12 million for the three months. Nobody thought it meant that the company was home free or even that it would come close to breaking even for the whole of 1981. But it was a profit, the first in more than two years. Iacocca trumpeted the news. "Chrysler has fought its way back to profitability, and everyone associated with this company has reason to be proud. . . . If we had earned a profit during booming economic conditions, it would have been remarkable. To accomplish that goal in the worst automotive recession ever is historic."[8]

But many industry analysts remained skeptical. Warned Peter Zaglio, a vice-president of Lehman Brothers: "It is very difficult for Chrysler to be consistently profitable because it's almost impossible to make money on small cars manufactured in North America." Harvey Heinbach, an auto analyst at Merrill Lynch, was even more dubious: "The main point is that they are not viable long-term. They can't service their huge amount of debt and develop enough new products to meet the competition."[9] By the end of the year, some of the skepticism seemed well founded. For all of 1981 the firm posted a loss from continuing operations of more than half a billion dollars—better than the previous year's $1.7 billion loss but still a staggering cash drain (see Appendix A, Figure 15A). Even if Chrysler was on the way up, it still had a very long climb ahead.

The losses for 1981 were not unexpected. But what had not been scheduled was a harrowing autumn cash crunch that brought the firm to the brink yet again. An automobile company's cash normally dwindles in the late summer—when sales slacken and launch costs rise—then swells again as the new-model cars hit showrooms. But in 1981 Chrysler inadvertently compounded this changeover crunch when, hungry for cash, it raised prices sharply on its 1982 models only to see Ford and GM post smaller increases. Then, when Chrysler announced it would reduce its prices soon, dealers were confused over what price they'd pay if they ordered immediately. The dealers decided to wait until the pricing mess was sorted out. Shipments nearly ceased, and Chrysler's cash dried up.

Chrysler executives discreetly tested the water in Washington: Would the Reagan administration be willing to issue the remaining $300 million in guarantees? The loan board staff would make no promises. "The message was 'If you put in for the three hundred million dollars, consider it betting the company,'" according to one government official.[10] Mindful of the havoc another public battle for government help would wreak on sales—even if the money came through—Iacocca decided against it. Instead, Chrysler launched what company officials called the internal drawdown. Executives intensified the search for production economies. A cash task force ferreted out ways to cut down on cash needs. Inventories were tightened. The accounts receivable process was streamlined. Procurement policies were revised with an eye to paring costs still further. "We simply began running the company differently," one official related. "There would be regular cash meetings—weekly, sometimes daily—with the operating guys. 'What can you do? And you? What about you? Go turn something into cash.'"[11]

Through it all the company just barely managed to stay liquid. One day in early November its cash balance brushed $1 million. "That's against an average daily expenditure of $50 million," Steve Miller explained after the crunch was safely past. "So we were kind of broke without telling anybody, and we went for a period of about sixty days with less than ten million dollars as a cushion. That was very tense because we couldn't go public with our problem. Otherwise, the sale of cars would stop again."[12]

The continuing efforts to trim costs, however drastic, were not enough. Chrysler decided it had to sell off one more major asset. Top managers debated whether it was to be the finance company, the New Process Gear operation, or the defense division. "I reluctantly came to the conclusion that it was a split house in the company, and you get paid for doing this," Iacocca related. "I had to be a tie breaker. I decided to sell the tank division. . . . At sixty million dollars [in profits] a year we hated to give it up, but it would never be the mainstream of our business. We were never going to try to be a defense contractor. Maybe that's a strategic mistake. I look back on it now, and if I knew that Reagan was going to be in there spending three hundred billion dollars a year, I should probably have gotten into the only business Japan can't get into."[13] The firm asked Lehman Brothers to find a buyer for Chrysler Defense. In February 1982 General Dynamics took the tank division for around $340 million—a sum that astonished observers, since most of the tank-making assets actually were owned by the government and only managed by Chrysler. Chrysler Defense was less a company than a license to do business with the Pentagon.

2.

The Reagan administration wanted to keep its distance from the Chrysler program. In part this was because Chrysler's failure appeared imminent through much of 1981, and the loan guarantees seemed sure to be seen as a shameful waste of public money. But probably more important was the grating dissonance between the Chrysler rescue and the free-market ideology that Ronald Reagan and his chief aides cherished. While still a Michigan congressman, David Stockman, now the President's budget director, had been among the most vehement opponents of the Loan Guarantee Act; in fact, his vigorous denunciations of the rescue had helped win him the top budget job. That the government was backing Chrysler's debt was an affront; that a team of bureaucrats in Reagan's own Treasury Department continued to monitor Chrysler's operations was an embarrassment. The administration would not abolish the program, but neither would it adopt it. "We never met one time in thirty months, and that really drove us nuts," Iacocca said in a late 1983 interview. "You can't run a government saying Coolidge or somebody put the program in and you don't like it."[14]

The repugnance with which the Reagan team contemplated the Chrysler rescue obscures a curious fact: Two initiatives by the new administration funneled to the troubled firm public subsidies that were probably larger, albeit far less overt, than the subsidies embodied in the loan guarantees.*

The first of the Reagan administration's subsidies to Chrysler

---

*The precise subsidy embedded in the guaranteed loans is difficult to quantify. It depends on four factors: (1) the amount of loans outstanding, which was never more than $1.2 billion; (2) the probability that the firm would collapse, or default, or otherwise force the government to pay off the noteholders; (3) the liquidation value of Chrysler's assets; and (4) the probability that the government would be able to exercise its claim on those assets. Depending on how one guesses about the uncertainties—factors two, three, and four—the subsidy could range from the whole $1.2 billion down to zero. Our interviews with participants persuade us that the government's claim on Chrysler's assets was quite firm, and their value would approach, and probably exceed, the amount of the guaranteed loans. Even if one judged Chrysler's survival to be a fifty-fifty proposition, the financial subsidy should probably be valued at something less than $100 million.

Formally, the value of a loan guarantee G follows the equation:
$$\tfrac{1}{2} \, o^2 v^2 G_{vv} + (rV - P)G_v - G_t - rG = 0$$
where V is the firm's total asset value and P is total claims on the firm. A rich theoretical literature exists on valuing loan guarantees (see, in particular, Philip Jones and Scott Mason, "Valuation of Loan Guarantees," *Journal of Banking and Finance*, 4 [1980]). We do not attempt to use this equation or its derivatives to estimate the government's risk mostly because the numbers hinge on the value of o, the variance of the return on the firm's assets. This parameter is tricky; the range of plausible values for o in Chrysler's case is broad, and it matters a good deal which we choose. Thus we opt for the less precise formulation based on informed guesses about the probability of default.

was a part of the enormous bundle of tax cuts known as the Economic Recovery Tax Act of 1981. Embedded in the legislation was something called safe-harbor leasing. In the past, money-losing firms could not take advantage of accelerated depreciation allowances and investment tax credits for the simple reason that they had no taxable income. They could "bank" them for the future when they might make money, but this was small consolation to firms that might well not survive that long. (Recall that Chrysler had first come to Washington in 1979 with a scheme to get a cash advance on future tax benefits.) There was a second alternative. Money-losing companies could sell and promptly lease back their plant and equipment to more profitable companies, which *could* use the tax benefits. There was a great deal of money to be made by both parties to these financial shuffles. But this paper transaction was permitted only if it could be shown to have an economic justification apart from the tax advantage. The Reagan administration wanted to loosen requirements so that *any* money-losing firm could have a legal safe harbor for such deals; it accomplished this in the 1981 legislation.

One remaining hitch was that many potential buyers were reluctant to negotiate sale-leaseback shuffles with sickly companies like Chrysler. They feared that if the seller of the tax benefits subsequently went bankrupt, the benefits would be lost as secured creditors seized back the leased plant and equipment. Chrysler sought a change in the rules. Its advocates in Treasury asked the Internal Revenue Service to allow money-losing companies to clear tax-leasing deals in advance with their secured creditors, so that the firms that purchased the equipment could be confident that the tax benefits would remain even in bankruptcy. The IRS—itself a part of the Treasury Department—complied with uncharacteristic speed. On November 10, just two weeks after Chrysler had made the request, the administration announced a new tax rule that opened the way for the firm to sell off its tax benefits.

Less than a week later Chrysler announced a deal with the General Electric Credit Corporation (GE's finance subsidiary) which transferred to GE tax benefits on $100 million worth of Chrysler equipment. Chrysler got $26 million; the cost to the public was rather more than this since General Electric as well as the investment bankers who engineered the swap obviously had to net something on the deal.[15] Chrysler would reap about $38.4 million from safe-harbor leased transactions in 1981, $10.1 million in 1982, and $19.8 million in 1983.[16] Unlike the guaranteed loans, these sums would never have to be paid back, and they came without strings.

In short, Chrysler got from the Reagan administration more than $68 million in the kind of quiet, clean tax subsidy it had originally asked for in 1979. But the Reagan administration's other intervention was by far the more important to Chrysler.

Since 1978 the U.S. auto industry had been lobbying for protection from Japanese imports. Ford had led the crusade, warning that without relief it would be compelled to abandon entirely its American operations. Japan's cost edge of $1,000 to $1,500 per car was an unfair advantage based on "slave labor," in the phrase of one Ford executive.[17] The Ford solution: a cap on Japanese imports of a million cars a year, roughly half the then-current rate. General Motors and Chrysler joined the campaign. With the United Auto Workers signed on, the coalition was formidable. As a candidate for President, Ronald Reagan had posed before a Detroit Chrysler plant in the fall of 1980 and proclaimed, "I think the government has a responsibility that it's shirked so far. And it's a place government can be legitimately involved, and that is to convince Japan that in one way or another, and for their own best interest, the deluge of their cars into the U.S. must be slowed while our industry gets back on its feet."[18]

By February 1981, a month after Reagan had taken office, the Japanese had captured nearly a quarter of the U.S. auto market (all other imports claimed 5 percent; see Appendix A, Figures 16A-1, 16A-2). A Commerce Department report prepared for the new President warned that continuing Japanese penetration of the U.S. market would pose a grave threat to the U.S. auto industry. In the absence of import restraints, "Chrysler could disappear."[19] Drew Lewis, Reagan's new secretary of transportation, bluntly told reporters that the level of Japanese imports was too high.[20]

Republican Senator John Danforth of Missouri, a major auto-producing state, promptly introduced legislation requiring a reduction in Japanese imports to 1.6 million cars a year. His intent was to incite the new administration to action. The strategy was well conceived: White House political operatives viewed with distaste the prospect of vetoing the Danforth bill and thus seeming to abandon the American automobile industry. At a Cabinet meeting in March 1981, Drew Lewis made the case for a quota. He was backed by Malcolm Baldrige, the secretary of commerce, and Raymond Donovan, the secretary of labor. But the supply-siders at the Treasury Department, along with David Stockman at the Office of Management and Budget (OMB), protested. The OMB proposed as a substitute to pare back federal regulations enough to save automakers as much as $5 billion over three years. But the protectionists feared this would not be enough. Finally, Edwin Meese, the White House counselor, and James Baker III, Ronald Reagan's chief of staff, worked out a compromise: The restraints would be imposed by the Japanese themselves. There would be no formal trade action, no demands, no bilateral negotiations, and no technical violation of international trade law. The White House simply would signal to the Japanese that they must restrain their auto shipments.

Officials in Japan balked at their assigned role. The Japanese government was reluctant to impose quotas on its exporters without an open and specific demand from the Americans. But as the Danforth bill gained momentum in Congress, the Japanese grew more receptive. William Brock, the administration's trade representative, embarked to counsel the Japanese. According to an aide, "[Brock] advised them on the political acceptability in the United States of various Japanese proposals. . . . [H]e was able to let them know whether he felt that [a specific level of restraint] would put off Danforth and others. The implementation of it was left to the Japanese."[21] On April 30, 1981, Japan's Ministry of International Trade and Industry (MITI) announced that it was imposing a limit of 1.68 million units on auto exports to the United States for the year beginning on April 1, 1981. In the next year the growth of Japanese imports would be limited to 16.5 percent of the total expansion of the market.

American reactions were mixed. Douglas Fraser called the restrictions a "modest but positive step." Senator Danforth said the quotas were "a step in the right direction . . . although personally I think that greater concessions should have been made." But a *New York Times* editorial scored the agreement: "President Reagan, being a champion of the free market and foe of inflation, 'volunteered' to inform the Japanese of the sad plight of the American auto industry. And now the Japanese have responded by 'volunteering' to limit their American sales. . . . All that remains is for the American consumers to volunteer to pay a billion dollars more for the cars they buy this year." The quotas let U.S. automakers raise prices without losing sales. This amounted to an automatic tax on both imported and domestic cars for the benefit of U.S. auto companies. By the third year of the restraints American consumers were paying as much as $5 billion a year in higher prices for cars than they would have paid without the quotas.[22] But unlike the Chrysler loan guarantees, this subsidy for the U.S. auto industry was unconditional: Nothing was asked in return from the automakers, their banks, their suppliers, or their employees.

Chrysler's shaky recovery gained stability in the spring of 1982. Once the money from the sale of the tank division was safely in the company's hands, its image with suppliers improved dramatically. And as its suppliers gained confidence, they relaxed their terms. "We got the cash, and all of a sudden I was awash in cash," Iacocca recalled. "I said, 'Where the hell is all this cash coming from?' They told me, 'We aren't paying the bills right away anymore; we're back to a normal forty days instead of twenty.' I never really planned it that way. I didn't think we could get the supplier who thought we were going bankrupt to change his attitude that quick."[23]

By the end of March 1982 Chrysler held $900 million in cash and marketable securities.[24] First-quarter profits came to $150 million. The quarterly gain was entirely due to the tank division sale—ongoing operations showed a $90 million loss—but the next three months saw a solid operating profit of $107 million. This was the first time in five years that Chrysler had posted net earnings for two quarters running. A jubilant Iacocca revealed the second-quarter gain to the press: "No sale of assets this time, no building of stocks, and, I might add, no help from the national economy. And the first of you guys out there that writes that that profit was in line with what most Wall Street analysts had estimated, I'm going to hit you right in the nose, okay?"[25]

The full-year results for 1982 were less gratifying: an operating loss of $70 million (see Appendix A, Figure 17A). But money from the Chrysler Defense sale offset the operating deficit to yield a net profit of $170 million during a year of deep recession. American carmakers sold only 5.8 million autos in 1982, the fewest in twenty-one years. Chrysler's share of the market, however, inched upward toward 10 percent. Had it not been for a five-week strike at Chrysler's Canadian plants at the end of the year, an operating profit would have been within reach.

There was no secret to the automaker's convalescence: Safe-harbor leasing and the quotas on Japanese cars had helped substantially. But most important, Chrysler's cost-cutting campaign was beginning to pay off. A Chrysler assembly line worker now earned $9.07 an hour, compared to roughly $11.70 at Ford and General Motors. (Chrysler's much larger pension fund burden—one pensioner for every employee still at work—reduced the net advantage over its rivals to $1.40 an hour.) What was more, Chrysler, long the least integrated of the Big Three, now was buying an even higher proportion of its parts from outside suppliers. It had closed many of its own component plants and was now contracting for parts with separate firms, many of them paying much lower wages. "We're integrated at about the same level that Toyota is," president Harold Sperlich explained in 1983. "Ford makes about fifty or fifty-five percent of its parts, and GM makes seventy percent. . . . Now we look at what's happening to UAW wages and the costs of UAW labor, and one of our secret weapons is the fact that seventy percent of the Chrysler parts come in from suppliers, most of whom are located in non-UAW plants. We've been moving our suppliers into right to work states. Most of them are paying not much more per hour than the Japanese are in wages."[26] Chrysler's own overhead was way down. Since 1978 the firm had pared its payroll by half and had closed one plant out of every three (see Appendix A, Figure 18A).

3.

When Chrysler's decline had accelerated into a vicious downward spiral in 1979, it had taken an act of Congress, a prodigious array of talent, and a staggering amount of organizational work to lighten the burden of claims that the stricken firm had to bear. Now as the company recovered, many of those same claims were being reasserted. The parties that had sacrificed to save Chrysler were understandably eager to recoup their losses. But—in a reprise of the wrangle over allocating the burden of renewal—a "fair" allotment of the benefit was elusive. Each party was keenly mindful of its own contribution to the turnaround but less aware of the roles others had played. As Chrysler gained a modest degree of financial slack, each set of constituents expected to be compensated for the lean years. These expectations intensified as the company, anxious to burnish its public image, trumpeted its recovery. The problem was the mirror image of 1979. Then the issue had been sharing pain; now it was sharing the gains of recovery. Each party expected its due. Yet there was no obvious way to divide the rewards. The firm was feebler than it appeared. But every dollar of spare cash was claimed by several parties, each of whom felt it had a right to it. The peril was that the sudden accumulation of claims would smother the automaker.

As the firm's fortunes perceptibly improved, Chrysler's unionized workers grew less content with their side of the deal. Each worker had forgone roughly $14,500 in wages and benefits, relative to what he would have collected under a pattern contract. In return, each had received around sixty shares of Chrysler stock—held in trust until death or retirement—under the employee stock ownership plan required by Congress.* By the terms of the separate profit-sharing plan negotiated in 1981, the company had agreed to give its workers stock valued at 15 percent of whatever profits the company achieved beyond a minimum return on net worth. But the profit-sharing plan was not to go into effect until Chrysler had earned $100 million for a full year, and it was to expire in September 1983.

Rank-and-file UAW members were irritated by raises bestowed on many Chrysler executives in the spring of 1981, only a few months after the union, at the government's insistence, had agreed to the biggest round of sacrifice. Lee Iacocca's annual pay was raised, retroactively, to $324,000. (When he came to Chrysler, he had agreed to accept $1 a year until the company became profitable again; he now promised to donate his retroactive salary to charity.) Paul Bergmoser, the company president, also received a retroactive salary increase to make up for previous pay cuts. Two levels of Chrysler managers were awarded new perquisites of cars, fuel, and insurance.

The UAW's Marc Stepp fired off an angry letter to Iacocca. When the union agreed to wage concessions, Chrysler had promised that its nonunion employees would not enjoy "any changes in compensation, benefits and other conditions of employment . . . more favorable" than the deal union employees accepted. Now, Stepp said, Chrysler was breaking that agreement. The 1982 round of collective bargaining would be difficult, he warned: "Certainly the granting of retroactive adjustments for the two top officers of the Corporation has legitimately raised demands by the membership for similar retroactivity or recovery." The letter went on:

Many of our Local Union leaders, those who had recommended ratification of the concessions, are now being defeated in re-election bids by a membership who feels that they have been betrayed. We had sensed that there was a new spirit of cooperation developing between the workers and management because of the most difficult times we have been through together. We had hoped we could have charted a new non-adversarial direction in labor-management relations in North America. . . . You have made a grievous mistake and perpetrated a serious injustice against the Chrysler workers. This breach of good faith on the part of the Corporation could result in long-term damage to our relationship.[28]

*By mid-1984 the plan would render each full participant 179 shares of stock worth $4,500.[27]

In a little publicized but significant concession the UAW leadership had agreed earlier not to authorize locals to strike Chrysler plants in response to purely local grievances. A few weeks after Chrysler had announced its executive pay and benefit increases, the union leaders ended this moratorium.[29]

As the 1982 contract negotiations approached, the union pushed the theme of recovery. It would seek to restore cost of living allowance payments and to narrow the $2.68 hourly pay gap between Chrysler and the other automakers. But the union leaders did not threaten a strike. "It would be ridiculous if we were driven to strike," said Stepp. "We would all be ashamed of ourselves, on both sides. We don't intend to commit economic suicide."[30] Nevertheless, Douglas Fraser was adamant on at least one point: "There will be absolutely no more concessions at Chrysler. None."[31]

Chrysler sought two things in the 1982 contract. First, it wanted to continue to hold down wage costs in order to avoid swamping the newly buoyant firm. It also wanted to limit the cost of health care benefits.

Because an unusually heavy proportion of covered workers were retired or furloughed, the firm's health care costs ran about $3.50 an hour per active worker. (Ford and GM paid around $2.50 an hour.) In fact, Chrysler's radical shrinkage since 1978 meant that almost half the people who depended on the company health plan were retirees and their spouses or survivors. In 1982 the average American company was paying about $1,250 per year in health insurance premiums for each active worker; Chrysler was paying close to $6,000.[32] Adding the health plan costs to the Medicare payroll taxes that Chrysler and its suppliers paid, total medical benefits accounted for about 10 percent of the sticker price of a Plymouth Horizon in 1982.

But health insurance, the prized achievement of decades of struggle, was sacred to the union. During the 1970's the company had conceded better health benefits with each contract, Iacocca later explained, "because we were a golden goose business. We were rich and fat and sloppy and lazy. The costs weren't so great then, and as long as I was making a ton of money, it didn't matter to me."[33] By the late 1970's, company-paid benefits covered all hospital and testing costs and most of the costs of outpatient dental, psychiatric, vision, and hearing care for active and retired workers and their dependents. For retirees and their spouses, the insurance paid nearly everything that Medicare did not—up to two years of convalescent care in a nursing home and all charges above $3 on prescription drugs. Workers who were laid off got full benefits for a year. "We have the best coverage in the country except maybe for the United States Congress," said Douglas Fraser.[34] But this coverage was hugely expensive. Hospitals were reimbursed for all their "customary and usual" costs, and doctors were paid on a fee-for-service basis. The more the hospitals spent and the more services the doctors performed, the more they were paid. No one had any interest in limiting costs. On the contrary, the pressures were all in the other direction. In reviewing its health costs in 1982, for example, Chrysler discovered that forty-one employees had been admitted to one hospital during the preceding year for lower-back pain. Most had received electromyograms, an elaborate test for disk disease. All the tests had been negative. None of the forty-one Chrysler patients had undergone surgery. The average stay was more than ten days. The average cost was more than $3,000. This sample, if not wholly typical, was suggestive. "What you have," Iacocca lamented, "is a huge vested interest. The doctors and the hospitals say this is a profession, this isn't a supplier, and you keep your cotton-picking hands off. If I want to buy steel, I can go to the lowest seller, but in health, the buyer-seller relationship doesn't exist. Yet, in fact, Blue Cross/Blue Shield is my biggest supplier."[35] Even during Chrysler's darkest days, health benefits remained untouchable.

Following an all-night session between company and union bargainers, a tentative accord was announced in September 1982. Cost of living benefits would be restored, and a new profit-based bonus system would be set up on top of the employee stock ownership plan begun in 1980 and the profit-sharing plan inaugurated as part of the 1981 deal. But there was to be no up front pay raise. Except for the cost of living adjustment, raises would be contingent on profits—that is, they would not be the rigid "productivity improvement" increases that by tradition had ratcheted up UAW wages in good times and bad. Chrysler workers, who had not had a wage increase since March 1981, would have to wait for a raise until December, when a cost of living adjustment was due. "We bargained with what the company could afford to do," said Chrysler's Harold Sperlich. "The worker is hurting, and the pain is real. But we're in no position to grant wage increases."[36]

The union's bargaining committee also agreed to a sweeping program of health care cost controls designed to save Chrysler $10 million by the end of 1983. Workers could still pick their own doctors and hospitals. But health care providers would have to meet tougher standards, and limits would be set on the cost of elective surgery, laboratory testing, and prescription drugs. A second opinion would be required before surgery.

Douglas Fraser and Marc Stepp knew that contrary to UAW tradition, ratification this time would be anything but automatic. Chrysler workers were getting restless. For two years they had been living with lower pay, leaner benefits, and fewer days off than their neighbors working for Ford and General Motors. Now Chrysler was showing signs of revival. A beaming, expansive Lee Iacocca appeared on television proclaiming the company's newfound health. Union members had heard about the restored salaries and perquisites for Chrysler executives. Douglas Fraser's membership on Chrysler's board of directors had given the union unprecedented access to the company books, and the leadership knew that the firm's recovery was precarious. But Chrysler's ballooning cash reserves and the chairman's calculated public crowing made it hard to convey this convincingly to the membership. Chrysler's rank and file felt they deserved some meaningful recompense for their years of sacrifice, and they were disinclined to wait. "Lee Iacocca is talking to the dealers and bankers and everybody," Fraser recalled, "and he's painting this glowing picture. And I told him, I says, 'Lee, you're getting the negotiations in trouble. You're speaking with forked tongue here. I understand what you're saying and why you're saying it, but you better explain to our committee. I'm not going to try to relay it for you. You've got to do it directly.' And he did. He came over and got up on that podium there. Our whole committee was there, and he just said, 'You know, things are not nearly as good as you've been hearing.' "[37]

The UAW's 250-member Chrysler Council was barely convinced. It recommended ratification of the September 1982 contract, but by a narrow margin. "It doesn't look good," said one Detroit area council delegate. "The bad thing was that all the big locals voted against it."[38] Union militants, like Bob Weissman, president of Local 122 at Chrysler's Twinsburg, Ohio, stamping plant, were opposed from the start. "No amount of selling is going to make a difference," Weissman warned.[39]

He was right. The contract was rejected by almost 70 percent of the rank and file—the first major contract to be voted down in UAW history. Marc Stepp attributed the loss to Iacocca's boosterism. "We were telling the membership that the profit sharing was a good deal, the best we could get from a company that was still in trouble," the UAW Chrysler chief said in 1984. "And here's Iacocca bragging all over the country that Chrysler's got a billion dollars. Now they needed that billion dollars for development and engineering and so on, fair enough, but the workers didn't give a damn about that. They see a man running all over the place talking about how healthy his company is, they figure that company can afford a little increase for them after so long without it. His mouth got us in trouble on that ratification vote."[40]

Douglas Fraser voluntarily suspended his membership on the Chrysler board of directors until the labor situation stabilized. Desperate to avoid a strike, Fraser and Stepp arranged for a referendum. A carefully worded ballot asked workers to choose between an immediate strike and a new round of negotiations. Most union members voted to continue working until a revised agreement was reached. But Chrysler's 10,000 employees across the river in Ontario refused to wait. These were the same workers who had declined to share in the 1980 round of concessions and had resisted the 1981 round, only to be outvoted. They also had objected more vigorously than the average Detroit worker to the original 1982 contract. Canadian unionists' normal militancy was now bolstered by the economics of the situation. The cheap Canadian dollar and government-subsidized health benefits lowered Chrysler's Canadian labor costs by nearly $7 an hour, they argued, while Canada's inflation was running at twice the U.S. rate, eroding real wages faster than in the United States. The Canadian workers struck.[41]

The strike instantly idled 2,400 U.S. workers, who made the components for cars and trucks assembled in Canada. Lost production cost the company $15 million. The strike also strained union relationships across the border. One member of the UAW's Chrysler bargaining committee said, "I'd like to take them [Canadian workers] by the head and throw them in the Detroit River."[42] But by the end of December 1982 company and union bargainers reached agreement on a new contract that offered Chrysler workers an immediate pay increase of, on average, seventy-five cents an hour in the United States, and $1.15 in Canada. In return, Chrysler workers gave up the profit-sharing plan arranged in 1981. The contract was scheduled to expire in January 1984.

4.

Chrysler's creditors had also endured two rounds of concessions. In 1980 they had converted $907 million in short-term credits into long-term loans, delayed or canceled some interest, and accepted a subordinate position to the government in the event of bankruptcy.

In return, Chrysler had given them 10.6 million warrants, as well as securing their much larger loans to Chrysler Financial. The following year the creditors had surrendered $1.3 billion in debt for $190 million in cash and preferred stock with a face value of $1.1 billion. Most creditors had assumed at the time that the preferred stock and the warrants—the values of which rose and fell in step with the firm's common stock—were close to worthless. By late 1982 this early assessment was manifestly mistaken. The stock began the year at $3.50; it was $18.50 by year-end (see Appendix A, Figure 19A).

Chrysler proposed that the banks exchange the preferred stock for a chunk of its booming common stock. The financial logic behind this proposal was convoluted but sound. The company would eventually need to return to the private capital market. To do this, it first would have to pay off its government-guaranteed loans. "It's very difficult to get a good credit rating and borrow money with government oversight and liens on all your property," one Wall Street analyst noted.[43] Once these loans had been retired, Chrysler would no longer be barred from paying dividends. This was the rub, because the company had pledged to pay dividends on the preferred stock just as soon as the government allowed it to. The upshot was that once the guaranteed loans had been paid off, just servicing the preferred stock, including a large chunk of dividends that had accumulated while the automaker was blocked from paying off any equity owner, would become a major drain on Chrysler's cash.

Chrysler and its creditors met on December 9, 1982, and Steve Miller told the bankers, "The last time I came to you there were forty thousand jobs on the line; this time there's only one—mine." After making the case for the new preferred-for-common stock swap, Miller left the room. A few minutes later he was summoned back in and handed a cigar: The deal was on. The creditors would surrender $1.1 billion in preferred stock—and the 10.6 million warrants—in return for around 35 million shares of Chrysler common.[44]

The bankers went along in part because they feared it could be many years before they would collect the full face value of the preferred. "If they had waited until after they paid back the guaranteed loans," one banker later explained, "Chrysler would have had to redeem the preferred out of their own pocket. In the stock deal, they didn't have to give us any cash. We got cash, but we got it from the market. They didn't have to spend a dime to get that monkey off their back."[45] Banks that cashed in their new

Chrysler common stock immediately netted about sixty cents for each dollar they had originally lent Chrysler; a few that held on to the stock as it rose came out substantially better than whole.[46]

The 35 million new shares represented a 44 percent increase in the amount of Chrysler common stock outstanding. The deal was a gamble. Chrysler hoped that the advantages of paying off the preferred would outweigh any ill effects from diluting the common stock. The gamble appeared to pay off; Chrysler's stock price continued to climb. Investors' hopes for the resurgent firm, bolstered, perhaps, by the recapitalization itself, overcame any potential concern about the amount of new common stock suddenly available.*

In the summer of 1983 Chrysler did something nobody could have anticipated two years earlier: It paid back all $1.2 billion in federally guaranteed loans. Lee Iacocca announced the repayment at a ceremony at Washington's National Press Club. Representatives of all of Chrysler's constituent groups attended to accept the chairman's thanks and hear him declare that the repayment would "tell the financial community, but especially the American car buyer, that we are here to stay and have the strength to compete with anybody in the world. But probably even more important than that, I think it shows that the system can work if everybody pulls together. We just got everyone working together. We cooperated; we fought for each other; we sacrificed equally. In a way maybe it was social democracy at its best. And we had help from all levels of government—Capitol Hill, the White House, the State House, and City Hall. And my question is simply this: What is so wrong with that?"[47]

Even after the preferred stock and the guaranteed notes both had been retired, there was still one major financial claim against Chrysler: the 14.4 million warrants held by the federal government. Each warrant conferred the right to buy a share of Chrysler common for $13.

The Treasury had collected the warrants in 1980 so that if the rescue were actually to succeed, Chrysler's stockholders would have to share some of the gain with the public. The banks also had received warrants—10.6 million of them—as part of the first restructuring but willingly traded them in for common shares early in 1983. When the government and the banks put the warrants in their vaults, Chrysler's stock was languishing at around $6 per

*Chrysler was officially readmitted to the capital market in June 1984, when fifty-seven U.S. and foreign banks eagerly signed on with a $1.1 billion credit syndicate headed by Manufacturers Hanover.

share. "The warrants were a complete throwaway," according to one banker. "The idea that they would be really valuable was almost completely foreign. 'Hey, how many Chrysler warrants do you want—a million? Sure. Have some more, what do you say? Ten million? Why not? Who cares? It's a joke; give them what they want.' "[48]

But the government had taken the warrants altogether seriously. "I thought we ought to grab a piece of the upside as a disincentive to the next bailout and because it was only fair," Brian Freeman explained in 1984. "But that idea didn't get too far until one day when Bill Miller got mad at Chrysler, heard I had a warrant proposal floating around, and called me in to tell him what it was about. As it happened, the day before was when the banks had made their demand for warrants. Miller decided if the banks got them, we should, too."[49]

Now, three years after that first restructuring, Chrysler's stock was rising toward $30 a share, and the government's warrants were increasingly valuable. If the Treasury exercised the warrants —bought a huge chunk of Chrysler stock at less than half the market price—the government stood to earn millions of dollars. The prospect made Chrysler queasy. It would have to issue 14.4 million new shares of stock to cover the warrants, thereby diluting existing equity by another 12 percent. This would likely depress the price of the shares already outstanding. The company decided to do something about the warrants.

Early in May 1983 Chrysler tried a direct approach. It simply asked the government to surrender the securities, on the ground that paying back the guaranteed notes early had terminated the financial ties between the firm and the Treasury. The request was summarily denied. Lee Iacocca was outraged. "It doesn't meet the test of fairness, or even decency. You can argue about the technicalities, but the operative line is that when you pay back a loan of that size seven years ahead of schedule, you often renegotiate the terms because there is no risk left."[50] Later, though, Iacocca conceded that the request had been impolitic: "We made one hell of a mistake. One of our guys went down and said, 'How about giving them back for nothing?' He wrote a letter to that effect. They believed it. And they creamed us. . . . Once that leak took place, it looked like we were trying to screw the government."[51]

In July Chrysler tried a new tack. It offered to pay the government about $218 million for the warrants. But some Treasury officials believed that the securities were worth much more. The warrant's value had two components. One was a simple matter of arithmetic

—how much profit could be collected by exercising the warrant right away. If the market price for a share of Chrysler was, say, $18, while the warrant let the holder buy a share for $13, the direct profit on the warrant was $5. The second component of the warrant's value was more difficult to figure. This was the possibility that the price of a share of Chrysler would go a good deal higher before the warrants expired in 1990. Treasury's financial experts couldn't agree on how to value this speculative component; some thought that Chrysler's stock would continue to increase dramatically in value, while others thought that it had about reached its peak. Treasury officials ultimately decided that the only sure way to find out what the warrants were worth was to sell them on the open market. That way, at least, several speculators would be bidding on Chrysler's future, and the Treasury Department would simply sell the warrants to the purchaser who was willing to pay the best price. The loan board notified Chrysler that the warrants would be sold at auction to the highest bidder.[52]

Lee Iacocca was appalled at the prospect of seeing the warrants transferred to private hands and "flopping around in the market until 1990," as Chrysler executive Frederick Zuckerman put it.[53] So he decided that Chrysler would itself join in the bidding. It would be a tricky call. If Chrysler's price turned out to be lower than any other bid, the firm would lose control of 14.4 million shares of stock. On the other hand, if the Chrysler bid were much higher, the company would have squandered a lot of money. It was easy to calculate that the minimum price would be around $16 for each warrant since Chrysler's stock was then selling at nearly $29 a share and exercising a warrant immediately would yield a $16 profit. The question was how big a speculative premium to add. Steve Miller and David Schulte, the Salomon Brothers investment banker who was now advising the company, decided to set the premium at $5 and to add on another dime to make sure that there was no tie, thus making the total bid just over $21 per share. At 4:20 P.M. on September 19, just ten minutes ahead of a deadline set by the Treasury, a Salomon agent dropped the bid into a slot in a conference room door at the New York Federal Reserve Bank building. Chrysler won. Its bid was 93.4 cents per share more than the second-highest. "It was worth it," Miller said. "We were finally able to get rid of the damn stuff."[54]

Chrysler's $311.1 million payment was deposited in the Treasury Department's Miscellaneous Proceeds account. "I can't tell you how the money will be spent," said Warren Carter, a deputy assistant secretary, "but it will reduce the Federal deficit by $311.1 million."[55] Nineteen members of the House Banking Committee had a different idea. In a letter to President Reagan they urged that the proceeds be used to establish a fund for retraining unemployed auto workers. (Nothing came of the proposal.) Iacocca still retained his view that the stated purpose of the warrants—compensating the public for risk incurred—was bogus. The government, he reasoned, "never had anything at risk because they had the first lien on everything. Even under bankruptcy, the worst scenario, they'd always get their billion two back. So that warrant issue turned out to be a sordid affair. They made three hundred eleven million dollars. I told the President this gave him a little over twenty-five percent [interest on the loan], which is illegal, really. It's usury. In six states if you're paid over twenty-five for anything, you're Mafia."[56]

5.

In the spring of 1983, Chrysler assured the union that it would close no more plants. Instead, it was trying to decide which plants to open again. The St. Louis truck assembly plant, shut down in 1980, was reopened and fitted with the old dies used to make big rear-drive New Yorkers. The venerable full-size car was suddenly back in demand as fuel prices stabilized and started to decline. Less than two years after shutting or selling a third of its factories, Chrysler decided to buy Volkswagen's Sterling Heights plant. Stephan Sharf, Chrysler's executive vice-president for manufacturing, told a press briefing that the company's Detroit forge and axle plant, previously scheduled to close in late 1983, might actually remain open because of increased demand for large rear-wheel-drive cars. Some furloughed employees were coming back to work. "At Newark we don't have a single guy on layoff," Sharf declared. "We are hiring from the street. In Windsor we're hiring from the street. We have only one city [Detroit] where we still have a lot on lay-off. But we really don't know how many of the 20,000 or so on lay-off in Detroit are still out there [looking for work]. You can't think of the people that were affected by plant closings. You have to think about the people that were saved."[57]

But once again, the more loudly Chrysler celebrated its newfound prosperity, the higher it raised workers' hopes for a share in the wealth. In May 1983, when the company announced that it had sufficient cash to begin early repayment of its federally guaranteed debt, the UAW demanded that Chrysler reopen the labor contract signed six months previously and begin to negotiate new terms. It was only fair, UAW leaders contended; they reminded Chrysler managers that the union had granted a "reopener" in 1981, when the company was facing bankruptcy and the federal government would not guarantee additional loans unless the workers shaved their earnings. The employees had shared in the pain; now they wanted to share the benefits. Joseph Zappa, president of Local 212 and a leader of the bargaining committee, said, "Lee Iacocca could have taken $100 million of that money they repaid [on the guaranteed loans] and given our members a dollar an hour. He could have taken $200 million and given us two dollars. Instead, he's a multimillionaire and my members are still making less than they were getting two years ago. How could they say no to us when we gave in to them two times when they needed it? It's inconceivable that they would say no. It would be unconscionable."[58] According to a Wall Street analyst, "Every time Chrysler opens its mouth to brag, it shoots itself in the foot. In some ways they were a lot better off when they were pleading poverty."[59]

The prospect of an early 1984 strike haunted Chrysler. New models it had spent years preparing, including an innovative small van, were scheduled for a January 1984 launch. Iacocca calculated that a sixty-day strike would bankrupt the company. Even a short walkout could poison the launch of the new models. Chrysler agreed in July to reopen the contract. But the early negotiations got nowhere. The company offered its workers increases worth $1.42 an hour for a one-year pact. The union rejected the proposal, holding out for a two-year deal with a $2.42 total increase, to match wage levels at GM and Ford by the end of the contract period. Chrysler refused. According to Marc Stepp, the ill will generated by this standoff wiped out whatever remained of a sense of common cause the company and workers had come to share while bankruptcy loomed. "Our members are mad as hell," Stepp recounted. "Iacocca goes in August to introduce a car in St. Louis. Not only don't the workers come up to talk to him, but they've got a picket line and a handbill that cuts his ass. That really hurt him; it played havoc with his ego. He called Owen Bieber [new president of the UAW] and said, 'We've got to work something out.' Then Owen and I announced that we'd strike in January 1984, when the contract ended. Now that's rare—we never announce in advance when we're going to strike a company. So they invited us back to the bargaining table to keep that from happening."[60]

A new round of negotiations took place over Labor Day weekend, after Iacocca personally had called Owen Bieber and suggested that Chrysler would be "responsive" to union demands. After a single six-hour bargaining session the company gave in. In addition to the $2.42 hourly wage increase, the new agreement in effect restored the 3 percent annual wage increase that had been in force in the auto industry since the 1950's. The new contract would cost Chrysler about $1 billion, or slightly in excess of $100 million more than the company's July proposal. It would raise its total labor costs about 29 percent by October 1985, to $27 an hour (about half that sum would be in wages; the rest, in benefits). But most of the cost would fall in 1985, by which time Chrysler hoped the car business would be booming. And Ford's and GM's hourly costs would be still higher since both companies would have negotiated new contracts in the interim. In any event, Chrysler had decided that it was essential to have two years of labor peace while introducing the new models. Said Thomas Miner, Chrysler's vice-president for industrial relations: "The situation we wanted to avoid was to go into negotiations in November and December with the threat of labor problems in mid-January disrupting a very important launch for us. The thing to do, we thought, was to get this over with, and that's what we did."[61]

Marc Stepp wrote to Chrysler union members:

> This victory is a direct result of the strong, principled position that our union took this summer when we asked that Chrysler reopen bargaining talks so that its workers could share equitably in the company's recovery, following the painful sacrifices that we made since 1979. . . . With your overwhelming demonstrations of support for our position, Chrysler finally got the message that its workers expected and deserved a fair share of the company's record profits.[62]

The new contract was ratified by a large margin.

Chrysler workers had a lot to celebrate. They had extracted two consecutive increases from the company. But some 42,000 of them were still on indefinite layoff in late 1983. Many of these former employees had not voted for the new contract because they had been laid off for so long that their union membership had expired. Had they voted, they might well have opted instead for lower wage increases and more jobs.

It is difficult to know with certainty how many of these former Chrysler workers were still jobless years after having been laid off and how many could find work only by taking dramatic pay cuts.

No studies were done; no one tracked the incomes or whereabouts of the employees who had been separated from Chrysler. But we can gain some sense of their fates from a detailed survey of 4,700 Ford workers undertaken in 1982, two years after they had been laid off when that company closed its assembly plant in Mahwah, New Jersey. Nearly half (48 percent) of these hourly workers were still unemployed. Of those over forty years old, 61 percent were jobless; for females, the figure reached 72 percent. Incomes declined substantially. Before the shutdown about 61 percent of these workers had a family income of at least $20,000 per year. Two years later, at the time of the survey, only 11 percent reported a current annual income of $20,000 or more. Nearly half earned less than $10,000. Median incomes fell from about $21,600 to $10,400.[63]

In other words, it seems a sadly sure bet that as the richer new contract was being ratified, a significant percentage of Chrysler's 42,000 former employees were still jobless or, if employed, were earning very much less than they had at Chrysler. Their sacrifices for Chrysler's revival would go unrecognized and unrewarded.

Nor did the new contract do much to allay the tension between workers and managers that had been growing through 1983 as Chrysler increased production faster than it recalled workers to its plants. To get maximum production without paying all the benefits associated with new hires, the company had been scheduling extensive overtime. An assembler at Jefferson Avenue complained, "They're trying to get quality and quantity at the same time, and it just doesn't work that way. As soon as you get a team going to where you can do the job right, like you want to, they figure you've got too much slack and they take one guy off and have him do something else. The main thing they're trying to do now is get the same work with fewer workers."[64] The discontent provoked by heavy overtime was exacerbated by the simple fact that after massive layoffs in reverse order of seniority, most of the younger workers were gone. Chrysler's assembly lines were staffed by middle-aged men.

At Chrysler's Twinsburg, Ohio, plant, where sheet metal was stamped into doors, side panels, and floor pans, workers were putting in seven-day weeks. The frantic pace of production left little time for regular maintenance or cleaning. Broken stamping presses, puddles of oil, and piles of scrap steel made the plant a hazardous workplace; one worker was crushed by a stamping press.[65] The president of the UAW local, Bob Weissman, was a militant. Between 1975 and 1978 Weissman had closed down Twinsburg three times. An old wisecrack in Detroit was that whenever Chrysler wanted to reduce its inventories, it had only to provoke Bob Weissman into action. But in the resurgent auto market of late 1983 Chrysler had no need to trim inventories. Weissman warned Chrysler that the involuntary overtime and unsafe working conditions at Twinsburg would result in a wildcat strike at the plant. He presented the company with a list of fifty demands, most of them concerning safety improvements and overtime. Chrysler executives refused to comply. Thomas Miner, Chrysler's vice-president for labor relations, said, "They were determined to strike no matter what."[66] When Miner asked UAW headquarters in Detroit not to authorize a strike at Twinsburg, he was told that union leaders "could handle" the local.[67]

On November 1, 1983, less than eight weeks after union members company-wide had ratified the new contract, 3,200 hourly workers at the Twinsburg plant went out on strike. Because metal stampings from the plant supplied almost all of Chrysler's assembly operations, the strike instantly paralyzed the company. All five of Chrysler's car assembly plants shut down. Half its blue-collar workers were laid off within three days. Each day the strike continued, Chrysler lost production of about 4,000 cars and trucks. To pay its bills without any revenue coming in, the company had to start dipping into its cash reserve at a rate of more than $45 million a day. If the strike lasted three weeks, this cushion would be gone.

Twinsburg workers returned to work six days later, after Chrysler had agreed to improve safety conditions, adhere to work rules, and make overtime voluntary. The strike had reduced Chrysler's fourth-quarter earnings by about $90 million.[68] But the real cost of the strike could not be measured in dollars and cents. It left a legacy of bitterness. It distanced the company still further from the brief era of cooperation and common cause that had prevailed during the worst of the crisis. And just as the firm was finishing the most profitable year in its history, it demonstrated how vulnerable Chrysler remained to recalcitrance on the part of any group that felt it was getting less than its due.

But such concerns seemed abstract in 1983. Despite the strike, Chrysler reported profits of $700 million for the year.

A few months after the billion-dollar increase to the wage bill, Chrysler's board of directors voted to offer its chairman, Lee Iacocca, a new long-term deal as well. The board had been rattled by rumors that Iacocca might leave the firm. "We had to do something to make sure that Lee would stay with Chrysler," explained board member Jean de Grandpré. "He is so intimately linked to the future success of the company that we couldn't take the slightest

FIGURE 12
Chrysler's Net Earnings

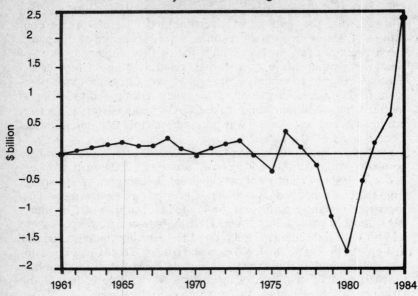

Source: Annual reports for 1961–1983;
analysts' estimates for 1984

chance he would leave. We heard that he was being approached by numerous organizations and companies."[69] The board decided to cement the chairman's ties to Chrysler by making it hugely lucrative for him to stay, offering a four-year package of stock and stock options worth $5.6 million.

Douglas Fraser's was the one dissenting vote on the board. "I really got agitated," he recalled. "I said, 'You know, the amount of money you're talking about is not important to Lee Iacocca, but the workers are going to view this as a retroactive recovery. You're making a goddamn mistake.' It was scandalous. It has not so much to do with compensation, but it has everything to do with ego. In Lee's case he was going to show the Ford Motor Company that he was going to earn more. It's crazy. It's goddamn insensitivity."[70]

If 1983 marked full recovery, 1984 was a triumph. Chrysler's new products met the market with perfect timing, and most of its factories ran full tilt. Wall Street analysts predicted earnings of $2.3 billion or more for the year (see Figure 12, opposite). (This meant that inflation aside, Chrysler would break even for the decade from 1974 to 1984.) Dividend payments to stockholders, halted by necessity in 1979 and by Congress from 1980 to 1983, were restored; in the first three quarters the company paid out $74 million in dividends, more than in any full year since 1974.[71] And Chrysler's unionized workers asked to reopen their contract once again to negotiate a fittingly richer deal.

VII

BEYOND CHRYSLER

1.

The Chrysler rescue marked a startling departure from political convention. A nation that by tradition masks its projects to succor ailing firms behind Byzantine tax subsidies or foreign trade quotas this time opted to countermand the market explicitly. Congress put public resources at the service of a private firm and subjected that firm to meticulous public oversight. The rescue was a symbolic watershed. But even among the few Americans familiar with the facts there would be no firm consensus on what lessons they offer.

Claims about what happened and what it implies are as various and as vigorously asserted as the crisp debunkings and the horror stories prepared for the 1979 congressional hearings on whether government help was needed to forestall disaster. In part this is because we tend to surrender our opinions to experience only under the most severe duress. But more important, here the experience itself is ambiguous. The Chrysler episode was sufficiently complex that by attending selectively to chosen facets of it, one can find support for practically any conclusion. To ask simply, "Did it work?" is to invite rounds of lively but inconclusive dispute revealing more about debaters' ideological proclivities than about the case at hand.

In 1979 commentators assessed the Chrysler Loan Guarantee Act as, variously, a requiem for American capitalism, an epochal refinement of our mixed economy, and an overblown version of industrial politics as usual. Six years later the debate continued, even as the rescue receded into the past. The act has been implemented. The Loan Guarantee Board has met for the last time. The loan board staff disbanded early in 1984. Chrysler's legal status is now the same as that of any other firm.

So did it work? At first blush the question seems silly. By 1985 Chrysler was thriving. Its 1984 profits approached $2.5 billion, and it reclaimed its spot among the fifty biggest firms in the world. Five summers after it had sold off its European operations to raise a few more months' worth of cash it bought a stake in Italian sports car maker Maserati. The goal of the act had been to save jobs: Six years later Chrysler was employing 83,900 Americans—far fewer than 1979's payroll of 121,800 but indisputably better than zero.

Yet debate persists. Uncertainty on how much and what kind of difference the rescue really made lets the old arguments thunder on with only token nods to the experience since 1979. Five years after his spirited rearguard action against the loan guarantee bill, Senator William Proxmire still dismissed as "absolute nonsense" claims that the program saved more jobs or factories than a reorganization would have. "Chapter Eleven would not close down the plants," said Proxmire. "You still would have the people working there. The owners would take a bath, but what the hell, that's what owners are supposed to do."[1] Five years after he had passionately argued for federal help, Detroit Mayor Coleman Young still supported the bailout. He conceded that Chrysler's Detroit work force had suffered a "pretty hefty decline" but insisted, "I don't think anyone would dispute the fact that if there's been a big job loss now, there would have been a hell of a lot bigger one."[2]

Two opposing strategists of the 1979 legislative battle were Chrysler's Wendell Larsen and Proxmire aide Elinor Bachrach. Both later went on to new positions unrelated to Chrysler. Both, interviewed five years later, echoed the themes of 1979. According to Bachrach, "It was oversold. I think that's one of the saddest things. There's no question that the company was saved by the loan guarantee package. Whether there were more jobs saved than there would have been, whether the guy on the assembly line was substantially helped by it, I don't know. The fact was, he was going to get it in the neck regardless. But nobody wanted to say that; it wasn't in anybody's interest to say it."[3] Larsen's conclusion was sharply different: "You've read the stories about swarms of people going from the Midwest to the Sun Belt and living in their cars while they look for work? Add a few hundred thousand more to that, and you'd have the 'natural' labor adjustment that would have followed Chrysler going broke. You can argue about the numbers, but the basic fact is layoffs or not, we saved a hell of a lot of jobs.'"[4]

Two submerged uncertainties frustrate simple assessments. The first concerns how much of what was valuable about Chrysler would have disappeared forever in a regular bankruptcy proceeding. How many of the people who are directly or indirectly working for Chrysler today would be making cars anyway—for Chrysler itself after Chapter 11 reorganization or for a successor or a competitor if the company had ended up in liquidation—had the government not come to the rescue? How much more of the firm would have been liquidated in bankruptcy than was in fact cut off under the aegis of the loan board? It is the *difference* between what would have happened otherwise and the disintegration that occurred that measures, as a first approximation, the effect of the bailout.

The second uncertainty concerns the alternative occupations that would have claimed the resources—including, especially, the people—that *would* have been permanently separated from Chrysler. Bailout or oblivion did not exhaust the options. Some displaced workers could have ended up in rewarding new jobs. Others, doubtless, would never have equaled their old wages. A few would surely have set up firms on their own, adding new dynamism to the economy. The problem, of course, is in knowing what that balance would have been between revivifying "creative destruction" and plain useless misery.*

Several points are worth noting.

First, Chrysler would have gone into bankruptcy—either reorganization under Chapter 11 or liquidation—at the start of a vicious recession, in one of the hardest-hit parts of industrial America. However happy the eventual fates of some displaced Chrysler workers, there would have been many bitter years of joblessness or underemployment for a large proportion of them. Even if we cannot know with precision how many jobs were permanently saved, it seems clear that in the chaos of a Chrysler bankruptcy *at that time*, there would have been a good deal of economically needless idleness. Suppose Chrysler had eventually been reorganized or its liquidated assets taken up by other firms. There would still have been thousands of workers laid off as the industrial structure was painstakingly reassembled, some no doubt only temporarily but many for good as competitors seized markets from the crippled

---

*The study of the Mahwah, New Jersey, Ford plant closing (see page 260) suggests that for blue-collar workers the balance went fairly strongly toward continued joblessness during the recession and, longer term, jobs that paid less than automaking.

organization. It is not just the *number* of jobs saved but their nature that makes the case for the rescue. Automaking is one of those few pursuits that reliably open a gateway to the middle class. Many of Chrysler's blue-collar workers were black. Helping such citizens retain their precarious middle-class status is a worthy achievement.

Second, one can argue that the rescue made budgetary sense. We avoided the loss of tax revenues and the burdensome rise in public assistance claims that would have attended secondary shocks to suppliers and creditors, regional economic decline, and the erosion of stranded communities. Indeed, the government came out ahead on the bottom line: Guarantee fees more than covered administrative expenses, and the $311 million from the warrant sale was a straight profit for the public fisc. Defenders of the rescue can also claim that the public really bore no appreciable risk. The government had first claim on Chrysler assets with a book value of $6.6 billion. Even in the chaos of liquidation, even in a depressed auto market, these assets would have been worth enough for the government to recoup most, and very likely all, of its $1.2 billion.

Proponents can also contend that the loan guarantees were hedged about with so many restrictions that fears of an epidemic of careless managers' clamoring for public help are baseless. No business executive looking to the Chrysler precedent would expect an easy, painless rescue or ask for assistance casually. The option of rigorously conditional aid will not make the prospect of failure appreciably more agreeable to American managers.

Pragmatic defenders urge attention to the simple but portentous fact that the rescue worked; Chrysler was saved. Senator Paul Tsongas, a drafter of the 1979 bill and something of a skeptic at the time, summarized this justification in a 1984 article: "Uncle Sam has no business throwing greenbacks at every skidding company [but] there may be circumstances when a bailout is in the national interest. Chrysler is such a case. It suggests that there are times when a bailout policy may be worthy of consideration. The challenge is going beyond ideological posturing and looking at the particular situation. 'Will it work?' should be the test. Happily, in Chrysler's case, it did."[5]

Some proponents, developing Tsongas's logic further, argue that the Chrysler model should be enlarged and extended. The rescue worked not, as some participants claimed, because it was novel and tension-ridden but because it was founded on accumulated experience from the Lockheed, Conrail, and New York City episodes. The New York Federal Reserve Bank had developed a system for monitoring troubled companies and identified Chrysler as a crisis in the making. Many of the officials who shaped the Chrysler pro-

gram had participated in these previous rescues and learned along
the way. Several members of Congress and congressional staffers,
having weathered the earlier crises, knew what sorts of conditions
had to be placed in the act. The main problem was that crucial data
and analysis had to be cobbled up on the run from hastily hired
studies and seat-of-the-pants appraisals. It would be imprudent to
count on such luck in the future, these observers contend; they
call for a durable institution to administer industrial rescues. A permanent office could monitor troubled cases before they become
crises. It could gather information more efficiently—and more
cheaply—than by hiring a herd of consultants as soon as an issue
heated up. And it would give government negotiators more legitimacy and hence more leverage. Arthur Burns in the early 1970's
called for such an institution; in the 1980's the cause was taken up
by Felix Rohatyn and other investment bankers.

Finally, some observers endorse the rescue, albeit without enthusiasm, out of a recognition that in our political system the alternative to the open rescue of a major firm is generally not the
bracing winds of the market but rather a covert bailout through
trade, tax, or regulatory policy. This is precisely how the Reagan
administration dealt with the automobile crisis. Such back-door interventions undermine democratic processes because most Americans remain in the dark about who is being subsidized, toward
what goal, and at what ultimate cost to the citizenry.

These arguments for the wisdom of the rescue must be balanced
against a weighty contrary case. First, even if we applaud Chrysler's
revival as a splendid turn of events, Treasury's rescue was not the
most potent force acting on the firm. There were tax subsidies and
protection from imports; there was an exceptional turnaround campaign within the company. But these factors aside, Chrysler was
a leaf tossed on the waves of macroeconomic policy. The Federal
Reserve Board's decision to clamp down on the money supply in
late 1979 turned the firm's transitional cash shortage into a mortal
threat. The looser policy launched in mid-1982, conversely, made
Chrysler's convalescence into a triumph. All three major American
automakers rode the same waves, but Chrysler, as the smallest
firm in this most cyclical industry, was subject to more violent ups
and downs (see Figure 13, opposite). Nor was the size the only
issue. John Riccardo had loaded up on debt to launch a risky make-
or-break strategy in 1978. The government did not alter the odds
on the strategy but stepped in with revivifying cash each time the
firm was about to go under for good. If Chrysler would never be
allowed to lose its risky bet, sooner or later it had to win. The

economy would eventually turn up. With a federal floor under its fortunes Chrysler surely would ride the cycle up again someday.

Nor did the intervention defend the most vulnerable of Chrysler's constituents. It was not blue-collar employees but stockholders, managers, lenders, consultants, lawyers, and lobbyists—all relatively wealthy—who benefited most from the bailout. Chrysler workers as a whole fared poorly compared to these groups. Despite the company's stunning revival, in 1984 its American work force was still smaller by a third than it had been in 1979. The number of hourly employees was down by 26,000; nearly 10,000 of these workers had been laid off the job so long they had lost all recall rights. The workers who *were* helped, moreover, were members of America's labor elite. By the mid-1980's auto workers were collecting wages and benefits 70 percent higher than what the average American manufacturing worker earned. Saving a few high-paying

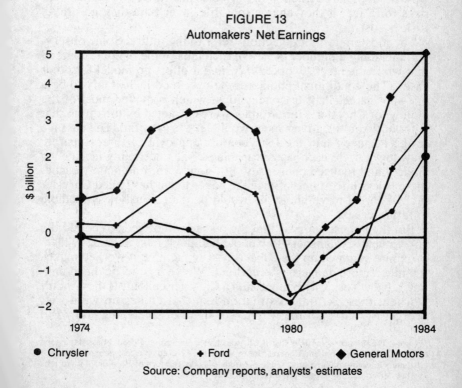

FIGURE 13
Automakers' Net Earnings

● Chrysler   ✦ Ford   ◆ General Motors

Source: Company reports, analysts' estimates

Chrysler jobs came at the expense of thousands of dispersed and anonymous workers—mostly unorganized, mostly poorer than average—who went jobless because federal guarantees shunted credit to Chrysler instead of to the businesses that would have hired them but that folded, or failed to expand, for want of affordable financing. Saving Chrysler clearly meant more layoffs at Ford and General Motors as well, especially once the quotas on Japanese imports had been imposed.* It is not hard to make the case that the rescue was distributionally perverse.

Nor was the rescue really without price to the public. The fact that the worst didn't happen—that Chrysler did not collapse and force the government to make good its guaranteed notes—does not mean the guarantees were costless. We got lucky this time; the odds of a game can't be judged by a single round. People also can win at Russian roulette—for a while. Had things gone a little differently for Chrysler, taxpayers could have lost. More broadly, if we as taxpayers make a habit of standing behind private firms' debt, we will lose a large fraction of our bets. Insurance companies bear risks for a fee; if they charge too little, over time they go broke. Risk is cost.

The most important objections refer to the future. Some observers, including a number of key participants in the bailout, contend that while the rescue worked *this time* it offers no model for other cases. The conditional public rescue may tend ineluctably to be a one-shot game. Private concessions, which provided most of the money for Chrysler's turnaround, were extracted by the threat that without them, the government would let Chrysler fail. The passage of the act itself and the loan board's approval of three separate drawdowns were each very near things. The uncertainty heightened anxiety and focused consensus. But now, after one major rescue, there is less uncertainty. Since the government has bailed Chrysler out, its threat to withhold aid would be dangerously less credible in future cases.

But the largest worry is that the rescue will be seen to herald the government's willingness to bail out bad managers. Senator William Proxmire summed up the concern: "The fact that it worked makes it a much more dangerous precedent. We've had a Lockheed bailout, a New York City bailout, and a Chrysler bailout. If they hadn't worked, the next time a situation like that comes up we'd say, 'Forget it; that's not the way to go; think of something else.' But

*Without the quotas, some jobs lost if Chrysler had collapsed would doubtless have gone to Japan; with them, Ford and General Motors would have picked up many more of Chrysler's customers and automaking jobs. While the trade-off between jobs at Ford or GM and jobs at Chrysler is not one to one, the trade-off is real.

now, when there's a national-scale firm in trouble, the word will be 'Look at Chrysler.' "[6]

Insurance company managers speak of "moral hazard," or a person's tendency to take more chances when the consequences of a misstep fall partly on other people. For example, car insurance may encourage careless driving if bad drivers aren't charged a proportionately higher premium; flood insurance may invite construction on vulnerable shores if the contractor shifts some of the risk to the insurer. Similarly, critics warn, Chrysler could set a precedent for sparing commercial losers that will alter economic behavior for the worse. The managers of large firms will fear failure less and take reckless chances. Workers, stockholders, and communities will pile ever heavier demands on firms, anticipating public rescues if the burdens become crippling. As market discipline is kept at bay, the economy will go slack, and we all will be worse off. The expectation that the government will step in to save large or well-connected firms will increase the strain on our already overburdened political system and reinforce public cynicism about the power of special interests.

It is here, on the issue of the precedent which the Chrysler bailout set, that the clashes are the sharpest. The stakes are high, touching the heart of our economic and political system. As Paul Tsongas hopes, and William Proxmire fears, the Chrysler rescue will be combed for guidance "next time," for Chrysler assuredly will not be the last politically salient firm to face collapse.

The real legacy of the rescue, then, can be understood only by appraising the subsequent behavior of the groups that participated in it. How has the rescue changed the institutional structure of the American system and, with it, the trajectory of our economy? How has it altered economic relationships within and among our core organizations—financial institutions, labor unions, corporate management, and government? We will have to wait decades for definitive answers, of course, and we cannot with full confidence attribute a given trend to the Chrysler precedent. But by 1985 there would be some useful, even if tentative and partial, evidence on how the lessons were being incorporated into the system.

2.

Institutions evolve. Laws, customary procedures, and organizations change over time. As the broader economic context evolves, organizations must adapt simply to avoid obsolescence even if their mandates remain unchanged. The emergence of foreign competitors, the opening or closing of outside markets, a shift in the prices of goods bought abroad—all can compel us to alter economic institutions. Learning guides this evolution. Lessons gleaned from experience alter how institutions perceive their goals and approach their tasks. The members of organizations discover new capacities. The members of the surrounding society observe, compare, and decide which innovations they consider worthwhile and legitimate.

Crises spur such institutional learning. Inertia is inherent in human organizations. Indeed, one serviceable definition of an institution is "a set of roles and codes that maintain old ways of doing things." Established procedures easily become enshrined; incumbent actors become entrenched. Crises threaten these arrangements. But improvisations born of crisis can also expand an organization's repertoire of response and alter the path and pace of its evolution.

Chrysler's crisis shook up America. The trauma of the firm's near collapse and the tension and novelty of the rescue strained old networks and compelled groups to cooperate in new and unaccustomed ways. The Chrysler experience—in alliance, of course, with other forces for realignment at work during the 1970's and early 1980's—disrupted economic organizations and the relations among them. It broke down some of the rigidities built up in more stable times. It induced old antagonists to make common cause. It invited organizations to experiment, and it compelled new thinking about goals. Within this accumulation of organizational experience lurk some of the most valuable lessons of the Chrysler episode.

The postwar decades of economic stability had witnessed an uneven but perceptible shift away from risky economic stakes to more certain, fixed claims: from small to large firms; from equity to fixed-rate loans; from day labor and local contracts to pattern bargaining and automatic cost of living adjustments; from corporate rivalry to safe oligopoly.* This trend should provoke neither surprise nor reproach. An intricate but substantially mature economy required predictability and control. A growing proportion of the populace attained a high degree of material comfort and became more anxious to secure its status than to advance it further. And the long respite from foreign competition let Americans indulge these preferences. Until the 1970's growth and stability seemed assured. Throughout

---

*In 1940, for example, proprietorships and partnerships were a little more than a quarter as important in the economy as corporations (measured by receipts). By 1975 these former categories together were less than a sixth as large as the corporate category.[7] See also note, p. 56, Chapter II, on the shift in proportions of debt and equity financing.

much of the economy, risky claims—bets on shared endeavors, stakes that paid off in step with the success of an enterprise—were exchanged for fixed expectations. Corporations grew more productive but also more heavily burdened with constituents. The accretion of claims made economic institutions rigid. The flight from risk sapped the economy's resiliency and, ironically, made the system more fragile.

Chrysler had been part of this pattern. Like other industrial firms, it had assembled obligations during the years of stability. As the weakest company in a cyclical industry it was the most vulnerable to shocks. It is not hard to find instances of managerial hubris, incompetence, or folly, particularly in the Townsend era. But efforts to identify the fatal blunders that brought Chrysler to the brink miss the point. Errors there were, but not so many more than we find when we dissect any other firm in the comfort of hindsight. Because of its position in the industry, Chrysler was simply the first to feel the forces of change. The interlocking networks of claims of which Chrysler was a part and an example were no longer supportable. Under pressure, they would either become more supple or crack.

The most telling lessons of the Chrysler saga concern responses to this pressure to adjust. Chrysler's agony, and the accommodations forced upon its constituents, illuminated alternative paths for some of the economic organizations that make the American system work. A few of these paths would be followed further; more would be abandoned after a few paces. But we can with profit trace the direction they lead.

Commercial banks had opted for bureaucratic stability in the postwar decades. Already barred from pure equity investments, they had dedicated their portfolios to the most conventional loans, with rates fixed or pegged to the prime. The sharp-eyed, flinthearted banker of folklore at least had a clear economic function: He produced *information*. He sorted bids for resources according to his informed judgment of the entrepreneurs' experience and talent and the plausibility of their projects. But as banking became more bureaucratized and as the organizational dynamics within and among banks were altered by the long postwar stretch of rapid and almost uninterrupted growth, this changed. Lending rates, in principle set by assessments of the borrower's *specific* riskiness, came to depend mostly on the type and size of the firm. There seemed little point in taking too great an interest in the borrower's business. Indeed, competition based on the gross amount of loans outstanding penalized overly fastidious lenders.

The Chrysler case challenged these implicit rules of commercial lending. The certain, high return that creditors had anticipated was no longer achievable, and Chrysler's bankers faced a choice: They could have a fairly certain *low* return in bankruptcy or a risky —but possibly rich—stake in a restructured Chrysler. By trading in loans for preferred stock, Chrysler's creditors willy-nilly became sharers in the firm's risks and rewards.

There were other lessons for lenders. As one banker recounts, "Before Chrysler, what caused so many problems in a workout was that many small banks thought that someone would buy them out. God love 'em, I'd do the same thing in their shoes. Experience told them if you're tough enough and just don't answer your phones, one morning you'd find a wire for so many millions of dollars and you're out of it. That's the expectation they used to work on. Chrysler came along and changed the expectations. The ground rules changed. We established that, no joke, everybody has to come to the party in these kinds of deals."[8] After Chrysler, creditors would enter workouts anticipating a requirement of unanimity. There would be fewer attempts to hold out for a separate, more favorable deal. The agreements also would be different in form: No longer would the lead bank come up with a plan and expect other lenders either to bolt or blindly to follow. Now negotiation and compromise among interested parties, geared toward consensus, would be required. The lenders, of necessity, would function as a group.

Substantially the same community of commercial bankers, investment bankers, and lawyers that worked on the Chrysler restructuring went on to handle troubled giants like International Harvester, foreign debt restructurings, and other reworked deals. This continuity promoted continued evolution. Even banks that had gone along with the Chrysler deal only reluctantly, such as Citibank, later learned to appreciate the merits of cooperation. A routine developed: Creditors formed into committees representing different interests, they classified different kinds of credits, they organized fact-finding missions, and they enforced the all-in rule.

There was yet another financial legacy of Chrysler, this one more for the investment bankers and other financial midwives than for the commercial bankers: a readiness to insist that governments "bring something to the party." The restructuring of International Harvester, following in the wake of Chrysler, illustrated this trend.

Harvester makes farm and construction equipment. It plodded through the 1970's with lackluster sales and disappointing profits. When Archie McCardell became chairman and chief operating officer in 1977, he set out to end overstaffing, pare inventories, and tighten purchasing policies. He also hoped to trim labor costs by changing what he saw as archaic and inefficient union work rules. But in early 1980 a devastating UAW strike closed down most of Harvester's domestic operations. Cash reserves eroded. Debt swelled. Competitors captured orders that Harvester was forced to refuse. Recession struck hard at building and farming, cutting sales and stifling recovery from the strike. High interest rates ratcheted up the cost of servicing the growing debt.

In December 1981 the company reached a new agreement with its 200 creditors on $4.2 billion in debt. By April 1982 it had already defaulted on the deal. The pact was revised, then quickly revised again. Many of the players in the Chrysler deal reappeared. Lehman Brothers, which had represented the creditors in Chrysler, represented the company in Harvester. Salomon Brothers had represented the company in Chrysler and now represented the creditors in Harvester. Many of the same law firms showed up at both restructurings. The consultants knew one another and had learned how to set up a deal. They arranged for wage concessions and breaks from suppliers. They orchestrated negotiations early in 1982 between Harvester and state and local agencies serving Fort Wayne, Indiana, and Springfield, Ohio, where the firm had its two domestic truck assembly plants. Within eight months the separate negotiations had escalated into a bidding war between the communities to retain existing Harvester investment and jobs.

In Fort Wayne, site of the firm's biggest plant for half a century, Harvester had laid off almost 7,000 workers since 1980. Fearing a total shutdown, the city suspended Harvester's $50,000 fire and utility fees in January 1982. Then the dealing began in earnest. The state of Indiana agreed to guarantee $2 million in loans to the company.* The city readied a sale-leaseback deal in which local investors would purchase Harvester's parts distribution center for $10 million. The investors would garner tax advantages from the new accelerated depreciation provisions in the 1981 tax law, and half the $10 million was covered by loan guarantees from Fort Wayne. The city lined up $10 million more from other sources, and the state offered $9 million in federal block grant money. Both Fort Wayne and the state of Indiana pressured local banks to participate through low-interest loans.

Harvester was also the largest employer in Springfield, Ohio; the truck plant there had a payroll of about 7,000 in peak periods. The

---

*Indiana's economic development statute authorized state investment if it would "be of benefit to the health, safety, morals and general welfare of the area where the project is to be located";⁹ loans could be guaranteed for up to 90 percent of a principal amount not to exceed $2 million.

local Chamber of Commerce estimated that the area would lose $100 million in business over the next few years if the plant closed. Ohio was determined to retain the plant. A group of local businessmen, backed by the state and local governments, offered a deal similar to the sale-leaseback offer from Fort Wayne: They would take over the plant and its tax benefits and would lease it long term to Harvester. (Aside from the tax advantages, this meant that if Harvester went into Chapter 11, the plant could be quickly transferred to a new manufacturer instead of staying tied up in court with the rest of the firm's assets.) About $30 million was needed to buy the plant. Ohio put up $20 million in guarantees. Local banks were persuaded to provide $7 million in low-interest credits.

Ohio won the bidding. International Harvester would consolidate its truckmaking in the Springfield plant owned by the new Community Improvement Corporation of Springfield. Harvester would extend the plant to accommodate the trucks previously produced in Fort Wayne. (The city also offered tax abatements on these improvements.)[10]

The financial community now routinely turned to state and local governments to help finance workouts of troubled major companies. Financiers became more experienced in dealing with government officials. At the same time, and for the same reason, states and cities became more vulnerable to firms' threats to decamp. By 1985, even in the bloom of economic recovery, communities were bidding against one another with increasing ferocity.

It is important not to overstate the changes in American finance. Even after Chrysler, banks continued to make loans to major companies without checking first on the firms' overall credit burdens or on the status of other lenders. In 1985 Manufacturers Hanover —Chrysler's battered lead bank—still did not require that major loan applicants list other outstanding credits. Pressures to secure new business still deterred lenders from insisting on full information. The next Chrysler would take many banks by surprise.

Creditors still moved in herds into currently fashionable deals. In the wake of Chrysler, International Harvester, and anxiety over foreign debts, American banks stepped up their loans for leveraged buyouts. In these deals a company's assets are offered as collateral for loans. The borrowed money is then used by a private group, usually led by management, that buys up the publicly held shares and thus acquires the company. Leveraged buyouts are inherently risky because they burden the newly private firm with debt. Much of the firm's cash flow in early years must be earmarked for debt service. A shortfall in revenue or a sharp rise in interest rates will make this burden insupportable. Manufacturers Hanover became one of the leading lenders for leveraged buyouts, with more than $2 billion tied up in such credits in mid-1984.[11] The record as these deals evolve will reveal how well the lessons of the last round of crises have been retained.

Finally, even after Chrysler, commercial bankers were still wary of taking an active role in counseling troubled borrowers *before* a crisis developed. This reluctance was in part rooted in legal strictures: A creditor who participates in management runs the risk of being considered in control of the debtor. Such financial "insiders" forfeit some of their rights in the event of bankruptcy and may even be sued by other claimants.* But part was simply due to the difficulty of understanding an industrial business and the anxiety stirred up by assuming responsibility for an uncertain proposition. Bankers, like the rest of us, prefer to live without risk if given a choice. Commercial bankers also declined, by and large, to develop the kind of in-house expertise that their compatriots in Japanese or West German banks possessed about the industries to which they lent money and about the regional economies in which they did business.

3.

Labor also learned from the Chrysler episode. Significantly, the evolution paralleled that of the banks. In the wake of the rescue, Chrysler's workers found themselves acting somewhat more like stake sharers and less like claim holders. They broke from the industry-wide pattern bargain, sundering forty years of tradition and taking a major step toward company-based unionism. New deals struck during the crisis blurred the status of blue-collar workers. Traditional rights and duties of hired manpower were suspended and mingled with some of the rights and duties of owners: The workers shared risk and reward. This evolution took two principal forms: profit sharing, instead of indexed wages, and board representation. It was replicated in other cases. One heir of Chrysler's legacy was Eastern Airlines.

Eastern faced collapse in 1983. Losses were crippling; it hinted publicly of a Chapter 11 filing. In October Eastern's chairman, Frank Borman, and its three main unions, representing machinists, trans-

---

*Bankruptcy Code Section 547. A lending institution in control of the debtor also is subject to primary liability under the Securities Exchange Act of 1934 for any antifraud violations committed in connection with its dealings with the debtor.

port workers, and pilots, agreed to commission an independent assessment of the firm's financial status. Hired negotiators assembled to strike a new deal. A former secretary of labor, W. J. Usery, advised Eastern. The former director of the Chrysler Loan Guarantee Board, Brian Freeman, advised labor. An agreement took shape: Unionized workers would take a pay cut of nearly 20 percent for a year, saving Eastern $367 million, in exchange for around a quarter of the company's stock. Labor also gained four seats on Eastern's board and the right to review and comment on management's operating and spending plans before they went to the directors.

But at Chrysler itself both these innovations—profit sharing and board representation—had begun to atrophy. Douglas Fraser's performance on Chrysler's board was generally celebrated as statesmanlike and astute. "Some people would say, 'No, you can never have a labor guy,' " Lee Iacocca said in 1982. "So then why can we have bankers and a top supplier? What the hell's the difference if the guy involved is a purveyor of labor? He's pretty key to making the joint run. The only guys who get mad at me are the other chief executives."[12] But Fraser retired from Chrysler's board in the summer of 1984, and the company only grudgingly agreed to transfer the board seat to Owen Bieber, Fraser's successor. Fraser was nominated as an individual, Chrysler contended, not as a labor leader, and no precedent for labor representation was set.

And Chrysler's workers willingly surrendered profit sharing for an immediate seventy-five-cent raise in the 1982 contract. The rejected formula would have paid each worker $2,350 in 1983, roughly four times the level of leaner profit-sharing plans at Ford and General Motors. (The employee stock ownership plan was retained, though, mostly out of concern for Congress's likely objection to abandoning a provision of the act.) "It's too abstract," Fraser said about profit sharing. "Once we can show that it means something, attitudes will shift."[13] Lee Iacocca was more emphatic: "The rank and file say, 'Hell, we don't want to own the company.' And some of the most unenlightened union leadership say, 'We don't want these bastards reading *The Wall Street Journal;* they'll think they're capitalists, and we've got to keep the troops in the corral here.' They didn't like that. Its time hasn't come. Don't let anybody tell you any different."[14]

More ominously for the notion of worker as partner, it is an odd and feeble sort of partnership that can be instantly dissolved at one party's initiative. By 1985 most blue-collar workers at Chrysler still lacked any meaningful job tenure. Job security had never become an issue in the Chrysler renegotiations. Management resisted any additional constraints on the struggle to stay solvent. But labor also declined to press the issue and never offered larger wage and benefit concessions—perhaps with a higher profit-sharing rate—in exchange for more job security. Harrowing job risk for some workers was chosen over greater wage risk for all. Chrysler wages and benefits fell only to a level midway between the auto pattern and the national average for manufacturing (see Appendix A, Figure 20A). Meanwhile, nearly half the firm's hourly workers were laid off, many of them permanently.

Union leaders insisted that no better deal could have been had. There were only so many auto jobs available, they argued, and further wage concessions would have conferred a windfall on Chrysler without saving any jobs. This is possible. But an alternative interpretation is this: Lower wages at Chrysler would have made the Auto Workers' vulnerable to similar demands for concessions from Ford and GM. Moreover, as base wages approached the manufacturing average, the rank and file might have begun to ask what benefits the union leadership was winning for them. High wages are seen as the product of leaders' negotiating skill; profit sharing is seen more as a bonanza from the firm. (It is also true, in fairness to the leadership, that the rank and file by tradition distrust management and discount job security pledges.)

The union's failure to press for job security in exchange for greater wage concessions could be blamed on the seniority system, too. The youngest workers are the first to go. Unless more than half the membership feels threatened, union ballots will generally yield a mandate for higher wage demands, even if one result is fewer jobs. In addition, supplemental employment benefits and early pensions—still built into labor contracts—sometimes are so enticing that senior workers can find it more advantageous to close a plant than to save it through wage concessions.

Two other factors would militate against a continuation of the labor transition the Chrysler crisis precipitated. First, before workers would willingly trade rigid claims for flexible stakes, they would need far better access to company information than they typically had and an ability to analyze such information. Otherwise, why believe management when it says the company needs a wage cut? Who's to be certain the money won't go for executive bonuses and perks or higher dividends? By 1985 labor negotiators still almost universally lacked such access. The new financial deals struck as part of the Chrysler rescue involved sophisticated analysis and detailed, current data and projections; labor's negotiations were primitive by comparison. For labor to negotiate at the same level of economic sophistication as finance required a leap in unions' analytical capacity and orientation.

Finally, by the mid-1980's the fraction of American workers organized into unions was shrinking precipitously. Unions represented less than a fifth of the private-sector work force. This shrinkage undercut labor's taste for participating in organizational change. Unions clung with desperate tenacity to earlier gains. Labor leaders were mounting a rearguard action against what they perceived—perhaps correctly—as a mortal assault by management against the principle of unionism. American unions were defensive, angry, and inclined to resist invitations to further innovations.

4.

What had management learned? The Chrysler episode demonstrated anew that a large corporation is fundamentally a network of claims and obligations. Managing such institutions is very much a *political* challenge of brokering claims among constituencies. Managers themselves are not only corporate claimants but also the arbiters and balancers of other constituents' claims. Chrysler's brush with bankruptcy offered a graphic reminder of the perils of letting claims exceed the organization's capacity to deliver. American managers drew lessons from the restructuring itself and from the broader downturn of which Chrysler's distress was only a single prominent instance.

But the lessons taken most to heart had little to do with *brokering* claims; few American managers showed much stomach for the political challenge of rendering durable corporate obligations more flexible and contingent. Instead, most sought ways to cut off claimants altogether.

American management came to view Chrysler's trauma as an object lesson in trimming down. Executives in many large companies took radical steps to lower the break-even point—the minimum level of sales necessary to cover fixed costs, the least flexible of the claims on a firm. Managers were slow to rehire workers as the 1983–1984 recovery progressed, resorting instead to overtime. Automakers and other basic manufacturers continued to reduce capacity and close older facilities. They pared head counts by replacing labor with advanced machines or buying parts from lower-wage concerns in this country and abroad. Thus they fell back on the simplest way of aligning claims with the ability to serve them: severing ties and canceling claims wholesale.

Lee Iacocca bluntly recounted the merits of shedding dependents in a session with securities analysts late in 1983: "Seventy percent is outside. What used to be a problem is now one hell of a deal, because you can go shop the world. You can look for Korean half-shafts, you can go to Mexico, you can go South if there's no union, because it's all out there. We don't have any investment. We had some, but we closed 21 plants, remember. We're out of all that crap. We're buying it on the outside."[15]

By 1985 American automakers were turning to low-cost suppliers for basic components and to Japan for key technologies. This trend was most apparent in the production of the smallest cars, which must be designed and manufactured with particular care. As the Japanese have learned in producing everything from televisions to semiconductors, innovations in products and manufacturing processes often occur at the most compact end of a product line, where the engineering challenges are the greatest. For the same reason, development expenses often are highest at the compact end. These costs make sense as part of a long-term strategy that centers on a highly skilled work force. But they are unduly burdensome for firms with no durable links to any particular nation or set of workers. Accordingly, by 1985 the Japanese were developing small-car technologies; the Americans were buying them. GM was seeking to import subcompacts from Suzuki and Isuzu. It had given up its plan to build an S-body Corsa in the United States, it was phasing out the Chevette, its futuristic Saturn model was barely off the drawing board, and it was relying on Toyota to supply the engines, transaxles, and other high-value components for its jointly manufactured car. Chrysler was quietly revising its long-term production strategy and dropping plans for building new lines of small cars in the United States; in the spring of 1985, it announced plans to boost imports from Mitsubishi to 200,000 cars a year—equal to one-sixth of 1984 U.S. car production. It was contracting with a South Korean automaker to supply a new line of small cars. Ford had announced a $500 million investment in Mexico, where it would assemble a Toyo Kogyo subcompact. American Motors was buying truck diesel engines from Nissan.

The trauma of Chrysler, in sum, contributed to a reshaping of the U.S. auto industry—and, less directly, of other basic industries—to reduce break-even points and thus to prepare to weather the next recession. This might better ready these organizations for a difficult future. Such strategies may well be in the best interests of their shareholders and executives. But as firms lightened the load, many of their workers and communities were left stranded. And in an imperfectly organized world, where economic adjustment is not the near-instant reflex of economic theory, it was far from obvious that decoupling firms from claimants improved the American standard of living.

In the network of rights and duties that is the corporation, expectations often depend less on the firm's ability to deliver—which is a complex and obscure matter—than on comparisons of the gains *other* claimants are collecting. Lofty rewards for one group of constituents cause the demands of other claimants to escalate, and the total burden on the firm ratchets upward. The decision by John Riccardo and Lee Iacocca to work, temporarily, for $1 a year had been a potent symbol. Austerity at the top—including lower pay and fewer perquisites for hundreds of top Chrysler managers—made it vastly easier to ask for restraint from the firm's blue-collar workers. But the return to prosperity reignited competition among all groups. By 1984 Chrysler was palpably regressing toward old ways. For the hugely profitable 1983, its executives shared almost $41 million in bonuses. And this generosity prompted workers, suppliers, dealers, shareholders, and other groups to demand equally generous treatment.

The slackness at top levels manifested itself in other ways as well. As one Chrysler official lamented in mid-1984, "We're living like fat cats again. I don't mean the bonuses. The Roger Smiths [of GM], Phil Caldwells [of Ford], and Lee Iacoccas of the world, and their subordinates, deserve a lot after what they've been through, and those top guys ought to make as much as the average ballplayer. I don't mean it that way. I mean, in the symbolic things like two-hundred-dollar-a-yard carpet on our fifth floor, leather sofas in the garage, huge corporate jets, all those things that are so visible to every manager. When he sees these things, then he in turn relaxes a little bit on trying to run his part of the business."[16] To the extent that the Chrysler episode represented a breakthrough in corporate relations with labor, middle-level management, and the public at large, by 1985 many of the lessons already were being forgotten.

5.

The central discovery for federal officials was the payoff from putting conditions on public help.

In the past, government involvement had often relieved a troubled firm's constituents of responsibility for recovery. As public money flowed in, private resources slipped away, and the government had to provide even larger subsidies. The New York City rescue and, even more decisively, the Chrysler rescue broke this pattern. Public involvement actually *increased* private commitment to the rescue. This was in large measure because the public money was strictly contingent on private sacrifice. If constituents came through with specified contributions, guaranteed loans would augment the turn-around fund. If constituents held back, the aid program would collapse. Once the deal had been struck, the company's performance was monitored by the government, and strict conditions had to be met as long as Chrysler retained any claim to public resources. In this way the rescue came to resemble a reorganization under bankruptcy with the government as an active participant.

Even those who criticized the system's details or who thought the goal of saving Chrysler was in itself profoundly wrongheaded agreed that the conditionality tactic worked well. It accomplished three things. First, it raised other groups' estimates of Chrysler's odds for survival *without* sparing them from responsibility to sacrifice. Thus it boosted their willingness to contribute. Second, it made it easier for Chrysler's managers to impose austerity by allowing them to blame the government for the stiff requirements. Third, the conditions radically altered whatever precedent the rescue set; attaching requirements for substantial private sacrifice would screen out many potential petitions for public help.

One aspect of conditionality concerns equity owners. Owning stock is *supposed* to be risky. It makes little sense for public rescues to confer windfalls on stockholders. When the rescue bill was taking shape, Senator John Heinz tried, unsuccessfully, to limit the windfall by requiring the company to turn over a little more than half of Chrysler's equity to a government board. The board would have gradually sold the shares to pay off guaranteed loans, simultaneously diluting existing holdings of Chrysler stock. The idea died in conference but was resurrected—though in a weakened form —when the Treasury Department required Chrysler to issue several million warrants to the government. The warrants did roughly the same thing as public stock ownership would have: They extracted from shareholders some of the benefits of the rescue. This kind of condition deters casual appeals for public help in hope of a better deal for shareholders than regular bankruptcy would offer.*

---

*The point of the warrant episode is often misunderstood. The Chrysler program was not a success because the government made money. Profitability should not be the criterion for selecting where to intervene; we can consign those deals to private investors. Nor, more subtly, was compensation for risk the main point. By taking a senior claim on assets, the government shifted most of the risk to Chrysler's creditors. The warrants made sense as a matter of fairness—paring the windfall to wealthier than average shareholders—and as a precedent to screen bids for public help.

Has the lesson endured? The evidence is mixed. The problem is the American penchant for delivering hidden subsidies to major firms through the tax code or trade barriers. This practice frustrates conditionality both because it obscures the public's contribution and because it makes it hard to exclude firms that flout the requirements. For conditions to be enforceable, there must be some way for the government to withhold or withdraw the subsidy from firms that fail to comply. Thus there must be a well-defined transfer to a single firm, or else transfers to separate firms must be separately controllable, or else all claimants to public funds must somehow be bound by the same conditions. These criteria seldom are met by chance, and in post-Chrysler rescues the federal government showed no effort to meet them by design.

When the Reagan administration arranged for the Japanese to limit their automobile exports to the United States, for example, the rescue benefited all American automakers indiscriminately and unconditionally. Here was an opportunity for the administration to gain assurances from the United Auto Workers and from executives of the Big Three that they would moderate wages, benefits, and executive compensation while the quota was in effect, reserving for retooling and retraining the financial fruits of protection. Instead, much of the extra money American consumers paid for new cars because of the quota went for executive bonuses and wage increases. The same failure to gain industry sacrifices characterized the administration's role in securing the tax subsidies embodied in the safe-harbor leasing rules of 1981.

Yet when *individual* firms were targeted for rescue after the Chrysler deal, the federal government displayed some willingness to impose rudimentary conditions. Two cases warrant mention.

Harley-Davidson, the only remaining American manufacturer of motorcycles, got a reprieve from failure in the spring of 1983. The firm could not compete with lower-priced imports from Japan. At Harley's request, the Reagan administration imposed a quota and a tenfold increase in tariffs on foreign motorcycles. American motorcycle buyers would fund this bailout by paying higher prices. But the rescue was not without conditions. In the course of negotiations with Harley, the staff of the U.S. special trade representative had obtained Harley's assurance that it would use the trade relief to make needed investments—upgrading its designs, plant, and machinery. Yet this informal agreement between the government and the firm merited applause only by comparison to the norm of wholly unconditional trade protection. It was a distinctly modest advance. It lacked, for example, any process for ensuring that Harley would comply with the deal. There was no provision for monitoring Harley's investment program or for withdrawing trade relief if the company reneged. The feebleness of the conditions was not entirely the fault of the administration. U.S. trade laws entitle firms and industries to virtually automatic, unconditional protection if they can establish eligibility for relief. But the lack of any visible effort on the part of the administration to impose firmer conditions on Harley-Davidson suggested that this particular legacy of the Chrysler rescue had not yet taken root.

Continental Illinois, in 1980 the nation's eighth-largest bank, had lent money aggressively to almost any large manufacturer that sought it. By the start of the 1980's the bank had a string of problem loans, including Chrysler and International Harvester. But it first faced serious trouble in July 1982, when the Penn Square Bank of Oklahoma City collapsed under the weight of bad energy loans.* This left Continental stuck with some shaky assets it had earlier acquired from Penn Square. Recession, deregulation, and high interest rates continued to buffet the bank. More loans went sour, and by the spring of 1984 rumors that it was in serious trouble spread. Continental's depositors became increasingly edgy.

The federal government had been bailing out troubled banks as a matter of course since a banking panic deepened the Great Depression in the 1930's. The Federal Reserve System served as a lender of last resort, standing by with funds to keep banks sufficiently liquid that depositors would not panic. The Federal Deposit Insurance Corporation (FDIC) insured the deposits directly. Prior to the crisis at Continental Illinois, the FDIC had handled more than 700 bank failures, either by paying off depositors or by arranging a merger with a stronger institution. Although the FDIC formally insured bank deposits only up to $100,000, the agency had backed *all* deposits in insured banks, even those above the limit. But since around the beginning of 1980 the agency had been pushing to restore more market discipline to the banks by covering only a fraction of the losses that large depositors suffered if—because of reckless lending or unsound management—their bank went under. As a result, depositors at Penn Square and six other banks had been only partly compensated for their losses, and major depositors were wary of the next collapse.

---

*Interestingly, Continental Illinois had been rescued from impending insolvency once before —in 1932, by Herbert Hoover's Reconstruction Finance Corporation. The RFC bought $50 million of the bank's preferred stock to save it from collapse and required as a condition of the rescue that the management be replaced. An assistant to the treasury secretary was named chairman.

The Continental, restricted from domestic branch banking by state and federal laws, had relied heavily on large foreign depositors. As rumors of its difficulties intensified in May 1984, these large depositors began to bolt. Then, at the urging of the Federal Reserve, a syndicate of major banks led by Morgan Guaranty offered Continental a $5.5 billion line of credit; the Federal Reserve banks backed these loans. The FDIC also put up $1.5 billion in capital. More important, it reversed the recent reforms and pledged that no depositor, of whatever size, would lose money in Continental. But the run continued. At the end of July the FDIC agreed to fortify Continental's balance sheet with another $1 billion and to buy for $3.5 billion the bank's portfolio of bad or questionable loans. It was the largest bank bailout in history. But the FDIC also imposed some strict conditions on the troubled bank: It replaced the bank's top officers and collected signed resignations—later accepted—from all its directors. It acquired preferred stock that could be converted into 80 percent of the bank's shares. Unlike the Chrysler rescue, the big losers here were the bank's shareholders. Not only would the value of their stock be sharply diminished by the plan, but the bank also was required to write off losses of $1 billion—about half the value of the shareholders' equity—and would have to endure additional losses if the FDIC ended up collecting less than it anticipated from the bad loans it bought.

The conditions that the government attached to the Harley-Davidson and Continental Illinois bailouts were designed only to revive the companies. They did nothing to help prevent similar crises from befalling comparable firms. In the Continental Illinois rescue, for example, there was no attempt to assure that banks provide depositors and shareholders with more accurate and timely information on their loans, a step that might motivate earlier adjustments and forestall sudden crises of confidence.

There was a second lesson for the government. It was found in the government's unanticipated capacity to extract information from private parties and to muster the talent to assimilate the data and put them to use. Consider that for three years one of America's largest firms had to check every move with a team of bureaucrats. (The loan board members themselves, especially during the Reagan administration, relied extensively on the civil service staff to run the program.) Yet, despite a good deal of grumbling, Chrysler managers complained in retrospect of precisely three instances in which federal oversight seriously interfered with their operations. The most mentioned by far was the rule depriving Chrysler of its fleet of jets, and this was a matter of policy, not business judgment.* In a nation in which the incompetence and commercial innocence of federal bureaucrats are assumed as a matter of course, this record merits attention.

A related bit of evidence is the absence of political pressures on the officials who implemented the program. Once the loan package was enacted, Treasury bureaucrats again and again consented to, and indirectly insisted on, drastic cutbacks in Chrysler employment. Yet we learned of no instance when any elected official intervened with the loan board or its staff in order to limit the pain. This, too, flies in the face of the conventional wisdom that governments cannot make or abide tough decisions the burdens of which fall on identifiable groups, and that Congress or the President will respond reflexively to the pleas of affronted constituents by curbing too blunt bureaucrats.

It is possible, of course, that the Chrysler episode was one of a kind. It worked because the particular public officials involved were so much more able and diligent than bureaucrats conventionally are. It couldn't happen again, at least not without the same configuration of players. This contention is only marginally creditable. While it is true that Treasury bureaucrats enjoy a reputation for exceptional ability, and Brian Freeman's team was considered exemplary even for Treasury, a more plausible interpretation is that such crises inspire officials and bureaucrats, who normally work well below their capacity, to unaccustomed energy and creativity. A gripping project like the Chrysler rescue also attracts talent to the agencies involved.

A final lesson concerns the *power* of public intervention.

The guaranteed loans were only a bargaining chip. What ultimately saved Chrysler was the sacrifice from labor, creditors, suppliers, and other constituents. The government's presence at the bargaining table radically changed the terms of the negotiations among claimants. It spurred greater sacrifice from these groups than they otherwise would have rendered. The government was able to broaden the terms of the bargain by threatening certain recalcitrant players, by verifying Chrysler's own threat to declare bankruptcy

---

*Chrysler managers cite the other two as moderate irritations: The government forbade Chrysler to buy back some bonds it had issued years earlier, which the market was discounting heavily. Managers saw this as an opportunity to eliminate debt obligations cheaply; the loan board disagreed. And the loan board delayed until it was too late permission for the company to buy insurance against a devaluation of the Mexican peso. (Both episodes occurred after the Reagan administration had virtually ignored the program and rendered the board staff a bureaucratic backwater.)

unless sacrifice was forthcoming, and by orchestrating a single grand bargain incorporating all major parties.

But the power of government to shape such deals raises deep questions and, at a minimum, implies still-uncodified responsibilities. There was a perceptible measure of bluff in the pressure that the government officials applied to suppliers and lenders. Bankers could not know with certainty, for example, what, if any, reprisal would come down on their heads if they refused to join the restructuring. But Paul Volcker's taciturn glowering cannot be an enduring instrument of industrial policy; if we repeat the Chrysler model, the consequences of refusing to go along must be laid out and understood. This is no small step for the American system. The prospect of invoking public authority to force concessions in a private firm's favor is—or should be—unsettling. Do we really want our elected and appointed officials to pressure small-town bankers to take on more risk so that giant firms can survive?

If we opt to replicate the Chrysler bailout, we will need to develop a clearer consensus on the proper limits of the government's power to coerce concessions. It is surely inappropriate, for example, for regulatory authority delegated by Congress to accomplish certain purposes (like ensuring the integrity and efficiency of the nation's banking system) to be applied by appointed officials toward very different ends (like persuading banks to go along with a corporate rescue). When the secretary of the treasury and the chairman of the Federal Reserve Board subtly threaten retaliation against perfectly legal private decisions, power is being used as an instrument of policy, not of law. Such practice invites abuse.

Guidelines must be drawn to protect the interests of less powerful players—the smaller banks, dealers, and suppliers—whose influence is dwarfed by that of the biggest and politically best-connected companies. There is an almost inevitable tendency in these situations for government to rely on the largest companies for information and proposals. The largest companies are best able to negotiate terms and conditions. But smaller organizations may face sharply different circumstances and bring a separate parcel of hopes and fears to the table. Unless special care is taken to ensure that their concerns have force, they may with reason assume from the start that such deals will be biased against them.

6.

Perhaps most important is a set of lessons concerning the processes of economic change. Underlying the debate over the fate of the

Chrysler Corporation was a more basic concern about the social network of employees, communities, and local businesses that depended on it. Surely keeping Chrysler viable was only one means of preserving that network and easing its adaptation. Public officials rightly feared in 1979 that reorganization under bankruptcy would leave unsettled this larger social problem. They erred in assuming that a corporate rescue *would* settle it. Yet no alternatives were ever fully aired. No major participant in the legislative debates had a clear stake in exploring other approaches, and those who implemented the act seemed relatively insensitive to them. Few of the lawmakers or bureaucrats recognized at the time that the problem of "Chrysler" may have been masking a more fundamental problem of economic adjustment.

The goal of microeconomic policy, broadly stated, is to keep national resources in the best possible alignment with the changing world economy. In an era when technology, capital, and management are ever less tied to any particular country, "national resources" means, primarily, people. Success lies in helping citizens secure desirable roles in an integrated world system. Saving firms makes sense only as an instrument in the service of this goal. Corporate rescues must be judged as one among many conceivable instruments.

Two fictions confound discussions of economic change in America. The first is the fiction of automatic adjustment. Those who recoil from any proposal to manage or buffer change—chiefly some breeds of economists and their fellow travelers—rightly observe that economic pain often prompts adjustment. Stagnant sales forcefully inform firms that they must produce better or cheaper goods if they hope to match the competition. Chronically low profits may be the cue to cut costs, drop old products, and develop new ones. Layoffs and unemployment may signal to workers that they need new skills or should move to a different part of the country. But economists often vault from this sound observation to the conclusion that such hardships or anxieties reliably and exclusively induce adjustment. This faith accords poorly with experience. Adjustments are costly. Existing bonds are valuable; there are reasons why firms do not liquidate each evening and reincorporate the next day. Uncertainty itself is painful. (This discrepancy in perception goes far to explain why economists are so often misunderstood and even abused by the laity and why so many of them learn to prefer swapping abstractions with their fellows.)

The other, opposite fiction is often embraced by labor leaders, many liberals, and business executives facing the sudden end of a subsidy or the unleashing of competitors. By this scenario, groups never adjust to change but simply suffer. Laid-off workers spend the rest of their days jobless or grossly underemployed; firms and communities wither; closed factories are reclaimed by the forests. And always the damage is said to extend to the public at large—customers and suppliers, when the injured party is a firm; taxpayers and communities, when labor makes the case. But in fact, wounded economies eventually heal, even if scars remain. In time, new businesses emerge to replace old ones. The most cited example is New England's transition from textiles to high technology.

All of us tend to prescribe for others the bracing tonic of change while perceiving for ourselves the virtues of constancy and the folly of meddling with a time-tested arrangement. Other situations are deplorably stagnant; our own is appropriately stable. We find these two fictions more appealing or less depending on our degree of vulnerability. But the question is not which is "right." Both are cartoons drawn from partial and highly selective perceptions. Adjustments eventually occur, *and* adjustments are costly. Practical rules to guide public policy must moderate the pain of transition without thwarting change. Pragmatists inhabit a middle, messier ground between the two fictions. We must neither try fecklessly to preserve the old nor assume away the peril and pain of adjustment. Our concern, in sum, should be finding the best way to get from here to there.

A reorganized but intact company can be one vehicle for channeling resources to better uses. But there are other ways, perhaps more efficient or direct than saving the corporate structure that currently envelops those resources. Adjustment programs are less dramatic, more prosaic than corporate rescues. They are hard to implement and hard to evaluate. But we can only gauge the wisdom of the Chrysler rescue—and appraise the next petition for help—by reference to the alternatives.

One approach, perhaps the simplest, is to ensure that displaced workers and stranded communities have either the time or the money to manage their own adjustments. Requirements for advance notice of a plant closing can be negotiated in individual union contracts or required by law. Almost twenty years ago George P. Shultz (the Reagan administration's second secretary of state) and Arnold R. Weber concluded that six months' or a year's advance notice was "a procedural prerequisite for constructive action. It gives the various organizations some time to organize their programs and permits employees to adjust their own plans as well as to consider the various available options with care."[17] Several unions—most notably the Steelworkers and the Rubber Workers— have included such advance notice provisions in master contracts. Warning of two scheduled closings of U.S. Steel's structural steel mills in western Pennsylvania did leave time for negotiating contract modifications that kept the plants open.[18] Two states—Maine and Wisconsin—require notice before plant closings. But such notice requirements are not without their own costs. The best workers may leave early; discipline and morale may erode; orders may dry up. This suggests two points. First, if some states require notice and others do not, firms may prefer to locate in states with fewer constraints. Any advance notice laws thus should apply at the national, not the state, level. Second, such laws should allow employers to opt for equivalent severance payments instead of advance notice if providing workers with cash instead of time is judged by the firm to be the less costly alternative.

A more active adjustment program would provide help in job placement. Most other industrialized nations help their workers find new jobs when a plant or company faces collapse. Canada's Manpower Consultative Service, for example, arranges for job interviews for vulnerable workers and monitors and coordinates manpower planning of regional firms.[19] In Sweden the Regional Labor Market Board takes primary responsibility for steering displaced workers to new jobs, and companies across the country are required to list vacancies with the board.[20]

Retraining and relocation assistance would be the next policy alternative. Relative to most other industrialized countries, the United States has never taken such programs very seriously. Nearly all efforts to retrain displaced workers have been indifferently designed and run, and most have been transmuted into income support measures. The reasons for this undistinguished record are fairly well known. First, there is no ready-made constituency for serious adjustment programs. Workers at risk of displacement often are unaware of their status and have no easy means of identifying and striking alliances with other vulnerable employees. Second, labor unions and managers have generally been unenthusiastic about such programs. Third, it is simply difficult to target the right people with the right kind of assistance. With loose monitoring and broad eligibility standards many workers and firms receive windfalls of "adjustment" aid for doing what they would have done anyway. Tighter standards, conversely, can exclude the workers most in need of help.

The story of trade readjustment assistance (TRA) in the 1970's is illustrative. The idea was to serve fairness and efficiency by subsidizing the adjustment of displaced workers by liberalized trade rules. The record is discouraging. Benefits were badly delayed; the average worker waited fourteen months after layoff to receive his first TRA check. There was never much emphasis on training. Indeed, only a third of potential beneficiaries in one study even knew that subsidized training might be available.[21] But the unconditional cash grant component of the program became hugely expensive: In fiscal 1980 the program cost the government $1.6 billion.

If we were to decide to devote substantial sums to *adjustment*, working out the details would remain a major project, but some reforms readily suggest themselves: There should be enough money. Income maintenance should be kept separate from adjustment assistance. Unemployment insurance payments should continue while workers are being retrained. Eligible workers should be able to select a wide variety of training opportunities, including community colleges, technical institutes, and on-the-job training. And for obvious reasons, programs designed to teach workers new tasks should not be wholly controlled by their present employers, programs to help people change fields should not be managed by the workers' present union, and programs to help workers relocate should not be run by the government of the locality where the workers presently reside.

When a region is threatened with a sudden surge in joblessness as a major firm fails, a bailout is not the only answer. There may be ways to encourage the wholesale transfer of a failing company's work force. Selective wage subsidies could entice new firms to enter an area or existing firms to increase hiring when a key employer collapses. Or companies in a region, possibly with government inducements, could agree to hire each other's displaced workers preferentially. A related option would be to expand the "failing company" defense under the antitrust laws. Present law lets a firm facing technical bankruptcy merge with another company within the same industry, even if the merger would normally be blocked as anticompetitive.[22] This law could be liberalized to allow easier mergers if firms pledged to maintain their employment or line up comparable new jobs for former workers.

None of these adjustment measures offers a simple solution; indeed, none is wholly new. What we have *not* had is a compelling political commitment to labor transition. Lacking that, training and adjustment programs have been either starved for resources or subordinated to other agendas. We have opted instead to protect failing enterprises through bailouts, tax subsidies, trade protection, and regulation.

7.

The proximate goal of the Chrysler program—saving the company through guaranteed finance and an austerity campaign—was at best linked by tenuous logic with, at worst substantially antipathetic to, its ultimate goal of saving good jobs. This pattern of holding one objective, substituting a more tractable and somehow related alternative, and hoping for the best is less rare in the United States than the serious-minded might think. America's microeconomic policies tend to rely on what might be called programmed serendipity. The tendency is general and often can be traced to the venerable struggle between a vigorous ideology and America's equally vigorous pragmatism. We shy away from open intervention, yet we often want results that only public action can achieve. So we proclaim for these programs goals that command instant political assent and arrange, often tacitly, that they will simultaneously achieve the sort of public economic ends we are loath to seek directly. Programmed serendipity was the guiding principle behind the huge highway effort of the 1950's and 1960's, in which we skillfully spurred the automobile and housing industries while claiming, out loud, that we were actually building routes for the supply trucks and runways for the fighters in the event of war. The civilian uses were welcome, we told ourselves, but incidental. Similarly, we educated a generation on "national defense" student loans. Programmed serendipity reached its peak in the space program. The goal of beating the Russians to the moon allowed all manner of useful things to be done. It generated whole new industries, although seldom by the most direct route. Our ideology forbade us to subsidize directly research in communications or computers or advanced materials. But we welcomed them as spin-offs of the moon race.

In a curious way programmed serendipity also shaped the exceptionally direct Chrysler rescue. The deciding political force came from workers and vulnerable communities. Direct labor adjustment—adequately supplied and seriously administered—commanded no political support. It fitted into neither the economist's fiction of instantaneous adjustment nor the liberal-labor fiction of the infinitely fragile status quo. But a tight and determined constituency could be mobilized for saving the company. For lack of a better chance at preserving their incomes, Chrysler's dependents signed on to the rescue campaign. So long as the choice was either bankruptcy and joblessness *or* a federal bailout, there was no doubt to which they would lend support.

Saving the firm was seized on as a proxy for saving workers' earning power and stabilizing regional economies. This proximate goal eventually took precedence over the ultimate goal. Chrysler is not the same company anymore. As the act was passed, Chrysler employed about 87,000 hourly workers in thirty-two production facilities in the United States, twenty-one of them in or near Detroit. In 1984 it employed about 60,000 (see Figure 14, below). Eighteen of its plants, including eight in the Detroit area, had been closed; only *two* new plants had been opened. In the crunch ties were severed, ending the link between the firm and many of its constituents and confounding the political logic of the Loan Guarantee Act. This is the drawback of programmed serendipity: Sometimes when we do not pursue a goal, we do not achieve it.

The Chrysler episode offers worthy lessons on how to preserve companies at moderate risk to the public. But it is less illuminating

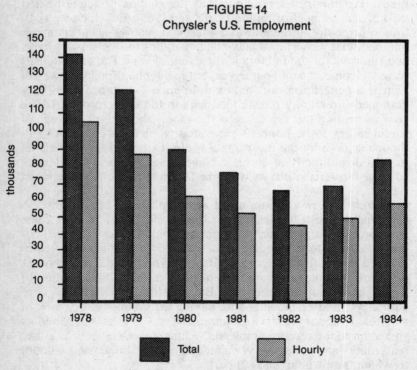

FIGURE 14
Chrysler's U.S. Employment

Source: Chrysler *Fact Book*, company estimates

about why—or when—we should want to. The act was for the most part wisely written. The bureaucrats who carried it out displayed admirable skill; the horde of legal and financial midwives who helped shape the deals were diligent; the union leaders who sold the membership on the new contracts showed vision. Lee Iacocca and Chrysler's management team exploited magnificently the reprieves from bankruptcy that the act provided. But something slipped. Many of the claimants whose vulnerability had motivated the rescue in the first place were simply cut off. With no explicit link between workers and communities and the corporate entity of Chrysler, the primary beneficiaries of the rescue were bound to be the company's managers, creditors, and stockholders. These are precisely the groups our economy rewards, and handsomely, for bearing risk. Protecting them from the consequences of failure— even if that failure is largely unmerited—is a dubious policy goal. The principal object should be to ease the process of adjustment, particularly for those least able to bear on their own the risks of economic change.

There is a symbolic realm of finance that shadows the real world of men and women at work. The economy encompasses both. But economic transformations are profoundly different in these parallel realms. Denizens of a world encompassing Wall Street, the Federal Reserve System, and the Treasury staff in any administration commonly share a pragmatic attitude toward markets. They understand that the market is a social artifact, established and maintained by rules. Most profess in public the folly of political meddling. But they concede that circumstances can require that some market rules be amended, reinterpreted, or cautiously suspended. When a Continental Illinois Bank teeters on the brink, when the intricate network of international lending becomes perilously tangled, then the code concedes that public action, *undertaken by people who know what they are doing,* is fitting. But such interventions must be limited to areas—chiefly the financial realm—where much can be accomplished quickly and cleanly, without too visibly undermining the majesty of market principles.

Former Treasury Secretary G. William Miller recounted the challenge of the Chrysler bailout as he saw it. "It was just a professional reorganization outside of bankruptcy," he recalled. "One of the problems of doing it as public policy is that you can't count on every administration to have people in place who can do that sort of thing. We happened to have a set of industrialists and lawyers who were not strange to deals like this."[23] From the government's perspective, the rescue was a financial deal. It was authorized by

Congress's banking committees. It was deemed the responsibility of the Treasury Department, the General Accounting Office, and the Federal Reserve. It was run by financial specialists trained in the minutiae of debt covenants, credit pacts, and balance sheets. They were not oriented to keeping people employed or easing social transitions; it was simply not their job.

Well after the rescue these officials—like Chrysler managers and labor leaders—would bridle at questions about the extent of Chrysler's shrinkage. Less brutal job cuts, they rightly assert, would have meant a greater risk of failure. They did what by their lights had to be done, and they did it well. It is hard not to recall the bad old joke about the brilliant surgeon whose contentment with a deftly done operation is only slightly diminished by the patient's death. It would be both misleading and unfair, however, to fault these officials for the hollowness of the program's success. When the crunch came, something had to give. Nearly every other claim on Chrysler, including wage levels and the government's stake, was fixed and defended by contract, covenant, or law. What gave was jobs.

Perhaps Congress should have added one more condition: Chrysler would maintain employment at some fraction of its 1979 level or forfeit the act's protection and go bankrupt. We are aware of the political difficulty of fixing and defending any such requirement. We are also aware that restricting Chrysler's ability to lighten the load would have increased the riskiness of the rescue. But surely at *some* point in corporate rescues the game is no longer worth the candle: The bailout saves no more jobs than a Chapter 11 reorganization would. It seems only reasonable to codify this concern.

In a world of perfect markets, financial adjustments would reliably induce parallel adjustments in the real economy. The symbols, once pushed into alignment, would tow reality along. But we inhabit no such world. The links between financial symbols and the world of work are often twisted and attenuated. If adjustment is our goal, which realm we attend to makes a difference.

Securities markets are highly efficient at transforming and transferring financial resources. Rights and duties are explicit. Risks are spelled out. Sophisticated means of spreading and hedging risks buffer the shocks of change. We have developed elaborate procedures to smooth the shifts of capital from failing undertakings to more profitable ones. As with Chrysler, armies of lawyers, investment bankers, and accountants attend these transitions. But our institutions for worker and community adjustment are still feeble. When a large firm like Chrysler begins to falter, there is no parallel process to arrange adequate training and alternative jobs for stranded workers or to establish new economic moorings for communities suddenly imperiled.

Our legal and financial system perceives only one central choice in a corporate crisis: Is the firm to be liquidated *or* is it to be reorganized? That choice may be thrashed out in formal bankruptcy proceedings, or in informal workouts with creditors, or by new owners who buy up prostrate companies and sell off the pieces. But the choices confronting *society* when a major employer falters often are broader and more complex. How can constituents' productive powers and standards of living be maintained as they undergo transitions? How can the fragile economic and social networks embedded in communities be preserved without blocking change? There are many options. Their relative merits can be discovered only through a mingling of careful analysis and robust political debate; to list or appraise them is not the purpose of this book. The central point is that these issues cannot be suppressed in a democracy; when the economic system submerges them, they resurface in the political process.

The two sets of choices—financial and social—often must be engaged simultaneously. But they are separable issues. It is possible to keep a firm in operation while stranding many of the people and communities that depend on it. It is equally possible to protect the status of people and communities without saving firms. The issue is one of what we want our economy and polity to do and what means we develop for pursuing our choices. There is no "neutral" system, but rather an intricate network of laws and institutions that sets the terms of economic choice. Both bailout and bankruptcy are social inventions. They will continue to evolve; indeed, they will likely continue to converge. But if we are chiefly concerned with the human consequences of economic change, we will invent other means for easing the adaptation of our citizens and our communities.

The Chrysler rescue worked, by the goal the rescuers served. Chrysler was saved. But the goal was narrowly conceived, and the costs were more subtle than we yet may know. Was the bailout, on balance, the best response we could make to the strains that caused the company's troubles? Probably not. Many of the participants in Chrysler's revival performed superbly, and merit our applause. But the episode left unprobed the messier issues of what obligations we owe each other to share the risks, costs, and rewards of economic change.

APPENDIX A

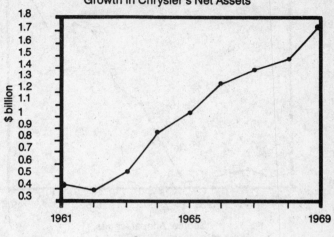

FIGURE 1A
Growth in Chrysler's Net Assets

Source: Annual reports

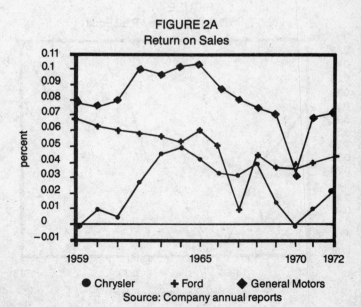

FIGURE 2A
Return on Sales

● Chrysler   ✛ Ford   ◆ General Motors

Source: Company annual reports

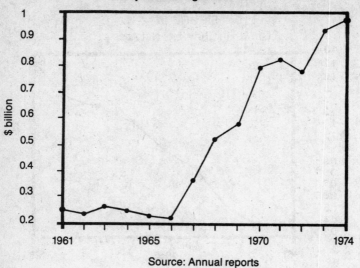

FIGURE 3A
Chrysler's Long-Term Debt

Source: Annual reports

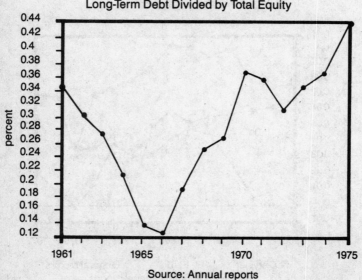

FIGURE 4A
Long-Term Debt Divided by Total Equity

Source: Annual reports

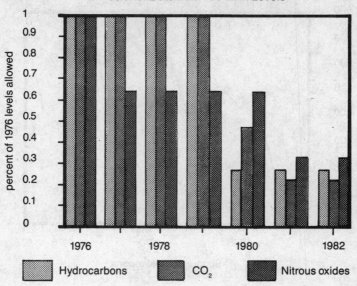

FIGURE 5A-1
Emissions: Cuts from Pre-EPA Levels

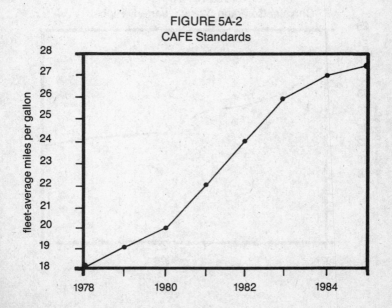

FIGURE 5A-2
CAFE Standards

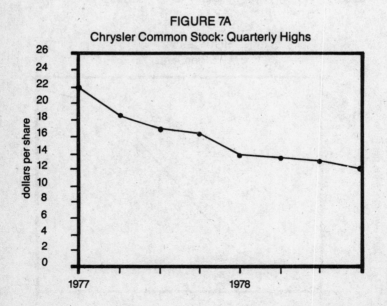

FIGURE 6A
Chrysler's Capital Spending

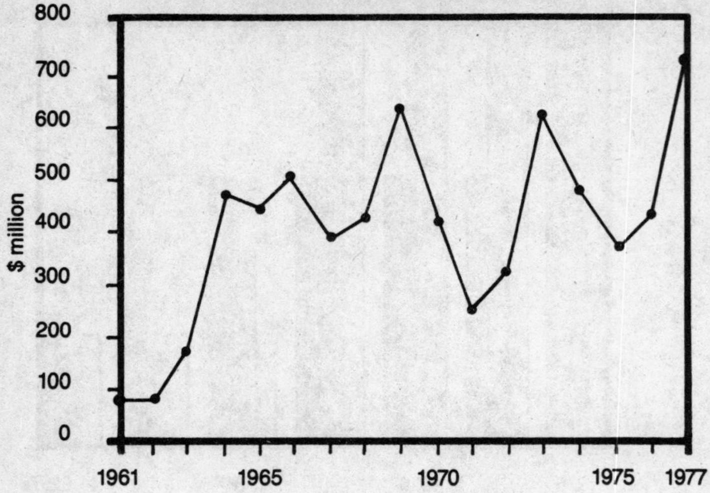

Source: Annual reports

FIGURE 7A
Chrysler Common Stock: Quarterly Highs

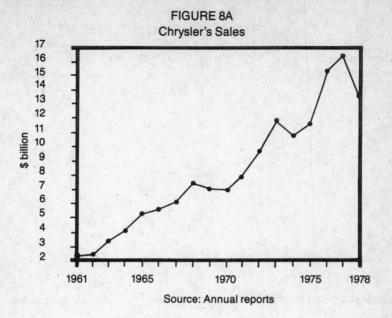

FIGURE 8A
Chrysler's Sales

Source: Annual reports

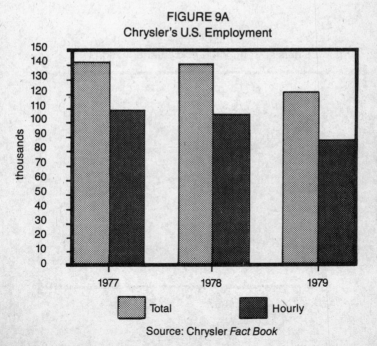

FIGURE 9A
Chrysler's U.S. Employment

Total   Hourly

Source: Chrysler *Fact Book*

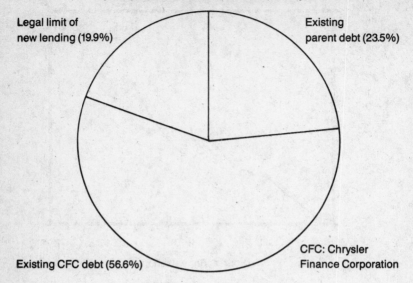

FIGURE 10A
Top Fifty U.S. Banks: Debt Limits to Chrysler

Legal limit of new lending (19.9%)

Existing parent debt (23.5%)

Existing CFC debt (56.6%)

CFC: Chrysler Finance Corporation

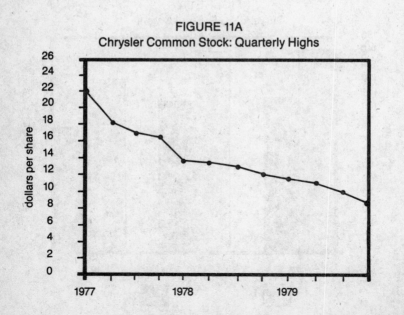

FIGURE 11A
Chrysler Common Stock: Quarterly Highs

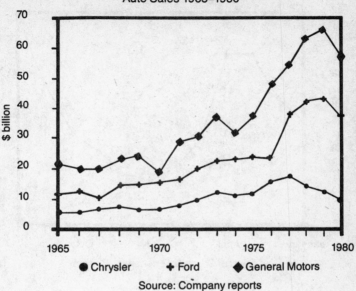

FIGURE 12A
Auto Sales 1965–1980

● Chrysler   + Ford   ◆ General Motors

Source: Company reports

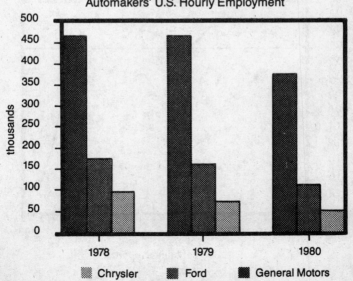

FIGURE 13A
Automakers' U.S. Hourly Employment

▨ Chrysler   ▨ Ford   ▨ General Motors

Source: Company reports

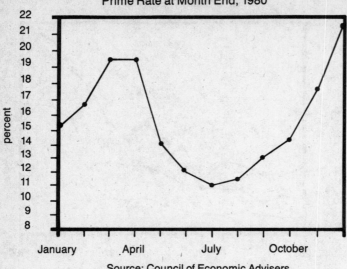

FIGURE 14A
Prime Rate at Month End, 1980

Source: Council of Economic Advisers

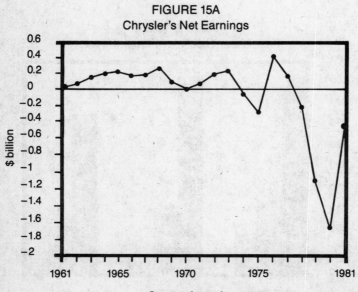

FIGURE 15A
Chrysler's Net Earnings

Source: Annual reports

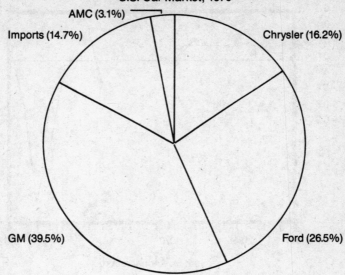

FIGURE 16A-1
U.S. Car Market, 1970

AMC (3.1%)
Imports (14.7%)
Chrysler (16.2%)
GM (39.5%)
Ford (26.5%)

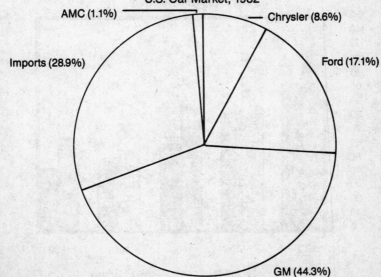

FIGURE 16A-2
U.S. Car Market, 1982

AMC (1.1%)
Chrysler (8.6%)
Imports (28.9%)
Ford (17.1%)
GM (44.3%)

FIGURE 17A
Chrysler's Net Earnings

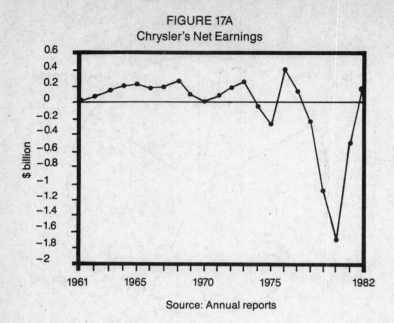

Source: Annual reports

FIGURE 18A
Chrysler's U.S. Employment

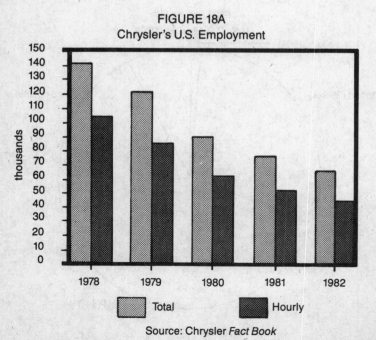

Source: Chrysler *Fact Book*

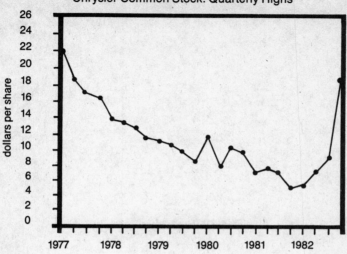

FIGURE 19A
Chrysler Common Stock: Quarterly Highs

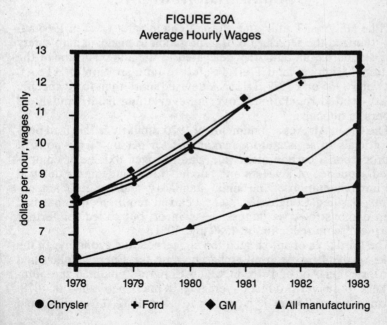

FIGURE 20A
Average Hourly Wages

● Chrysler   ✚ Ford   ◆ GM   ▲ All manufacturing

APPENDIX B

The 1979 Studies

THE WAINWRIGHT STUDY[1]

The National Traffic and Motor Vehicle Safety Act of 1966 authorized the secretary of transportation to mandate auto safety standards, an authority delegated to the administrator of the National Highway and Traffic Safety Administration (NHTSA). Between 1966 and 1977, NHTSA devised more than forty specific safety-related regulations covering everything from windshield wipers to hubcaps.

The Clean Air Act amendments of 1970 similarly authorized public officials to set statutory maximums for per mile emissions of hydrocarbons, carbon monoxide, and nitrogen oxides. A complicated sequence of lawsuits and administrative judgments delayed the implementation of the initial standards, and the 1977 amendments clarified Congress's intent, relaxed requirements that had been demonstrated as impossible to meet, but called for further sharp emission reduction in 1980 and 1981.[2]

The third area of auto regulation concerned fuel economy. In the wake of the 1974 Arab oil embargo came the Energy Policy and Conservation Act of 1975, in which Congress enjoined the automakers to deliver products averaging 18 miles per gallon in 1978, 19 miles per gallon in 1979, on up to 24 in 1982, 27 in 1984, and

27.5 in 1985 and beyond. These figures are averages for all offerings of each automaker; hence the term "corporate average fuel economy," or CAFE. Significantly for Chrysler, "captive" imports —foreign-made cars imported by a U.S. firm and sold under the American company's label—would not be counted toward compliance with CAFE regulations after 1980.

Chrysler engaged the Boston consulting firm of H. C. Wainwright & Company to prepare analytical support for its claim that these regulations were particularly debilitating to the smallest of the Big Three. The result, a handsome and well-written (if intermittently baroque) document entitled "The Impact of Government Regulations on Competition in the U.S. Automobile Industry," was delivered on May 4, 1979. The principal authors were Charles W. Kadlec, a Wainwright associate; Kenneth W. Clarkson, from the University of Miami; and Arthur B. Laffer (of the curve), from the University of Southern California. The authors, as they set out their case, "assumed, without prejudice, that the environmental, health, safety and fuel-efficiency regulations . . . are necessary and appropriate, reflecting a consensus of the desires of the American people" but that "the regulatory design may be suboptimal . . . unnecessarily subtracting from the economic welfare of the regulated firms or unduly burdening one or more of the firms relative to the others."[3] The core of the analysis was this: "All regulations create a wedge between prices paid by consumers and the prices received by producers. When compliance with a regulatory wedge involves a common or fixed cost, it is equivalent to a lump sum tax. As a result, there is a differential impact on the profitability of large versus small firms. This differential increases for industries characterized by economies-of-scale production." The emission control, fuel economy, and safety rules introduced since 1967 had imposed "extensive fixed costs for development systems and/or retooling plants on all auto producers." But the government, anxious to keep the auto industry as competitive as possible because of the small number of firms, had forbidden auto companies from pooling their efforts to develop the innovations the regulations called for. The Wainwright team argued that this "shifted the nature of the tax from proportionate to a lump sum which hurts the smallest firm the most."[4]

The study concluded that over the 1978 to 1985 period the cost of new regulations would cut Chrysler's real economic rate of return from an average of 4.4 percent to an average of −14 percent; GM and Ford, able to spread the costs over many more units, would see their rates of return go from strongly positive to moderately positive over the same period.[5] (Different analyses, using different assumptions about the automobile industry and the economy as a whole, generally reinforced this conclusion.) On the basis of these results, the study warned that "Chrysler, in order to have a chance for survival as a full-line domestically based auto manufacturer, at the very least must have removed the regressive regulatory bias it now faces in competition with Ford and, especially, General Motors."[6]

A separate analysis of the fuel economy regulation issue was released by Harbridge House, Inc., a Boston economics consulting firm, at about the same time as the Wainwright study was issued. The Harbridge report corroborated Wainwright's (and Chrysler's) contention that CAFE standards were particularly, even cripplingly, burdensome for a smaller firm: "The rapid and frequent reshaping of product lines and the development of technological fixes has proved to be much more demanding of capital resources than ever imagined by either government agencies or the automakers themselves. The burden of this development falls somewhat disproportionately on the smaller full-line companies. . . . Experience is also illustrating that the penalties to the smaller companies, either from strategic errors or product development difficulties, are extremely severe in terms of market share loss."[7]

Without some kind of relief, the Wainwright study contended, Chrysler would falter and shrink if it did not fail altogether. A 10 percent cutback in Chrysler production, according to the study, would mean layoffs of 8,425 workers. This would imply a $38 million rise in welfare payments, a $27 million fall in federal income taxes, and $199 million in lost wages. Were Chrysler to cut back by 50 percent, idling 38,230 workers, welfare costs would rise by $171 million, tax revenues would fall by $182 million, and nearly $1 billion worth of wages would be lost.[8]

Wainwright devised several possible revisions to the regulatory regime that could help forestall these grim denouements. Five changes would lower regulatory costs for all firms: counting captive imports in CAFE totals; taxing gas to boost the small-car market; adjusting the timetable for CAFE standards; simply delaying the deadline for all regulations, especially fuel economy requirements; and freezing standards at current levels. Four other changes would differentially benefit smaller firms—that is, Chrysler: allowing joint research and development; granting small firms special lenient treatment; allowing extra time to meet industry-wide standards; or giving subsidies to cover regulatory costs.[9]

Without some combination of these changes, the study concluded, "it is unlikely that the domestic auto industry will remain as healthy, competitive, or diverse as it is today. The chance that Chrysler could continue to exist in its present form . . . is extremely small. . . ."[10]

THE DATA RESOURCES STUDY

Anticipating the demand for some kind of legislative action, the Congressional Budget Office commissioned Data Resources, Inc. (DRI) to estimate the effects of a Chrysler failure. The study was delivered in August 1979. Data Resources is a Lexington, Massachusetts, firm founded by the late Harvard economist Otto Eckstein and known for sophisticated quantitative analysis.

A DRI team composed of Allen Sinai and Terry Glomski defined a scenario, "Chrysler Default," translated it into quantitative terms, cranked it through the company's vast macroeconomic model, and compared the results with what the model predicted would happen if Chrysler went on making cars as before. This analytical enterprise, Glomski and Sinai acknowledged, inevitably involved some perilous assumptions since no company as large as Chrysler had ever suffered a complete collapse.

The researchers crafted this scenario: Throughout the second half of 1979 Chrysler tries to ease its short-term financial load by curtailing its reliance on commercial paper and increasing its bank debt. This maneuver unnerves the commercial paper markets, and some investors abandon paper for safer securities. The interest rate on commercial paper rises by six-tenths of a percent in the third quarter of 1979 and stays somewhat higher than it would otherwise be for a full year. Meanwhile, the extra strain on the banking system causes bank lending rates to rise as well (though the Federal Reserve is assumed to limit this pressure on lending rates by pumping more reserves into the banking system). The rise in interest rates puts a crimp in housing starts for the rest of 1979. The stock market wobbles somewhat, with the Standard & Poor's 500 index losing three points in late 1979 and seven points in early 1980, relative to the baseline; it recovers fully only in mid-1981.[11]

Chrysler shuts plants and drops workers in its last struggle to survive. Layoffs total 30,000 in the third quarter of 1979 and another 30,000 in the last quarter. The refinancing and job cuts are in vain; Chrysler collapses completely in the first quarter of 1980. Between Chrysler itself and dealers, suppliers, and others affected by its failure 250,000 workers are out on the streets in the first quarter of 1980, and another 90,000 lose their jobs in the second quarter. As the effects ripple through the economy, total unemployment rises by 600,000 in the third quarter and only gradually subsides. It is still 200,000 higher than the baseline at the end of 1981, when unemployment is 6.9 percent instead of the 6.8 percent it would otherwise be.[12]

Ford and GM already have excess capacity in any product lines Chrysler plants are suited to, so they decline to purchase the closed Chrysler facilities. The Big Two share between themselves 60 percent of Chrysler's old market. The other 40 percent is picked up by imports, and the trade balance worsens by $2.1 billion in the first quarter.

Chrysler's product development plan dies with the company, and the Big Two see no need to increase their own new-product efforts to accommodate their market-share bequest from Chrysler, so total new investment falls by at least $500 million in 1980; secondary shocks cut investment by another $1.3 billion.[13] As the effects of the collapse spread throughout the economy, the slump of the second half of 1979 worsens—growth drops from −1 percent to nearly −1.5 percent—and the recovery expected to begin in early 1980 is weaker, with average 1980 growth of 2.35 percent instead of 2.75 percent.

In sum:

> . . . a Chrysler collapse produces temporary instability in the U.S. economy, with sizeable near-term employment, income, and output effects, some of which last throughout the forecast horizon. The near-term weaker economy, in typical cyclical fashion, reverses itself by late 1980 and is slightly stronger by the end of the forecast horizon. There is a longer-term employment loss of some 200,000 to 300,000 persons even though most Chrysler employees are assumed to be reabsorbed into the economy. A shift in automobile sales toward imported and away from domestic cars occurs, under the assumption that the current foreign producer share of the market applies to Chrysler's share of the market. The unemployment rate is permanently higher and automobile production is lower throughout the forecast horizon.[14]

Glomski and Sinai note that the actual situation would be more serious if the shock to the stock market turned out to be worse than they assume, if financial markets tightened more than moderately, or if a "domino effect of fallouts and bankruptcies" laid many other firms low. On the other hand, it would be better than the scenario modeled if the Federal Reserve took more than the minimal steps to buffer the shock or if foreign carmakers rushed in to buy Chrysler's assets and hire its workers to produce or at least to assemble cars in the United States. They conclude, though, with the warning that "potential and uncertain ripple impacts on the large number of smaller firms related to the auto industry should not be minimized, so that the results reported here might well be a conservative assessment for the economic impacts of a Chrysler collapse."[15]

A separate study using the DRI model predicted the change in government revenues and expenses stemming, directly and indirectly, from a Chrysler failure. Over the three-year period from 1979 through 1981, personal income tax revenue would fall by $6 billion, corporate taxes by $4.4 billion, Social Security contributions by $3.4 billion. Government spending for welfare and other programs would rise by $1.4 billion. City governments would lose $75 million in Chrysler property taxes. The federal government would be liable for $800 million in Chrysler pensions it guaranteed. In total, lost taxes and bigger burdens would mean a net loss to the federal government and cities and states of $16.5 billion over three years, according to the model.[16]

THE TRANSPORTATION SYSTEMS CENTER STUDY

As the Chrysler issue assumed greater salience, the Department of Transportation directed researchers at its Transportation Systems Center (TSC) in Cambridge, Massachusetts, to prepare their own report of the impact of a Chrysler failure. The study was completed in mid-August 1979. Following a conscious choice not to repeat or revise the more quantitative and macroeconomic DRI study, the TSC team drafted an analysis that "builds upward from plant and community data, rather than moving downward from macroeconomic or corporate level data."[17] The rationale for a "plant-based" analysis was the team's concern that "macroeconomic analysis can obscure critical data: by ignoring the local dependence upon Chrysler, by simplifying the apparent re-employment of Chrysler workers . . . and by avoiding important constraints such as the capacity of other companies to pick up Chrysler workers or sales."

Of the 97,000 auto production workers in Chrysler's U.S. plants, all but 6,000 to 12,000 would lose their jobs if the company failed, the study assumed. Broadening the data to include secondary effects, the TSC team identified 292,000 additional "related jobs potentially lost, at least temporarily'': 180,000 with supplier firms, 100,000 with dealers, and 12,000 with shipping and other service operations.[18]

Standard economic reasoning would suggest that this increased unemployment would be strictly temporary; while there would doubtless be some transitional hardship, the laid-off workers would ineluctably be drawn into new jobs that would be about as lucrative and productive as making Chryslers. Most of the TSC study is devoted to developing arguments why, in this case, that benign dynamic of automatic adjustment could not be expected to occur.

If Chrysler collapsed, would not Ford and GM rush in to fill the production and sales gap in the auto market? And to do this, wouldn't they hire Chrysler workers and buy Chrysler plants? Not likely, according to the TSC team. Most of the cars that would go unbuilt if Chrysler failed would be larger cars. The remaining Big Two already had huge levels of excess capacity in this market segment; they could pick up Chrysler's share without even reopening all their own plants. Moreover, ''as GM and Ford picked up those sales, they would be drawing from their own employment rolls, currently on layoff, and they would have little need for Chrysler labor.''[19] The situation was different for small cars, the authors argued, but no more hopeful. Here the problem was a shortage of physical capacity. The other automakers were running their small-car factories at full tilt. It would take at least a year, and probably two or more years, to add capacity to take up the slack left when the Omni/Horizon line disappeared.[20]

The fortunate few thousand Chrysler workers who would keep their jobs or speedily regain them would be those at the four plants likely to be useful to other car companies. The New Process Gear plant in Syracuse, New York, already sold a majority of the drive trains it made to GM, Ford, AMC, or International Harvester. The Belvidere, Illinois, assembly plant, where Omnis and Horizons were put together, was Chrysler's best assembly operation, and another auto company might well buy it. But, the TSC team cautioned, ''we doubt that other producers would want to continue Omni/Horizon production, and therefore one could expect job losses while the takeover company retooled the plant.''[21] The Introl division in Ann Arbor made instruments and emission control devices for AMC, GM, and Peugeot as well as for Chrysler, and it would likely stay in operation even if Chrysler folded. Finally, parts of the Kokomo transmission facility—which sold transmissions and trans-axles to AMC, International Harvester, Simca, Mitsubishi, and Peugeot—would likely be bought up and kept in business. In sum, at least 6,000 Chrysler workers and maybe as many as 12,000 could expect to keep their jobs.

The rationale for projecting layoffs from Chrysler suppliers as high as 180,000 was that only Chrysler relied so heavily on outside component sources. GM made almost everything that went into its cars; Ford went outside only sparingly. Thus "Chrysler suppliers are making very specific parts for Chrysler products, their markets would be instantly removed, and there would be little relief available from the other domestic manufacturers."[22]

The study also noted that a Chrysler shutdown would mean the cancellation of around $2 billion in tooling orders. It noted that other orders would likely fill some of the gap but declined to calculate the net effect on output or employment since there had never been so large a wave of cancellations before.[23]

The point the TSC team stressed most was that Chrysler's plants and workers were extraordinarily concentrated in a few areas, principally Detroit but also in several smaller cities in the Northeast and Midwest.

A little more than half of Chrysler's auto workers (52,000 out of 101,000) were in Detroit. (This was unlike Ford, which had never had any plants in Detroit proper and was gradually moving away from the whole area, and GM, which had only Cadillac production left in central Detroit.) Moreover, the study noted, Chrysler's Detroit facilities were "old, inefficient in their spatial layout, limited in their potential for expansion, and located in areas known to have some of the most inefficient and troublesome workforces available."[24] These considerations would presumably reinforce the Big Two's reluctance to adopt Chrysler plants.

Chrysler jobs were 3 percent of total employment in metropolitan Detroit and 9 percent of total manufacturing employment.[25] A shutdown would immediately raise unemployment from 8.7 percent to between 16 percent and 19 percent.[26] No one doubted that Chrysler's failure would benefit Ford and GM to some extent; economic analysis would view this as a more or less neutral transfer. But the TSC team, pointing to Chrysler's concentration in Detroit and the dispersion of the other car companies' plants, called this "an instantaneous redistribution of wealth, primarily away from Chrysler dominated areas."[27] The implications for black jobs and income were particularly grim. A majority of Chrysler's Detroit workers were black; 38,000 could lose their jobs. Indeed, the TSC team drew on Chrysler payroll figures and Census Bureau statistics and calculated that around 1 percent of the total income paid to blacks in the United States came from Chrysler.[28] Since auto jobs paid exceptionally well, "even if minority workers were able to find other jobs, the net economic loss would be large in both cash and social benefits terms." Alluding to the riots of 1967, the study said, "[I]t takes little imagination to envision the results of such massive economic reductions in the inner city."[29]

While Detroit would be the city most grievously affected by a Chrysler collapse, several other local economies relied heavily on its facilities. Chrysler counted for 9.4 percent of all manufacturing jobs in the Belvidere-Rockford, Illinois, area; for 7.2 percent in the Newark-Wilmington, Delaware, area; for 6.7 percent in Huntsville, Alabama; for 5.5 percent in Syracuse, New York; and for 3.6 percent in St. Louis, Missouri. In Kokomo, Indiana, work at the Chrysler transmission plant and foundry represented 14 percent of *all* local employment, not just manufacturing, and in New Castle, Indiana, making power trains for Chrysler cars employed 11.6 percent of the working population.[30]

The report listed total employment (hourly and salaried), annual payroll, and production for each of Chrysler's forty-six plants in eight states and estimated the number of family members dependent on breadwinners working for Chrysler. (It also listed all congressmen and senators with constituents vulnerable to a Chrysler shutdown.)

Some other calculations and conclusions:

—Total U.S. output would fall by something like $30 billion. This would be only 1.5 percent of the gross national product, but it would be concentrated. The report held that "Economic growth in the sunbelt has little relationship to losses in the midwest manufacturing belt, and therefore a regional assessment is the relevant measure. . . . In the case of smaller cities, such as New Castle, Indiana, the economy could easily shut down."[31]

—Welfare costs would rise by $1.5 billion in the first year.[32] A separate study by Michigan's Department of Social Services predicted that a Chrysler shutdown would mean 26,400 new aid-to-families-with-dependent-children cases in Michigan; 18,500 new general assistance cases; and 54,800 more families receiving food stamps by fiscal year 1981. The cost for these categories of public assistance would increase by $340 million in fiscal year 1981, about evenly split between Michigan and the federal government.[33]

—Personal income taxes would fall by $500 million.[34]

—The U.S. trade balance would worsen by $1.5 billion per year.[35]

—The pension system for retired Chrysler employees would be disrupted, and the government would be bound by law to pick up much of the slack.[36]

—The existing Chrysler capacity to produce 300,000 small cars would be lost, and planned capacity to produce 500,000 K-cars would never be realized, thereby undermining national fuel economy goals.[37]

—People who owned Chrysler cars—an estimated 17 million—would lose access to spare parts and service. This stock of cars, worth between $30 billion and $70 billion, would quickly lose its value.[38]

THE CONGRESSIONAL RESEARCH SERVICE STUDY

The Congressional Research Service (CRS), an operation of the Library of Congress, delivered its report on the Chrysler situation early in September 1979. The study was prepared by a team of more than a dozen specialists in various branches of economic analysis and finance. Following the tradition of CRS studies, the report was scrupulously factual, and the team took pains to offer both sides of any disputed point. Much of the study summarized other publications. But it added to the background by clarifying three topics: the eligible criteria for federal assistance, the different mechanisms open to the government, and alternatives to government help.

Criteria: A decision to help Chrysler would presumably rest on one or more of three potential motives: First, saving Chrysler promised net social gains over letting it fail; second, distributional considerations outweighed strict efficiency criteria; third, the government was to blame for Chrysler's predicament and fairness impelled redress. On the first point, CRS suggested that while a Chrysler failure would surely disrupt the industry and cause a short-term drop in auto jobs and output, "there is considerable doubt as to the extent of these decreases in the longer run."[39] Americans would want roughly the same number of cars with or without Chrysler, and adjustment to Chrysler's demise would involve some combination of domestic or foreign firms buying Chrysler plants and hiring Chrysler workers; domestic firms stepping up production with their own factories and workers; and imports increasing. The team left it to Congress to assess what the mix would be and how it judged the desirability of each type of adjustment. Another consideration was competition in the auto industry. The CRS team termed it "possible, but by no means certain, that the decrease in competition accompanying a Chrysler demise would be accompanied by a higher industry price path and lower output" than otherwise.[40] The report called attention to the potential for competition from imports to blunt this threat, however.[41] To compare the benefits of saving Chrysler against the costs, the CRS suggested that Congress consider two kinds of rescue costs: (1) the losses to society attendant on shifting funds from other endeavors to keep Chrysler going; (2) the probability that other firms would appeal for assistance successfully by citing Chrysler as a precedent.[42]

Aside from a strict weighing of costs and benefits, the CRS noted that Congress might want to consider the distribution of costs. The team did judge that "loss to the stockholders . . . is not a reasonable basis for public intervention [since] part of dividends and interest is compensation for bearing risk." But "Congress may judge that anticipated output and employment decreases are unacceptably concentrated by State, region, income class or some other important distribution classification."[43] Aside from the clustering of Chrysler operations in Detroit, the report referred to the exceptional share of parts Chrysler bought from suppliers, mostly small businesses.[44]

The third potential criterion was compensation. A subsidy might be justified if "the Government's tax, spending, and regulatory policies have either by design or inadvertence discriminated against Chrysler. . . ."[45] CRS recorded Chrysler's contention, documented in the Wainwright study, that equal absolute costs of complying with regulation meant higher per unit costs for Chrysler. Yet "it needs to be added that American Motors and foreign competitors have been able to meet these standards and still maintain profitability."[46] It was also possible, the team conceded, that the tax code hampered unprofitable firms competing with profitable ones by denying equal access to credits against profit taxes; there was no firm evidence on the importance of this effect, however.[47]

Mechanisms: The tax advance idea that Chrysler originally favored would amount to an interest-free loan from the government. Moreover, since "repayment of the principal . . . would depend on the future profitability of the firm . . . the tax advance would basically involve a subordinated, unsecured loan.'' The study did acknowledge a precedent, however: In 1967 the government gave American Motors a special extension of the carry-back period, a ruling worth $22 million to AMC. This meant that AMC could collect a refund on taxes paid previously—farther in the past than the law normally allowed—in order to offset current tax deductions that would otherwise be worthless in an unprofitable year. Chrysler's proposal, though rather more complicated, would have a roughly similar effect.[48] A further feature of the tax advance option is that it would involve no oversight or control by the government.

The administration's preferred mechanism, loan guarantees, could be seen as an extension (albeit a significant extension) of the many programs that backed loans to enterprises and activities to which private credit markets, for one reason or another, lent too little in light of broader social goals and criteria. Examples the CRS cited include mortgage guarantees by the Federal Housing Administration and Veterans Administration, business loan guarantees by the Small Business Administration and Farmers Home Administration, and special incentives for lending to shipbuilding and railroad operations.[49]

There were fewer precedents for firm-specific guarantee programs; indeed, ''if a strong precedent does exist, it is *not* to grant Federal assistance to an individual private enterprise. However, where Federal assistance has been granted, there appears to be a precedent for requiring a substantial management reorganization or financial restructuring . . . as a basis for receiving such Federal assistance.''[50] The main precedent was Lockheed.

A third eligible mechanism for aiding Chrysler was regulatory relief. The CRS study cited several analyses—including the Wainwright report—suggesting that Chrysler's cost of compliance with health, safety, and fuel efficiency regulations could be $300 or more per car greater than Ford's or GM's cost. Chrysler was requesting a two-year extension on the deadline for meeting emissions standards; lower fuel economy standards, at least in 1981 and 1982; and a reconsideration of the requirement for passive-restraint devices on all cars built after September 1983. Weighed against the studies suggesting that Chrysler bore a disproportionate burden, the CRS said, were two considerations: First, smaller car companies than Chrysler had been able to meet the standards; second, ''a very expensive precedent will be set if taxpayers are obliged to subsidize financially weak corporations' compliance with Federal laws and regulations . . . the steel companies for the costs of making their chimneys less smokey, the paper and chemical companies for not dumping hazardous wastes into rivers, the cotton mills for protecting their workers from brown lung disease, etc."[51]

Alternatives: The CRS study listed—without much detail or analysis—six conceivable alternatives to government help. First, Chrysler's banks could increase their lending. The study noted that the real emergency concerned short-term debt to cover the slump in sales and the costs of maintaining a large inventory. The banks were reluctant to extend themselves further, however. The Chrysler Financial Corporation had been selling receivables as a partial substitute for commercial paper borrowings or bank loans; perhaps if the CFC "succeeds in raising funds outside commercial banks, it may free bank funds for the parent company."[52] Second, Chrysler could sell more assets, such as its 15 percent stake in Peugeot-Citroën, its 15 percent of Mitsubishi, its Argentinian and Mexican division, or profitable domestic operations like New Process Gear, the Marine division, or Chrysler Defense; the defense division, in particular, was guaranteed profitability well into the 1980's by its contract to make the XM-1 tank.[53] Third, Chrysler could follow the American Motors strategy and transform itself into a specialty producer. But giving up on trying to "compete, model for model, with General Motors and Ford . . . has thus far been firmly resisted by the Chrysler management."[54] Fourth, Chrysler could persuade the United Auto Workers to reduce or defer wage increases, change work rules and practices, or buy more Chrysler stock.[55] Fifth, Chrysler could solicit help from various state governments, from Canada and the province of Ontario, where major Chrysler plants were located, and from its suppliers in the form of easier payment terms and lower prices.[56] Sixth, Chrysler could seek protection from creditors under the bankruptcy laws and undergo reorganization. "It is argued that if Chrysler disappeared as a separate entity, other companies can be expected to acquire most if not all of its productive facilities, hire many if not most of its workers, and replace it as a customer for parts suppliers. The industry as a whole could well be fully as competitive as before."

This scenario would be the sole subject of the next major study of the Chrysler issue.

THE KENNEDY STUDY

Professor Frank Kennedy of the University of Michigan Law School prepared for the Treasury Department task force an appraisal of the prospects for reorganizing Chrysler under the bankruptcy code. The study was delivered in the early fall of 1979.

Kennedy began by summarizing Chrysler's precarious financial position, noting that creditors and suppliers had "taken steps to restrict or withhold future credit" and contending that the "prospect for the foreseeable future for Chrysler without some form of dramatic assistance from outside is indeed dismal."[57] His study weighed the advantages and disadvantages of Chapter 11 as the vehicle for that assistance.

Chapter 11 offered Chrysler three broad categories of relief: postponing and restructuring debt, retaining substantial control of the business, and extending the company's rights to enforce or cancel contracts.

Debt relief: Chapter 11 of the Bankruptcy Reform Act lets a petitioner file for protection from creditors without demonstrating technical insolvency. Simply filing a petition would give Chrysler immediate relief from servicing its $4.2 billion in debt "except under a plan providing for their payment in whole or part which has been confirmed by the court of bankruptcy."[58] Since Chrysler was not in fact insolvent—as of October 1979 its assets exceeded liabilities by over $1.8 billion—it would eventually have to pay off its prepetition debts, but it would be spared for the present a heavy drain on its cash flow. Moreover, interest would cease to accrue on unsecured debt.

The plan Chrysler would submit to the bankruptcy court must, in order to be approved, meet several tests of priority among claimants: Since Chrysler had a positive net worth, every claimant "is entitled to at least as much . . . as he would receive on liquidation."[59] (Since the liquidation value of a firm can be much less than its "going concern" value, this might not be a very stringent constraint.) Each class of claim holders must approve the plan by specified majorities. Secured creditors have priority rights to be repaid either in full or in an amount equivalent to their collateral. Unsecured creditors have second priority. Stockholders come last and are paid only if Chrysler's assets are shown to be "in excess of what is required to pay all creditors and all the expenses of administration."[60] (Within the group of stockholders, owners of preferred stock have a claim prior to common stockholders.)

Debts to workers for wages earned in the ninety days prior to filing a petition (up to $2,000 per worker) as well as money owed consumers for undelivered goods (up to $900 per customer) would take priority over everything but administrative costs.

Debtor rights: Management could continue to run Chrysler under Chapter 11 either as the agents of stockholders or as the employees of the special trustee that the bankruptcy court could, at its discretion, appoint. The Securities and Exchange Commission might press the court to appoint a trustee; it had tried to have written into law that "a disinterested trustee should always be in the saddle when a company is publicly held."[61] Instead of a trustee to oversee operations and authorize management decisions, the court might appoint an examiner to report on the enterprise. (Any unsecured creditor with $5 million or more outstanding to Chrysler could demand such an examiner be appointed.)

Kennedy speculated that Chapter 11 might open up access to capital by giving new lenders first claim on Chrysler's assets. Any potential claimant "bumped" by the new lien would have a right to alternative security, however; because Chrysler had plenty of assets not currently serving as anyone's collateral, it could easily offer such alternative security. But the company "has the ability now, quite independently of the bankruptcy law, to borrow on such security." This option for attracting new money seemed to Kennedy to be unhelpful in Chrysler's case.[62]

Selectively honoring contracts: Chrysler (or its trustee) would also be enabled by Chapter 11 "to assume and enforce advantageous executory contracts and to reject burdensome contracts." For example, suppliers might be enjoined from stopping shipments even if Chrysler violated its side of the contract. Dealers, too, may be "compelled . . . to honor their executory contracts . . . notwithstanding bankruptcy clauses and other provisions entitling them to terminate," although Kennedy judged that "practical problems" would make it hard to force a dealer to sell Chryslers against his will.

Similarly, Chrysler could unilaterally abandon contracts with or without bankruptcy. The difference with Chapter 11 protection is subtle: The other party could still sue, still win, and still be awarded damages, but the claim for damages would be put in the queue along with other unsecured claims, to be paid off when a repayment plan was worked out or, if Chrysler went into liquidation, after more senior claimants had been satisfied.[63] Among other contracts, Chrysler could use this provision to escape from collective bargaining agreements.[64]

One reason Kennedy doubted that Chapter 11 could save Chrysler was the track record of reorganization efforts. "Most [reorganization] cases have been converted into liquidation, and most re-

organized debtors do not survive long even after confirmation. . . .
Experience warrants a presumption that a company that files a petition for reorganization will not make it." Beyond this presumption,
Kennedy offered four specific reasons why Chrysler would be unable to escape liquidation once it had entered the bankruptcy process.

First, filing a petition could instantly shrivel Chrysler's sales.
"When a petition under Chapter 11 is filed, the headlines . . . will
trumpet the news that Chrysler is 'bankrupt'. . . . The word 'bankrupt' carries a stigma. . . . It is not easy to sell a Chrysler product
now, but the difficulty will be greatly magnified. . . ."[65] Ford and
GM salesmen "can be expected to exploit the 'folly' of buying from
Chrysler to the fullest. . . . A person who buys a Chrysler automobile will be needled by his friends, neighbors, and relatives."[66]
Moreover, warranties on Chrysler cars already on the road would
technically be unsecured claims. Under Chapter 11 all unsecured
creditors must have equal priority, and all take back seat to secured
and priority creditors. In other words, Kennedy judged, warranties
on Chryslers sold before filing for protection would likely go un-
honored. Warranties on cars sold once Chrysler had filed for protection would take precedence over old creditors' claims, but "the
fact that the warranty is made by a 'bankrupt' company will be the
most salient fact about it," particularly once the network news
shows have interviewed a large enough number of furious Chrysler
owners left in the lurch by Chapter 11.[67]

Second, Chrysler dealers would likely desert the company. As
the stigma of bankruptcy shrank sales, dealers would see better
prospects with another brand; as dealers dropped Chrysler and diminished the opportunities to test, buy, or—most important—get
service for the products, sales would shrink further. While the news
of Chrysler's financial crisis was by itself already provoking dealer
attrition, "the pendency of the petition adds an element of hope-
lessness that makes these developments more dire."[68]

Third, reorganization would likely disrupt Chrysler's management. Indeed, Chapter 11 was intended, in part, as "a means of
getting incompetent or dishonest management . . . displaced." Were
a trustee to be appointed, he could in principle delegate most managerial tasks to the current managers, but it would be difficult to
keep "capable managerial talent in subordination to a disinterested
trustee"; many top officers would probably leave. The appointment
of a trustee and the predictable exodus of talent expose the firm
to "the risk that knowledgeable, capable people will be replaced
by a person who knows nothing about the business, never learns

what is required to operate it successfully, and expedites its descent into hopeless insolvency."[69] Even if a trustee were not appointed, Kennedy worried that the creditors' committee and the court itself could intrude on management discretion, hampering officers and perhaps inspiring the more talented into flight.

Finally, the reorganization process itself would involve heavy —perhaps crippling—direct and indirect costs. Dealers and customers might cease to worry about keeping up their credit with a bankrupt firm and force Chrysler to sue to collect receivables. Chrysler would have to pay the administrative costs of bankruptcy; while Kennedy could not provide an estimate of what these would be, administrating liquidation typically took a quarter of the proceeds collected. Perhaps more immediately threatening would be the thicket of legal proceedings that would slow Chrysler's response to markets and render rigid its operations. Not only does Chapter 11 begin in a court—"a setting that is conducive to much litigation"—but—an important point—the Bankruptcy Reform Act was barely a year old. Because it was new, it "frequently employs language difficult to understand, and leaves sizable gaps to be filled in by Rules of Bankruptcy Procedure that have not yet been promulgated." Thus "many issues will be litigated to establish the law. . . . Litigation is expensive and engenders delay."[70]

Among the issues inviting legal action: the constitutionality of the broad powers granted the bankruptcy court; the inconsistency between the old Rules of Bankruptcy Procedure and the new Bankruptcy Reform Act; whether a trustee should be appointed; which creditors should be exempt from the automatic stay against collecting claims; whether and to what extent collateral secured a claim in each given instance; under what conditions old claims can be subordinated to entice new money into the firm.

In sum, Kennedy judged, "a Chapter 11 case for Chrysler is fraught with hazards to its future survival."[71]

NOTES

Chapter I

1. Walter P. Chrysler, written in collaboration with Boyden Sparks, *Life of an American Workman* (New York: Dodd, Mead & Company, 1937), p. 1.
2. *Ibid.*, p. 20.
3. *Ibid.*, p. 40.
4. *Ibid.*, pp. 102, 105.
5. *Ibid.*, pp. 141–142.
6. *Ibid.*, p. 161.
7. *Ibid.*, p. 164.
8. *Ibid.*
9. *Ibid.*, p. 170.
10. *Ibid.*, p. 166.
11. *Ibid.*, p. 167.
12. *Ibid.*, p. 171.
13. *Ibid.*, pp. 175–176.
14. *Ibid.*, pp. 180–181.
15. *Ibid.*, pp. 188–189.
16. *Ibid.*, p. 191.
17. *Ibid.*, p. 196.
18. *Ibid.*, p. 217.
19. National Academy of Engineering, *The Competitive Status of the U.S. Automobile Industry* (Washington, D.C.: National Academy Press, 1982), p. 84.
20. *Detroit Free Press*, June 24, 1979.
21. Chrysler, *op. cit.*, p. 200.
22. *Ibid.*

23. *Ibid.*, p. 219.
24. *Detroit Free Press*, June 24, 1979.
25. *Fortune* (March 1948), p. 12.
26. Michael Moritz and Barrett Seaman, *Going for Broke: The Chrysler Story* (Garden City, N.Y.: Doubleday, 1981), p. 52.
27. *Ibid.*, p. 55.
28. *Ibid.*, p. 56.
29. Laurence Steadman, "Chrysler Corporation (A)," Harvard Business School case, 1971, p. 1.
30. *Ward's Automotive Yearbook*, 1961, p. 81.
31. *Fortune* (November 1968), p. 165.
32. Steadman, *op. cit.*, pp. 11–13.
33. *Ibid.*, pp. 12–13 and Exhibit 5.
34. *Ibid.*, p. 12.
35. Moritz and Seaman, *op. cit.*, pp. 71–78.
36. Anonymity requested.
37. Steadman, *op. cit.*, Exhibit 3.
38. *Fortune* (April 1970).
39. *Detroit Free Press*, June 24, 1979.
40. *The New York Times*, August 9, 1968.
41. *Fortune* (November 1968).
42. Steadman, *op. cit.*, Table 5, p. 18.
43. *Fortune* (November 1968), p. 167.
44. Moritz and Seaman, *op. cit.*, pp. 103–104.
45. *Detroit Free Press*, June 8, 1980.
46. Interview with Shep Lee, New England Chrysler dealer, January 24, 1984, Boston, Massachusetts.
47. *Detroit News*, November 1979, quoting Eugene Cafiero.
48. *Fortune* (April 1970), p. 105.
49. *Ibid.*
50. *The Wall Street Journal*, July 10, 1969.
51. Steadman, *op. cit.*, p. 12.
52. *The Wall Street Journal*, February 3, 1971.
53. *Ibid.*
54. *Ibid.*
55. Moritz and Seaman, *op. cit.*, p. 120; *Business Week* (December 14, 1974).
56. Code of Federal Regulations (CFR) 571.113, 571.211.
57. 472 F.2d 659 (Court of Appeals 6, 1972).
58. National Academy of Engineering, *op. cit.*, p. 84.
59. *The Wall Street Journal*, February 7, 1973.
60. *Ibid.*
61. *Ibid.*
62. *Ibid.*
63. *The New York Times*, October 5, 1973.
64. *Ibid.*, December 14, 1974.
65. *The New York Times*, January 14, 1975, and February 19, 1975.
66. *Ibid.*, August 12, 1979; Chrysler's annual reports.
67. *The New York Times*, April 27, 1975.
68. *Ibid.*
69. *Ibid.*, August 10, 1975.
70. *Ibid.*, March 22 and 26, 1975, and April 27, 1975.
71. *Ibid.*, April 27, 1975.

72. *The Wall Street Journal,* July 7, 1976.
73. *Ibid.,* February 10, 1976.
74. *Ibid.*
75. *Ibid.*
76. *Ibid.*
77. *Ibid.,* July 7, 1976, quoting David Eisenberg.
78. *The New York Times,* March 3, 1976.
79. *The Wall Street Journal,* July 7, 1976.
80. *Ibid.*
81. *The New York Times,* March 3, 1976.
82. *Ibid.*
83. *The Wall Street Journal,* July 7, 1976.
84. *The New York Times,* October 24, 1976.
85. *Ibid.,* February 22, 1977.
86. *Ibid.,* May 4, 1977.
87. Interview with Wendell Larsen, March 8, 1984, Chicago, Illinois.
88. Chrysler's 1977 annual report to shareholders, p. 5.
89. Interview with Harold Sperlich, September 26, 1983, Highland Park, Michigan.
90. *Ibid.*
91. *Fortune* (June 19, 1978), p. 56.
92. *The New York Times,* February 24, 1978.
93. Chrysler's 1977 annual report to shareholders, pp. 5–6.
94. *Fortune* (June 19, 1978), p. 55.
95. *The New York Times,* April 27, 1978.
96. Chrysler's 1977 annual report to shareholders, pp. 4–5.
97. *Ibid.,* p. 2.
98. *The New York Times,* May 7, 1978.
99. *Fortune* (June 19, 1978), p. 55.
100. *The New York Times,* June 18, 1978.
101. Interview with Wendell Larsen, March 8, 1984, Chicago, Illinois.
102. *Fortune* (June 19, 1978).
103. *The Wall Street Journal,* November 2, 1978.
104. Jeffrey Hadden, *Detroit News,* 1979 (no date available).
105. Interview with Lee Iacocca, November 9, 1983, New York, New York.
106. *The Wall Street Journal,* November 2, 1978.
107. *Ibid.*

Chapter II

1. Code of Hammurabi, Sections 115, 116.
2. S. Scott, *The Civil Law,* vol. 1 (1932), pp. 63–64.
3. 4 Anne, Ch. 17, 1705.
4. C. Warren, *Bankruptcy in United States History* (1935), pp.19–21.
5. Ford, "Imprisonment for Debt," 25 *Michigan Law Review* (1926), pp. 24, 29.
6. Nehemkis, "The Boston Poor Debtor Court," 42 *Yale Law Journal* (1933), pp. 561, 576.
7. Constitution of the United States, Article I, Section 8.
8. Morton Horwitz, *The Transformation of American Law 1780–1860* (Cambridge: Harvard University Press, 1977), p. 228; J. Gallison, *Considerations on an Insolvency Law* 4, 1814.
9. J. Dorsey, *Treatise on the American Law of Insolvency* 16, 1832.

10. Horwitz, *op. cit.*, p. 229.
11. The Torrey Bankruptcy Bill, Fifty-fourth Congress, 1st Session, Senate Document 237, 1896.
12. Dan Dimanescu, *Deferred Future* (New York: Ballinger, 1983), pp. 24–26.
13. Richard Austin Smith, *Corporations in Crisis* (Garden City, N.Y.: Doubleday, 1963), pp. 13, 25.
14. Robert B. Reich, *The Next American Frontier* (New York: Times Books, 1983), Chapter VIII.
15. *The New York Times*, November 6, 1983, p. 11.
16. *National Labor Relations Board* v. *Bildisco and Bildisco*, No. 82-818, decided on February 22, 1984.
17. *Fortune* (May 14, 1984), pp. 34-38.
18. John Harr, *The Great Railway Crisis: An Administrative History of the U.S. Railway Association* (Washington: National Academy of Public Administration, March 1978).
19. *Time* (May 12, 1968), p. 14.
20. *Philadelphia Inquirer*, April 30, 1981, p. 1.
21. *Business Week* (April 16, 1984), p. 80.
22. *The New York Times*, January 8, 1971, p. 30.
23. *Business Week* (June 26, 1971), p. 14.
24. *The New York Times*, August 1, 1971, Sec. 4, p. 2.
25. "Guidelines for Rescuing Large Failing Firms and Municipalities," Report to the Congress by the Comptroller General (Washington, D.C.: General Accounting Office, March 29, 1984), p. 12.
26. *Business Week* (March 17, 1975), p. 22.
27. "Implementation of Emergency Loan Guarantee Act," Report to the Congress by the Comptroller General (Washington, D.C.: General Accounting Office, April 25, 1977); Emergency Loan Guarantee Board, 6th Annual Report, January 31, 1978; Nonna A. Note, "Financial Conditions Surrounding the Federal Loan Guarantee to Lockheed" (Washington, D.C.: Congressional Research Service, August 20, 1979).
28. General Accounting Office report, March 29, 1984, pp. 14–15; Stacey M. Kean, "The New York City Financial Crisis" (Washington, D.C.: Congressional Research Service, August 2, 1976); Christopher R. Conte, "New York City Aid: The Bargaining Begins," *Congressional Quarterly*, February 25, 1978, pp. 545–47.
29. *The Wall Street Journal*, July 3, 1984, p. 8.
30. "Development Incentives: State Financing Programs for Industry," Site Selection Handbook, Council of State Governments, 1982.
31. *The New York Times*, May 23, 1981, p. 24, and January 28, 1982, p. 18.
32. *1983 Guide to Government Resources for Economic Development* (Washington, D.C.: Northeast-Midwest Institute, 1982), p. 102.
33. *Forbes* (July 18, 1983), pp. 30–31.
34. Letter from Richard Demers to James Angevine, Small Business Administration, dated December 9, 1982.
35. Howard Baker-Smith, Lucy Gorham, and Linsay French, "Adams Print Works," a case study, Cambridge, Mass.: March 22, 1984.
36. *The Wall Street Journal*, April 11, 1975, p. 1.
37. "British Leyland: The Next Decade," report presented to the secretary of state for industry by a team of inquiry led by Sir Donald Ryder, House of Commons, April 23, 1975, p. 3.
38. *The New York Times*, April 25, 1975, p. 45.
39. *The Economist* (February 4, 1978), p. 110.
40. *Ibid.* (January 31, 1981), p.48.

41. *The Wall Street Journal,* October 3, 1974, p. 11.
42. "Where Is Toyo Kogyo Going?" *Toyo Keizai (The Oriental Economist)* (February 14, 1976), p. 14.
43. Sam Jameson, "The Turnaround at Mazda—Is There a Lesson for Chrysler?" *Los Angeles Times,* October 25, 1981, p. 81.
44. "Where Is Toyo Kogyo Going?" *loc. cit.*
45. Interview with Satoshi Yamada, general manager of the Sumitomo Bank, September 16, 1983, Osaka, Japan.

Chapter III

1. *Detroit Free Press,* June 10, 1979.
2. *The New York Times,* December 2, 1978.
3. Stuart Eizenstat notes, December 4, 1978.
4. Interview with Philip Loomis, April 27, 1984, New York, New York.
5. *The New York Times,* February 3, 1979.
6. *Ibid.,* May 24, 1980.
7. *Ibid.,* February 3, 1979.
8. *Ibid.,* April 13, 1979.
9. *Detroit Free Press,* June 10, 1979.
10. Interview with Wendell Larsen, February 14, 1984, Chicago, Illinois.
11. Eizenstat notes, August 10, 1979.
12. *Detroit Free Press,* May 16, 1979.
13. *Ibid.,* June 10, 1979.
14. *Ibid.*
15. *Ibid.,* May 31, 1979.
16. *Ibid.,* July 5, 1979.
17. *Ibid.,* and *Detroit News,* May 30, 1979.
18. *Detroit News,* May 30, 1979.
19. *Detroit Free Press,* July 24, 1979.
20. *Ibid.*
21. *The New York Times,* June 23, 1979.
22. *Detroit News,* June 29, 1979.
23. Midwestern banker, anonymity requested, January 1984.
24. Data are from Manufacturers Hanover Trust.
25. Interview with Brian Freeman, February 2, 1984, Cambridge, Massachusetts.
26. Eizenstat notes, July 25, 1979.
27. United Automobile Workers memo, dated May 25, 1979.
28. *Detroit News,* July 24, 1979.
29. Interview with Marc Stepp, January 10, 1984, Solidarity House, Detroit, Michigan.
30. *The New York Times,* August 1, 1979.
31. Internal Chrysler memo, dated August 28, 1979.
32. *Ibid.*
33. *The New York Times,* August 1, 1979.
34. *Detroit Free Press,* August 5, 1979.
35. Eizenstat notes, July 26, 1979.
36. *Ibid.,* July 31, 1979.
37. Interview with Robert Carswell, October 19, 1983, New York, New York.
38. Interview with Tommy Boggs, January 30, 1984, Washington, D.C.
39. Interview with Wendell Larsen, March 8, 1984, Chicago, Illinois.

40. Interview with G. William Miller, February 3, 1984, Washington, D.C.
41. Interview with Wendell Larsen, March 8, 1984, Chicago, Illinois.
42. Interview with Tommy Boggs, January 30, 1984, Washington, D.C.
43. Eizenstat notes, August 9, 1979.
44. Interview with Coleman Young, January 13, 1984, Detroit, Michigan.
45. Eizenstat notes, August 9, 1979.
46. Interview with Roger Altman, November 26, 1983, New York, New York.
47. Eizenstat notes, September 5, 1979.
48. *Ibid.*, September 6, 1979.
49. Interview with Gerald Greenwald, November 9, 1983, New York, New York.
50. Chrysler Corporation, "Analysis of Chrysler Corporation Situation and Proposal for Government Assistance," September 15, 1979, p. 6.
51. *Ibid.*, p. 8.
52. *Ibid.*, pp. 10–12.
53. *Ibid.*, pp. 13–18.
54. Interview with Philip Loomis, April 27, 1984, Washington, D.C.
55. Chrysler Corporation proposal, pp. 19–20.
56. *Ibid.*, pp. 28–29.
57. *Ibid.*, p. 20.
58. *Ibid.*, p. 27.
59. *Ibid.*
60. *The Wall Street Journal*, September 6, 1979.
61. *Detroit Free Press*, August 1, 1979.
62. *The New York Times*, September 12, 1979.
63. Interview with Brian Freeman, April 23, 1984, Newark, New Jersey.
64. Interview with Tommy Boggs, January 31, 1984, Washington, D.C.
65. Interview with Wendell Larsen, February 14, 1984, Chicago, Illinois.
66. *Congressional Quarterly*, August 18, 1979, p. 1697.
67. *Detroit Free Press*, October 11, 1979; *The New York Times*, October 25, 1979.
68. *Detroit Free Press*, September 15, 1979.
69. James Blanchard, as told to Jennifer Holmes, "How Chrysler Went to Washington and Blanchard Went to Bat," *Detroit Free Press*, May 25, 1980.
70. *Detroit Free Press*, September 15, 1979.
71. *The Wall Street Journal*, September 4, 1979.
72. *Detroit News*, August 26, 1979.
73. *Congressional Quarterly*, September 22, 1979.
74. Interview with Elinor Bachrach, March 13, 1984, New York, New York.
75. Interview with G. William Miller, February 3, 1984, Washington, D.C.
76. *Detroit News*, October 18, 1979.
77. *Congressional Quarterly*, October 27, 1979, p. 2421.
78. Lee Iacocca, "Testimony before House Committee on Banking, Finance, and Urban Affairs, Subcommittee on Economic Stabilization, October 18, 1979"; printed and distributed by Chrysler Public Affairs, p. 2.
79. *Ibid.*, pp. 5–6.
80. *Ibid.*, p. 13.
81. *Ibid.*, pp. 4, 11; and *Congressional Quarterly*, October 27, 1979.
82. Iacocca testimony, *loc. cit.*, pp. 16–17.
83. *Congressional Quarterly*, October 27, 1979, p. 2422.
84. Quoted in *The New York Times*, October 20, 1979.
85. Interview with Dorothy Brody, September 26, 1984, Detroit, Michigan.
86. Hearings before the Subcommittee on Economic Stabilization of the House Committee on Banking, Finance, and Urban Affairs, Ninety-sixth Congress, 1st Session, pp. 342–44.

87. *Ibid.*, pp. 342–43.
88. *Ibid.*, p. 346.
89. *Detroit Free Press*, October 24, 1979.
90. *Detroit News*, October 24, 1979.
91. *The New York Times*, November 2, 1979.
92. Eizenstat notes, October 24, 1979.
93. Interview with Douglas Fraser, April 26, 1984, Cambridge, Massachusetts.
94. *Detroit News*, October 26, 1979; *Detroit Free Press*, October 26, 1979; *The New York Times*, October 26, 1979; text of October 25, 1979, contract.
95. *Detroit News*, October 26, 1979.
96. *Detroit Free Press*, October 26, 1979.
97. *Detroit News*, October 26, 1979.
98. *Ibid.*
99. *Ibid.*, October 27, 1979.
100. Statement appended to United Auto Workers Chrysler *Newsgram*, November 1979.
101. *The New York Times*, October 31, 1979.
102. *Ibid.*
103. *Congressional Quarterly*, October 27, 1979, p. 2423.
104. Chrysler Corporation, "Modification of Loan Guarantee Request," October 17, 1979 (hereafter Chrysler's October 17 plan), Table 4, p. 14.
105. *Ibid.*, p. 15.
106. *Ibid.*, Table 1, p. 11.
107. *Ibid.*, p. 16.
108. *The New York Times*, October 7 and 14, 1979.
109. Blanchard and Holmes, *op. cit.*
110. Eizenstat notes, October 31, 1979.
111. Interview with Philip Loomis, April 27, 1984, New York, New York.
112. Anonymity requested.
113. *Congressional Quarterly*, November 3, 1979, p. 2453.
114. Interview with Roger Altman, November 26, 1983, New York, New York.
115. *Congressional Quarterly*, November 3, 1979, p. 2506.
116. *The New York Times*, November 2, 1979.
117. *Congressional Quarterly*, November 3, 1979, p.1979.
118. *The New York Times*, November 3, 1979.
119. Hearings before the Committee on Banking, Housing, and Urban Affairs, United States Senate (hereafter Senate Hearings), November 14, 1979, p. 3.
120. *Ibid.*, p. 605.
121. *Ibid.*, p. 601. See Lee Iacocca's comment to securities analysts four years later, p. 281.
122. Interview with Elinor Bachrach, November 10, 1983, New York, New York.
123. Senate Hearings, pp. 1414, 1416.
124. *Ibid.*, pp. 780–82.
125. *Ibid.*
126. *Detroit News*, November 17, 1979.
127. *Ibid.*, November 22, 1979, and Senate Hearings, p. 1286.
128. Senate Hearings, p. 1140.
129. *Congressional Quarterly*, December 1, 1979, p. 2752.
130. Senate Hearings, p. 1196.
131. *Ibid.*, p. 1264.
132. *Ibid.*, p. 78.
133. *Ibid.*, pp. 657–58.
134. *The New York Times*, October 25, 1979.

135. Chrysler's October 17 plan, p. 74.
136. 12 United States Code 24(7).
137. Interview with Wendell Larsen, February 14, 1984, Chicago, Illinois.
138. Interview with Gerald Greenwald, November 9, 1983, New York, New York.
139. *The New York Times,* November 23, 1979.
140. Senate Hearings, p. 1300.
141. Chrysler's 1979 annual report to shareholders.
142. *The New York Times,* November 11, 1979.
143. Senate Hearings, p. 1415 ff.
144. *Detroit Free Press,* November 20, 1979.
145. *The New York Times,* November 19, 1979.
146. *Ibid.*
147. Stock figures as of December 31, 1979, from Chrysler's 1979 annual report, p. 25.
148. Senate Hearings, p. 342.
149. *Ibid.,* p. 341.
150. *Ibid.,* p. 638–39.
151. *Ibid.,* p. 843.
152. Interview with Brian Freeman, April 22, 1984, Newark, New Jersey.
153. Senate Hearings, p. 1046 ff.
154. *Detroit Free Press,* November 4, 1979.
155. *Detroit News,* November 14, 1979.
156. *Detroit Free Press,* November 21, 1979.
157. Senate Hearings, pp. 1017–18.
158. *Ibid.,* p. 1018.
159. Interview with Elinor Bachrach, November 10, 1983, New York, New York.
160. *Detroit Free Press,* November 12, 1979.
161. *The New York Times,* November 8, 1979.
162. Interview with Kenneth McLean, October 19, 1983, Washington, D.C.
163. *The New York Times,* December 1, 1979.
164. *Ibid.*
165. *Ibid.,* June 29, 1980.
166. *Ibid.,* November 30, 1979.
167. *Congressional Quarterly,* December 1, 1979, p. 2751.
168. *Ibid.*
169. *Ibid.,* December 15, 1979, p. 2820.
170. *Detroit Free Press,* December 19, 1979.
171. *The New York Times,* December 11, 1979.
172. *Ibid.*
173. Interview with Wendell Larsen, February 14, 1984, Chicago, Illinois.
174. *Detroit Free Press,* December 18, 1979; *The New York Times,* December 19, 1979.
175. Interview with Lee Iacocca, November 9, 1983, New York, New York.
176. *The New York Times,* December 11, 1979.
177. *Detroit News,* December 23, 1979.
178. Interview with Gerald Greenwald, November 9, 1983, New York, New York.
179. *The New York Times,* December 11, 1979.
180. Interview with Howard Paster, October 10, 1983, Washington, D.C.
181. *Congressional Record,* Vol. 125, H11900.
182. *Ibid.,* H12194.
183. Interview with Lee Iacocca, November 9, 1983, New York, New York.
184. *Congressional Record,* Vol. 125, H12138-9.

185. *Ibid.,* H12139.
186. *Ibid.,* H12182.
187. *Ibid.,* H12188 ff.
188. *Ibid.,* H12188.
189. *Congressional Quarterly,* December 22, 1979, p. 2872.
190. *Congressional Record,* Vol. 125, H12222.
191. Interview with Wendell Larsen, February 14, 1984, Chicago, Illinois.
192. *Detroit Free Press,* December 15, 1979.
193. Interview with Gerald Greenwald, November 9, 1983, New York, New York.
194. *Congressional Record,* December 1979, S19110.
195. *Congressional Quarterly,* December 22, 1979, p. 2872.
196. *Congressional Record,* December 1979, S19113.
197. *Ibid.,* S19155.
198. *Ibid.,* S19156–7.
199. Interview with Elinor Bachrach, November 10, 1983, New York, New York.
200. *The New York Times,* December 19, 1979; *Detroit News,* December 20, 1979.
201. *Congressional Record,* December 1979, S19172.
202. Interview with Gerald Greenwald, November 9, 1983, New York, New York.
203. *Congressional Record,* December 1979, S19182.
204. *The New York Times,* December 20, 1979.
205. Moritz and Seaman, *op. cit.,* p. 263; interview with Wendell Larsen, February 14, 1984, Chicago, Illinois.
206. *Congressional Quarterly,* December 22, 1979, p. 2873.
207. *Congressional Record,* December 1979, H12489.
208. *Ibid.,* S19406.
209. *Ibid.,* S19409.
210. *The New York Times,* December 21, 1979.
211. Interview with Pierre Gagnier, May 3, 1984, Highland Park, Michigan.
212. *The New York Times,* December 21, 1979.
213. *Congressional Quarterly,* December 22, 1979, p. 2873.
214. *The New York Times,* January 7, 1980.

Chapter IV

1. Interview with Elinor Bachrach, November 10, 1983, New York, New York.
2. Thomas C. Schelling, *The Strategy of Conflict* (Cambridge: Harvard University Press, 1960, 1980), p. 37.
3. PL 96-185, Chrysler Corporation Loan Guarantee Act of 1979, Section 6(a)1.
4. *Ibid.,* Section 4(c)1.
5. *Ibid.,* Sections 4(a) and 4(d).
6. *Ibid.,* Section 4(c).
7. Interview with Gerald Greenwald, November 9, 1983, New York, New York.
8. *The New York Times,* January 19, 1980.
9. *Detroit Free Press,* January 5, 1980.
10. Letter from Chrysler Corporation to Marc Stepp of the United Automobile Workers, dated January 5, 1980.
11. United Automobile Workers press release, dated January 5, 1980.
12. Interview with Dan Luria, January 12, 1983, Solidarity House, Detroit, Michigan.
13. Figures from letter from United Automobile Workers to Department of Labor, dated January 8, 1980.

14. *Ibid.*
15. *Detroit Free Press,* February 2, 1980.
16. Interview with Bill Daniels, January 10, 1984, Local 7 headquarters, Detroit, Michigan.
17. *Detroit Free Press,* February 2, 1980.
18. Statistics from a letter from Paul Volcker to Senator William Proxmire, dated November 26, 1979.
19. *Detroit Free Press,* February 19, 1980.
20. Chrysler's October 17 plan, p. 74.
21. Gary Hector, *American Banker* (October 22, 1980).
22. *Ibid.* (October 13, 1980).
23. Moritz and Seaman, *op. cit.,* p. 306.
24. Quoted in John Dizard, "Trying to Put Chrysler Back on the Road," *Institutional Investor* (March 1980); p. 45.
25. *Ibid.,* p. 44.
26. *Ibid.,* p. 45.
27. *Ibid.*
28. Hector, *loc. cit.* (October 22, 1980).
29. Senate Hearings, p. 1328.
30. Interview with Leonard Rosen, April 16, 1984, New York, New York.
31. Interview with Gerald Greenwald, November 9, 1983, New York, New York.
32. Memorandum presented to bankers, dated December 23, 1979.
33. *Ibid.*
34. Interview with Gerald Greenwald, November 9, 1983, New York, New York.
35. Interview with James Wolfensohn, April 16, 1984, New York, New York.
36. Interview with J. Philip Lowman, January 11, 1984, Detroit, Michigan.
37. Steve Miller's personal notes.
38. Interview with Leonard Rosen, April 16, 1984, New York, New York.
39. Hector, *loc. cit.* (November 3, 1980).
40. *Ibid.*
41. Interview with Luke Lynch, April 27, 1984, New York, New York.
42. Hector, *loc. cit.* (November 3, 1980).
43. Interview with Gerald Greenwald, November 9, 1983, New York, New York.
44. Senior official of a major regional bank, anonymity requested.
45. *The New York Times,* April 1, 1980.
46. Hector, *loc. cit.* (November 10, 1980).
47. *Ibid.*
48. *The New York Times,* April 3, 1980.
49. Chrysler Corporation Loan Guarantee Board, Report to Congress for the Period Through March 31, 1980, p. 18.
50. Hector, *loc. cit.* (November 10, 1980).
51. Report of the Chrysler Corporation Loan Guarantee Board to Congress, July 15, 1980, p. 301.
52. Interview with a major regional bank officer, anonymity requested.
53. Interview with Walter Watkins, January 11, 1984, Detroit, Michigan.
54. Hector, *loc. cit.* (October 11, 1980).
55. Interview with Brian Freeman, April 23, 1984, Newark, New Jersey.
56. Interview, March 1984, anonymity requested.
57. *Los Angeles Times,* May 13, 1980.
58. *The Wall Street Journal,* April 21, 1980.
59. Interview with Lee Iacocca, November 9, 1983, New York, New York.
60. *The New York Times,* June 29, 1980.

61. Hector, *loc. cit.* (November 18, 1980).
62. *Detroit Free Press,* April 16, 1980.
63. *The Wall Street Journal,* April 21, 1980.
64. *Ibid.*
65. *The New York Times,* April 11, 1980.
66. *Detroit Free Press,* May 1, 1980.
67. *The New York Times,* May 1, 1980.
68. *Detroit Free Press,* May 6, 1980.
69. *The New York Times,* May 7, 1980.
70. *Ibid.,* May 10, 1980.
71. *Detroit Free Press,* April 15, 1980.
72. *The New York Times,* May 10, 1980.
73. *Ibid.,* May 1, 1980.
74. Interview with Douglas Fraser, October 19, 1983, Washington, D.C.
75. *Detroit Free Press,* May 11, 1980.
76. *The New York Times,* May 11, 1980.
77. *Detroit Free Press,* May 12, 1980.
78. United States of America and Chrysler Corporation, Agreement to Guarantee $1,500,000,000 Aggregate Principal Amount of Indebtedness, dated May 15, 1980 (hereafter Agreement to Guarantee); Sections 2.01, 2.02, 2.03, and Exhibit J.
79. *The New York Times,* May 21, 1980.
80. *Ibid.,* May 26, 1980.
81. Interview with Steve Miller, September 26, 1983, Highland Park, Michigan.
82. Interview with Brian Freeman, April 23, 1984, Newark, New Jersey.
83. Interview with G. William Miller, February 3, 1984, Washington, D.C.
84. Interview with Leonard Rosen, April 16, 1984, New York, New York.
85. Interview, January 1984, Manufacturers Hanover Trust, New York, New York, anonymity requested.
86. Hector, *loc. cit.* (November 18, 1980).
87. *The New York Times,* June 29, 1980.
88. Hector, *loc. cit.* (November 25, 1980).
89. *Ibid.*
90. Company memo, dated January 24, 1980.
91. Company memo, dated April 14, 1980.
92. *The New York Times,* June 17, 1980.
93. *Ibid.,* June 18, 1980.
94. *Ibid.*
95. Interview with Wendell Larsen, February 14, 1984, Chicago, Illinois.
96. Moritz and Seaman, *op. cit.,* p. 316.
97. Hector, *loc. cit.* (November 25, 1980).
98. *The New York Times,* June 29, 1980.
99. Interview with Charles Struve, May 3, 1984, Highland Park, Michigan.
100. Chrysler Corporation Loan Guarantee Act of 1979, Section 5(a).
101. *Ibid.,* Section 11 (i).
102. *Ibid.,* Section 11 (a).
103. *Ibid.,* Section 4 (a) 3 and 4.
104. *Ibid.,* Sections 5(c) and 5(d).
105. Interview with Brian Freeman, February 2, 1984, Cambridge, Massachusetts.
106. *Ibid.,* April 23, 1984, Newark, New Jersey.
107. Interview with Pierre Gagnier, May 3, 1984, Highland Park, Michigan.
108. Interview with Charles Struve, May 3, 1984, Highland Park, Michigan.

109. Interview with Wendell Larsen, February 14, 1984, Chicago, Illinois.
110. Interview with Federal Reserve official, March 13, 1984, New York, New York.
111. Former loan board staff member, anonymity requested.
112. Interview with Frederick Zuckerman, May 25, 1984, Boston, Massachusetts.
113. Interview with Pierre Gagnier, May 3, 1984, Highland Park, Michigan.
114. Interview with Brian Freeman, February 2, 1984, Cambridge, Massachusetts.
115. Interview with Michael Driggs, January 30, 1984, Washington, D.C.
116. Interview with Cyrus Friedheim, February 14, 1984, Chicago, Illinois.
117. Interview with Gerald Greenwald, November 9, 1983, New York, New York.
118. Interview with G. William Miller, February 3, 1984, Washington, D.C.
119. Loan Guarantee Board's Report to Congress, July 15, 1980, p. 28.
120. Interview with Brian Freeman, April 23, 1984, Newark, New Jersey.
121. Interview with Donald Hammond, January 18, 1984, Washington, D.C.
122. Interview with Pierre Gagnier, May 3, 1984, Highland Park, Michigan.
123. Interview with Wendell Larsen, March 8, 1984, Chicago, Illinois.
124. Interview with Pierre Gagnier, May 3, 1984, Highland Park, Michigan.
125. Agreement to Guarantee, Director's Agreement, Exhibit K.
126. Interview with Pierre Gagnier, May 3, 1984, Highland Park, Michigan.
127. *The New York Times,* June 29, 1980.
128. *Ibid.*
129. *Ibid.,* June 25 and June 29, 1980.
130. Statement by Lee Iacocca at press ceremony, June 25, 1980.
131. *The New York Times,* June 29, 1980.
132. Chrysler Corporation *Fact Book,* p. Q-4.

Chapter V

1. *Detroit News,* February 16, 1980; *Detroit Free Press,* April 16, 1980.
2. *Detroit Free Press,* May 13 and 16, 1980.
3. *The New York Times,* July 17, 1980.
4. *Los Angeles Times,* May 13, 1980.
5. *Detroit Free Press,* May 13, 1980.
6. "The Automobile Industry: Outlook and Options for Government Action," submitted to the Economic Policy Group by Neil Goldschmidt, June 13, 1980.
7. "The U.S. Automobile Industry, 1980: Report to the President from the Secretary of Transportation," January 1981, Table 7.3.
8. *Detroit Free Press,* May 13, 1980.
9. Statement by Lee Iacocca to reporters at Highland Park, Michigan, July 2, 1980.
10. *Detroit Free Press,* July 25, 1980.
11. Loan Guarantee Board's Report to Congress, November 10, 1980, p. 8.
12. *Ibid.,* p. 19.
13. *The New York Times,* July 17, 1980.
14. Chrysler submission to Loan Guarantee Board, September 1980.
15. Speech by J. Paul Bergmoser to Detroit Rotary Club, November 12, 1980.
16. *Detroit Free Press,* June 2, 1980.
17. *Ibid.*
18. *The New York Times,* August 30, 1980.
19. Interview with Douglas Fraser, October 19, 1983, Washington, D.C.
20. Interview with Thomas Miner, September 26, 1983, Highland Park, Michigan.
21. Interview with Richard Gross, December 22, 1983, Kokomo, Indiana.
22. *The New York Times,* October 20, 1980.

23. Interview with Michael Driggs, January 30, 1984, Washington, D.C.
24. Interview with G. William Miller, February 3, 1984, Washington, D. C.
25. Interview with Brian Freeman, April 23, 1984, Newark, New Jersey.
26. Interview with Lachlan Seward, January 17, 1984, Washington, D.C.
27. *The New York Times,* August 1, 1980.
28. *The Wall Street Journal,* November 7, 1980.
29. Interview with Wendell Larsen, March 8, 1984, Chicago, Illinois.
30. Transcript of Lee Iacocca remarks to the press, dated September 23, 1980.
31. Chrysler's October 17 plan, p. 11.
32. *The New York Times,* October 30, 1980.
33. *The Wall Street Journal,* November 7, 1980.
34. *Ibid.*
35. Moritz and Seaman, *op. cit.,* pp. 328–29; *The Economist* (November 29, 1980), p. 62.
36. Memo from Office of Chrysler Finance staff to board on Section 5 (a) 4 of act, dated January 19, 1981.
37. Interview with Lee Iacocca, November 9, 1983, New York, New York.
38. Interview with Luke Lynch, April 27, 1984, New York, New York.
39. Interview with G. William Miller, February 3, 1984, Washington, D.C.
40. Interview with Brian Freeman, April 23, 1984, Newark, New Jersey.
41. Press conference, December 17, 1980, Highland Park, Michigan.
42. Loan Guarantee Board's Report to Congress, January 19, 1981, p. 124.
43. *The New York Times,* December 11, 1980.
44. Press conference, December 17, 1980, Highland Park, Michigan.
45. Interview with Luke Lynch, April 27, 1984, New York, New York.
46. Interview with Lee Iacocca, November 9, 1983, New York, New York.
47. *The New York Times,* December 18, 1980.
48. *Detroit Free Press,* January 18, 1980.
49. *The New York Times,* December 23, 1980.
50. *Ibid.,* December 24, 1980.
51. *Ibid.,* December 23, 1980.
52. Interview with Luke Lynch, April 27, 1984, New York, New York.
53. *The New York Times,* December 22, 1980.
54. Interview with Pierre Gagnier, May 3, 1984, Highland Park, Michigan.
55. Interview with G. William Miller, February 3, 1984, Washington, D.C.
56. *Detroit News,* January 16, 1981.
57. *Detroit Free Press,* January 10, 1981; *The New York Times,* January 9, 1981; *Detroit News,* January 10, 1981; interview with Luke Lynch, April 27, 1984, New York, New York.
58. *The New York Times,* January 12, 1981.
59. *Ibid.,* February 6, 1981.
60. Interview with Steve Miller, September 26, 1983, Highland Park, Michigan.
61. Interview with Charles Struve, May 3, 1984, Highland Park, Michigan.
62. Interview with Luke Lynch, April 27, 1984, New York, New York.
63. Steve Miller's personal notes.
64. Interview with David Schulte, August 11, 1983, Martha's Vineyard, Massachusetts.
65. Interview with Douglas Fraser, October 19, 1983, Washington, D.C.
66. *The New York Times,* January 13, 1981.
67. Interview with Douglas Fraser, October 19, 1983, Washington, D.C.
68. Interview with Luke Lynch, April 27, 1984, New York, New York.
69. *Detroit News,* January 14, 1981; *Detroit Free Press,* January 14, 1981.
70. *Detroit News,* January 14, 1981.
71. *Detroit Free Press,* January 14, 1981.

72. Interview with Marc Stepp, January 10, 1984, Solidarity House, Detroit, Michigan.
73. Interview with Douglas Fraser, October 19, 1983, Washington, D.C.
74. Interview with Marc Stepp, January 10, 1984, Solidarity House, Detroit, Michigan.
75. Letter of agreement, T.W. Miner for Chrysler Corporation to Marc Stepp for UAW, dated January 14, 1981.
76. *Ibid.*
77. Interview with Marc Stepp, January 10, 1984, Solidarity House, Detroit, Michigan.
78. *The New York Times*, January 16, 1981.
79. *Detroit Free Press*, January 15, 1981.
80. Calculated from data in memorandum from Office of Chrysler Finance to Loan Guarantee Board, reprinted in House Subcommittee on Banking, Finance, and Urban Affairs, "Findings of the Chrysler Corporation Loan Guarantee Board," January 19, 1981, pp. 114–29.
81. Interview with Luke Lynch, April 27, 1984, New York, New York.
82. *The New York Times*, January 20, 1981.
83. *Labor Notes* (January 27, 1981).
84. *Ibid.*
85. *Detroit News*, January 30, 1981.
86. *Detroit Free Press*, January 31, 1981.
87. *Ibid.*
88. *The New York Times*, February 3, 1981.
89. *Detroit Free Press*, February 3, 1981.
90. *Ibid.*, February 8, 1981.
91. Interview with Steve Miller, September 26, 1983, Highland Park, Michigan.
92. Interview with Luke Lynch, April 27, 1984, New York, New York.
93. *Ibid.*
94. *The Washington Post*, February 25, 1981.
95. *The New York Times*, February 27, 1981.
96. *Ibid.*
97. *Detroit Free Press*, February 28, 1981.
98. Interview with Michael Driggs, January 30, 1984, Washington, D.C.
99. Interview with Brian Freeman, April 23, 1984, Newark, New Jersey.
100. *Ibid.*
101. Interview with Wendell Larsen, March 8, 1984, Chicago, Illinois.
102. Interview with Michael Driggs, January 30, 1984, Washington, D.C.

Chapter VI

1. *Detroit Free Press*, February 28, 1981.
2. Interview with Ellen Seidman, January 17, 1984, Washington, D.C.
3. *The New York Times*, March 15, 1981.
4. *Ibid.*
5. *Ibid.*, April 11, 1981.
6. Interview with Lee Iacocca, November 9, 1983, New York, New York.
7. *The New York Times*, April 1, 1981.
8. *Ibid.*, July 23, 1981.
9. *Ibid.*, pp. 1, D6.
10. Interview with Luke Lynch, April 27, 1984, New York, New York.
11. Interview with Pierre Gagnier, May 3, 1984, Highland Park, Michigan.
12. Interview with Steve Miller, September 26, 1983, Highland Park, Michigan.

13. Interview with Lee Iacocca, November 9, 1983, New York, New York.
14. *Ibid*.
15. *The New York Times,* November 14, 1981, p. 31.
16. Chrysler's 1983 annual report to shareholders, p. 19.
17. *Fortune* (May 4, 1981), p. 156.
18. David Jernigan, "Restrictions on Japanese Auto Imports," Kennedy School of Government, 1983, p. 45.
19. *Ibid*.
20. *Fortune* (May 4, 1981), p. 161.
21. *Ibid.,* p. 55.
22. *The New York Times,* April 8, 1984, p. 12; figures estimated by Wharton econometrics.
23. Interview with Lee Iacocca, November 9, 1983, New York, New York.
24. *The New York Times,* April 13, 1982.
25. *The Economist* (July 24, 1983), p. 60.
26. Interview with Harold Sperlich, September 26, 1983, Highland Park, Michigan.
27. *The New York Times,* July 10, 1984.
28. Letter from Marc Stepp to Lee Iacocca, dated May 29, 1981.
29. *Automotive News* (July 27, 1981), p. 8.
30. *Detroit Free Press,* May 30, 1982; *Business Week* (July 26, 1982), p. 22.
31. *Business Week* (July 26, 1982), p. 22.
32. *The New York Times,* March 5, 1984, pp. A1, B7.
33. *Ibid.,* p. B7.
34. *Ibid*.
35. *Ibid.,* p. B8.
36. *Business Week* (November 4, 1982) p. 46.
37. Interview with Douglas Fraser, April 26, 1984, Cambridge, Massachusetts.
38. *Detroit Free Press,* September 18, 1982.
39. *Business Week* (October 4, 1982), p. 46.
40. Interview with Marc Stepp, January 10, 1984, Solidarity House, Detroit, Michigan.
41. *Business Week* (November 22, 1982).
42. *Ibid.,* p. 31.
43. *The Wall Street Journal,* July 15, 1983, pp. 1, 12.
44. Figures from Chrysler's 1982 annual report to shareholders.
45. Interview with Walter Watkins, January 11, 1984, Detroit, Michigan.
46. *The Wall Street Journal,* June 25, 1984.
47. *Congressional Record,* July 14, 1983, S10015.
48. Interview with J. Philip Lowman, January 10, 1984, Detroit, Michigan.
49. Interview with Brian Freeman, February 2, 1984, Cambridge, Massachusetts.
50. *National Journal* (August 13, 1983), p. 1697.
51. Interview with Lee Iacocca, November 9, 1983, New York, New York.
52. Interview with Warren Carter, January 17, 1984, Washington, D.C., and Treasury financial files.
53. Interview with Frederick Zuckerman, May 25, 1984, Boston, Massachusetts.
54. *Institutional Investor* (December 1983), p. 171.
55. *The New York Times,* September 13, 1983, p. D5.
56. Interview with Lee Iacocca, November 9, 1983, New York, New York.
57. *Detroit Free Press,* April 20, 1983.
58. *The New York Times,* June 27, 1983.
59. *The Wall Street Journal,* June 9, 1983, p. 5.
60. Interview with Marc Stepp, January 10, 1984, Solidarity House, Detroit, Michigan.
61. *The New York Times,* September 7, 1983, p. A18.
62. Letter from Marc Stepp to Chrysler UAW members, dated September 15, 1983.

63. "The Closing of a Ford Motor Company Plant in Mahwah, New Jersey," prepared for the New York State Department of Labor by the New York State School of Industrial and Labor Relations, Division of Extension and Public Service, Cornell University, January 1983.
64. Interview with Anthony Moore, January 10, 1984, Local 7 headquarters, Detroit, Michigan.
65. *The Wall Street Journal,* November 4, 1983, p. 6.
66. *Ibid.,* November 9, 1983, p. 6.
67. *Ibid.*
68. *Ibid.,* November 14, 1983.
69. *Ibid.,* December 9, 1983.
70. Interview with Douglas Fraser, April 26, 1984, Cambridge, Massachusetts.
71. Chrysler Corporation, report to shareholders, Third Quarter 1984, p. 10.

Chapter VII

1. Interview with William Proxmire, January 31, 1984, Washington, D.C.
2. Interview with Coleman Young, January 13, 1984, Detroit, Michigan.
3. Interview with Elinor Bachrach, December 10, 1983, New York, New York.
4. Interview with Wendell Larsen, March 8, 1984, Chicago, Illinois.
5. Paul E. Tsongas, "Did the Chrysler Bailout Work?" *The New York Times,* August 2, 1983.
6. Interview with William Proxmire, January 30, 1984, Washington, D.C.
7. Richard Caves, "The Structure of Industry," in Martin Feldstein, ed., *The American Economy in Transition* (Chicago: University of Chicago Press, 1980) Table 7.5.
8. Interview with J. Philip Lowman, January 11, 1984, Detroit, Michigan.
9. Indiana Statutes Anno 4-4-11-17 (d).
10. Details on International Harvester from a draft case prepared for the Kennedy School of Government by Robert P. Haney, Jr.
11. *The New York Times,* June 9, 1984, p. 33.
12. *Ward's Auto World* (December 1982), p. 43.
13. Interview with Douglas Fraser, October 19, 1983, Washington, D.C.
14. Interview with Lee Iacocca, November 9, 1983, New York, New York.
15. Transcript of speech by Lee Iacocca to securities analysts, Highland Park, Michigan, December 1, 1983.
16. Anonymity requested.
17. George P. Shultz and Arnold R. Weber, *Strategies for the Displaced Worker* (New York: Harper & Row, 1966), p. 190.
18. William L. Batt, Jr., "Canada's Good Example with Displaced Workers," *Harvard Business Review* (July–August 1983), p. 8.
19. *Ibid.*
20. *Ibid.*
21. Steve Charnovitz, "Trade Adjustment Assistance: What Went Wrong?" *The Journal of the Institute for Socioeconomic Studies,* vol. 9, no. 1 (Spring 1984).
22. Clayton Antitrust Act, Section 7.
23. Interview with G. William Miller, February 3, 1984, Washington, D.C.

Appendix B

1. Charles W. Kadlec, Kenneth W. Clarkson, and Arthur B. Laffer, "The Impact of Government Regulations on Competition in the U.S. Automobile Industry" (Boston: H. C. Wainwright & Company, 1979), pp. 10–11.

2. *Ibid.*, pp. 15–16.
3. *Ibid.*, p. 1.
4. *Ibid.*, p. 3.
5. *Ibid.*, p. 49.
6. *Ibid.*, p. 7.
7. "Energy Conservation and the Passenger Car: An Assessment of Existing Public Policy" (Boston: Harbridge House, Inc., June 1979), pp. 4–5.
8. *Ibid.*, Appendix F, pp. 75–76.
9. *Ibid.*, pp. 58–60.
10. *Ibid.*, p. 8.
11. Terry Glomski and Allen Sinai, "Chrysler and the U.S. Economy: A Simulation Study" (Lexington, Mass.: Data Resources, Inc., 1979), pp. 2–3.
12. *Ibid.*, Table 1.
13. *Ibid.*, p. 4 and Table 10.
14. *Ibid.*, p. 6.
15. *Ibid.*
16. Figures cited in Chrysler Corporation, September 15 submission, Exhibit XIII.
17. Martin Anderson, George Byron, and John O'Donnell, "Employment and Economic Effects of a Chrysler Shut Down or Major Reduction in Business: Preliminary Data and Analysis," Transportation Systems Center, Department of Transportation, August 15, 1979, reprinted in U.S. Congress, House of Representatives, "Hearings Before the Subcommittee on Economic Stabilization of the Committee on Banking, Finance, and Urban Affairs: The Chrysler Corporation Financial Situation," Ninety-sixth Congress, Part 1A (Washington, D.C.: Government Printing Office, 1979), pp. 187–227; quote from p. 188.
18. *Ibid.*, pp. 189–190.
19. *Ibid.*, p. 190 and Exhibit 8.
20. *Ibid.*, p. 191.
21. *Ibid.*, pp. 192–93 and Exhibit 10.
22. *Ibid.*, p. 191 and Exhibit 9.
23. *Ibid.*
24. *Ibid.*, p. 192.
25. *Ibid.*, Exhibit 2.
26. *Ibid.*, p. 196.
27. *Ibid.*, p. 197.
28. *Ibid.*, p. 194.
29. *Ibid.*, p. 196.
30. *Ibid.*, Exhibit 2.
31. *Ibid.*, p. 197.
32. *Ibid.*, p. 198.
33. Mark Murray, "The Impact of a Collapse of Chrysler Corporation on Public Assistance Caseloads and Costs in Michigan," Michigan Department of Social Services, Policy Analysis Division, November 13, 1979.
34. Anderson, Byron, and O'Donnell, *op. cit.*, p. 198.
35. *Ibid.*
36. *Ibid.*, Exhibit XIII.
37. *Ibid.*, p. 199.
38. *Ibid.*, p. 200.
39. Congressional Research Service, Economics Division, "The Question of Federal Assistance to the Chrysler Corporation," September 5, 1979, p. 32.
40. *Ibid.*, p. 33.
41. *Ibid.*, p. 30.

42. *Ibid.*, p. 33.
43. *Ibid.*, p. 34.
44. *Ibid.*, pp. 30–31.
45. *Ibid.*, p. 34.
46. *Ibid.*
47. *Ibid.*, pp. 34–35.
48. *Ibid.*, pp. 41–43.
49. *Ibid.*, pp. 35–36.
50. *Ibid.*, p. 36.
51. *Ibid.*, p. 49.
52. *Ibid.*, pp. 51–52.
53. *Ibid.*, p. 52.
54. *Ibid.*, p. 53.
55. *Ibid.*
56. *Ibid.*, pp. 54–55.
57. Frank Kennedy, "The Impact of a Chapter 11 Bankruptcy Proceeding on Chrysler Corporation," reprinted in Anderson, Byron, and O'Donnell, *op. cit.*, p. 1351.
58. *Ibid.*, p. 1357.
59. *Ibid.*, p. 1359.
60. *Ibid.*, p. 1360.
61. *Ibid.*, p. 1368.
62. *Ibid.*, pp. 1363–64.
63. *Ibid.*, p. 1367.
64. *Ibid.*, p. 1378.
65. *Ibid.*, p. 1380.
66. *Ibid.*, pp. 1381, 1379.
67. *Ibid.*, p. 1379.
68. *Ibid.*, p. 1382.
69. *Ibid.*, p. 1390.
70. *Ibid.*, p. 1393.
71. *Ibid.*

ACKNOWLEDGMENTS

This book could not have been written without the cooperation and goodwill of a vast number of people. Some of them occupy well-appointed offices in law firms, investment banks, accounting firms, commercial banks, corporate headquarters, and at the highest levels of government. Others spend their days in more modest surroundings. All of them offered their time and their recollections. Several opened personal files and lent papers and diaries. Some of our sources' names appear in the text or footnotes; many others preferred that their assistance remain anonymous. To all we owe our thanks.

A few must be singled out for contributions that were particularly useful. In this category we would include four people who were instrumental in shaping the events of the Chrysler rescue: Wendell Larsen, Elinor Bachrach, Brian Freeman, and Douglas Fraser. Each has since left the post he or she held at the time of the rescue; each exercised his or her memory for us—with generosity and candor—more than once. Stuart Eizenstat allowed us unqualified access to his daily White House notes; Steve Miller, to his personal diaries of the Chrysler debt restructuring. We are similarly in the debt of several highly placed officials in the Reagan administration who were remarkably helpful in reconstructing certain of the events of the last few years.

Not a few companies and organizations also opened their files. Manufacturers Hanover Trust Company, the United Auto Workers, and the city of Detroit were particularly cooperative. But it is to the Chrysler Corporation itself that we are most indebted. It freely arranged access to all the managers we sought to interview. It opened its corporate files and archives and answered queries with dispatch and precision. All this and more was organized by the incomparable Tim Yost.

Several people surrendered weekends to read earlier versions of the book and provided helpful suggestions and criticisms. We are especially indebted to Jeffrey Garten, Alan Webber, Howard Frant, Kim Clark, Malcolm Salter, Richard Neustadt, Herman "Dutch" Leonard, Joseph Bower, and Mark Moore. A small army of students gamely traced down obscure data and references; special thanks for high morale and performance in the face of tedium goes to Miriam Messenger, Eugene Sperling, and Frank Ostroff. Finally, but not least, we owe great thanks to Mrs. Elizabeth Miele, whose extraordinary secretarial abilities kept us organized throughout.

The research on which the book is based was supported by a generous grant from the Center for Business and Government of Harvard's John F. Kennedy School of Government.

INDEX